THE Lite SWITCH

by
June McLean Jeter

Cover design and artwork by Kim Cathro, Arlington, Texas

Photograph by Paul Knudson, Portfolio Studio, 519 W. Main, Arlington, Texas

Nutritional Analysis of Recipes and Preface by Michael McAllister, M.S., R.D., L.D., C.D.E.

Cookbook design and typesetting by Lazara & Douglas Abernathy, CustomType Designs, Fort Worth, Texas

Printed in the United States of America

Chariot Press, Inc.
1300 W. Arkansas Lane
Arlington, Texas 76013

First Printing October 1992

ISBN 0-9634783-0-3

In Loving Memory

... To my father, Dr. R.N. McLean, who loved life and family as passionately as he did his patients and study of medicine, and who strived to make this world a better place.

Dedicated

... To my husband, Ross, a true gift in my life... without your unconditional love and friendship combined with your wonderful sense of humor, patience, encouragement, and support, this project would not have been possible.

To my daughters, Holly and Stephanie, two of the most precious joys of my life... who give me the privilege of seeing everything through their eyes and who keep me focused on what is really important in life.

To my mom... who instilled in me the ability to keep trying even if the going was rough, who always told me I could do anything if I put my mind to it, but most of all who taught me the beauty of love and the joy of friendship between a mother and a daughter.

To God above... with Whom all things are truly possible.

My Sincerest Gratitude

... To Ross (my husband) and my daughters Holly and Stephanie; Margaret (my Mom) and Elmer Nooner; and Lillian and Jack Neal (my second parents) who helped and supported me in more ways than I could possibly count. Without you there would be no "**Lite Switch**."

To family and friends who contributed their time and efforts to help make this cookbook a reality: Doug and Lazara Abernathy, Kim Cathro, Chris Houston, Kim Lindsey, Mike McAllister, Shannon McAllister, Jeff McLean (my brother), Amy McMichael, David Mullinax, and E. Faye Williams.

To other family and friends whose faith and encouragement kept me going: Deb Biggs, Debbie Brown, Marlane Burns, Susan Cooper, Carol Dominguez, Pat Ezell, Lori Hamilton, Annette King, Peggy Jeter, Pam Mycoskie, Helen Nooner, Trish Selgrath, Karen Streater, Debbie Vernon, members and staff of Maverick Athletic Club including Glynda Hatton, Yelan Smart, and Ilene Thomas.

Preface

For thousands of people, nutrition in the nineties represents an evolutionary process. We are leaving the days of eating everything in unending quantities at a moments notice, and moving towards a new found realism that diet does indeed affect us physically and emotionally.

Fueling this realism are major health concerns of obesity, diabetes, heart disease, and hypertension. We know the consequences of these diseases are vastly lessened by improved nutrition practices and physical activity.

However, changing nutrition practices, (choices), in our quest optimal health is a challenge. Change is nearly always difficult particularly with something (nutrition), we have had little experiencewith, aside from the mere act of eating.

The challenge of change can best be met with an attitude or a desire to change, or evolve. An awareness of our lifestyle areas in which we could improve will greatly enhance change performance.

June's book, The Lite Switch, has focused on many of these lifestyle areas which can aid you in your evolution of dietary practice and management. Not only does her book offer wonderfully tasting low fat recipes, but useful information that can be implemented to meet our fast-paced lifestyle and still produce positive outcomes.

Michael McAllister, M.S., L.D., R.D., C.D.E., currently divides his busy schedule between his practice at the Irving Health Care Center, Infectious Disease Home Care Programs, and his personalized nutritional and diabetes counseling.

Before Beginning

... this or any other nutritional or physical fitness program, consult your physician to be sure it is appropriate for you. The information in this book is not intended to take the place of any medical advice. It reflects the author's experiences, studies, research, and opinions regarding healthy eating and physical fitness. The information provided is true and accurate to the best of the author's knowledge.

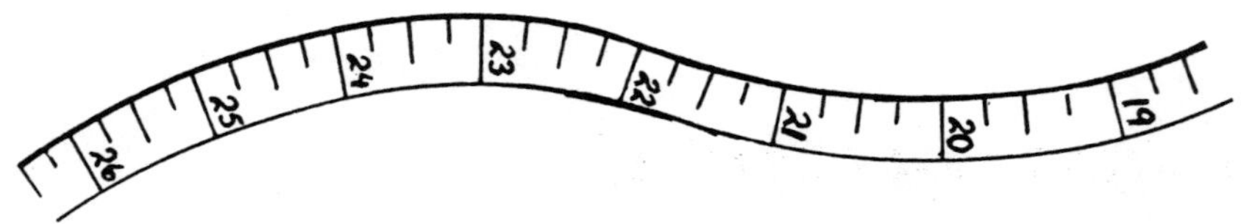

CONTENTS

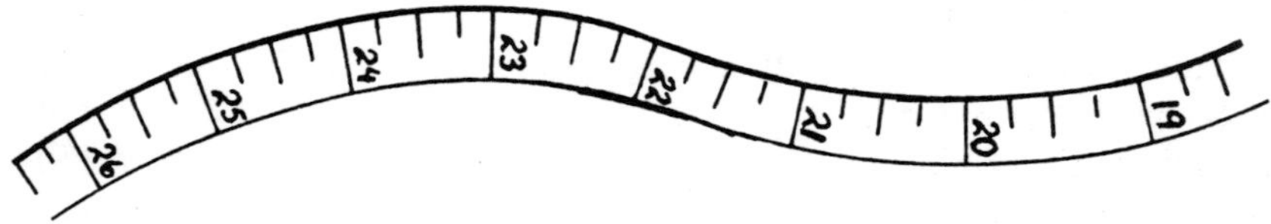

INTRODUCTION

Welcome to freedom. Yes, freedom is how I describe the principles outlined in this book. "**The Lite Switch**" can show you how easy it is to make a change in your life will alter the rest of your life for the better.

ABOUT THE BOOK

Ask yourself these questions: • Would you like to look and feel better? • Would you like to lose weight without really trying and without feeling deprived? • Would you like to be able to eat all those great foods you've grown up with without feeling guilty? • Would you like to update your low-fat lifestyle with some new recipes and fresh ideas? • Would you be relieved to know that you can eat out at restaurants, fast food establishments, and other places you thought you had to avoid? • Would you like to reduce your risk of heart disease, high blood pressure, or even cancer? • Would you like to know how to feed your family right and know you might be saving them from future health problems? • Would you like to share your low-fat lifestyle with your friends? • Just once, wouldn't you like to say "I CAN have this or this or this, instead of I can't have this or that? • Isn't it time you took charge of your body and how you treat yourself? • Wouldn't it be great to have choices that are easy to live with?

I am sure you answered "Yes" to at least one of these questions. All these things are possible with "**The Lite Switch!**" I have tried to give you the tools you need to begin and continue a realistic plan for healthy living, not a plan you try for a week or two and then return to your old eating habits. For those of you who are just beginning, a gradual change is encouraged; do not consider going from a high fat diet directly to a completely fat free one. You must give your body (your taste buds), a chance to get accustomed to some of the new tastes. By using the substitutions listed in the "How Do I Begin" section and by using the great variety of recipes and ideas, you will see how to begin slowly and on an individual basis to fit your own needs. Those of you already on the right track can find new recipes, helpful hints, and maybe some things that you didn't know or at least a reinforcement of things you're doing right. Remember this process is always changing. New ideas, recipes, low-fat and fat free foods continue to give us choices for a healthier lifestyle.

ABOUT THE AUTHOR

Today it is so much easier to live a healthy lifestyle, with so many available choices, than when I began almost 9 years ago. I began exercising regularly after the birth of my first daughter. With the encouragement of several friends I joined an aerobics class. At first, it was hard to make myself go to class; there are so many excuses not to go and I probably used every one of them. Then I decided to give myself one month; I would attend class 3 times per week faithfully and then make a decision whether or not to continue.

Something amazing happened to me in those few weeks. I began to see a change in my body that I had never seen before. Naturally I was losing the body fat I had gained during my pregnancy, but it was more than that. I started feeling better; I had more energy and I couldn't wait until the next class. I guess you could say I became "hooked". Not only was my body toning up gradually, but I was having fun. The instructor was so encouraging; she gave an intense, yet safe and fun workout that made me want to come back.

I did go back. I even became an instructor. I had finally found something that I could do to keep unwanted pounds from creeping back and I wanted to share it with others. All of my life I have had to watch my weight. As a child I was always considered "chubby". I have been on every diet from Scarsdale to Slim Fast, but those were only temporary. As soon as I lost the weight, I returned to my old eating habits. I never really learned how to eat normally. The exercise did help keep the weight off but, because I did not change my eating habits, I was still borderline overfat (24%). The scale showed a lower weight, but when my body fat was tested, I was overfat. I had to make some changes.

At that time, some members of my family got results from their cholesterol tests showing their counts to be well above 200; there also is a history of heart disease in my family. These two risk factors meant there could be a higher chance for the development of heart disease. With the help of my mother, reading all I could find, and attending continuing education classes and seminars, I got seriously interested in modifying my diet and that of my family. My cholesterol was borderline at 199. I'm sure it would have been higher; regular exercise probably helped keep it intact. I had always used skim milk, except with my children when they were under age 2, but more changes were needed.

I changed gradually by using many of the same substitutions mentioned in the "How Do I Begin" section, although the choices were not as good then as they are now. I have continued making changes throughout the years to see that most of the fat in our diet comes from foods such as complex carbohydrates, followed by skinless chicken breast or lean fish and lean beef in moderation, not from added margarine, oils or other fats. As a result of theses changes, usually consuming no more than 10%-20% of my calories from fat (plus regular aerobic exercise), I have seen my body fat go from about 24% to around 16%. If I can make these changes, anyone can! Making a change for your life is not hard if you follow the guidelines outlined in this book.

I tried to write **"The Lite Switch"** so it would be easy to use and easy to read. The recipes have been developed through many hours of trial and error. Some recipes are named after friends and relatives who had asked that their favorite recipes be modified so they could enjoy them on a regular basis. A few others that had already been developed and modified were given to me to use in the book. I hope you will find this book helpful and enjoyable. Please write to me and let me know how you are doing and how you like **"The Lite Switch."**

HOW TO USE THE COOKBOOK

The cookbook is designed for you and your special needs. If you glance at the Table of Contents and Index, you will notice different topics. Recipe names are listed twice in the index, once under the category they fall under and once in alphabetical order. If you are already on a low-fat plan, you might wish to skip directly to the recipes. However, if this is your first attempt at low-fat or you are fairly new to low-fat eating, I suggest you begin at the "How Do I Begin" section.

NUTRITIONAL ANALYSIS:
Each recipe comes with special nutritional information. This information is based on the ingredients listed in the recipe. For convenience and because of my preference, I listed specific brand names. For example, lite cake and brownie mixes used in the recipes are Pillsbury brand Lovin' Lites; also, when "Nonfat Yogurt Cheese" ✔ is listed, feel free to substitute No Fat sour cream. If you wish to substitute another brand for any of the ingredients, whether to save

money or because you prefer another product, you can do so easily comparing fat and calorie content for the most accurate substitution.

Nutritional values are listed for each recipe in calories per serving along with the amount in grams of protein, carbohydrates, and fat, plus the amount of cholesterol and sodium in milligrams. Also included is the percentage of calories that come from fat. Nutritional analysis was done by Michael McAllister, R.D., L.D. and are assumed to be as accurate as possible. Other food counts in the "Restaurant Choices" and "Fast Food" sections are based on comments directly from the facilities or from nutritional booklets provided by the company. These allow you to keep tabs on what you are eating. Notice the recommended daily servings of foods at the end of the "Daily Nutritional Needs" section.

In the recipe breakdown, optional ingredients and spices are not counted in the nutritional breakdown; and, if two food items are listed (for example ground turkey breast or Healthy Choice ground beef), the first one mentioned is the one used in the calculation. Also, if two quantities of an ingredient are listed, for example, ½ C or ¾ C, the first one is the one used in the nutritional breakdown. These options are mainly to give you more freedom and variety to better meet your needs.

At the beginning of each recipe section, notice there are "Time Savers" - quick and healthy recipes low in fat (without nutritional analysis) and "Helpful Hints." Within each section you will notice the terms "Quick Fix" and "Easy Prep" beneath some of the recipe titles. A "Quick Fix" should be easily prepared in 30 minutes or less. An "Easy Prep" may or may not take 30 minutes but is easy to prepare. Those recipes with "Quick" or "Easy" as a part of the recipe title imply that they are either "Quick Fix" or "Easy Prep."

LITE SWITCH SYMBOLS:

A word or group of words that has quotation marks around it and a ✔ at the end indicates that the recipe is listed in the index: "Recipe Name"✔ = check index

T = Tablespoon
t = teaspoon
C = Cup

Notes and Extra Recipes:

Notes and Extra Recipes:

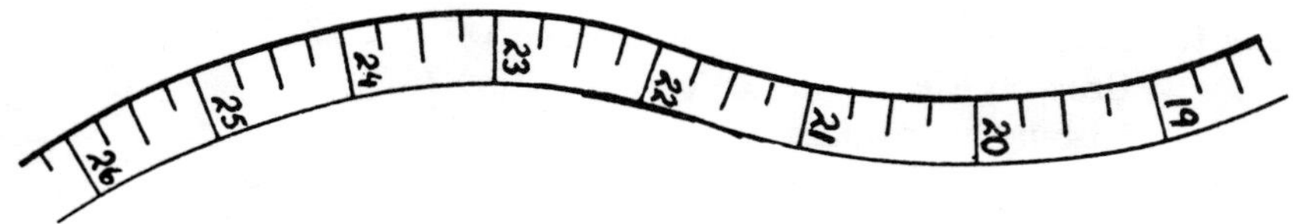

HOW DO I BEGIN?

Getting started on your eating plan is easy, whether you are trying to lose weight or just reduce your fat intake. In this section I have included a one-week menu plus a grocery list to take the guesswork out of beginning. The lists of substitutions and equivalents at the end of the section will help you make changes one step at a time.

ONE-WEEK MENU PLAN

Here is a one-week sample menu to get you started, followed by a grocery list to make finding the new products easier. Recipes are noted using quotation marks and check marks beside it so you can check the index to find recipes quickly. Menus include some of my favorite recipes. This 1-week menu will probably take you through a 2-week period because a lot of the foods can be frozen or eaten again on other days. Desserts are included every other day with suggested substitutes at the end of this portion. Feel free to mix and match food items to your taste. If you need an appetizer or pre-meal "munchy", I've listed several favorites.

APPETIZERS

Munch on:

"Pita or Bagel Chips"✔
Fat free pretzels
Sliced raw vegetables
Guiltless Gourmet No-Oil Tortilla Chips (serve with "Bean Dip Olé"✔ or "Susan's Cheese Dip"✔
"Potato Skins"✔ or "Pasta Crunch"✔; or, dip Pillsbury breadsticks in fat free spaghetti sauce

Also see Hors D'oeuvres Section "Time-Savers" for other quick ideas.

DINNER MENUS

Day 1: "Frances Foley's Crock Pot Chicken"✔
"Broccoli Rice Casserole"✔
Pillsbury breadsticks
"Millionaire Cookies"✔

Day 2: "Taco Soup"✔
"Stephanie's Favorite Cornbread"✔
"Fresh Fruit Salad with Poppy Seed Dressing"✔ (dressing optional - ingredients not in grocery list)

Day 3: "Layered Cheese Pasta"✔
"Easy Focaccia Bread"✔
"Fresh Green Salad"✔
Fat Free dressing
"Mamie's Orange Pineapple Cake"✔

Day 4: "Super Meatloaf"✔
"Bikini Potatoes"✔
"Mema's Quick Sizzle Beans"✔
Pillsbury Hearty Grains Wheat and Honey Twists

Day 5: "Oven Fried Catfish"✔
"Hash Brown Casserole"✔
"Fresh Green Salad"✔
"Homemade Banana Pudding"✔

Day 6: "Lite Monte Cristo Sandwich"✔
"Creamy Split Pea Soup"✔
"Pita or Bagel Chips"✔

Day 7: "Ross's Chicken on the Grill"✔
"Carol's Cornbread Salad"✔
"Green Bean Casserole"✔
"Baked Yellow Squash"✔
"Karen's Favorite Chocolate Peanut Butter Pie"✔

DESSERTS

(These are extra desserts included in your grocery list.)

"Strawberry Surprise Dessert"✔
"Coconut Banana Cream Pie"✔
"Lillian's Angel Food Cake"✔

ONE-WEEK GROCERY LIST

This list includes all items you will need for the menu plans Day 1 through Day 7 including spices, condiments, etc. If one recipe calls for 1 medium green pepper and one recipe calls for half of a small green pepper, I listed 1 large green pepper for convenience. (As stated before, you may want to spread these menus out by eating some as leftovers or freezing leftovers for weeks to come. Many can be carried over for lunches.)

Produce Section:
4 medium tomatoes
16 whole mushrooms plus a few more for green salad (if desired)
2 large onions
1 medium zucchini
6 new potatoes
2 medium baking potatoes
4-5 celery stalks
1 large green pepper
1 small red pepper
1 head of lettuce
1¾ lbs. yellow squash
1 small bunch carrots
Assorted vegetables of your choice for "Fresh Green Salad"✔
5 large bananas
Assorted fruits of your choice for fruit salad

Cereals:
4 cups cornflakes
2 cups Honey Bunches of Oats
1 small box Grape Nuts
2½ cups dry oatmeal

Dry Goods:
4 cups dry split peas
4 (14½-oz.) cans stewed tomatoes
1 (6-oz.) can tomato paste
1½ cups Healthy Choice Spaghetti Sauce
6 oz. garden pasta spirals
2 cups cooked rice
2 cups dry vermicelli (about 4 oz.)
1 packet McCormick/Schilling gravy mix

1 packet lite Taco seasoning mix
1 packet lite ranch dressing mix

Refrigerated foods:
1 (20-oz.) bag Simply Potatoes (hash browns)
1 small package Healthy Choice or equivalent brand turkey or ham--need 2 oz. for recipe
1 can Pillsbury breadsticks
1 can Pillsbury Hearty Grains Wheat and Honey Twists

Cake Mixes, Frostings, Jello and Puddings:
2 boxes Butter Buds butter flavored mix (each box contains 8 packets and sometimes are found with the butter)
1 box Pillsbury Lovin' Lites yellow cake mix
1 box Pillsbury Lovin' Lites white or yellow cake mix
2 boxes Betty Crocker Fluffy White Frosting Mix
1 box Pillsbury Hot Roll mix
6 cups sugar
1 cup powdered sugar
brown sugar
4 cups flour
2 cups cornmeal
¼ cup peanut butter chips
1 small box Swans or Softasilk cake flour
1 large box instant sugar-free chocolate pudding and pie filling
4 tsp. Bac-Os artificial bacon bits
1 (3-oz.) box instant vanilla pudding
4 (12-oz.) cans evaporated skim milk
chili powder
Butter flavor Pam no stick cooking spray
salt (see note)
Light corn syrup (2 T)
½ cup cumin

Spices:
baking powder
basil
celery salt
clove garlic
coconut extract
cornstarch
dill
garlic powder
garlic salt

Spices (continued):
ginger
mace
minced onion
oregano
parsley
pepper
salt (you may use lite salt or a non-salt substitute)
vanilla extract
(Small amounts of dried spices, herbs, baking products, or flavorings will be used)

Refrigerated Dairy Products
2 dozen large eggs
12 oz. Healthy Choice Fat Free mozzarella cheese (you can buy it packaged whole or grated)
1 (12-oz.) package plus 3 slices Healthy Choice Fat Free cheese singles
1 quart fortified skim milk
1 cup 1% fat buttermilk
2 containers Truly Lite Fat Free ricotta cheese
3 cups nonfat plain Dannon yogurt or Land O'Lakes No Fat sour cream
4 tsp. Parmesan cheese

Frozen Foods:
4 (8-oz.) cartons Egg Beaters or fat free egg substitute (some are found in the dairy section)
2 (10-oz.) packages frozen chopped broccoli

Beef, Poultry and Seafood:
3 lbs. Healthy Choice ground beef (packaged in 1-lb. rolls - sometimes in frozen section)
4 (4-oz.) boneless, skinless chicken breasts
4 (4-oz.) catfish fillets
1 whole (3 lbs.) Louis Rich (or equivalent brand) boneless skinless turkey or chicken breast

Condiments:
1 small jar crunchy peanut butter
1 bottle fat free salad dressing
1½ cup Kraft-Free (fat free) mayonnaise
3 T Worcestershire Sauce
dash hot pepper sauce (opt.)

Canned Fruits, Vegetables, Beans, and Soups:
1 (15-oz.) can kidney beans
1 (15-oz.) can pinto beans
1 (14-oz.) can artichoke hearts
4 cans cut green beans
1 (14½-oz.) can hominy
5 cans Weight Watcher's cream of mushroom soup (sometimes this is found with the diet foods) You may also make your own using "Basic Cream Soup"✔ recipe.
1 can low-fat tomato soup
1 (8-12 count) jar chicken bouillon cubes or granules
1 small jar beef bouillon cubes or granules
4 oz. chopped green chiles
1 large can water chestnuts
¾ cup unsweetened applesauce
1 large can lite mandarin oranges
1 large can unsweetened crushed pineapple

Breads, Cookies, Baked Items:
1 package pita pocket bread (sometimes in deli)
2 loaves Wonder Lite Fat Free reduced calorie bread
1 package bagels (sometimes in deli or freezer section)
1 box vanilla Teddy Grahams (need 40 cookies)

Miscellaneous Items:
Yogurt strainer or cheesecloth for yogurt cheese (or use nonfat sour cream and omit yogurt strainer)

SUBSTITUTIONS
(For Modifying Recipes, Snack Substitutes, and Equivalents)

When modifying your recipes to reduce any or all of the following, (fat, sugar, and sodium), start by substituting one ingredient at a time so that you will know what changes need to be made, if any, and where to begin. If you are new to lowfat eating, some ingredients have an in-between substitute, for example, instead of going straight from whole milk to nonfat milk, try mixing half 2% milk with half fortified skim milk. This way you are able to make a gradual change, eventually changing to fortified skim as a lifetime choice. Don't get discouraged; make gradual changes.

Eventually, all those high fat favorites you have enjoyed for so long will not taste as good as you once thought. You will start to taste the true food and not the fat in the food. The same thing will occur in your recipes. It's really easy once you get started; it's a lot of fun to see those old family recipes get healthier so you are still able to enjoy them without the guilt. You'll be surprised, they still taste great — even better, I think.

Use equal amounts of foods listed unless otherwise specified. Check the index for recipes in the book for great substitutions for foods such as cream soups, salad dressings, cookies, sour cream, etc. Check the Grocery Section for specific brand names of healthy food items and where they can be found.

Instead of This:	Try This:	Then This:
1 Whole Egg	1 Whole Egg plus 2 Egg Whites	2 Egg Whites, ¼ C Egg Beaters egg substitute or fat free egg substitute equivalent
2 Egg Yolks		¼ C Egg Beaters per yolk
Whole Milk	Half 2% Milk plus Half Fortified Skim Milk	Fortified Skim Milk, Skim Milk, or Sanalac powdered milk (Less Expensive)
Sour Cream	Reduced Fat Sour Cream or Half Sour Cream plus Half Nonfat Plain Yogurt	"Nonfat Yogurt Cheese"✔, "Mock Sour Cream"✔, or No Fat Sour Cream
Half and Half	Poly Rich or Mocha Mix or Half of Poly or Mocha plus Fortified Skim Milk	Half Evaporated Skim Milk plus Half Skim Milk

Instead of This:	Try This:	Then This:
Cream	Poly Rich or Mocha Mix or Half of Poly or Mocha plus Fortified Skim Milk	Evaporated Skim Milk
Mayonnaise	Half Mayonnaise or Salad Dressing plus Half Kraft Free Mayonnaise	Kraft Free Mayonnaise, Fat Free Miracle Whip, Fat Free Salad Dressings, or Fat Free cream cheese
Whole milk cheese	Reduced Calorie and Reduced Fat or Lite Cheese such as Weight Watchers or Kraft	Healthy Choice Fat Free Cheese and Cheese Slices or other Fat Free cheeses
Pastry and Pie Crusts		Phyllo (Filo) Dough in freezer section (spray with butter flavor Pam no stick cooking spray instead of brushing pastry sheets with butter or margarine); or, "Basic Pie Crust"✔ or "Hearty Grains Pie Crust"✔
Cream Cheese	Lite Cream Cheese or Half Weight Watcher's Cream Cheese plus Lite Cream Cheese	Weight Watcher's Cream Cheese or Healthy Choice Fat Free cream cheese spread, or a mixture of the two spreads. Also mix half fat free ricotta cheese with half Weight Watcher's or Healthy Choice cream cheese
4% Fat Cottage Cheese	Lowfat Cottage Cheese Such as Weight Watcher's	Nonfat Cottage Cheese or Polly-O Free Fat Free Ricotta Cheese
Whole Milk Ricotta Cheese	Part-Skim Ricotta Cheese	Truly Lite Fat Free Ricotta Cheese
Bacon Grease		Bacon Flavor Molly McButter (dry or mixed with a little warm milk or water for liquid form.
Cooked Bacon	Turkey Bacon or Healthy Favorites Bacon	Bac-Os Artificial Bacon Bits, Hormel Canadian Bacon, Healthy Choice Ham, Healthy Favorites Lean Breakfast Ham
Oil Used in Preparing Salad Dressings	Reduce Amount By Half or Less	Omit Oil; experiment with water, flavored wine vinegars, fat free salad dressings, Butter Buds liquid, etc.

Instead of This:	Try This:	Then This:
Cooking Oil for Frying	Reduce Oil By Half or Less	For Sautéing: Butter Buds Liquid, "Defatted Beef or Chicken Broth"✔, Vegetable Bouillon, Wine, Pam No Stick Cooking Spray - all flavors including Plain, Olive Oil Flavor, and Butter Flavor, or a Combination of one or more of the above.
Butter, Margarine, Shortening, or Oil in Baked Goods*	Reduce Amount of Fat Called for in Recipe by ½ or ¾; Replace the reduced amount of oil with Smart Beat margarine or canola oil	Kraft Free Mayonnaise, ½ Each Unsweetened Applesauce and Fat Free Mayonnaise, Corn Syrup, and Liquid Butter Buds, sometimes Promise Fat Free margarine. Occasionally, as a substitute for the fat, double the fruit in recipes already containing fruit.
Oil, Butter, or Margarine used for basting, coating, or marinating foods, or for greasing pans	Reduced Calorie Margarine	Pam No Stick Cooking Spray (all flavors), Liquid Butter Buds for Basting or Coating Foods
Real Whipped Cream, Cool Whip, Dream Whip, or other Similar products containing highly saturated fats	Reddi Wip Lite (Aerosol) Whipped Topping (**See Note Below Table)	"Nonfat Whipped Cream"✔, prepared Betty Crocker Fluffy White Frosting mix (does not harden when frozen), "Never Fail Meringue"✔
1 oz. unsweetened or semi-sweet chocolate	3 T Dry Cocoa plus 1 T Canola Oil	3 T Dry Cocoa Powder plus 2 T Butter Buds Liquid (May use Braum's Lite Fudge Topping or any fat free chocolate topping in place of the Butter Buds Liquid
1 C chocolate or peanut butter chips	¼ C Chocolate or Peanut Butter Chips	Use Sparingly and Save for Special Occasions

Instead of This:	Try This:	Then This:
Nuts	Reduce Amount By Half or Less	Grape Nuts Cereal
Avocados		Frozen Asparagus, Cooked and Drained
Peanut Butter	Spread on very thin and try to use as a snack, not a main meal	Truly Lite Fat Free Ricotta Cheese mixed with a little Peanut Butter
Salad Dressings	Use Less and Instead of Pouring the Dressing on Your Salad, Dip Your "Bite" of Salad into the Dressing	Fat Free Salad Dressings (Read Labels - some contain Cream), or See Cookbook Recipes
Ice Cream and Ice Cream Bars and Whole Milk Yogurt	Lowfat Ice Cream, Lowfat Ice Cream Bars, and Lowfat Frozen Yogurt	Nonfat Frozen or Sugar Free Nonfat Frozen Yogurt or Nonfat Dietary Frozen Dessert, Popsicles, All Fruit Frozen Juice Bars, Italian Ices
Spaghetti Sauce		Healthy Choice Spaghetti Sauce or product equivalent, or nonfat homemade
Canned Soup	Choose Broth Based Soups as opposed to Cream Soups	Healthy Choice or Health Valley low fat and fat free soups, "Defatted Beef or Chicken Broth"✔ or Vegetable Bouillon
Chicken with Skin	Chicken Without Skin	Boneless Skinless Chicken (Breast Meat Only)
Sweetened Condensed Milk		"Mock Sweetened Condensed Milk"✔ in Time Saver Dessert Section
Beef	Lean Cuts Such As Top Round, Eye Of Round, etc. (See Helpful Hints - Beef)	Boneless Skinless Chicken Breast
Ground Beef	Ground Round and Ground Turkey	Ground Turkey Breast or Chicken Breast or Healthy Choice ground beef

Instead of This:	Try This:	Then This:
Ground Sausage	Same as above, mixed with Sausage Seasoning	Same as above, only mix seasoning used in "Spicy Hamburger Cheese Balls"✔ into meat.
Deviled Ham	See "Margaret's Famous Ham Ball"✔ Recipe or "Ham Salad for Sandwiches"✔ - In place of Kraft Free Mayonnaise, use Half Kraft Free Mayonnaise and Half Regular Mayonnaise	Same as in previous column, but use all fat free mayonnaise
Prepared Pre-baked Cakes from Bakery or Deli or Commercially Prepared Baked Items		Prepared Angel Food Cakes, Entenmann's Fat Free cakes, Health Valley baked goods, or recipes from the cookbook
Sugar	Reduce Sweetener by ½ or ⅔ in most recipes	For every cup of sugar try substituting ¾-1 C honey or corn syrup, ½ C frozen fruit juice concentrate, or 1 C unsweetened applesauce. Increase spices such as vanilla, cinnamon, nutmeg, ginger, etc. Start slow - change 1 thing at a time.
Commercially Prepared Bread Crumbs or Croutons		"Basic Bread Crumbs"✔ or "Crunchy Croutons"✔
Commercially Prepared Cracker Crumbs		Premium Fat Free cracker crumbs or cornflakes
Coconut		Coconut Extract to taste
Salt	Reduce Amount by Half or Use Lite Salt	Salt Free Substitutes such as Papa Dash or fresh or dried herbs and spices such as onion, garlic, celery seed, lemon juice, parsley, low sodium soy sauce, etc.

Instead of This:	Try This:	Then This:
Prepared Cream Soup	Weight Watcher's Cream Of Mushroom Soup - One of the ingredients in the soup is cream; however, it is listed near the end of the ingredients. So far it is the best commercially prepared soup on the market that I have found.	"Basic Cream Soup Base"✔
Guacamole		"Great Guacamole"✔
1 C Regular Buttermilk		1 C 1% or less Fat Buttermilk or 1 C plain nonfat yogurt or 1 C skim milk plus 1 or 2 T white vinegar (mix and let thicken about 5 minutes).
Snack Chips, Snack Crackers, Popcorn (over 3 grams fat, 100 calories), and Commercially Prepared Snack and Cereal Mixes	Lite Chips (30% or less of calories from fat) or snacks containing fat but no partially hydrogenated oils. Acceptable varieties include some Eagle and Charles Chips, and low-fat popcorn	Air Popped Popcorn - Coat hot cooked popcorn with Butter Flavor Pam; sprinkle with dry Butter Buds and/or your favorite nonfat seasonings; also, plain or flavored rice cakes or rice bites or rice crackers, nonfat or lowfat crackers, Guiltless Gourmet No Oil Tortilla Chips, "Pita or Bagel Chips"✔, lowfat or nonfat pretzels, SnackWells snacks
Brownies and Cakes		Lovin' Lites Brownie or Cake Mixes or recipes from cookbook
Doughnuts		"Doughnut Muffins"✔, Bagel Doughnuts (See Kid's Stuff - Time Savers Section), Bagels or nonfat English Muffins with jelly
Candy Bars and Granola Bars		Fresh Fruit, Canned Unsweetened Fruit, Jelly Beans, Gummi Fruits, Raisins, Hard Candy, Suckers
Commercially Prepared Bean Dip		"Bean Dip Olé"✔, Guiltless Gourmet Bean Dip

Instead of This:	Try This:	Then This:
Cookies	Lowfat Cookies such as ginger snaps, animal crackers, fig bars	Fat Free Entenmann's, Health Valley, Frookie or other fat free Cookies or ones from cookbook like "Lemon Whippersnaps"✔ or "My Favorite Oatmeal Cookies"✔
Sweet Rolls	Entenmann's Fat Free coffee cakes and sweet rolls	Fat Free or low-fat muffins, breads, English muffins, or bagels topped with fruit jelly and/or cinnamon and sugar
High Fat Rolls like Crescents	Soft White or Wheat Rolls	Bagels, corn or flour tortillas, soft Pretzels, Low or no fat cornbread (See recipes)
Milk Shakes		Frozen Yogurt Shake or One made from nonfat milk, ice, and fruit
French Fries	Use oven french fry recipe, add 1-3 t Canola oil and bake as directed	Baked potato or "Fantastic Fries"✔ - using this recipe, may sauté fries in Pam in nonstick skillet instead of cooking in oven
Lunchmeats and Hot Dogs		Healthy Choice Lunchmeats and Hot Dogs or equivalent
Packaged Macaroni and Cheese, Pasta, Rice, and Vegetable Mixes such as scalloped potatoes	Use only half or less of the fat called for in recipe; use half of cheese sauce in macaroni and cheese.	Omit Butter, Oil, or Margarine that package directions call for
Dry Salad Dressing Mixes		Fat Free Salad Dressing Mixes (Read Labels) Good Seasons is a good choice
Commercially Prepared Dips and Cheese Spreads	Lowfat or Lite Dips and Cheese Spreads	Healthy Choice fat free Pasteurized Processed Cheese Spread and Garlic and Herb Cheese Spread or prepare cookbook recipes
Egg Noodles		No Yolks Egg noodles containing no yolks

Instead of This:	Try This:	Then This:
Commercially Prepared Baking Mix	Bisquick Low fat Baking Mix	"Best Baker's Mix"✔; Pioneer Fat Free Biscuit Mix
Olives		Pickles, pickled okra, water packed artichoke hearts, baby corn, hearts of palm
Oil-packed Canned Tuna, Seafood, and Chicken	Rinse Oil-packed Tuna, Seafood and Chicken well and drain	Water-packed Canned Tuna, Seafood and Chicken
Toppings for Nonfat Frozen Yogurt and Desserts (like candy, nuts and cookies)		Fat Free or Low-fat Cereals like Grape Nuts, cornflakes, or Health Valley Fat Free Granola, Braum's Lite Fudge topping, Fruit
Tortilla Chips	Lite Tortilla Chips or Restaurant Style containing no partially hydrogenated oils	No Oil baked tortilla chips - (See Grocery list)
Sausage, Hamburger, Pepperoni, Extra Cheese Pizza	Cheese Pizza or Vegetable Pizza or ask for Cheese or Vegetable Pizza made with only half the cheese	Plain Breadsticks not topped with butter, oil, or margarine or cheese (Dip in nonfat spaghetti sauce); Healthy Roman Fat Free frozen pizza - GREAT!

* Sometimes it takes a little experimenting with the substitutions to make recipes turn out right. Notice substitutions made in recipes such as "Quick Fix Brownies"✔ and "Stephanie's Favorite Cornbread"✔. The cornbread took a lot of trial and error to get it right. I replaced the oil with applesauce and corn syrup. The brownies were easier. Kraft Free mayonnaise took the place of shortening and gave it the moistness it needed. Cocoa replaced 2 unsweetened squares of chocolate; Grape Nuts replaced the nuts. The key to having the right texture in lowfat baked goods is to mix just until ingredients are combined; overmixing makes them dry or tough.

** The Reddi Wip is only 6 Calories per serving, however a little over half of the calories come from fat. I do think it makes a good choice, used in moderation, because the fat is not saturated like it is in the Cool Whip, Cool Whip Lite, and Dream Whip and other whipped topping mixes. The latter 3 products contain coconut and/or palm oil.

TABLE OF EQUIVALENTS:

For This:	Try This:
1 T prepared mustard	1 t dry mustard
2 t fresh minced herbs 1 T fresh herbs	½ t dry herbs 1 t ground or crushed dry herbs
1 C white rice	1 C long grain brown rice
1 clove garlic	½ t garlic powder
1 C tomato sauce	½ C tomato paste plus ¾ C water
2 T flour or 1 T cornstarch plus enough water to form a paste for thickening soups, gravies, sauces, etc.	2-3 T instant dry potato flakes or pureed vegetables
1 C all-purpose flour	1 C whole wheat flour less 2 T
1 envelope unflavored gelatin	1 T gelatin
1 large onion	¾-1 C chopped onion
1 package dry yeast	1 T dry yeast
1 (10-oz.) pkg. frozen vegetables 1 (16-oz.) " " " 1 (20-oz.) " " "	About 2 C frozen vegetables " 3 C " " " 4 C " "
2 oz. dry spaghetti	About 1 C cooked (spaghetti)
4 oz. grated fat free cheese	1 C Grated Nonfat cheese
1 T cornstarch	2 T All-Purpose Flour
1 C cake flour	1 C All-Purpose Flour minus 2 T
1 C self-rising flour	1 C All-Purpose Flour plus 1 t Baking Powder and ½ t Salt (Opt.)
1 lb. fresh mushrooms	6 oz. Canned Mushrooms

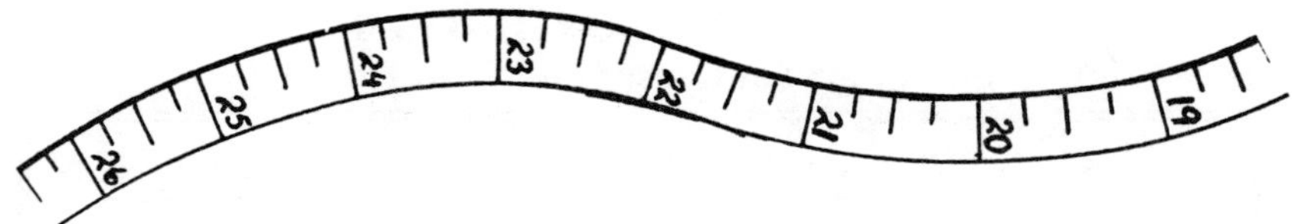

MAKING A LIFESTYLE CHANGE

In this section you will learn about healthy eating, which can affect your weight or body fat thus affecting your health. If a healthy plan is not followed, you are at great risk for developing high blood cholesterol, heart disease, cancer, and other health problems. The best plan is one that includes a variety of foods to be sure your body gets the proper amount of nutrients, vitamins, and minerals for a proper balance.

DAILY NUTRITIONAL NEEDS

To be able to make good choices, you need to be aware of what they are. The "Daily Nutritional Needs" in the following chart guides you through the food groups by showing you the serving size of healthy choices and how many servings you need each day for a healthy lifestyle. Learning about fat, carbohydrates, protein, etc. and how these affect your body fat and weight, along with cholesterol, heart disease and other health concerns, will help you understand how the whole plan works.

The best plan is one that includes a variety of foods to be sure our bodies get the proper amount of vitamins and minerals. Foods listed are suggestions; choose suitable equivalents according to taste.

Higher fat alternatives to these products are marked (*). If you choose these higher-fat foods, or go over the recommended servings of fat, simple carbohydrates or saturated fat, make sure you balance them with other low fat foods throughout the day or week. Also, choose low sodium products and sugar-free products as needed, if desired.

DAILY NUTRITIONAL NEEDS For a Low Fat Lifestyle & Good Health	
FOOD GROUPS & SERVING SIZE	SERVINGS
Complex Carbohydrates:	
Grains - 1 slice bread or 2 slices reduced calorie bread; 1 oz. cold or cooked cereal; ½ C cooked rice or pasta; ½ medium bagel or English Muffin; 1 low fat muffin or pancake (average 80-100 calories)	**6-11**
Vegetables - ½ C cooked, raw, or canned vegetables; ½ medium baked potato; 1 C raw leafy vegetables; ¾ C vegetable or tomato juice	**3-5**
Fruits - 1 medium piece of fruit; ½ C unsweetened cooked, canned or chopped fruit; ½-¾ C unsweetened fruit juice (preferably not from concentrate)	**2-4**
60%-75% of your daily calories should come from grains, vegetables and fruits	
Simple Sugars or Simple Carbohydrates:	
High sugar foods: soft drinks; sugary cereals; cakes; pies; jams & jellies; hard candy; cookies; candy	**Optional**
Only 10% of your daily (60%-75%) carbohydrate intake should be from simple sugars	
Protein:	
Meat, Poultry, Fish, Beans, Eggs & Nuts - 1 oz. boneless skinless chicken or turkey breast; 1 oz. Healthy Choice lean ground beef or lean beef; ½ C cooked beans; 1 egg*, 2 egg whites, or ¼ C Egg Beaters; 1-2 T Peanut Butter* or ¼-½ C nuts*	**2-3**
Dairy Foods - 1 C Skim or Nonfat Milk; ½ C Evaporated Skim Milk (undiluted); 1 oz. fat free cheese products (cream cheese, cheese singles, cheese sticks, etc.); 1 C nonfat yogurt or nonfat frozen yogurt (some contain large amounts of sugar); ½ C nonfat Ricotta or nonfat cottage cheese	**2-3**
12%-15% of your daily calories should come from protein foods	

DAILY NUTRITIONAL NEEDS For a Low Fat Lifestyle & Good Health	
FOOD GROUPS & SERVING SIZE	SERVINGS
Fats*: Salad dressings, margarine, oil, butter, cream, olives, avocados, fried foods, and any food that contains fat (meat, peanut butter, high-fat cheese, etc.) **No more than 25%-30% of your total daily calories should come from fat (15%-20% if you are trying to lose weight or body fat). Of the total percent of fat, no more than 10% should come from saturated fat. When choosing the lower percentage of fat, replace it with complex carbohydrates**	**Optional**

NUTRITIONAL TIPS AND INFORMATION

ALCOHOL
It contains no fat grams, however, your body absorbs alcohol the same way it does fat. If you do indulge, do so in extreme moderation.

CARBOHYDRATES
A major source of energy for the body. It's not carbohydrates that are fattening, it's what you put on them that makes them high in fat.

SIMPLE SUGARS OR SIMPLE CARBOHYDRATES
Check your labels for ingredients ending with the letters -ose like fructose, sucrose, dextrose, etc. If these are listed as the first, second or third ingredient on a package, this product is considered to be high in simple sugars and should be used in moderation.

PROTEIN
Used to fuel growth and repair the body. One (3-oz.) serving of lean meat is about the size of a deck of playing cards. It's easy to eat too much protein; you don't need that much. Nonfat cheese and skim milk usually contain more protein and calcium than higher fat alternatives.

CALCIUM
Extremely important during the childhood and teen years for growing

bones and to protect against osteoporosis in elderly women. Currently, the recommended daily allowance is 800-1200 mg per day from foods like: skim milk (2 C = 600 mg), nonfat yogurt (1 C = about 350 mg), canned salmon (3 oz. with bones = 195 mg), broccoli (½ C = 80 mg), and green beans (½ C = 50 mg).

IRON

For healthy blood cells; can be acquired through eating foods other than meat such as whole grains, vegetables, and legumes for a lower fat alternative.

SODIUM

Try to consume no more than ½-1½ t daily or 1000-3000 mg. Try to reduce table salt and buy no-salt or low sodium products. People with high blood pressure or who have a history of high blood pressure should try to consume no more than 2000 mg or 1 t.

FIBER

The National Cancer Institute recommends 25-30 grams of fiber each day. Most get less than half that amount. Get your fiber from foods like: beans and lentils - 7-9 grams per ½ C; fruit like an apple or pear - skin on, ½ C bananas or blueberries, or 1 C strawberries - about 3 grams; oranges or peaches - about 2 grams; whole wheat and bran cereals - about 12 grams per ounce; ⅔ C corn - 6 grams; other vegetables - about 3 grams; 2 slices whole wheat bread - about 3 grams; and ⅔ C brown rice - 3 grams. (It is best not to get your fiber from supplements). It sometimes takes time for your body to adjust to the extra fiber; be patient and drink plenty of water.

CAFFEINE

A drug found in coffee and other products. Caffeine stimulates the heart and sometimes produces extra heartbeats. Use caffeine in moderation; no more than 250-300 mg or less is recommended. Some major sources with approximate levels include: drip coffee (1 C = 145 mg); percolated coffee (1 C = 110 mg), instant coffee (1 C = 55 mg), tea (1 C = 40), and diet and regular cola (12 oz. = 35).

BETA CAROTENE AND VITAMIN C

Many fruits and vegetables contain Beta Carotene and Vitamin C, which have been known to reduce the risk of cancer. Best sources include spinach and other dark green leafy vegetables, red peppers, sweet potatoes, cantaloupe, mangos, carrots, pumpkin, broccoli, apricots, etc. Have at least one serving of beta carotene a day.

WATER

Drink a minimum of 8 glasses per day; more is better. Drink before you think - you're actually thirsty before you know it. Drink small amounts of cool water before and during exercise. Replenish your body with more cool water after exercise.

ALL ABOUT FAT

Fats are fuels for body functions and exercise. They contain over twice the calories of carbohydrates and protein; fats have 9 calories per gram and the latter two each contain 4 calories per gram. To illustrate the difference, for example, 1 Tablespoon of fat has about 120 calories; the same amount of carbohydrate = about 54 calories. Fats take longer to digest and when not used, are stored in our fat cells for later use. If those reserves are not used enough, and the body stores more than we need over a period of time, we become overfat. Complex carbohydrates, on the other hand, are the main source of fuel for our bodies and are used up quickly. Nutritionally speaking, the equivalent of 1 Tablespoon of fat a day is really all the fat we need for good health; most people consume 8-10 times that amount. We need to be aware of our nutritional needs and apply them to our lives so we can make a lifestyle change for the better. Since it is suggested that we consume 30% or less of our calories from fat, we need to learn how to figure how much fat is contained in a recipe or a serving of food. To figure this percentage:

Multiply Total Grams of Fat Per Serving by 9 (Calories in 1 Fat Gram) = Total # of Fat Calories Per Serving.

Divide Total # of Fat Calories by the number of Calories Per Serving

For example: A (½ oz.) serving of Wheat Thins crackers has 3 Fat Grams and 70 Calories.

3 (Total Fat Grams) X 9 (Calories per Fat Gram) = 27
(27 of those 70 Calories is Fat)
27 divided by 70 ≈ 0.38 or 38% Fat.
This means that 38 percent of those 70 calories comes from fat.

If you reduce your fat intake to less than 30%, make up the extra percent with complex carbohydrates. For example, if you are deriving 55% of your daily intake from Complex Carbohydrates, 15% from Protein, and 30% from fat and you want to reduce the fat and up the Carbs, make an adjustment of 60% Carbohydrates, 15% Protein, and 25% Fat. As you continue to reduce your intake of fat, up the Complex Carbohydrates. There are 3 types of fat consumed in the diet:

Saturated Fat - Fats from animal products (meats, cheese, lard, beef fat, cocoa butter found in chocolate, etc.); and some other highly saturated vegetable sources (Coconut and Palm Kernel Oil, Palm Oil, and hydrogenated oils which are hardened oils found in stick margarine, commercially prepared baked goods, peanut butter, etc.). Consume no more than 10% of your daily fat intake from saturated fat.

Polyunsaturated Fat - Found in plants (Safflower, sunflower, corn, soybean, cottonseed, etc.).

Monounsaturated Fat - Found in plants (Canola - which contains the lowest percentage of saturated fat - is the best choice if you do use oil or fat. Other good choices are Olive Oil or olives, and Peanut Oil or peanuts. It is very important to reduce the amount of saturated fat in your diet; however, don't forget the importance of keeping your TOTAL fat intake at (or, preferably, below) 30%. The chart below will make this easier.

Grams of Fat Needed to Stay Within Desired Percentages of Fat				
Calories	15%	20%	25%	30%
1200	20 g	27 g	33 g	40 g
1500	25 g	33 g	42 g	50 g
1600	27 g	36 g	44 g	53 g
1800	30 g	40 g	50 g	60 g
2000	33 g	44 g	56 g	67 g
2200	37 g	49 g	61 g	73 g
2500	42 g	56 g	69 g	83 g
2800	47 g	62 g	78 g	93 g

IDEAL BODY FAT PERCENTAGES AND IDEAL BODY WEIGHT

Most of us have a bad habit of relying on the bathroom scale to tell us if we're successful at dropping those extra pounds. But, what ARE those extra pounds? Are they mostly made up of fat?

Ideal Body Fat Percentage:

Our goal toward losing body weight should actually be re-focused on losing body fat. Concentrating on fat loss means the weight you're losing is mostly fat and not water or lean muscle tissue. As you begin an exercise program, you will start to build muscle thus adding a little more weight, not more fat. (Don't worry, just because the muscles are toning up, it doesn't mean you're adding more bulk.) This can be deceiving. You're scales may show a gain in weight, but you're body is actually getting leaner. The most accurate method to measure body fat is Hydrostatic or underwater weighing. Fees vary and it can be done at some universities and hospitals. Some charge only $25.00. The easiest next most accurate method is by Calipers. This is a test which measures your skinfolds at 3 different sights on your body. Many exercise specialists or health professionals can do this for you. Sometimes there is a fee. Some health clubs provide that service and, if you are a member, there may be no charge. Make sure you get someone who: 1) measures each of the three designated sights 3 times to get an average for a more accurate reading; 2) gets a good reading by pinching the fat away from the muscle; 3) does this type of testing frequently.An easy, inexpensive way to measure your progress is by using a tape measure. Measure your upper arms, chest, waist, abdomen, hips, and legs before you start your new eating and exercise plan. Measure again in 3-4 weeks. Notice how your body looks and how your clothes fit.

RECOMMENDED BODY FAT

	EXCELLENT	GOOD	OVERFAT
WOMEN	16%-22%	23%-25%	26%-30%
MEN	6%-18%	19%-21%	22%-25%

* It is not recommended that body fat go below these levels, except in special cases due to risk of health problems and amenorrheic in women.

Ideal Body Weight:

Now that you have an idea of what your body fat is or how to measure your progress, you need to know approximately how many calories you will need to maintain, lose, or even gain weight.

Calories Per Day For Weight Maintenance:

To determine how much your body needs daily to maintain your weight in terms of calories, use these general guidelines for normal healthy adults and teens recommended by The National Academy of Sciences:

GROUP	CALORIES PER DAY*
Sedentary Women and Elderly Adults	1600
Active Women (Women who exercise aerobically at least 3 times per week), Teenage Girls, and Some Sedentary Men	2200
Active Men, Teenage Boys, and some Extremely Active Women	2800

*(Adjust calories to fit your lifestyle and keep percentage of fat under 30%).

Calories Per Day Recommended For Effective Weight Loss:

The American Dietetic Association recommends that women consume 10 calories per pound of current body weight, (Men - 12 Calories per pound). For example, if a woman weighed 140 pounds, she should consume about 1400 Calories per day. Fat Percentage should be dropped to between 15%-25% of daily calories if possible for optimal fat loss.

Choose servings from the "Daily Nutritional Needs" chart for a well-balanced diet. If your caloric needs are low, choose the smaller number of servings on the chart; if caloric needs are larger, choose the larger numbers of servings. For good health, calories for women should not fall below 1200 (1500 for men). Use these numbers and charts in conjunction with the provided eating plans for losing weight.

CHOLESTEROL, HEART DISEASE, AND SPECIAL HEALTH CONCERNS

High cholesterol, heart disease, and other health problems can be reduced if people would take a few steps to improve the way they eat and take care of themselves. It is important to have regular check-ups with your doctor every year, more frequently if your doctor recommends. Following are some basic facts that should be used as a guideline to help you understand how important a healthy diet and exercise program is for your life. Have your blood cholesterol and blood pressure tested; pay close attention to your level of HDL's (High Density Lipoproteins), LDL's (Low Density Lipoproteins), and Triglycerides. It is best to have this checked with a fasting blood test; it is more accurate. Listen to your body and watch for abnormalities in body change or how you feel. Women need to do regular breast self-examinations as well as with their doctors. Remember, a history of heart disease, high blood pressure, cancer, etc. increases your risk of developing such illnesses. Learn to take care of yourself. Your diet and exercise plan for life can be the key.

Cholesterol:

A wax-like substance produced by the body, cholesterol is made up of several elements. LDL's (referred to as Bad Cholesterol) carry cholesterol to your arteries and leave it to be absorbed into the growing plaque. HDL's (Good Cholesterol) pick up those deposits and carry them away from the arteries and may even prevent the development of plaque. Triglycerides are a type of fat in the blood. By adding your level of HDL + LDL + VLDL (Very Low Density Lipoproteins), or by adding HDL + LDL + 20% of your Triglycerides, you can calculate your total cholesterol.

Most doctors suggest total cholesterol levels be 200 or below for good health, however, more and more physicians are looking at each individual element involved (LDL, HDL, and Triglycerides). Consult with your doctor and agree upon a level that is best for you. A good guide is: LDL should be less than 125, and HDL should be over 45.

HDL, LDL, and Triglycerides, which are contributing factors in heart disease, can usually be controlled by 1) eating a healthy balanced diet made up of complex carbohydrates and a little protein, with less than 30% of the caloric intake coming from fat (no more than 10% of that being saturated fat); 2) reducing your intake of simple sugars to 10% of your daily calories; 3) consuming no more than 250-300 mg of dietary cholesterol daily. (Less is even better); 4) exercising regularly; and 5) not smoking. Some individuals have bodies that overproduce cholesterol and must regulate it with medication prescribed by their doctor.

Studies show that a diet restricted to 10% of calories from fat and regular aerobic exercise can lead to reversal of heart disease in some cases. However, this is very restricted, and not recommended normally due to the fact that you need a plan that is easy to stick to for a lifetime.

Being overfat increases your chances of developing heart disease, high blood pressure, diabetes, and some cancers. This hazardous condition contributes directly to heart attacks; add smoking and high cholesterol to this and the body becomes a time bomb waiting to explode.

Remember that children need to be educated at an early age about the importance of eating right. Studies show that children as young as age 9 are already showing signs of plaque build-up in the arteries due to cholesterol. Check the "Kid's Section" and check with your pediatrician for more ideas on how to feed your kids right.

Keep your blood pressure intact. Recommended readings are *equal to or less than* 120/80. Readings are expressed by a fraction S/D, where:

S = SYSTOLIC PRESSURE
(Pressure produced when heart contracts)

—

D = DIASTOLIC PRESSURE
(Pressure produced when heart relaxes)

Notes and Extra Recipes:

Notes and Extra Recipes:

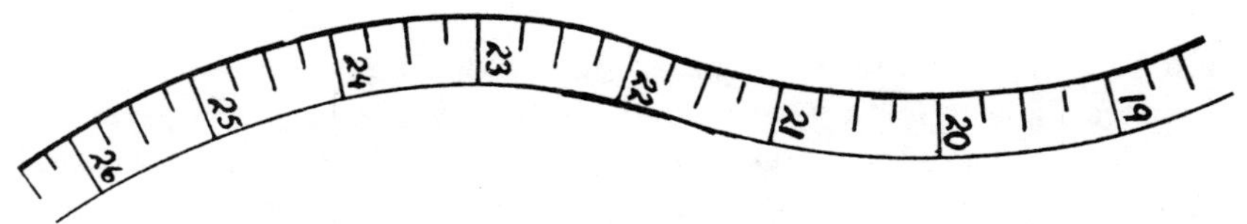

LOSING WEIGHT AND KEEPING IT OFF: A NO-NONSENSE PLAN!

After having read the "Making A Lifestyle Change" section, you should have all the tools you need to plug in to the plan for losing weight. Now you can keep the extra body fat off forever, without dieting!

This section includes basic information, tips, helpful hints on behavior modification, and an Eating Plan that has three levels. Since everyone is different, and we all have different needs, these levels encourage you to choose the plan that will help you be successful in losing that extra body fat. Millions of people every year go on diet after diet in an attempt to lose weight. Most diets leave you feeling depressed and deprived so you don't stick to them or, when you finally do go off the diet, you gain the weight right back. Crash diets only make you fat. You go on the diet temporarily and you lose weight, however, not necessarily body fat. **DIETS DON'T WORK because:**

1) Their weight loss evolves around the scale and not your percentage of body fat.
2) They are so restrictive that you can't stick to it and don't want to.
3) You lose more muscle and water than you do fat.
4) Because of #3, when you do gain the weight again, you gain more fat.
5) You do not learn eating habits that you can stick to for a lifetime, so you go on yet another diet, repeating the process. This process is called **YO YO Dieting**.

How To Get Off The Fat Track:

Counting fat grams is the easiest way I have found to lose the weight and keep it off because it is based on a lifetime plan, not one which temporarily lasts for a week or month. Keeping track of fat grams is easy and once you learn how and are comfortable with it, there is really no counting involved, just a healthy awareness. This program allows YOU to be in charge. It gives you the freedom to choose what you eat so you don't feel deprived. It helps you make permanent, positive changes in the way you eat so you can stay with it for the rest of your life and feel good about it.

Losing weight with the "**Lite Switch**" is about CHOICES. You can have most anything in moderation if you work it into your fat budget, balance it throughout the day or week, and exercise aerobically at least 3 times a week. Occasionally, not every day, allowing yourself to splurge relieves the guilt most diets offer. However, once you really get involved with your low-fat plan and begin using the low-fat alternatives, you will see how quickly your taste buds change. Given time, you will no longer crave many of the high fat foods you are accustomed to eating. You may take a bite of a rich dessert, for example, that you once craved and find that all you really wanted was a bite, and not the whole thing. The richness, the fatty taste, will no longer appeal to you as it once did. It is a great feeling and believe me it does happen. Eat smart and be in control; lose the body fat and keep it off.

TIPS AND PROBLEM SOLVERS:

1. **Decide why you need to lose weight and if it is for the right reasons.** -If it is for your health and well-being, great! - that's the best reason of all! If you are trying to lose for someone else or to try to look like someone else, ask yourself if you are being realistic. People are made differently. Even if you weighed the same as someone you admired, and worked out religiously, it doesn't mean you are going to look like that person. Genetics play a big role in how your body responds to exercise and weight loss. However, this does not give you an excuse to give up and continue poor eating habits. I encourage you to set realistic healthy goals to be the best you can be. Look at the recommended body fat percentages and try to stay within those guidelines. Having body fat that is too low is as dangerous as being overfat.

2. **Make the decision to make a lifetime change,** a change based on healthy choices that you make. Look at it as freedom to choose and freedom to win by losing, not drudgery or deprivation. Take your time, make gradual changes. This is a plan you can stay with; and, YOU WILL see RESULTS!

3. **Exercise aerobically at least 3 times per week to maintain your weight; at least 4-5 times per week to lose.** Healthy eating, restricting your fat intake to 15-20% of your total caloric intake, replacing the fat with complex carbohydrates, plus regular aerobic exercise is the only way to permanent weight loss and, more importantly, to body fat reduction. Read the "Exercise" section for tips on getting started with your exercise plan.

4. **Try not to eat while standing up; make it your new "policy".** Make mealtime a pleasant, not hurried one, if possible. If you must hurry, try not to overeat.

5. **Get out of the habit of nibbling while fixing food in the kitchen.** If you need help, chew gum, suck on a piece of hard candy, munch on raw vegetables or brush your teeth before preparing meals.

6. **Drink at least 8-12 glasses of water each day.** It is especially helpful to drink a glass before meals to help curb your appetite. Listen to your body. Sometimes we think we are hungry, but all our body is asking for is something to drink. Try drinking water, maybe with a squeeze of lemon juice, before reaching for food.

7. **Decide that you will not try to lose more than 2 pounds per week and that you will relax and take your time.** Worrying about dropping 10 pounds in a week or two not only is unrealistic, it will only result in a loss of more muscle than fat and will be gained back quickly. Each time you do this, you end up with more fat and less muscle. Remember, as I said previously, this is called yo-yo dieting which makes you fat! Your scales may show you have lost weight; you did, but it wasn't fat.

8. **If you really want to keep an accurate account of your weight or fat loss, start by getting your body fat tested.** The section "Making a Lifestyle Change" has more on body fat testing.

9. **If you must use the scale, weigh no more than once a week, on the same scale, the same time of day, preferably without clothes or with the same clothes each time to be more accurate.** Use your scale in conjunction with the body fat tests. Since muscle weighs more than fat, you may see a slight weight gain after several weeks if you are exercising and building more lean muscle; however, your clothes should start to fit more loosely.

10. **If you begin to gain weight and your clothes start to fit tighter, and you feel you are not losing body fat for several weeks, keep track of**

everything you eat by writing it down. Keep track of fat grams and calories so you can see where the problem lies. Some-times little things add up. (A good book for use in calculating fat and calories is by Corinne T. Netzer; it is called "The Complete Book of Food Counts." If you need a more structured eating plan to help you get back on the right track, follow the "Eating Plan (Level III)" for losing weight in this section.)

11. Think before you eat! Are you really hungry? Perhaps you are eating out of boredom, habit, stress or for other emotional reasons. Pinpoint your weaknesses and make them strengths. For example, tell yourself, "I used to eat when I was depressed, now I go for a walk or walk up and down the stairs or paint, etc." Make a list of activities you like to do; do these instead of overeating.

12. If you really are hungry, remember, we eat to live, not live to eat! Decide what it is you really want and have that. If it is something you shouldn't have, ask yourself these things. Do I have room for it in my eating plan for today or this week? Is it worth it or is there a substitution that is just as good? Will it satisfy my hunger or only make me want more? How will it make me feel once I have eaten it? If it's something you shouldn't have, but you have decided you really want it, then, it probably is a good idea to go ahead and eat it. Otherwise, you are liable to go through the kitchen devouring everything else to try to satisfy your craving and end up eating more calories and perhaps more fat in the long run. (Moderation and balance are the key).

13. Give yourself positive feedback. Tell yourself (write it down if it helps) what the benefits are of losing weight. Make a list and keep it on the refrigerator. Keep reminding yourself of all the choices you have. Never say I can't have this or that; say I can have anything I choose and learn to make the right choices.

14. Try to eat six mini meals a day, if possible, instead of three large meals; do not skip meals. This keeps you from getting too hungry and keeps your metabolism going. Also, studies show that people who eat too much at one sitting are more apt to gain fat, than those who spread their calories and fat out throughout the day.

15. Try to eat your evening meal as early as possible so as not to go to bed on a full stomach. Better yet, take a walk after your meal; it is a great way to keep your metabolism going to help burn up what you have eaten.

16. If breakfast only makes you hungry, try eating a high carbohydrate breakfast with a little protein. It will stay with you longer.

17. If you come home and you are extremely hungry, stop yourself. Don't begin eating everything in sight. Drink a large glass of ice water with lemon and have some fruit. The fructose in the fruit will curb your appetite by bringing up your blood sugar a little until you are able to have your meal. Drinking something warm like defatted broth also tends to curb your appetite.

18. Be prepared, make sure you have plenty of low fat foods on hand for snacks and meals. (See the Grocery Shopping Section.)

19. Try not to go grocery shopping when you are hungry. Make a list, but keep an eye out for new choices on the market. If you go when you are hungry, take a glass of water, iced tea, or diet soda.

20. Let your conscious not your sub-conscious control your eating. Think about what you are about to put in your mouth. Eat slowly.

21. Make your meals attractive. Don't just prepare a bowl of soup for lunch. Add a few low-fat or fat free crackers and a fruit salad. Make an attractive place setting; you are worth the extra effort. This also tells your mind that you have treated yourself to a nice meal; you are not deprived and now you're finished.

22. Leave food on your plate; you don't have to eat every bite. Push yourself away from the table before you feel full. Give your stomach a chance to tell your brain you've had enough to eat.

23. To lose 1 pound of body fat, you must take 3500 calories away from your stored body fat reserves. Reduce your normal caloric intake by reducing the fat in your diet, and by increasing exercise which will use up your energy stored as fat. For example:

Let's say that you figure your normal daily calories to be around 2000 calories a day, (That's 14,000 calories a week.) If you consume 300 calories less per day (eating only 1700 calories); and, you exercise aerobically (in your Target Zone for about an hour 5 times per week, burning approximately 300 calories each time (total 1500 calories burned); you will reduce your weekly intake. Take your total weekly intake (14,000 calories); Subtract 300 calories per day (300 X 7 Days) = 2100; and subtract the 1500 calories burned during exercise, you have reduced your weekly intake by 3600 Calories (2100 Calories + 1500

Calories). All you needed to do was reduce it by 3500 Calories, so you should easily lose 1 pound a week. Obviously, if you reduced your calories a little more (staying above 1200 for a woman and above 1500 for a man) and exercised one or two more days, you would drop 2 pounds in a week. That's how it works - that's how it stays off - because you're doing it right!

CHOOSING THE PLAN THAT'S RIGHT FOR YOU:

LEVEL I: Follow this plan if you fall into this category:

You do not currently follow a low fat eating and/or exercise plan.
You are overfat or overweight.
You have always dieted and have not been able to stick to anything for very long.

1. **Read the "How Do I Begin" section.** Notice the list ot substitutions. Find several items in the first column that you enjoy; choose a substitution for each of your choices in the second column when snacking or preparing meals. (A few good suggestions to start with are the suggested substitutions for chips and hot sauce, butter, whole milk, and cream cheese. Try these, or any you choose for the first two weeks, adding others gradually when you are ready. Eventually you will graduate to the third column.

2. **Choose some of the menus in the "How Do I Begin" section and prepare them for yourself and your family.**

3. **Keep your changes gradual.** Reduce the amount of fat you consume daily and increase the amount of complex carbohydrates. Replace the amount of fat you normally consume in fried foods, chips, cookies, pastries, mayonnaise, butter, etc. and replace it with pasta, grains, vegetables, potatoes, and fruit. Remember it's not the previously mentioned food items that are unhealthy, it's what most people put on them. Consider some of the "Pizza, Pasta and Potato Toppers"✔ in the recipe section. Most people eat entirely too much protein. Remember, there are other sources of protein like beans and skim milk or nonfat milk products.

4. **Read the section on exercise and make a commitment to exercise at least 3 days a week.** Schedule your time to exercise just like you would any other appointment and keep it.

5. Read the section on "Making a Lifestyle Change" to help you learn how to eat healthy and why it's so important. Start scanning the grocery shopping section and become aware of some of the new low fat products on the market.

6. If you go out to eat, look at the section on "Eating Out The Low Fat Way." Try to begin making wise choices. Remember, gradual change is the key.

LEVEL II: Follow this plan if you fall into this category:

You have been trying to follow a low fat plan without consciously counting fat grams like in Level I and you have seen many changes; you are ready for more positive changes.
You try to exercise at least 3 times a week.
You want to get more serious about your eating and exercise habits.

1. Read "How Do I Begin," "Making a Lifestyle Change," and the section on exercise.

2. Notice the "Substitutions" list in the "How Do I Begin" section. What other changes can you make to reduce your fat intake? Begin choosing foods from the third column.

3. Using the grocery list and menu plans in the section on getting started, shop for the ingredients and prepare the meals. Pay close attention to the new low fat products on the market as you shop. The Lite Shopping Guide under "Eating Lite for Life" will be helpful. Read labels to see where the hidden fats and sugars lie.

4. Decide how many calories you need each day and what percentage of those calories should come from fat. (Remember, as stated before, a good caloric guideline for women trying to reduce their body fat is 10 calories for every pound of current body weight (12 for men); and, percentage of fat between 15 - 25%). If you choose to eat 1500 calories a day and only 20% of those calories comes from fat, figure it by multiplying .20 X 1500 = 300 Calories from fat. To figure the grams you should have, divide 300 by 9 (calories in 1 fat gram). Therefore, at 20%, you should consume 33 grams of fat. To make it easier, the chart on page 26 has numbers done for you. Also, to make counting fat grams easier, The Complete Book of Food Counts by Corinne T. Netzer, is a good choice. You need to become aware of how much fat foods contain, so you are able to make the right choices. You'll be surprised, at some of the things you once thought were low fat. You will quickly become familiar with fat grams and will not need to keep a daily count; you will know how to eat right and be free from dieting forever.

5. Read the section on exercise and make sure you are exercising aerobically with the correct frequency, time, and duration. To lose weight, you should try to exercise at least 4-5 times a week. Doing something every day is even better. Try to vary your workout for the best results.

6. Read the "Kid's Stuff" section to help make this more of a family plan. Healthy eating is for everyone.

LEVEL III: Follow this plan if you fall within this category:

You have been eating low fat for quite awhile and you are at a standstill; you cannot seem to lose those extra 5 or 10 pounds.
You exercise at least 4 - 5 times a week or more.
You are tired of trying to lose weight or body fat; you feel discouraged. After all, you have been really trying.
You need a more structured Step-By-Step plan to help get you on the right track.

1. Make sure you really have a few more pounds to lose. This could be muscle weight, not fat. Recheck your body fat; re-evaluate.

2. Make sure you are eating enough calories. If you restrict your calories too much, your body will go into a starvation mode, so to speak, holding onto everything for dear life. Your body thinks you are trying to starve it and it's natural reaction is to protect itself. Your metabolism slows down and becomes more efficient at running on less fuel; therefore, it's harder to lose weight. Then, when you eat normally it's possible you might even gain weight. Eat at least 1200 calories - more if you work out, mainly of complex carbohydrates, reduce your fat, and exercise to rev up your metabolism.

3. Write down everything you put in your mouth for one week. Don't cheat; be honest and write down everything! Include the calories and fat content (see the recommended book in #4 of the previous section.)

4. Keep a record of your exercise activity that week.

5. Once you have a record of your behavior, you should be able to see where the problem is. Possibilities include:

a) You are eating over 25-30% of your calories from fat and are not aware of it.
b) You are not consuming enough calories.
c) Even though you are consuming very little fat, perhaps you are consuming too many calories. Unfortunately, anything not used by your body will go to your fat cells, causing you to gain weight or body fat.
d) You are not exercising as much as you thought or perhaps you are not doing the proper exercise for fat burning results. If you are in a rut, try some cross-training for an added boost.
e) You are exercising too much, and like in #2, your body is protecting itself from starvation.
f) As you get older, your metabolism slows down more; you need fewer calories and you need to exercise regularly, if possible.
g) Your body has reached its "setpoint" which is a weight at which your body feels comfortable. It is largely determined by genetics. Your body decides where you should be, which may not be where you want it to be, and works at controlling your appetite so you will stay at that point.

By following the tips above, you should be able to lose those last unwanted pounds of body fat. The 1200 and 1500 calorie eating plan which follows helps to take the guesswork out of what you are going to prepare or have to eat. I have talked with so many people who asked that this type of plan be included. It helps people get a focus on how to eat for a healthy lifestyle and stick to it. It shows you that dieting this way is not deprivation, but re-education. Following the plan, which also gives <u>you</u> choices, you get focused again if you have strayed from your healthy plan.

There are many reasons why this eating plan is included. It is not a diet; diets are restrictive and dictate your every move. It is a plan with choices. Many people need a more structured plan to help guide them through something that is new or unfamiliar. Others need something to keep them focused. Some, who have been eating low fat for a long time may have hit a plateau; they may be struggling to lose those last 5-10 pounds. These eating plans help focus on areas that perhaps have been ignored or forgotten. For example, perhaps someone has been eating all or most of his/her calories late at night, or has been eating low fat but consuming way too many calories and not burning them off. Another person may not be losing due to the fact that he/she has not been eating enough calories. Yes, the emphasis nowadays is on fat and not really on calories. This plan does focus on fat; however, if you consume more calories than your body uses, it will be stored as fat in your body. Also, by showing calories and fat, you can see what a tremendous savings you have when you leave off most of the fat. If you used higher fat products you would not only see the fat count go up, but the calorie count as well. Many people have asked for a plan of this kind; thus I felt there was a need for one. This is a guide; the calories and fat grams can be adjusted as needed.

How To Use The Eating Plan:

Included are two plans; one is for 1200 calories and the other is for 1500 calories; both are geared toward 20% of the calories from fat. (Total fat grams for 1200 calorie plan = 26 Fat Grams; 1500 calorie plan = 33 Fat Grams). The breakfast, lunch, and dinner menus are done for you and include calories and fat counts for each meal. Daily calorie and fat totals are not complete. You get to choose additions to meals by selecting extra food servings per meal or adding snacks or other foods whenever you need them. Following these instructions you will find a list of suggested snacks or food additions for meals or anytime. Try some of the other recipes in the book to give yourself even more variety. Enjoy yourself and feel good about what you're learning on your way to a new lifestyle.

The 1200 calorie plan is the basic plan. The 1500 calorie plan is basically the same with extra servings and sometimes additional foods added. Each day you will find the total fat and calories for the day, plus the number of fat grams and calories left for your choice of added food servings, snacks, or meal additions. For example, in the Day 1 Menu for 1200 calories, you have 288 calories left and 18.21 fat grams left that you may use anywhere you please. Let's say you wanted a piece of fat free reduced calorie toast with your breakfast (40 Calories, 0 Fat) and 1 T Heartbeat margarine (75 Calories, 9 Fat). After lunch you decided to have 3 gingersnaps (90 Calories, 1.5 Fat) and a cup of skim milk (80 Calories, 0 Fat). At dinner, you wanted another serving of "Country Market Soup" (34 Calories, 0.21 Fat). Add the total number of calories and fat grams from your snacks and meal additions to the total calories and fat at the end of each day's plan. In this case, the total is 1231 calories and 18.5 grams of fat. The percentage of calories from fat is 13.5. Remember, this is just a sample; you have many choices and you may use your extra calories and fat any way you please. Hopefully, you will make wise choices that will keep you in your calorie and 20% fat range. This plan has the freedom you need so you don't feel deprived.

Snacks or meal additions:

During each day add these to meals or use as snacks when desired. Choose 3 each day or calorie/fat equivalent to what each menu plan has left after the main meals have been calculated. These figures are located at the end of each dinner menu. Again, use these calories and fat grams as you desire at any time during the day. As a guide, following is a list of suggested snacks to choose from. Choose these or something equivalent. Also see "Lite Grocery Shopping."

	FAT	CAL.
1 serving fruit = (½ C canned unsweetened 1 medium whole piece, ½ or medium-size melon)	0	80
1 frozen juice bar or nonfat yogurt bar	0	25-90
I Can't Believe It's Yogurt:		
1 (6¾-oz.) Yoglacé Nonfat yogurt	0	68
1 (9⅓-oz.) Yoglacé Nonfat yogurt	0	93
1 (12-oz.) Yoglacé Nonfat yogurt	0	120
1 (6¾-oz.) Sugar Free Nonfat yogurt	0	115
1 (9⅓-oz.) Sugar Free Nonfat yogurt	0	158
1 (6¾-oz.) Nonfat yogurt	0	135
1 (9⅓-oz.) Nonfat yogurt	0	186
7 Nabisco Garden Crisp Crackers	2	60
½ of a 2-oz. bagel	<1	114
Sliced fresh vegetables approximately	0	35
With 2 T fat free salad dressing	0	67
1 oz. dry nonfat or lowfat cereal (approx.)	0-2	110
with ½ C skim milk	0-2	150
1 serving sugar free jello	0	8
1 serving regular jello	0	80
1 C low sodium defatted chicken or beef broth	0	8
5 C Orville Redenbacher Air Pop Popcorn	1	70
2 rice cakes (corn, wheat, nacho, etc.)	0	80
1 Hostess Lite Cupcake	1	140
1 Hostess Lite Twinkie	1	30

	FAT	CAL.
4 oz. Jello Free pudding	0	100
6 oz. lowfat hot chocolate	1	110
1 (8-oz.) cup non-frozen sugarfree nonfat yogurt	0	90
1 oz. Guiltless Gourmet No Oil tortilla chips	1.4	110
with ¼ C nonfat picanté sauce	1.4	130
1 oz. Mister Salty fat free pretzels	0	100
½ C sugarfree nonfat frozen dietary dessert	0	80
1 C 1% buttermilk	2	100
1 "Blueberry Bran Muffin"✔	<1	146
3 "My Favorite Oatmeal Cookies"✔	1.4	114
¼ C "Pasta Crunch"✔	0	83
½ C "Oscar's Trash Can Mix"✔	1.6	80

A Note For Those of You Who Need to Gain Weight:

Just because you need to gain weight, it doesn't necessarily mean you need more fat. Your goal should be to consume 30% of your calories from fat. The fat you do consume preferably should be canola or olive oil and not fat that is highly saturated. You also should have your body fat tested do see if you are within a healthy range. The main thing is to focus on consuming more calories and maintaining an exercise program 3 times per week.

Finally, if you have special problems in losing body fat or gaining weight and you need more personal assistance, consult a registered dietician, personal trainer, or health professional for help.

DAY 1	Fat	Calories
BREAKFAST		
1200 Calorie Plan:		
¼ of a 5-inch cantaloupe	0	40
1 C oatmeal (cooked)	2	145
½ C skim milk	0	40
Total for 1200 calorie plan:	**2**	**225**
1500 Calorie Plan Add the Following:		
¼ of a 5-inch cantaloupe	0	40
1 slice reduced calorie fat free bread	0	40
1 oz. Healthy Choice Fat Free cream cheese	0	30
Total for 1500 calorie plan:	**2**	**335**
LUNCH		
1200 Calorie Plan:		
2 oz. Louis Rich boneless skinless turkey breast	2	70
1 corn on the cob (½ C)	1	70
1 T liquid Butter Buds	0	6
Mixed green salad plus 2 T fat free salad dressing	0	57
1 Pillsbury soft breadstick	2	100
½ C grapes	0	60
Total for 1200 calorie plan:	**5**	**363**
1500 Calorie Plan Add the Following:		
½ C grapes	0	60
1 Pillsbury soft breadstick	2	100
Total for 1500 calorie plan:	**7**	**523**
DINNER		
1200 Calorie Plan:		
1 serving "Country Market Soup"✔	0.21	34
1 C boiled rice	0	180
1 serving "Stephanie's Favorite Cornbread"✔	0.58	85
¼ C EACH sliced onions and tomatoes	0	25
Total for 1200 calorie plan:	**0.79**	**324**
1500 Calorie Plan Add the Following:		
1 serving "Stephanie's Favorite Cornbread"✔	0.58	85
½ of a 5-inch cantaloupe, sliced	0	80
Total for 1500 calorie plan:	**1.37**	**489**
DAY 1 1200 CALORIE PLAN TOTALS:	**7.79**	**912**
Calories and Fat Grams left for Snacks or Meal Additions:	**18.21**	**288**
DAY 1 1500 CALORIE PLAN TOTALS:	**10.37**	**1347**
Calories and Fat Grams left for Snacks or Meal Additions:	**22.63**	**153**

DAY 2	Fat	Calories
BREAKFAST		
1200 Calorie Plan:		
½ pink grapefruit	0	40
1 plain medium bagel	2	228
1 oz. Healthy Choice Fat Free cream cheese	0	30
Total for 1200 calorie plan:	**2**	**298**
1500 Calorie Plan Add the Following:		
2 t no sugar jelly	0	80
1 C skim milk	0	30
Total for 1500 calorie plan:	**2**	**410**
LUNCH		
1200 Calorie Plan:		
2 slices fat free reduced calorie bread	0	40
1 slice Healthy Choice Fat Free cheese	0	27
1 T Kraft Free mayonnaise	0	12
2 slices fresh tomato	0	10
Mixed green salad plus 2 T fat free salad dressing	2	57
1 peach	0	60
Total for 1200 calorie plan:	**0**	**206**
1500 Calorie Plan Add the Following:		
1 serving Healthy Choice minestrone soup	2	160
Total for 1500 calorie plan:	**2**	**366**
DINNER (At Jack-In-the-Box)		
1200 Calorie Plan:		
1 Chicken Fajita Pita	8	292
1 serving Sesame Breadsticks	2	70
Total for 1200 calorie plan:	**10**	**362**
1500 Calorie Plan Add the Following:		
No added foods		
Total for 1500 calorie plan:	**10**	**362**
DAY 2 1200 Calorie Plan Totals:	**12**	**866**
Calories and Fat Grams Left for Snacks or Meal Additions:	**14**	**334**
Day 2 1500 Calorie Plan Totals:	**12**	**1138**
Calories and Fat Grams Left for Snacks or Meal Additions:	**19**	**362**

DAY 3	Fat	Calories
BREAKFAST		
1200 Calorie Plan:		
6 oz. tomato juice	0	35
1 slice Wonder Light Fat Free reduced calorie bread	0	40
8 oz. nonfat fruit yogurt	0	100
Total for 1200 calorie plan:	**0**	**175**
1500 Calorie Plan Add the Following:		
1 slice Wonder Light Fat Free reduced calorie bread	0	40
Total for 1500 calorie plan:	**0**	**215**
LUNCH		
1200 Calorie Plan:		
1 medium baked potato with skin	1	220
2 t Bac-Os artificial bacon bits	3	68
½ C liquid Butter Buds	0	48
1 slice Healthy Choice Fat Free cheese slices	0	27
1 C diced raw vegetables with 2 T fat free dressing	0	60
Total for 1200 calorie plan:	**4**	**423**
1500 Calorie Plan Add the Following:		
1 apple	4	70
Total for 1500 calorie plan:	**4**	**493**
DINNER		
1200 Calorie Plan:		
2 servings "Vegetarian Lasagna"✔	0.6	106
2 servings "Tossed Italian Vegetables✔	0	68
1 Pillsbury soft breadstick	2	100
Total for 1200 calorie plan:	**2.6**	**274**
1500 Calorie Plan Add the Following:		
1 Pillsbury soft breadstick	2	100
Total for 1500 calorie plan:	**4.6**	**374**
DAY 3 1200 CALORIE PLAN TOTALS:	**6.6**	**872**
Calories and Fat Grams Left for Snacks or Meal Additions:	**19.4**	**328**
DAY 3 1500 CALORIE PLAN TOTALS:	**8.6**	**1082**
Calories and Fat Grams Left for Snacks or Meal Additions:	**24.4**	**418**

DAY 4	Fat	Calories
BREAKFAST		
1200 Calorie Plan:		
½ of a medium banana	0	50
¼ C (1 oz.) Health Valley Fat Free Granola cereal	0	90
½ C skim milk	0	40
Total for 1200 calorie plan:	**0**	**180**
1500 Calorie Plan Add the Following:		
No added foods	0	0
Total for 1500 calorie plan:	**0**	**180**
LUNCH (At McDonalds)		
1200 Calorie Plan:		
1 McLean Deluxe	10	320
1 Side Salad	0	30
½ oz. Lite Vinaigrette Dressing	0.5	15
Total for 1200 calorie plan:	**10.5**	**365**
1500 Calorie Plan Add the Following:		
1 small vanilla yogurt shake	1.3	290
Total for 1500 calorie plan:	**11.8**	**655**
DINNER		
1200 Calorie Plan:		
1 serving "Stir Fry Garden Chicken"✔	3.5	360
Mixed green salad plus 2 T Fat Free salad dressing	0	57
1 C "Fresh Fruit Salad"✔	.3	143
Total for 1200 calorie plan:	**3.8**	**560**
1500 Calorie Plan Add the Following:		
No added foods	0	0
Total for 1500 calorie plan:	**3.8**	**560**
DAY 4 1200 CALORIE PLAN TOTALS:	**14.3**	**1105**
Calories and Fat Grams left for Snacks or Meal Additions:	**11.7**	**95**
DAY 4 1500 CALORIE PLAN TOTALS:	**15.6**	**1395**
Calories and Fat Grams left for Snacks or Meal Additions:	**17.4**	**105**

DAY 5	Fat	Calories
BREAKFAST		
1200 Calorie Plan:		
1 Special K Eggo Waffle	0	80
½ C sliced strawberries	0	80
3 T Reddi Wip Lite Whipped Topping	2	18
½ C skim milk	0	40
Total for 1200 calorie plan:	**2**	**218**
1500 Calorie Plan Add the Following:		
½ C skim milk	0	40
Total for 1500 calorie plan:	**2**	**258**
LUNCH		
1200 Calorie Plan:		
1 (2.5 oz.) Healthy Choice breaded fish fillet	4	120
⅔ C boiled rice, cooked in water mixed with 1 chicken bouillon cube	.5	128
1 T dry Butter Buds	0	6
1 C mixed vegetables	0	70
Total for 1200 calorie plan:	**4.5**	**359**
1500 Calorie Plan Add the Following:		
⅓ C boiled rice	0	60
1 T dry Butter Buds	0	6
Total for 1500 calorie plan:	**4.5**	**425**
DINNER		
1200 Calorie Plan:		
1 serving "Pasta Bean Casserole"✔	1.5	326
¼ of a 5-inch cantaloupe	0	40
Total for 1200 calorie plan:	**1.5**	**366**
1500 Calorie Plan Add the Following:		
½ of a 5-inch cantaloupe	0	80
Total for 1500 calorie plan:	**1.5**	**446**
DAY 5 1200 CALORIE PLAN TOTALS:	**8**	**943**
Calories and Fat Grams left for Snacks or Meal Additions:	**18**	**257**
DAY 5 1500 CALORIE PLAN TOTALS:	**8**	**1129**
Calories and Fat Grams left for Snacks or Meal Additions:	**25**	**371**

DAY 6	Fat	Calories
BREAKFAST		
<u>1200 Calorie Plan:</u>		
Apricot Oat Bran Muffin	0.3	118
6 oz. orange juice	0.1	84
1 oz. Healthy Choice Fat Free cream cheese	0	30
Total for 1200 calorie plan:	**0.4**	**232**
<u>1500 Calorie Plan Add the Following:</u>		
4 oz. nonfat fruit yogurt	0	45
Total for 1500 calorie plan:	**0.4**	**277**
LUNCH		
<u>1200 Calorie Plan:</u>		
1 whole pita pocket bread	<1	180
1 serving "Terrific Tuna Salad"✔	0.18	61
Shredded lettuce and diced tomatoes	0	10
1 oz. Mr. Salty Fat Free pretzels	0	100
Total for 1200 calorie plan:	**<1.18**	**351**
<u>1500 Calorie Plan Add the Following:</u>		
1 oz. pretzels	0	100
Total for 1500 calorie plan:	**<1.18**	**451**
DINNER		
<u>1200 Calorie Plan:</u>		
1 serving "Crispy Quesadillas"✔	1	114
½ C pinto beans	0	100
1 serving "Fiesta Rice"✔	1.3	78
1 serving "Broccoli Cauliflower Salad"✔	0	57
Total for 1200 calorie plan:	**2.3**	**349**
<u>1500 Calorie Plan Add the Following:</u>		
1 serving "Crispy Quesadillas"✔	1	114
Total for 1500 calorie plan:	**3.3**	**463**
DAY 6 1200 CALORIE PLAN TOTALS:	**3.88**	**932**
Calories and Fat Grams left for Snacks or Meal Additions:	**22.12**	**268**
DAY 6 1500 CALORIE PLAN TOTALS:	**4.88**	**1191**
Calories and Fat Grams left for Snacks or Meal Additions:	**28.12**	**309**

DAY 7	Fat	Calories
BREAKFAST		
1200 Calorie Plan:		
½ C scrambled Egg Beaters	0	50
1 (1-oz.) slice Healthy Choice ham	1	35
1 Pillsbury Hearty Grains biscuit	2	80
½ C fresh blueberries	0	45
½ C skim milk	0	40
Total for 1200 calorie plan:	**3**	**250**
1500 Calorie Plan Add the Following:		
1 t Smart Beat Margarine	3	25
1 C skim milk	0	80
Total for 1500 calorie plan:	**6**	**355**
LUNCH		
1200 Calorie Plan:		
1 fajita size flour tortilla	2	100
½ C Old El Paso vegetarian refried beans	1	70
Shredded lettuce and diced tomatoes	0	10
1 oz. Guiltless Gourmet No Oil tortilla chips	1.4	110
¼ C nonfat picanté sauce	0	20
Total for 1200 calorie plan:	**4.4**	**310**
1500 Calorie Plan Add the Following:		
⅔ C boiled rice	0	120
Total for 1500 calorie plan:	**4.4**	**430**
DINNER		
1200 Calorie Plan:		
2 servings "Chicken in A Biscuit"✔	4.4	254
1 serving "Margaret's Vegetable Medley"✔	0.4	87
½ C lite fruit cocktail	0.1	40
Total for 1200 calorie plan:	**4.9**	**381**
1500 Calorie Plan Add the Following:		
½ lite fruit cocktail	0.1	40
Total for 1500 calorie plan:	**5.0**	**421**
DAY 7 1200 CALORIE PLAN TOTALS:	**12.31**	**941**
Calories and Fat Grams left for Snacks or Meal Additions:	**13.7**	**259**
DAY 7 1500 CALORIE PLAN TOTALS:	**15.4**	**1206**
Calories and Fat Grams left for Snacks or Meal Additions:	**17.6**	**294**

EXERCISE - THE FINISHING TOUCH TO MAKE YOUR ROAD TO A HEALTHY LIFE COMPLETE

Exercise is important to everyone from children to older adults. Whether you're trying to lose weight/body fat, increase your flexibility, tone up your body, strengthen your cardiovascular system, or do a combination of these things, exercise is the last piece of the puzzle that will make your healthy lifestyle complete. There are many activities to choose from and many benefits from exercise, not just physical, but also mental. Beginning should be a gradual process; find the activity that is right for you and make the necessary preparations to do it. Focus on the benefits and do everything you can to help yourself be successful. If you have certain health or physical limitations or if you have not exercised aerobically in a long time, again please consult with your doctor before beginning an exercise program. It is a lot of fun once you give yourself a chance; you will see your efforts pay off quickly if you gradually follow the guidelines below.

You're Number 1 goal in beginning an exercise plan should be for you to get your cardiovascular system (body systems relating to the heart and blood vessels) in shape. That is why aerobic exercise is so important. Other benefits will appear just by beginning this plan first.

Use These Tips to Make Your Exercise Plan a Success:
1) Choose an aerobic activity in an atmosphere you will enjoy; choose something you can stay with. Have a list of alternate activities you can do in case something interferes with that activity. For example, if you choose swimming as your activity and you swim in an outside pool, then you need to have an alternate activity when you are unable to swim due to weather. It is also a good idea to keep this list handy so you can choose from a variety of activities to keep you from getting bored. As you become more and more fit, alternating between different activities is a great challenge to yourself. This variety is called cross training. Your body is challenged by different activities, so your fitness abilities tend to be strong in different areas. For example, your cross-training schedule might look like this (the first activity listed would be for someone who is in fairly good shape, the activities in parenthesis would be for someone just beginning):

Monday - 1 hour low impact aerobics - (30-minute moderate walk)
Tuesday - 30 minutes resistance training - (Rest)
Wednesday - 1 hour bench aerobics - (45 minutes low intensity low impact aerobics)

Thursday -	30 minutes resistance training - (Rest)
Friday -	Brisk walk - 1 hour - (30-minutes moderate walking)
Saturday -	1 hour bench aerobics (weekend - walk if you want to)
Sunday -	Rest

2) Set realistic goals; begin gradually and evaluate your progress as you go. You did not get out of shape in a week. Don't expect to get back into shape that quickly. You will get there. Do it gradually; do it right this time so you will stay with it.

3) Make an exercise appointment. Schedule it just like you would schedule getting your hair cut or a business meeting. Put it on your calendar and plan other things around it. Plan a time with the least distractions.

4) Make exercise a family affair and a regular part of your life. That way you always have a support system and you are teaching good habits. Remember there is always an excuse not to do something; focus on the reasons to get in shape!

5) Measure your success by getting your body fat tested before you begin or by using your tape measure so you can see proof of results other than the obvious changes. Keep a log and record your progress.

6) Exercise with a friend for added support, motivation, and fun. You can do this at home or at a health club. At home, for example, let one person ride the exercise bike, while the other person does a step workout with a video for 2-3 minutes; change activities quickly and repeat until the aerobic session is over. This helps the workout go by faster.

7) Don't overdo. When you are first beginning, just because something is great, more is not necessarily better. Progress gradually performing moderate aerobic exercise from 3 days a week to eventually 1 time each day if you like, varying the activities (see cross-training above).

8) If you have to skip your workout for any reason, begin again as soon as possible, especially when you are just starting. It is extremely important when beginning a fitness program to workout during your scheduled 3 times per week; if you have to change your schedule, that's okay, as long as you do it. Make a commitment to yourself to start with 3 days a week at least for 4-6 weeks. Do not miss for any reason unless it is absolutely necessary. Once you miss, it's just too easy to miss again and again. I promise you that you will see results if you follow a gradual plan of reducing the fat intake and doing moderate aerobic exercise.

You will see and feel a difference in yourself. I think you'll be hooked. You can do it!

9) Don't use exercise as a punishment. It is your reward. Your body loves it!

10) You can do a few things to supplement your workout and keep your metabolism revved up: a) Do some abdominal crunches, push-ups, or a few resistance activities with weights while watching T.V.; b) Take the stairs whenever you can instead of the elevator; c) Walk or bicycle instead of driving when possible; d) Keep moving after a meal.

What Activity is Best For You and How Do You Begin For Best Results:
1) Choose something aerobic first. Aerobic, meaning with oxygen, is an activity that can be done steadily for a sustained period of time, (a minimum of 20 minutes), that elevates your body temperature and increases your need for oxygen. Performed in the right amount of Frequency (F), Intensity (I) and Time (T), aerobic exercise has many benefits. (See Exercise Benefits as you continue this section.) Choose an activity where you can apply the FIT principles:

Frequency - At least 3 times per week when beginning a program or to maintain your fitness level (4-5 times at least per week if your goal is to lose body fat and condition more cardiovascularly).

Intensity - Is the level you stay in (within your Target Heart Rate - see following chart) every time you exercise, which promotes maximum fat-burning results and conditioning of the heart and lungs. Exercising out of the zone is anaerobic; activities that stop and start or which do not last a long enough Time (see below) are considered anaerobic. Activities such as tennis, volleyball, sprinting, football, golf, ballet, bowling, etc. are a great part of a fitness program but don't do much for the cardiovascular system.

Time - Time spent on your aerobic workout. Beginners try 20 - 30 minutes at first. You can do more if you keep the intensity very low and listen to your body. Don't overdo. Gradually build up to 45 - 60 minutes. The longer duration (in your target zone) the more fat burning benefits you get. Also, the reason you need to work out for minimum of 20 minutes is because your body needs a little time to get it's fat burning process in gear. The more you work out, the quicker it will start.

TO FIND YOUR PULSE TO CHECK YOUR HEART RATE (see Intensity above) - Place your forefinger and middle finger against the inside of your opposite wrist; press gently to feel the pulse. You may also check it by placing those same fingers on the opposite side of your neck. Find your Adam's apple; slide your fingers over about 2 inches and press lightly to find the pulse. Count each beat (the pulse) for 10 seconds (beginning with zero) and count up. Walk around as you check your pulse.

To figure your target heart rate use this formula:

Subtract your age from 220 = X (your maximum heart rate)
Multiply X by .6 (60% of your maximum) = Y
Multiply X by .85 (85% of your maximum) = Z

To make it even easier, use this chart (the first number represents a 10-second count; the second number represents a 60-second count):

Average Target Zones (These values represent a 10-second pulse count)			
AGE	**60%**	**70%**	**85%**
20	20 (120)	23 (140)	28 (170)
25	20 (117)	23 (137)	28 (166)
30	19 (114)	22 (133)	27 (162)
35	19 (111)	22 (130)	26 (157)
40	18 (108)	21 (126)	26 (153)
45	18 (105)	21 (123)	25 (149)
50	17 (102)	20 (119)	24 (145)
55	17 (99)	19 (115)	23 (140)
60	16 (96)	19 (112)	23 (136)
65	16 (93)	18 (108)	22 (132)
70	15 (90)	17 (105)	21 (127)
75	14 (87)	16 (101)	20 (123)

Check the chart on the previous page to make sure you are in your zone for maximal cardiovascular and fat-burning effect. Obviously if it is too high, you are working too hard, to low, not hard enough. Check your heart rate near the beginning of your workout, in the middle, and at the end. It should start out low and increase gradually and stay at about the same moderate level, then decrease as you begin to cool down. Be sure your pulse is 20 or below before you sit or lie down.

Stay within the 60%-70% level for the first 4 - 6 weeks when starting out, then progress up if desired. As you work out more, you will become more familiar with how it feels to be in your Target Zone. Then, you may use the Perceived Exertion Scale. Basically, this is a scale that rates how you feel while exercising. You should exercise at a level that is rated as "somewhat hard"; you should still be able to talk or carry on a conversation without huffing and puffing and gasping for breath. This scale is good for people on medication that alters the heart rate.

2) Know that choosing the right aerobic activity for you can have many benefits that should keep you motivated. Exercise:

- Burns up some of the calories we take in by increasing your basal metabolic rate.
- Creates a sense of well-being and accomplishment.
- Relieves stress. This is a very important benefit, especially in today's society where undo stress seems to be the norm. Too much stress or tension within the body can cause overeating, drinking, smoking, sleep disorders, and severe health problems. Stress can be relieved by first pinpointing what is causing the stress and then trying to remove or reduce it as much as possible. Try to learn to say "No", and not overextend yourself. Make a list of 5 or 6 things you have to do each day in order of preference; check them off one at a time and only do those things you can do today; write other things down on the "tomorrow list" and save them until them. Save some time for you. We all are guilty of not taking the time to relax and set aside time for the little things that are most important in life. Laughing and smiling with good friends and family plus lots of love and hugs are great stress relievers.
- Helps you lose or maintain your body weight/body fat.
- Raises HDL (good cholesterol), important in the reduction of cholesterol in your body.
- Lowers your body fat percentage along with a low fat eating plan by increasing lean muscle mass.
- Helps control your appetite.
- Helps increase your stamina.

- Can lower high blood pressure.
- Lowers resting heart rate.
- Reduces your risk of heart disease, especially when accompanied with a low fat diet.
- Helps in the prevention of osteoporosis in elderly women if the exercise is weight bearing in nature and is accompanied with prober calcium intake.
- Helps you gain strength, tone up, and improve cardiovascular fitness, thus increasing energy level.
- Increases flexibility.

3) Choose an aerobic activity depending on:
a) How fit you are
b) If you have any physical or health limitations or handicaps
c) How long it has been since you exercised
d) If what you enjoy doing involves being with a group as provided by a health club, or if what you enjoy is working out by yourself or with a close friend.

Examples of some aerobic activities include high intensity aerobics, low impact aerobics, dancing, bench stepping, brisk walking, bicycling, chair aerobics (discussed below) jogging, cross-country skiing, rowing, rebounding (mini trampoline), water aerobics, swimming, stair climbing, jumping rope, safe exercise video, etc. - (Something that keeps you moving).

4) If you have a physical or health limitation or a handicap, I encourage you to do something that will help keep your body moving. Walking, water aerobics, and some low impact aerobics are a few activities that can accommodate most people. If you are able to do these activities, try "Chair Aerobics". It is something almost anyone can do. All you need is some of your favorite music, on a tape or on the radio, and a chair.

a) Sit in your chair.
b) Do some slow rhythmic movements using your arms and legs. If you are not able to lift your legs, pull them up gently using your arms. If you are not able to do this, just use your upper body.
c) Begin slow stretching exercises like reaching up, down, over to the side, and in front. Stretch out your legs. Moves in (a), (b) and (c) are your warm-up and should last about 5 minutes.
d) Begin moving rhythmically a little faster according to your abilities. Point and flex your toes and feet. Rotate your ankles. Do the same with your arms, wrists, and shoulders. Extend your lower legs one at a time and put them down. Then lift your legs one at a time.

Continue these types of movements for about 10 minutes. Don't overdo the first time. Gradually build up your strength and endurance. Do not do anything that hurts or is extremely uncomfortable. Listen to your body; do what you can do. Soon you will be able to do your workout for at least 20-30 minutes, which is the recommended time.

e) Cool your body down in much the same way that you warmed up. Don't just stop completely. Gradually reduce your intensity, then stretch. Drink sips of cool water during exercise and plenty afterwards.

5) Whatever activity you do, begin with a warm up for about 3-5 minutes of rhythmic movement as mentioned in # 4, only standing up. Then stretch without bouncing for another 3 minutes or so, making sure your back is supported at all times. Do not stretch past your point of tension. The old theory "No pain, no gain" does not apply. If you feel pain during the cool down, or any part of your workout, stop, change what you are doing to something that is mildly hard but not uncomfortable. This holds true for any exercise.

6) If you decide on working out at home, you can do many of the listed activities. Set a time just for you with the least amount of distractions. Turn on the answering machine and make this time count. Four safe, highly effective and motivating exercise video tapes are by Susan Cooper and Madeleine Lewis. If you do aerobics at home, just make sure you have a space to move freely. When doing bench or step, you can make your own bench or have someone make one for you. Begin with a 4-inch bench, especially if you are short. If you are tall, over 5'6", try a 6-inch bench. If you have knee problems, keep the bench height low and check with your doctor to make sure it is the right activity for you. If you are having your bench made, a good size is 32 inches across X 13½ inches deep and 4-6 inches tall.

7) Before you begin your activity, make sure you have the proper clothes and shoes to prevent injury. Having the proper shoes, clothes, equipment makes a difference. If you get injured because you did not have the proper shoes, for example, then you will not be able to exercise.

8) If you have decided on joining a health club, check to make sure the aerobics instructors are certified; also check out the classes. Ask questions to make sure they are informed about safety and the newest techniques. Check to make sure the equipment is in good shape. Join with a friend to help keep each other motivated to keep going.

9) In addition you may decide to do some weight training along with your aerobic exercise to help tone your muscles and increase your strength. By building lean muscle you also burn more fat because it requires more calories per day to support lean muscle tissue. When I say "build muscle", I don't mean like a body builder. That takes very specialized training. Some of you may wish to progress to that type of training; I am simply talking about toning and strengthening the muscles. Choose some form of resistance (start out just using your body weight, then hand weights, exercise bands or tubing). The weight should be heavy enough so that when you start to do the 12th or 15th repetition of the exercise, it is extremely difficult. Adjust your resistance up or down; repeat up to 3 times (3 Sets). Move slowly when using resistance; be careful not to hyperextend joints. Breath out on the exertion; inhale on the release. Try using the exercise equipment provided by a health club, but make sure you get accurate, safe instruction from a professional before beginning.

Exercise Review:

1) Choose an aerobic activity you will enjoy and make a schedule to stick with.

2) Warm up rhythmically by walking or moving around, then by stretching the muscles slowly (about 5-10 minutes - the latter when the temperature is cold, and cool down properly, about 5 minutes) each time to prevent injury. (Note: some exercise professionals are saying that the warm-up can be shorter, however, until more facts are out, I suggest the longer time just to be safe.

3) Sustain aerobic activity from 20-60 minutes.

BodyBusiness
COOPER-REEVES WORKOUT©

GET A JUMP ON THE ACTION!

Get faster results from your workouts with fitness techniques developed by internationally recognized fitness leader Susan Cooper, M.A., co-owner of BodyBusiness, Inc. and BodyBusiness Education Services and Training in Austin, Texas.

Turn on the POWER and fire up the intensity in a traditional Bench class. The 75 minute PowerMetrics workout and instructional video incorporate power moves with advanced Bench choreography to challenge your physical potential.

Does Your Muscle work pack a punch — or is it down for the count? The BodyBusiness KNOCK-OUT Series is sculpting that "hits" the muscle where it counts!

BELOW THE BELT

The 30 minute UPPER CUT workout takes the upper body through innovative muscle sculpting combinations and introduces the unique D.O.A. technique. Developed by BodyBusiness, D.O.A. — Definition using Opposite Action, is guaranteed to shock the muscle and tone the body faster than any program on the market. BELOW THE BELT takes the "floor" out of floorwork with 30 minutes of intense lower body sculpting incorporating D.O.A. and PowerMetric techniques on and off the Bench.

The KNOCK-OUT Series includes both the 45 minute UPPER CUT Workout/Instructional Video and the 45 minute BELOW THE BELT Workout/Instructional Video. See reverse side for ordering information.

POWER*METRICS*

BodyBusiness
2700 W. Anderson Lane, Suite 102
Austin, Texas 78757
(512)459-9424

Please send me:

___**KNOCK-OUT Series** which includes: The 45 minute UPPER CUT Workout/Instructional Video and the 45 minute BELOW THE BELT Workout/Instructional Video. Each: $32.95 (includes postage/handling). Texas residents add $2.40 sales tax per order.

___**UPPER CUT Workout/Instructional Video** only. Each: $22.95 (includes postage/handling). Texas residents add $1.60 sales tax per order.

___**BELOW THE BELT Workout/Instructional Video** only. Each: $22.95 (includes postage/handling). Texas residents add $1.60 sales tax.

Send check or money order to:

BodyBusiness
2700 W. Anderson Lane
Suite 802
Austin, Texas 78757.

Credit card phone orders accepted by calling **(512) 459-9424**

BodyBusiness
2700 W. Anderson Lane, Suite 102
Austin, Texas 78757
(512)459-9424

Please send me:

___**KNOCK-OUT Series** which includes: The 45 minute UPPER CUT Workout/Instructional Video and the 45 minute BELOW THE BELT Workout/Instructional Video. Each: $32.95 (includes postage/handling). Texas residents add $2.40 sales tax per order.

___**UPPER CUT Workout/Instructional Video** only. Each: $22.95 (includes postage/handling). Texas residents add $1.60 sales tax per order.

___**BELOW THE BELT Workout/Instructional Video** only. Each: $22.95 (includes postage/handling). Texas residents add $1.60 sales tax.

Send check or money order to:

BodyBusiness
2700 W. Anderson Lane
Suite 802
Austin, Texas 78757.

Credit card phone orders accepted by calling **(512) 459-9424**

MADHOUSE PRODUCTIONS
5525 West 123rd Street
Hawthorne, California 90205

❐ YES! Please send me _____ copies of the California Calorie Burner Video by Madeleine Lewis. For each copy send $19.95 plus $3.00 (shipping/handling).

_____ copies × $19.95 . . . . $______

$3 P&H per Video . . . . $______

Total . . . . $______

✂ ____

MADHOUSE PRODUCTIONS
5525 West 123rd Street
Hawthorne, California 90205

❐ YES! Please send me _____ copies of the California Calorie Burner Video by Madeleine Lewis. For each copy send $19.95 plus $3.00 (shipping/handling).

_____ copies × $19.95 . . . . $______

$3 P&H per Video . . . . $______

Total . . . . $______

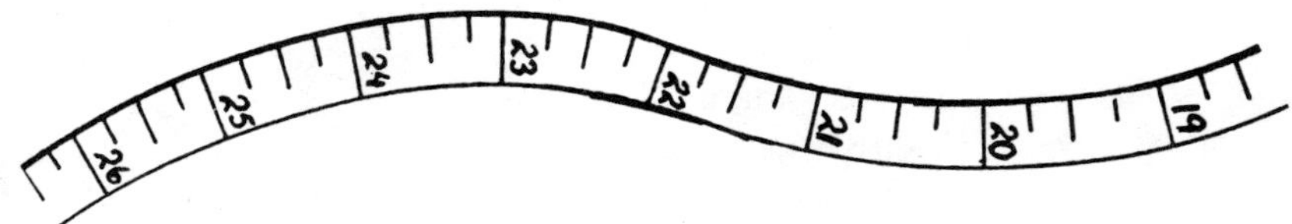

EATING LITE FOR LIFE

Making the lifestyle change for a lifetime is easier now more than ever, with all the new low-fat products to choose from on the market. This change for the better not only involves what you eat at home; it spills over into every aspect of your life. Whether you're serving low-fat creations to your friends, entertaining guests, preparing for the holidays, or eating away from home - this guide will make your life a little easier.

COMPANY'S COMING - DON'T PANIC!

Most people do very well when changing to low-fat eating; however, they panic when company is coming for dinner. Surprisingly enough, there are many dishes you can serve easily for even your hardest-to-please "customers". Listed below are several suggested menu plans. These are some of my favorites that have been "tested" on people other than family. It's great to see them enjoy the meal, then tell them they have just eaten a low-fat, low-cholesterol meal. Keep in mind that these are suggestions. I do not always serve dessert after a heavy meal. Feel free to mix and match.

Mexican Fiesta:

Guiltless Gourmet baked No Oil tortilla chips
Picanté sauce (containing no oil)
"Great Guacamole"✔
"Ross's Chicken Fajitas on the Grill"✔
"Mild Mexican Rice"✔
Old El Paso vegetarian refried beans
"Lillian's Margaritas"✔ (optional)
"Fresh Fruit Compote"✔

Elegant Dinner:

"Melt in your Mouth Eye of Round Roast"✔
"Scalloped Potatoes"✔
"Meme's Famous Carrots"✔
"Fresh Green Salad"✔
"Cheesecake to Diet For"✔ topped with fresh fruit

Italian Specialty:

"Best Baked Lasagna"✔
"Tossed Italian Vegetables"✔
"Quick Focaccia Bread"✔
"Easy Meringues"✔ topped with fresh fruit, 2 squirts of Reddi Wip

Seafood Spectacular:

"Aunt Maggie's Shrimp Casserole"✔
"Just Plain Ol' Cooked Vegetables"✔(choose broccoli or any favorite and cook as directed)
"Lite Fresh Strawberry Shortcake"✔ or "Surprise Peach Cobbler"✔

Casual But Special:

"Taco Puff Pie"✔ any variety is great
"Fresh Green Salad"✔ or "Shoe Peg Vegetable Salad"✔
"Lillian's Angel Food Cake"✔ serve plain or ice with prepared Betty Crocker Fluffy White frosting and serve with fresh fruit.

Quick As a Flash

"Quick Chicken Spaghetti"✔ or "Easy Chicken Parmesan"✔
"Fresh Green Salad"✔
1 loaf sour dough bread
1 quart nonfat frozen yogurt topped with fat free chocolate syrup and a squirt of Reddi Wip

HAPPY HOLIDAYS

Most people seem to overindulge during the holidays. Prepare yourself mentally before the holidays arrive. Remember holidays don't have to be hard on your fat budget. When eating at someone else's home, try to stay away from the sauces or casserole-type dishes. These usually contain butter or margarine, cheese, or other high fat items. Choose bread, plain green salad, vegetables, lean meat, jello, fruit, angel food cake, even fruit pies and cobbler's - but leave the crust. Adding fat-laden salad dressings and margarine or butter to some of these good choices is where you add the extra fat (also see section on "Eating Out The Low Fat Way").

If, however, you are unable to avoid some of these tempting foods, try to balance out your meals prior to and after you know you'll be eating more fat. Make sure you continue your exercise program and perhaps add an extra day around the holidays. No time to exercise, you say? Take the stairs whenever possible, park as far as you can from the door to the mall or grocery store and walk briskly (using safety precautions of course). Wouldn't it be nice to come away from holidays still looking and feeling great, not dreading looking at the bathroom scale?

Here are some suggestions for holiday recipes. Other menus including delicious appetizers are listed under "How Do I Begin"✔. Choose from these or other recipes in the book to make your holidays a special time.

Turkey (see "Main Dish - Poultry Time Savers"✔ section)
"Melt in Your Mouth Eye of Round Roast"✔
"Company Turkeyloaf"✔
"Grandaddy Rousse's Syllabub"✔
"Heavenly Ambrosia"✔
"Lillian's Cranberry Salad"✔
"Aunt Jodie's Cornbread Dressing"✔
"Creamed Potatoes"✔
"Aunt Jodie's Favorite Sweet Potatoes"✔
"Holiday Asparagus"✔
"Honey Glazed Carrots"✔
"Mema's Quick Sizzle Beans"✔
"Nana's Never-Fail Hot Rolls"✔
"Pumpkin Spice Bread"✔ with "Nonfat Whipped Cream"✔
"Ruby's Pecan Pie"✔
"I Can't Wait Cake"✔
"Chocolate Lover's Dream Torte"✔

LITE SHOPPING GUIDE

Be a Label Reader:

Food labels can be confusing and deceiving. That's why it pays to be informed so you can make good, healthy food choices. Always look at the labels to make sure you know what you are eating.

Most food labels contain serving size, number of servings per container, calories, fat, carbohydrates, protein, sodium, and cholesterol per serving, and information on other nutrients and vitamins.

Many products claim to be healthy, lean, 90% fat free, etc. but may be misleading. For example, many products that say "Cholesterol-Free", contain highly saturated fats like coconut oil, palm kernel oil, palm oil, and hydrogenated oils or fats. Presently, the Food and Drug Administration is working on a new labeling system that is more specific, states the fact more clearly, and should be easier to understand.

Avoid foods containing large amounts of sugar. Some key words besides sugar are corn syrup, honey, or words ending in -ose like fructose, lactose, glucose, sucrose, etc. Many processed or prepackaged foods contain large amounts of sodium. Most people need no more than 3000 mg per day (1½ t). People who are at risk for high blood pressure or who have high blood pressure should try to consume no more than about 2000 mg per day (½ t).

Look for products containing lots of fiber, such as bran cereals, beans, and other products.

Check products for the number of fat grams compared to the calorie count per serving (percentage of calories from fat). Remember, a good rule of thumb is no more than 3 fat grams for every 100 calories. Limit saturated fat to 10% or less each day. To calculate percentage of calories from fat, use the following formula:

(9 calories) × (number of grams of fat per serving) = X
X ÷ (total calories per serving) = Y
Y = percentage of calories from fat

Labels list ingredients in descending order by weight. Main ingredients are listed first, followed by the ones used in smaller amounts. Thus, the first 2 or 3 items listed make up the majority of that food item. For example, in a can of Old El Paso Vegetarian refried beans the list of ingredients are: Cooked beans, water, salt, soybean oil, and onion powder. This product is made up mostly of beans and water. It does contain a small amount of polyunsaturated fat; but, by looking at the label you can see that the amount of fat is small, only about 12%. The nutritional information per serving is:

Serving Size: . . . . . . 4 oz.

Servings Per Container	4	Fat	1 g
Calories	70	Cholesterol	0 mg
Protein	6 g	Sodium	590 mg
Carbohydrate	15 g	Potassium	320 mg

You can see that there are 4 (4-oz. or ½ C) servings in the can. Each serving has 70 calories with 1 fat gram. There are 9 calories in every fat gram. Using the formula shown on page 66, we can calculate total calories from fat:

$$(9 \text{ calories}) \times (1 \text{ gram of fat per serving}) = 9$$
$$9 \div (70 \text{ calories per serving}) = .12$$

Which means that about 12% of the calories are from fat. As you can see, this is a good choice.

Going Shopping:

The food items on the grocery list beginning on page 70 are here as a guide to keep you on the right track to living a healthy lifestyle. The list includes a wide variety of fat free and low-fat products currently available in most major supermarkets. A few items over 30% fat, indicated with an *, are still good choices used in moderation with a low-fat plan.

The list is as up-to-date as possible as of this printing, Fall 1992. However, there are newer and better products hitting the shelves each day. For example, Land O'Lakes now makes a fat free sour cream; feel free to substitute this in any recipe calling for "Nonfat Yogurt Cheese"✔ if desired. Nonfat buttermilk is also available in some places; please substitute this for the 1% buttermilk called for in some recipes as an added bonus. Improvements are made even on healthy products already on the market to make them better choices. A product that may not have been a healthy choice one day, may have been revised or changed the next day so please keep reading those labels.

Making the right Choices - The purpose of this section is to show you that you do have choices; and, it shows how to find them in the stores. In reading the labels, notice that some low-fat items I listed may be higher in sodium and sugar than some others; a few may contain small amounts of saturated fat such as partially hydrogenated oils, whole milk, chicken fat, etc. Please use these products in moderation and remember to keep your saturated fat intake and consumption of simple sugars (sweets sweetened with sugar and sugar equivalents) to 10% or less of your total fat and carbohydrate intake respectively.

It is important especially for those of you just beginning a low-fat plan to know about choices so you can stick to your plan without feeling deprived. These products are so much better than the high fat alternatives; and, if you are following a healthy eating plan, you can occasionally budget some of these fat grams and milligrams of cholesterol into your daily intake thus adding more variety to your choices. It also keeps you from feeling deprived; it's kind of a way to feel you're cheating but you're really not. Again, let me say that I am showing you that there are more choices than ever before. There is no excuse anymore for not trying to eat better and eat better for life. The choice is yours; happy shopping.

Where to Find Products - For convenience, I tried to list food items like you might find them in the stores. Most of the major grocery stores carry or will soon carry these items. In shopping I have found that most Tom Thumb and Albertson's stores seem to be leaders in carrying the products sooner than some of the others. However, other major stores such as Food Lion, Kroger, Minyards and Winn Dixie carry many of the low-fat products. Also, as you know, just because one Tom Thumb carries a product, it doesn't mean the one on the other side of town will carry it. Talk with your store managers where you shop; they will pay attention to your requests if you keep telling them they need to order more healthy products. Healthy products can also be found at Sam's Wholesale Club. They have many low-fat items found in bulk that can save you money.

Saving Money - While on the subject of saving money - some low-fat foods are more expensive than their higher fat competitors. However, I feel that as more products come out on the market, the prices will come down; in fact some prices are already doing so. Cooking your meals at home will definitely save you money as opposed to eating out, and many leftovers can be used the next days. Use your coupons and shop wisely, stocking up when the store has "specials". Don't forget about bread stores; they have special days when their food items are even cheaper than on regular days and many take coupons.

Try not to shop when you are hungry; you may buy more than you need or buy things that are not healthy. If you'd like to buy foods in bulk but are afraid you'd never use them all or they might go to waste, why not share with a friend who feels the same way. Cut your groceries and your grocery bill in half. To save cooking time, find a friend that is cooking healthy too. One night a week or month cook double the amount you usually cook. Give half to a friend and let your friend do the same for you.

The bottom line is your health and the health of your family. Perhaps you spend a little more in one area; aren't you worth it, especially if it might help prevent an illness or medical costs in the future. Isn't it worth it just to feel better? Your body feels better and you feel better about yourself. I find these things to be true in our family and friends have shared with me these same statements. I hope you find these things to be true for you and your family as well. There are no guarantees but studies show that a healthy lifestyle brings a better quality of life which is what we all strive for anyway.

With all of these elements to consider, shopping for healthy foods may seem a daunting task. The grocery list on the following pages is designed to make that task easier. To help you further, I have included phone numbers of some of the food companies should you need to know where their products are sold in your area. Numbers of companies whose foods are used frequently are listed below. Other numbers are listed on the following pages with their products. As always, if you need help, please don't hesitate to call (817) 460-2280.

Health Valley (800) 423-4846
Healthy Choice (800) 323-9980
Kraft Light & Lively Dairy Products (800) 551-5557

♥ This symbol designates products that have been added to the grocery list since the first printing.

PRODUCE SECTION

Fresh herbs and spices such as garlic, basil etc.
Marie's Lite & Zesty Fat Free Dressings

DELI

Butterball Lite Lunchmeats
Healthy Choice Lean Lunchmeats
Louis Rich Lean Lunchmeats
Plantation Turkey Meat Products and Skinless Chicken Products
Weight Watcher's Lean Lunch meats

Afghan Kabuli Gourmet Natural Pizza Crust
Afghan Natural Bread (Long Whole thin bread - Use for pizza crusts, slice into thin pieces and make breadsticks) (214) 247-9835♥
A11 Natural Crackle Rice Snacks by Jacquet
Alpine Lace Free 'N Lean Fat Free Cheese
Bagels
American Grains Rice Bites
Bialys - No Fat Bagels♥
Crispini Mediterranean Snacking Crisps
International New York Style Soft Breadsticks
Kangaroo Pocket Bread
Light & Tasty Fat Free Crackers by Jacquet
Mr. Pita Bread or any brand without fat
Water Crackers

BREADS, BAKED GOODS COOKIES, CRACKERS, DRIED FRUIT. RICE CAKES

Earthgrain's Honey Wheatberry, Whole Grains and Nuts, and French Bread, English Muffins, etc.
Orowheat (English) Muffins
Pepperidge Farm Stuffing (Herb Seasoned, Cubed Country Style, and Cornbread)
Pepperidge Farm Raisin Bread with Cinnamon, Light Style and Soft Whole Wheat Breads
Wonder Light Fat Free Bread, Low-Fat Rolls and Hamburger and Hot Dog Buns

Archway Gingersnaps
Comet (Ice Cream) Cones and Cups
Del Monte Orchard Fruit Mix Fruit Snacks
Entenmann's Fat-Free Cakes and Cookies
Featherweight Crackers
Fifty 50 Cookies and Crackers (Sometimes in Diet Section)
Frookie Fat-Free and Low-Fat Cookies and Gourmet Fat-Free Crackers (Sometimes in Diet or Gourmet Section)
Gardetto's Mustard Flavor Pretzel Mix (800) 257-3663♥
Hain (Mini Cheddar, Apple Cinnamon, Cheese, and honey Nut Rice Cakes)
Health Valley Graham Crackers (All Varieties) and Rice Bran Crackers (Sometimes in Diet or Gourmet Food Section)
Health Valley Cookies and crackers (Most Varieties and sometimes in Diet or Gourmet Section)
Heart Lover's Popped Corn Cakes♥
Hol-Grain Crackers and Lite Snack Thins (sometimes in Diet or Gourmet Section)
Honey Maid Graham Crackers
Hostess Light Cupcakes, Twinkies, and Cinnamon Crumb Coffee Cake
Jacquet Crackle Rice Snacks
Keebler Elfin Delights Lowfat Cookies and Crackers♥
Keebler (Ice Cream) Cones, Cups, and Waffle Cones
Kroger Fat-Free Crackers

Kroger Vanilla Wafers
Melba Toast
Mother's Dinosaur Grahams and Fat Free Fig Bars♥
Mr. Phipps Pretzel Chips and Tater Crisps (BBQ, Sour Cream and Onion and Original - GREAT!♥
Nabisco Fat-Free Saltine Crackers
Nabisco Garden Crisps Vegetable Crackers
Nabisco Harvest Crisps Crackers
Nabisco SnackWells (All Varieties Reduced Fat and Fat Free Crackers and Cookies These are great!) (800) 932 - 7800
Nabisco Cookies (Devil's Food Cakes, Fat-Free Newtons, Old Fashioned Ginger Snaps, and Teddy Grahams)
Rice Cakes (Chico San, Pacific Grain, President's Choice (Tom Thumb), Pritikin, Quaker, S&A - Snack Attack, etc.) Try the new caramel corn and honey nut fat free rice cakes! They're definitely not the same old rice cakes - GREAT SNACK!♥
Rycrisp
Stella D'Oro Plain (crunchy) breadsticks
Sunshine Animal Crackers
Tasty Kake Tasty Lights Cupcakes
Tender Toasts (Wheat) (Sometimes in Gourmet Food Section)
Wasa Crispbread
Zesta Fat Free Saltine Crackers (708) 782-2532♥

DIET FOODS OR HEALTH FOODS

Alba Dairy Shake Mixes
Barbara's Moist & Chewy Nature's Choice Real Fruit Bars and Granola Bars (Oats 'N Honey, Cinnamon, & Raisin (707) 765-2273♥
Estee Crackers, Cake Mixes, Snack Crisps, Salad Dressings, and Sauces
Featherweight Crackers, Microwave Popcorn, Pretzels, FI-BARS, Snack Bars, and Sauces
Featherweight Low Calorie and Low Sodium Dressings (ALL Varieties Except Creamy Dijon,Oriental Spice, and Italian Cheese)
Featherweight Soups Except Instant Bullion
Health Valley (Granola and Granola Bars, Chili and Soups, Cookies, Caramel Corn
Lite Munchies (ALL Varieties Sometimes In Snack Foods and Chips)
Pritikin (Soups, Salad Dressings, and Spaghetti Sauces, etc.)
Skinny Munchies (Chocolate Fudge)
Toast 'N Jammers toaster pastries by Auburn Farms
Weight Watcher's Instant Nonfat Dairy Creamer (in small individual packets)
Weight Watcher's Honey Roasted Peanuts* (good kid's snack in moderation)
Weight Watcher's Cocoa Mix and Shake Mixes
Weight Watcher's Cookies (Oatmeal Spice, Shortbread, Apple Raisin Chocolate Chip, Fruit Filled, Oatmeal Raisin) and (Chocolate* and Chocolate Sandwich*)
Weight Watcher's Cooking Spray
Weight Watcher's Croutons (Fat Free and found in individual packets)
Weight Watcher's Snacks (Apple Snacks, Corn Snackers, Crispbread, Fruit Snacks, and Microwave Popcorn)
Weight Watcher's Soups and Microwaveable Meals
Weight Watcher's Fat Free Salad Dressings and Spaghetti Sauce

BEVERAGES, DRINK MIXES

Alba Shake Mixes (usually in Diet Foods)

Albertson's Hot Cocoa Mix
Swiss Miss Hot Cocoa and Sugar Free Hot Cocoa Mix
Weight Watcher's Hot Cocoa and Shake Mixes (usually in Diet Foods)

DRY BEANS, PASTA, AND RICE, TOMATOES, GRAVIES, AND SALAD SEASONING MIXES, BOXED OR PACKAGED DINNERS OR SIDE DISHES

Note - Many boxed or packaged pasta, rice, or vegetable mixes, etc. are low in fat but do contain small amounts of saturated fat such as cream, beef or chicken fat, cheese, egg yolk, and etc. as well as Monosodium Glutamate (MSG).

Please be aware of these things and check the labels before you buy. On the macaroni and cheese mixes, try using only half the dry cheese or cheese sauce mix. When preparing some of the products calling for margarine or butter, omit it completely and add Butter Buds or Molly McButter if desired. When calling for added milk and/or eggs, use nonfat or skim milk and egg substitute or egg whites. Again, these are some choices.

Carnation Kid's Macaroni (shaped pasta)
De Fino No Boil Lasagna
Hodgson Mill Whole Wheat Spaghetti
No Yolks Cholesterol-Free Egg Noodle Substitute
R F Garden Spirals Vegetable Macaroni Product
Taboule Wheat Salad Mix (Prepare by using only 1 T of canola oil. To make without fat, add extra lemon juice, tomatoes, and/or water to replace oil.)
Kraft Macaroni and Cheese
Noodle Roni (Chicken and Mushroom, Oriental- prepared without nuts and use fish or chicken breast)
Rice-A-Roni (Spanish) and Savory Classics - omit butter - and Rice-A-Roni Pasta with less fat directions♥
Pritikin Dinners (Sometimes in Diet Section)
Uncle Ben's (Brown and Wild Rice - Mushroom Recipe, Long Grain and Wild Rice Original)
Velveeta Shells and Cheese (use only half the cheese sauce to reduce fat)

SPAGHETTI SAUCES, PARMESAN CHEESE PREPARED RECIPE SAUCES AND PIZZA CRUST MIX

Note - Use boneless skinless chicken breasts with chicken recipe sauces; saute' chicken in nonstick skillet with cooking spray or use defatted chicken broth instead of oil or margarine.)

Campbell's Healthy Request and No Fat Spaghetti Sauce♥
Hain Pasta Mixes and Sauces (Sometimes in Gourmet Section or in Health Food Stores)
Hunt's Chunky Style Spaghetti Sauce
Hunts Light Spaghetti Sauce
Healthy Choice Spaghetti Sauce
Kraft Grated House Italian Topping* (1/3 less fat)♥
Mama Rizzo's Marinara Sauce
Ragu Today's Recipes Spaghetti Sauces
Ragu Pizza Quick Mix for Homemade Crust (omit oil in preparation)
Betty Crocker Recipe Sauces (Cacciatore, Pepper Steak, Sweet & Sour, Teriyaki)
Ragu Chicken Tonight (Salsa Chicken, Spanish Chicken, Oriental Chicken, and Chicken Cacciatore

Weight Watcher's Fat Free Grated Parmesan Italian Topping♥

CEREALS AND CEREAL BARS

All Bran
Bran Buds
Bran Flakes
Cheerios
Fiber One
Frosted Mini Wheats
Grape Nuts Cereal
Health Valley Fat-Free Granola, Hot cereals, and Ready-to-Eat Cereals (Sometimes in Diet Section)
Health Valley Hot Cereals
Honey Bunches Of Oats Cereal
Kashi Puffed Cereal and Breakfast Pilaf (619) 454 - 6186♥
Kelloggs Lowfat Granola (contains coconut) and Low Fat Granola Bars♥
Kelloggs Raisin Squares
Nutrigrain Cereals and snack bars
Oatbran
Pritikin
Quaker Grits, Oatmeal and other hot cereals, Oat and Oat Bran Squares
Raisin Bran
Shredded Wheat and Shredded Wheat 'n Bran
Wheat Chex

CANNED FRUITS, VEGETABLES, BEANS

DelMonte Lite Fruit in Snack Cans
Food Club Natural Applesauce
Motts Natural Applesauce
Bush's Vegetarian Beans♥
Del Monte Pasta Classics Microwave Ready (Italian Style and Broccoli Marinara)
B & M Beans (Vegetarian)
Guiltless Gourmet No Fat No Oil Bean Dips (Sometimes with chips)
Health Valley Boston Baked and Vegetarian Beans
Libby's Lite Fruit-in snack cans♥
Old El Paso Vegetarian and Fat Free Refried Beans♥
Rosarita Vegetarian and Fat Free Refried Beans♥
Van Camps Vegetarian Style Beans

CANNED CHICKEN, SEAFOOD, PACKAGED SEASONINGS, SOUPS AND READY-TO-SERVE DINNERS

Bumble Bee Tuna Mix-Ins (Lemon Herb, Garlic & Herb, Zesty Tomato)
Campbell's Healthy Request Lowfat Soup
Hain Canned Soup (All Varieties Except Chicken Broth and Italian Vege-Pasta)
Hain Dry Soup Mix (Lental, Minestrone, Vegetable, and Split Pea Savory)
Health Valley Lowfat and Fat Free Soups and Chili
Healthy Choice Low-Fat Soups
Lipton Cup-A-Soup Lite
Lipton Cup-A-Soup Lots-A Noodles (Garden Vegetable and Hearty Beef and Noodles)
Ramen Noodle Lowfat Cup a Ramen (All Varieties)
Starkist Tuna packed in Water
Sweet Sue 98% Fat Free canned Chicken Breast in Broth
Weight Watcher's Cream of Mushroom Soup and All Other Varieties (Check Diet Section)
Weight Watcher's Microwaveable Chicken Noodle Soup, Vegetable Beef, New England Clam Chowder'' (Sometimes in Diet Section)

SPICES, COOKING PRODUCTS, CAKE AND BAKING MIXES, FROSTINGS, TOPPINGS, JELLO, PUDDINGS

Aunt Jemima Lite Buttermillk Complete Pancake Mix (312) 222-7843

Betty Crocker "Light" Cake and Muffin Mixes
Betty Crocker regular and Chocolate Swirl Angel Food Cake Mix♥
Betty Crocker Fluffy White Frosting Mix (in a box)(800) 328-6787
Bisquick Reduced Fat Variety Baking and Pancake Mix with Buttermilk♥
Duncan Hines Angel Food cake mix
E.Z. Baker Bread Mix (Country White and Garden Vegetable)♥
Fast Shake Pancake Mix
Health Valley Buttermillk Biscuit and Pancake Mix
Hungry Jack Extra Light Pancake and Waffle Mix♥
Krusteaz Blueberry Muffin & Almond Poppyseed Muffin Mix (206) 872 - 8400♥
Martha White Oat Bran & Double Blueberry Lite Muffin Mix♥
Pillsbury Gingerbread Mix
Pillsbury Lovin' Lites Cake, Fudge Brownie and Muffin Mixes
Pillsbury Lovin' Lites Frostings (in can)
Pillsbury Hot Roll Mix - Also use for making quick pizza crust (Prepare without the oil or margarine called for in the directions) (800) 767-4466
Pioneer No-Fat Biscuit Mix (210) 227-1401♥
Quick Loaf Fat Free Bread Mix (Cinnamon-Raisin, Garlic & Herb, Cracked Wheat & Hearty (800) 635-5668♥

Lite Evaporated Skim Milk (Carnation and Pet)
Lucky Leaf Lite Pie Filling
Nabisco Premium Fat Free Cracker Crumbs
Pet Evaporated Skim Milk
Quick Loaf Fat Free Bread Mix (Cinnamon-Raisin, Garlic & Herb, Cracked Wheat & Hearty (800) 635-5668♥

Shake 'N Bake Chicken, BBQ Chicken, and Hot & Spicy Chicken
Mrs. Richardson's Fat Free Caramel and Fudge Toppings♥ (312) 222-8354
Smucker's Light Hot Fudge Fat Free Topping (216) 682-0015

Baker's Joy Vegetable Oil and Flour Spray
Butter Buds Butter Flavored Granules (Comes in a box with 8 (1/2/oz) packets enclosed to make in liquid form or sprinkle. Also comes in a shaker bottle. Sometimes the box of Butter Buds is found with the real butter and margarine.)(800) 231-1123
Kroger Nonstick Cooking Spray
Mazola No Stick Cooking Spray
Molly McButter Butter Flavored Sprinkles (Other flavors include Bacon, Cheese, Sour Cream, and Garlic - In shaker bottle or also comes in small individual packets so you can take it with you.)
Mrs. Dash Herb and Spice Blends
Papa Dash Lite Salt and No Salt Sprinkles
Pam No Stick Cooking Spray (Plain, Butter-flavor, and Olive Oil flavor)
Weight Watcher's Cooking Spray
Wesson Lite No Stick Cooking Spray

FROZEN FOODS - FROZEN DINNERS AND ENTREES

Armour Classics Lite Frozen Dinners♥
Banquet Healthy Balance
Birds Eye Custom Cuisine (Chow Mein vegetables in Oriental Sauce)
Celentano "Great Choice" Italian Entrees(201) 239-8444♥
Chun King Entrees and Side Dishes

Dining Right
Kraft Eating Right (All Varieties)
Featherweight Healthy Recipes (All Varieties)
Green Giant "Create A Stir" Meal Starters (Teriyaki, Sweet and Sour, & Lo Mein)♥
Health Valley Fast Menu Dinners (ALL Varieties)
Healthy Choice (All Varieties)
Healthy Roman Fat Free Pizza - Delicious! (903) 581-6233♥
Jack's Cheese and Pepperoni 9 inch Pizza
Kid Cuisine (Cheese Pizza and Mini-Cheese Ravioli)
Lean Pockets
Le Menu Light Style
Le Menu Healthy
Midland Harvest All Vegetable Harvest Burgers (217) 424 - 5200
Old El Paso (Beef and Bean Burrito and Beef Enchilada)
Patio (Cheese Enchilada Mexican Dinner)
Rosita Fiesta Lite (Chicken Suiza and Shredded Beef Enchilada)
Stouffer's Dinner Supreme (Roast Turkey Breast)
Stouffer's Right Course
Swanson Homestyle (Seafood Creole with Rice)
Tombstone Light Sausage Pizza, Vegetable Pizza, and Supreme
Totino's Microwaveable Cheese Pizza
Tyson Gourmet Selection (Chicken and Beef Luau, Mesquite,Oriental, A L'Orange)
Tyson Healthy Portion
Weight Watcher's Smart Ones

FROZEN FOODS – VEGETABLES, SIDE DISHES;S, PLAIN MEAT, POULTRY, SEAFOOD

Birds Eye Easy Recipe for Chicken (Chicken Teriyaki)
Birds Eye International Rice Recipes
Broken Arrow Ranch Lowfat Venison (800) 963-GAME♥
FLAV-R-PAC Stir Fry Vegetables, Plain Vegetables and Vegetable Combinations
Gorton's Specialty Butterfly Shrimp
Green Giant One Serving Size (ALL Rice Varieties)
Green Giant Vegetables in Fat Free Butter Flavored Sauce
Green Giant Microwave Garden Gourmet (Asparagus Pilaf, Sherry Wild Rice)
Green Giant Pasta Accents (Garlic Seasoning and Pasta Primavera)
Healthy Choice Breaded Fish Fillets and Fish Sticks
Healthy Choice Ground Beef (Sometimes in Refrigerated Meat Section)
Mrs. Paul's Healthy Treasures Breaded Fish Fillets and Fish Sticks
Take Stock Fat Free Vegetable and Chicken Stocks (214) 503-SOUP♥
Tyson Chicken Fajita Kit
Tyson Boneless Skinless Chicken Meat (cooked)
Van de Kamps Crisp and Healthy Breaded Fish Sticks and Fish Fillets (314) 622-7700♥

FROZEN FOODS - SWEETS, BREADS AND PASTRY, BREAKFAST, EGG SUBSTITUTES

Albertson's Brand Fat-Free Frozen Dessert
Blue Bell Non-fat Frozen Yogurt
Blue Bell Extra Light Fat-Free Frozen Dessert
Blue Bell Free Fat Free Frozen Dessert (409) 836 - 7977
Blue Bunny NonFat Dairy Dessert and Nonfat Yogurt (All Varieties)
Blue Bunny Sherbet

Blue Bunny Nutrasweet Bars and Pops (All Varieties)
Borden Fat Free Frozen Dessert
Dole Sorbet
Food Lion Fat Free Frozen Dessert
FrozFruit Nonfat Frozen Yogurt Bars
Fudgesicle Fudge Pops (Sugar Free and Original)
Healthy Choice Frozen Lowfat Dairy Dessert (When You're in the mood to splurge - still low fat)
Kemps Nonfat Frozen Yogurt
Kroger Delme Fat Free Frozen Dairy Dessert
Light 'N Lively Low Fat Dairy Dessert♥
Luigi's Italian Ice
Popsicle Ice Pops (Original and Sugar-Free)
Simple Pleasures Light Frozen Dairy Dessert
Weight Watcher's Grand Collection Ice Milk (All Varieties)
Welch's Fruit Juice Bars (All Varieties)

Sara Lee Free and Light Frozen Desserts

Aunt Jemima Lowfat Waffles and Pancakes (312) 222 - 7843
Egg Beater's Egg Substitute (Comes in small cartons)
Bridgford Frozen Bread dough
Healthy Choice Muffins and Breakfasts
Pepperidge Farm Wholesome Choice Muffins
Phyllo (Filo) dough
Lenders Bagels
SUPERPRETZELS Microwaveable Soft Pretzels

REFRIGERATED FOODS (LUNCHMEAT, MEAT PRODUCTS, SAUSAGES, BISCUITS. SPREADS, ETC.)

Armour Deli Tray (Honey Ham and Smoked Turkey Breast)
Bryan Healthy and Flavorful
Butterball Fresh Boneless Turkey Tenderloin & Breast Strips♥
Butterball Fresh From the Deli Oven Roasted Turkey Breast
Chicken By George (Lemon Oregano, Roast Chicken, and Teriyaki)
Dubuque Extra Lean Ham♥
Healthy Choice lunchmeats and hot dogs
Healthy Choice Ground Beef (Extra Lean; 130 Calories, 4 Fat Grams - Comes packaged in a roll; Found sometimes in Freezer Section)
Healthy Choice Smoked Sausage and Polska Kielbasa
Healthy Favorites Bacon*♥
Healthy Favorites Lean Breakfast Ham♥
Hillshire Farms Deli Select
Hormel Canadian Style Bacon*
Hormel Light & Lean 97% Fat Free Hot Dogs
Hormel Light & Lean 97 ham, chicken and turkey breast cuts for salads (diced in package)♥
Jimmy Dean Light Grilled Chicken Sandwiches (in a box)
Jones Dairy Farm Canadian Bacon and Ham Slices
Ledbetter Turkey, Smoked Ham, and Honey Ham
Louis Rich Turkey Bacon* (still over 30% fat but a better choice than regular bacon)
Louis Rich Turkey Breast and Turkey Pastrami♥
Oscar Meyer "Our Leanest Cuts" Cold Cuts
Sandwich Shop Thin Sliced Meats
Turkey Store Boneless Breast Tenderloins
Weaver Turkey Breast and Turkey Ham
Wilson Extra Lean Boneless Smoked Cooked Ham

REFRIGERATED FOODS (CANNED BISCUITS, BREAD, PACKAGED VEGETABLES AND CHILLED FRUITS)

Food Club Ready-to-Bake Buttermilk and Homestyle Biscuits
Pillsbury Hearty Grains Low fat Biscuits and breadsticks (all varieties) (800) 775 - 4777
Pillsbury Soft Breadsticks and Crusty French Loaf
Simply Potatoes (Hash Browns, With Onion, and Shredded Plain)
Tortillas - Mission, Tom Thumb and others containing no lard

REFRIGERATED BEVERAGES AND FRUITS - CHOOSE JUICES AND JUICE BLENDS PREFERABLY NOT MADE FROM CONCENTRATE AND CONTAINING NO ADDED SUGAR

Minute Maid Premium Choice Juices
President's Choice Juices (Tom Thumb)
Sun Fresh Chilled Fruits (No Sugar and Light Syrup Varieties)
Tropicana Pure Premium Juices

REFRIGERATED DAIRY PRODUCTS (CHEESE, MILK, PUDDING. YOGURT. ETC.)

Alpine Lace Free 'N Lean Fat Free cheddar and mozzarella cheese (found grated and hanging in 6 oz. packages or whole; some stores also carry it in the deli)
Alpine Lace Free 'N Lean Fat Free Cheese Singles
Alpine Lace Free 'N Lean Fat Free Cream Cheese Spread, Plain, With Chives, Party Spread with Garlic and Herbs
Alpine Lace Free 'N Lean Fat Free Pasteurized Process Cheese Spread (plain, cheddar and jalapeno)
Better 'N Eggs Fat Free Egg Substitute
Butter Buds Butter Flavor Sprinkles (individual packets in box) (800) 231 - 1123
Borden Fat Free Cheese Slices
Churney Lite Reduced Fat Cheeses*
Coffee-mate Fat Free creamer (800) -NESTLE -4♥
Dannon Lite Yogurt
Egg Beater's Fat Free Egg Substitute♥
Food Lion Nonfat Cottage Cheese
Healthy Choice Fat Free Cheddar and Mozarella Cheese (grated and whole packaged)
Healthy Choice Fat Free Cheese Singles and Cheese Sticks
Healthy Choice Fat Free Cream Cheese Spread, Strawberry Cream Cheese, Garlic and Herb Cream Cheese, and Pasteurized Process Cheese Spread -(In block form like Velveeta, only Fat Free!)
Hershey Fat Free Pudding
Jell-O Fun Packs♥
Jell-O Free Pudding (Fat Free)
Kaukauna Cheese Lite 50 Cold Pack Cheese Product* (800) 558 - 3500♥
Kraft Free Cheese Slices
Kraft Healthy Favorites Reduced Fat Cheese*
Kroger Nonfat Cottage Cheese
Lactaid Nonfat Milk (Lactose Reduced)
Land 'O Lakes No Fat Sour
Lifetime by Lifeline Lowfat Cheddar *♥
Lifetime by Lifeline Nonfat Pasteurized Process Cheese (block form); Monterrey Jack, Cheddar, Garden Vegetable, Mild Mexican (408) 899 - 5040♥

Lite-Line Fortified Skim Milk
Lite-Line Nonfat Cottage Cheese
Mootown Snackers Light String Cheese*♥
Polly-O Free Fat Free Mozarella and Fat Free Ricotta Cheese (800) 845-FREE♥
Reddi Wip Lite Whipped Topping* (in aerosol can) (414) 782 - 2750
Sargento Pot Cheese*
Schepps 1% Buttermilk, 1% Cottage Cheese, and Protein Fortified Skim Milk
Smart Beat Fat Free Cheese Slices
Smart Beat Margarine (18% Vegetable Oil Spread)
Tom Thumb 1% Buttermilk and Protein Fortified Skim Milk
Truly Lite Fat Free Ricotta Cheese
Weight Watcher's Cream Cheese* and Cottage Cheese
Weight Watcher's Lowfat Cheese Slices and Natural Cheese*
Weight Watcher's Ultimate 90 Yogurt
Yoplait Fat Free Yogurt

CONDIMENTS, ETC. (SALAD DRESSINGS, MAYONNAISE, JELLY)

Catalina Reduced Calorie Dressing
Good Seasons Nonfat Salad Dressing Mix for Fat Free Dressing
Kraft Free Mayonnaise and Miracle Whip (Nonfat Mayonnaise and Salad Dressing)
Weight Watcher's Fat Free Whipped Dressing
Kraft Free Tartar Sauce (Fat Free)
Kraft Free Nonfat Salad
Dressings, and No Oil Italian
Marie's Lite & Zesty Fat Free Salad Dressings (In Produce Section)
Medford Farms Fat Free Dressings .(609) 654-7904 -MY Favorite!
Mrs. Dash Salad Dressing Mix♥
Pfeiffer Fat Free salad Dressing♥
Pritikin Salad Dressings
Seven Seas Free Nonfat Salad Dressings
Skinny Haven Creamy Garlic and French Salad Dressing
Take Heart Dressings
Weight Watcher's Fat Free Salad Dressings (Also found in individual serving packets ; sometimes in Diet Section)
Wish-Bone Healthy Sensation Fat-Free Salad Dressings

Kraft Barbecue Sauces
Lawry's Dijon & Honey Barbecue Sauce
Pritikin Fat Free Bar-B-Que and Cooking Sauce

Polaner All Fruit Spread
President's Choice Ultra Light Fruit Spread (Tom Thumb)
Smucker's Simply Fruit
Weight Watcher's Fruit Spreads
Welch's Totally Fruit

CHIPS, POPCORN, SNACK FOODS

American Grains Rice Bites (Sometimes Found in Diet or Gourmet Food Section)
Broken Pretzels by Wege
Bugles "Crisp Baked" (800) 328 - 6787♥
Charles Light Popcorn* (717) 285 - 5981
Childer's Natural Potato Chips (No Fat - usually in health food stores (704) 377 - 0800♥
El Galindo Baked No Oil Tortilla Chips
El Paco Restaurante Style Tortilla Chips*
Guiltless Gourmet No Oil Baked Tortilla Chips and White Corn Tortilla Chips (512) 443 - 4373♥

Guiltless Gourmet Bean Dip (Fat Free)
Hain Mini Rice Cakes
Keebler Pop Deluxe Honey Caramel Glazed Popcorn
Louise's Fat Free Potato Chips (original flavor is best!) (502) 495 - 0494♥
Mister Salty Fat Free Pretzels
Orville Redenbacher Hot Air Gourmet Popping Corn
Any variety pretzels (preferably those containing no partially hydrogenated oil and 1 gram of fat or less per serving)
PopSecret "By Request" microwave Popcorn - 3 c = 1 g Fat (800)328 - 6787♥
Pop Weaver's Gourmet Light Microwave Popcorn (Found usually at Target -(800) 634 - 8161♥
Pringles Lite Potato Chips*
Quaker Rice Cakes
Rolo Gold Pretzel Chips♥
Ruffles Light Choice Potato Chips*♥
Smart Temptations Baked No Oil Tortilla Chips (The Best so Far!) (708) 647 - 0787♥
SnackWells Fat Free and Lowfat Crackers and Cookies (800) 932 - 7800
Tostitos No Oil Baked White Corn Tortilla Chips♥
Tostitos Low Fat Baked Cool Ranch Tortilla Chips (My kids love these!) (214) 334 - 7000 ♥
Weight Watcher's Microwave Popcorn
Comet Ice Cream Cones
Keebler Ice Cream Cones

SAM'S WHOLESALE CLUB

CANNED AND PACKAGED FOODS

Act II Lite Microwave Popcorn
Bush's Pinto Beans
Campbell's Healthy Request Soups♥
Fig Newtons
Healthy Choice Soups♥
Honey Maid Graham Crackers
Hunt's All Natural Thick & Rich BBQ Sauce♥
Leonardeo Enriched Macaroni and Cheddar (Use half the cheese sauce packet to reduce &t under 30%)
Leonardo Pasta Veggie Spirelle
Mrs. Dash Products♥
Musselman's Natural Applesauce
Nutrigrain Bars
Old Farmer's 15 - Bean Soup Mix♥
Rosarita Vegetarian Refried Beans♥
Thank You Brand Sliced Apples in Water
3-Minute Brand Quick Oats and Oatmeal
Tyson Canned White Chicken in Broth
Tyson Canned White Turkey in Water

REFRIGERATED VEGETABLES AND FRUIT

Fresh Cut Up Raw Vegetables and Salad (Packaged and Ready-to-Serve)
Fresh Whole and Cut Up Fruit
TCBY Traditional Style and Low Fat Yogurt

REFRIGERATED MEATS AND CHEESE (FOUND IN DELI AND IN REFRIGER-ATED MEATS SECTION)

Alpine Lace Low Fat* and Fat Free Cheese♥
Bryan Sliced Smoked Turkey Breast
Dak Sliced Ham and Turkey
Eckrich Deli Lite Roast Beef Slices♥
Hafnia Cooked Ham

Healthy Choice Sliced Lunchmeat or Whole Turkey or Chicken Breast
Hillshire Farms Smoked Turkey Breast
Hudson Boneless Skinless Breast Portions
Louis Rich Turkey Boneless Skinless Chicken or Turkey Breast
Wilson Continental Deli Lite Turkey Pastrami, Lite Turkey and Chicken Breast and Ham
Wilson Extra Lean Ham

FREEZER SECTION - MEATS AND VEGETABLES

Avalon Bay Ocean Perch and Orange Roughy
Delinix Chicken and Beef Taquitos (Bake without oil; do not fry)
Del Mario's Vegetable Lasagna*
Delta Pride Farm Raised Catfish Nuggets and Fillets
FLAV-R-PAC Stir Fry Vegetables, Plain Frozen Vegetables and Vegetable Combinations
Flavor Land Fruit and Mixed Fruit (No Sugar Added)
Galletti Orange Roughy and Flounder Fillets
Meridian Peeled & Deveined Shrimp♥
Pasta Perfect Rotini with Vegetables
Pierre Grilled Chicken Sandwiches on buns♥
Shanghai Brand Shrimp and Oriental Stir Fry
Texas Smoked Chicken for Fajitas
Treasure Isle Ready to Cook and Ready to Eat Peeled and Deveined Shrimp
Tyson Boneless Skinless Chicken Breast Portions
Tyson Chicken Vegetable and Pasta Salad Kit (Ranch Style, Italian Style, Shanghai Shrimp and Oriental Vegetables)
Tyson Lemon-Pepper Flavored and Mesquite Flavored Boneless Skinless Chicken Breast Portions♥
Tyson Glazed Chicken in Mushroom Sauce
Tyson Resolutions Beef Stir Fry (Oriental Style)

FREEZER SECTION FRUIT AND SWEETS

Mama Tish's Original Italian Ices
Welch's Fruit juice Bars

COMMERCIALLY BAKED BREADS AND BAKED PRODUCTS

American Classic A High Energy Bar (The Original High Energy Bar from California)
Fig Newtons
Honey Maid Graham Crackers
Honey Wheatberry Bread
Italian Soft Breadsticks
Wonder Light Fat Free Bread

BAKING PRODUCTS

Krusteaz Buttermilk Pancake Mix and Oat Bran and Apple Cinnamon Muffin Mix
Molly Mc Butter Butter-Flavored Sprinkles
Morton's Lite Salt
Mrs. Dash Salt Substitute
Pam No Stick Cooking Spray

BAKERY

Angel Food Cake Sour Dough, French Bread, and Bagels

EATING OUT THE LOW FAT WAY

(Please read this section before going on to specific restaurants!)

More people eat away from home than ever before. Thus, the thought of dining out when trying to eat healthy or lose weight usually brings an attitude of defeat even before you get out of the house or away from the office. Where to go..., what to eat..., salad again..., why bother, there's nothing I can eat anyway; these are some of the things that may cross your mind. In today's society, even though many people choose a diet high in fat and cholesterol, restaurants are beginning to offer choices (some very good ones). All you have to do is know where to look and what to look for.

This guide will help you make the right choices so you can dine out without feeling deprived, remain on your healthy plan, and actually look forward to eating away from home. If you normally follow a healthy eating plan, sometimes you may feel the need to splurge and order something that may not be recommended. That's okay, sometimes, as long as you don't make it a weekly habit.

Remember, just because you splurge, (let's say for example that you'd like to have a hamburger for dinner), you don't have to "blow it" totally. Have your hamburger, (leave off the mayonnaise) and instead of french fries, have a baked potato using your low-fat substitutions. Or, perhaps you'd like a luscious dessert; usually once you've tasted it, all you really wanted was one or two bites anyway. Try sharing the dessert with friends, or ask the waiter for a small portion if you are by yourself. Better yet, treat everyone to nonfat yogurt on the way home.

Visualize dining out as an adventure and look at all the things that you CAN have instead of focusing on all the things you shouldn't have.

My main goal in presenting this section for you is to show you that you DO have choices. Some choices, of course, are better than others. Choose the ones best suited for you and your health needs and discover new ones on your own. First, let's start with a few good rules of thumb which apply to many types of restaurants and some fast food places (following the restaurant guide).

GENERAL TIPS

1. **BE PREPARED** - Take a few items with you so you are not tempted to cheat:
   a. Small packets of Molly McButter butter-flavored sprinkles
   b. Small packets of Fat Free salad dressing
   c. Small packets of Weight Watcher's croutons
   d. Small packets of Weight Watcher's nonfat coffee creamer
   e. I keep a small container of fat free cereal in the car to use as a topping for frozen yogurt.

2. **SALADS** - When ordering salads, if there is no fat free dressing available, ask for your dressing on the side. High fat dressings average about 80 calories and 8 grams of fat per tablespoon. One ladle at the salad bar holds between ¼ cup to ½ cup of dressing which adds up to either 320 or 640 calories and between 32 and 64 grams of fat respectively; and, that's only if you use one ladle. Instead, dip your bite of salad into a small bowl of the dressing instead of pouring the dressing on your salad. All you really want is a little added flavor. You will be surprised how much dressing is left in the bowl. Other good salad toppers are cracked pepper, lemon juice, and low-fat cottage cheese. Also, some chicken taco salads are not too bad if the shell, sour cream, cheese, and guacamole are omitted.

3. **SALAD BARS** - At the salad bar, choose vegetables and other accompaniments such as spinach and lettuce, broccoli, cauliflower, radishes, sprouts, pickles, baby corn, pickled okra, garbanzo beans, tomatoes, cucumbers, onions, mushrooms, green and red peppers, etc. Try to avoid pre-made salads such as chicken or tuna and vegetable or pasta salads that contain oil or mayonnaise. In addition, avocados, eggs, bacon, olives, croutons, cheese, sesame seeds, chinese noodles, crispy onions and high fat items such as these can add a tremendous amount of fat to a salad, making that once healthy salad derive over half its calories from fat.

4. **GETTING EXACTLY WHAT YOU WANT** - Check the menu for

any lite or heart-healthy items. Then, ask your waiter exactly how your selection is prepared to make sure it meets your expectations. (People have different definitions of "healthy".) Try ordering items that are grilled, broiled, boiled, or baked. Ask them not to add any butter, margarine, or fat in preparation. If the vegetables are steamed, ask whether or not they add butter or fat to them before serving. When dishes have a sauce, ask what kind it is. Usually, the tomato sauces or marinara sauces, followed by a wine or bouillon-based sauce, are the best choices. Some teriyaki and soy sauces are okay. It pays to ask; some chefs insist on adding that extra touch of butter. Make sure you praise the management for offering a healthy menu; this encourages them to continue to provide healthy choices.

5. **FINDING NEW CHOICES** - When trying a new restaurant, call ahead to find out what choices they offer to the health-conscious consumer.

6. **PLAN AHEAD FOR EATING OUT** - Some people, when they know they will be dining out in the evening, will avoid eating all day. This is not a good idea. Your body needs nourishment to keep you going and get your metabolism moving. By the time you reach the restaurant, you will be so hungry that you may overeat and/or eat something you would normally have avoided. Eat sensibly and cut back on your other meals during the day; add an extra workout to burn more calories and keep your metabolism going strong.

7. **ORDERING YOUR MAIN MEAL** - Remember, you do not have to order the traditional meal. Create a delicious meal by ordering an appetizer such as a shrimp cocktail and side dish such as a baked potato or salad. Baked potatoes make a great main dish meal. I like to order vegetable soup and a baked potato; then, spoon a little of the soup into the potato for a new creation. Experiment; baked potatoes go with almost anything. They're great with butter-flavored sprinkles sprinkled on top, a spoonful of Bac-Os, a dash of Parmesan cheese, onions, vegetables or any of the OK foods found at the salad bar, low-fat cottage cheese, salsa, etc. If you just aren't hungry for a hot meal, choose salad and a low-fat dessert. Decide what it is you are really hungry for and eat that item (preferably the low-fat version). You don't have to eat the entire meal just to get to the dessert; and, on the other hand, you don't have to have dessert after every meal. Listen to your body; maybe it's not the peach cobbler you want, just the sweet fruit.

8. **AN ALTERNATIVE TO ALCOHOLIC BEVERAGES** - Instead of ordering alcoholic beverages, try choosing mineral water with a squeeze of lemon or lime or other nonalcoholic fat free beverages to take the edge off your appetite and add fewer calories than those containing alcohol. Beverages which quickly add many calories and sugar to your daily intake are soft drinks. One (32 oz.) cola, for example is approximately 384 calories with no fat. Some people drink diet drinks with or without caffeine; this is a personal decision as some feel artificial sweeteners are unhealthy. If you drink diet drinks, coffee and tea, do so in moderation.

9. **DINNER DELAY** - If you know that dinner will be delayed once you arrive at the restaurant, try eating a lite snack before you leave home. Fruit, fat free crackers and fat free cheese, or a bowl of fat free cereal and skim milk are a few suggestions.

10. **SOUPS** - When ordering soups, choose broth-based soups such as vegetable, tortilla (without the tortilla chips and cheese), onion (without the cheese), and minestrone. Thick soups or cream soups usually contain extremely high amounts of fat and cholesterol. If you order a broth-based soup and it looks like there is a lot of fat in it, take part of a lettuce leaf and float it on top. Remove the leaf; along with the leaf goes a lot of the fat.

11. **BREAKFAST** - Breakfast is relatively simple to order when eating out. Choose cold low-fat cereal with skim milk, bagels or English muffins with jelly (omit the cream cheese), hot oatmeal, oatbran, or grits, fresh fruit, omelettes and scrambled eggs made from egg substitute, and toast without butter or margarine. Don't forget your Butter Buds or Molly McButter.

12. **SANDWICHES** - When ordering sandwiches, choose lean meats such as turkey breast, chicken breast, lean roast beef and ham. Avoid chicken or tuna salad sandwiches due to the added mayonnaise. Hot dogs, sausage, bologna, salami, pastrami, knockwurst, and bratwurst derive most of their calories from fat and also should be avoided. Try a veggie sandwich; order sandwiches without mayonnaise and cheese. Avocados, olives, and sour cream are high in fat and should be avoided. Ask instead for extra vegetables such as sprouts, mushrooms, tomatoes, pickles, onions, etc. and choose mustard, low or nonfat barbecue sauce, and ketchup as a substitute for the mayonnaise.

13. **HOW FOOD IS PREPARED** - Order your foods grilled, broiled,

baked, or boiled without added fat. Fried foods, even when fried in canola oil, still contain a high amount of fat and should be avoided. Besides, all you really taste is the fat, not the true taste of the food.

RESTAURANT CHOICES:

Below are some suggestions on what you might eat at specific restaurants and in general. Some of the nutritional data is provided by the information in the book "The Incredible Edible Metroplex (A Nutrition Guide to Eating Out) by Sandra Carey, R.D., L.D., and Tamra Boteler, R.D., L.D. The fat and calorie counts listed also include the percent of calories from fat (in parenthesis after the fat grams). Serving size is one serving as prepared by the restaurant unless otherwise specified. All of the restaurants mentioned are located in the Dallas/Fort Worth metroplex; some have locations in other cities in Texas and other parts of the country. There are hundreds of restaurants not mentioned; however, this does not mean some do not have equally good choices on their menus. See the box at the end of the this section for a list of common low-fat menu items found at many restaurants.

I hope the following can be used as a guide and that more restaurants will follow the trend with healthy selections. For more information on choosing healthy, low-fat menu items such as salads, potatoes, soups, etc., see "Eating Out - General Tips."

AMERICAN RESTAURANTS:

American restaurants serve a variety of foods including steaks, chicken, pasta, and sandwiches

THE BACK PORCH - Fort Worth, Texas - This is a great place to dine. What a variety they offer in salad, vegetables, and fresh fruit. They also offer plain baked potatoes and baked french fries. However, the fries do have oil, so they still contain quite a bit of fat I'm sure. They also have a variety of lean meats for sandwiches and a very good "Veggie Burger".

BLACK-EYED PEA - They offer grilled chicken that is part of their low-fat choices. Stay with vegetables prepared by themselves as opposed to ones prepared as a casserole or with a sauce. Mashed potatoes are not too bad; order them without gravy. The rolls probably have less fat than the cornbread. If you do choose to have fruit cobbler leaving off the crust will help hold down the fat content.

DENNY'S - They offer a huge variety of delicious foods including Stir-Fry /Chicken with Vegetables cooked on a "dry grill" without oil. 1 serving is about 400 calories with 10 grams of fat (23%). They also offer Spaghetti with rich and zesty meat sauce for 600 calories and 16 grams of fat.(24%). Other good choices include Sliced Turkey Sandwich (omit the mayonnaise) with 281 calories and 5 fat grams (16%)., Halibut Dinner (without tartar sauce), 315 calories, 3 fat grams, (9%)., and Grilled Chicken Dinner on a toasted bun with vegetables and a plain baked potato (without dressing), 312 calories, 3 fat grams, (9%). Extras include applesauce (½ C) 97 calories, less than 1 fat gram (4%), and for a little splurge, try 10 French Fries for 111 calories, 4 fat grams, (32%). Denny's also offers a nice selection of extras such as Egg Beaters egg substitute for breakfast, nonfat milk, and low calorie syrup.

FRIDAY'S - They have several great selections on their Lite menu containing the calorie, fat, and cholesterol count of each item on that menu. Choose from grilled chicken or tuna with steamed vegetables, a Garden Burger or Vegetable Baguette Sandwich. They also have a great steamed vegetable platter with a baked potato and soup or salad. Order the vegetables and potato without added fat or cheese and salad as mentioned in "Eating Out - General Tips."

GOOD EATS CAFE - This is a great place to go for good "down-home" cooking. They even have hearts on the menu to highlight the healthy choices. Choose from a wide variety of steamed vegetables such as Corn (½ C) 84 calories, 2 fat grams (21%), Broccoli, 69 calories, 1 fat gram (13%), New Potatoes, 150 calories, 4 fat grams (24%), Pinto Beans (½ C) 133 calories, less than 1 fat gram (3%), Dirty Rice and Beans, 210 calories, 1 fat gram (4%), and Dirty Rice, 77 calories, 1 fat gram (12%). Other good choices include Chicken Sandwich (served with 1 vegetable, not included in analysis), 468 calories, 13 fat grams, (25%), Vegetable Soup (1 Cup), 52 calories, less than 1 fat gram (8%), Wheat Roll, 187 calories, 6 fat grams, (29%), and for a delicious dessert try the Banana Pudding, 250 Calories, 7 fat grams, (25%). Other vegetables and side dishes, although a little over the 30% mark, are good choices when eaten with other lower fat foods. These include Carrots, 52 calories, 2 fat grams (34.6%), Mashed Potatoes, no gravy, 111 Calories, 5 fat grams, (40%), Broccoli Rice Casserole (½ C), 132 calories, 5 fat grams, (34%), Baked Squash (½ C), 135 calories, 6 fat grams, (40%), Chicken Fried Chicken Sandwich (fried in canola oil, as prepared, without added vegetable), 663 calories, 23 fat grams, (31%), and Cornbread, 198 calories, 7 fat grams, (32%). Try their salads without cheese and croutons. They also offer grilled fish; ask them to prepare it without fat. Breakfast items on the list include grits, 96 calories, 0 fat, Banana

Muffin, 357 calories, 12 fat grams, (30%), Country Potatoes, 132 calories, 4 fat grams, (27%), and for a splurge, Strawberry Pancakes, 1269 calories, 43 grams of fat, (30.4%). Instead, try the bagel, skip the cream cheese, and add fruit jam or jelly to save on fat and calories.

STEAK AND ALE - Favorites include Shrimp Cocktail with cocktail sauce plus 2 packages of crackers, 213 calories, 2 fat grams, (8%), Chateau for One (without hollandaise sauce on vegetable), 609 calories, 20 fat grams, (30%), 8 oz. Beef Filet served with plain baked potato and vegetable of the day (no sauce), 648 calories, 21 fat grams, (29%), Shrimp Pilaf (without hollandaise and lobster sauces), 407 calories, 7 fat grams, (15%), and English Dip Sandwich (without cheese or french fries), 669 calories, 18 fat grams, (24%). Usually, other selections are offered such as plain grilled chicken breast or grilled seafood. Again, ask that both are prepared without added fat. Side dishes which make a meal by themselves include salad bar (add suggested toppings), Rice Pilaf (2/3 C), 208 calories, 5 fat grams, (21%), Vegetable of the Day (without added sauce), 17 calories, less than 1 gram of fat, Garlic Sub Roll (without garlic spread), 328 calories, 3 fat grams, (8%), Baked potato (without butter or margarine), 219 calories, less than 1 fat gram.

BAR-B-QUE RESTAURANTS:

Choose green salad when available, plain baked potato instead of potato salad, sliced vegetables such as tomatoes, onions and pickles instead of slaw. Ask for thin-sliced chicken breast. If they only have chicken pieces, select breast portions and remove the skin. Some bar-b-que sauces are fine, but ask just to make sure they contain no oil or fat. Choose beans that do not contain bacon or added fat and plain corn or corn on the cob.

COLTER'S BAR-B-Q & GRILL - Colter's has more than just a traditional barbecue menu; they offer several grilled chicken dishes, one a "LIGHTER SIDE" that comes with fettuccine, two vegetables and a roll. Smoked turkey is also available. The best vegetable is a plain baked potato; corn, green beans, and barbecue beans are better alternatives than cole slaw, fried okra, and potato salad.

CAFETERIAS:

Cafeterias offer a huge variety of foods. Some of the more familiar, of course, are fresh fruit, green salad, baked potato, and vegetable or chicken and rice or chicken noodle soup. Other low-fat items include plain gelatin and gelatin combinations that contain fruit and/or diced vegetables (these lower fat congealed salads usually are clear), shrimp cocktail, ambrosia (avoid the coconut), plain vegetables (not vegetable casseroles; try to avoid the vegetables that are cooked in butter, margarine, or oil), plain or stir-fried rice and plain beans (cooked without bacon), Shrimp Creole, baked fish (scrape off breading or coating), grilled skinless chicken breast, plain spaghetti with tomato sauce or salsa, breads such as jalapeño corn bread (without cheese), cornbread, and soft or hard white or wheat rolls. Best choices for dessert are fruit, gelatin, baked apples without butter, angel food cake, and strawberry shortcake (omit whipped cream). If you must have pie, choose the ones with fruit and without nuts; avoid the crust. If cholesterol is not a problem, egg custard or rice pudding usually make good choices.

FRENCH CUISINE:

The French are known for their wonderful bread among other things. Choose plain French bread without added fat; avoid croissants which are loaded with butter. Ask for dishes prepared without the high fat cream sauces. Plain pasta dishes or pasta served with a broth-based sauce or tomato sauce are more acceptable. Of course, salad without dressing, once again, is always a good choice. Don't forget to bring along your own additions (see #2 and #3 in "Eating Out - General Tips").

LE CHARDONNAY - They offer many French items as well as a variety of salads and soups that can be modified to fit into a healthy eating plan. Black Bean soup, plain, is a good choice for a main dish; add a salad and bread for a complete meal. Several salads, including grilled chicken breast or shrimp, make a wonderful meal (order without dressing and guacamole). Other popular healthy items are steamed vegetables and plain baked potatoes. When ordering grilled chicken or fish ask that no extra fat be added and omit heavy sauces.

ITALIAN CUISINE:

Eating in Italian restaurants is really easy. Choose plain pasta and salad (bring your toppers) and choose tomato or marinara sauces on the side. Order chicken breast or seafood dishes without the sauces, unless they are low-fat, such as broth-based without oil. Minestrone soup is usually a good choice. When ordering pizza, ask for a vegetable pizza, minus the olives, and opt for no cheese or at least a reduced amount. Bread sticks are low in fat, if you ask them to make yours plain without added oil, butter, or margarine. Many times, for dessert, they offer fat free Italian Ices or sherbet.

BIRRAPORETTI'S - They offer a wide variety of steamed vegetables and plain pasta, a la carte. Other healthy items are found in some of their salads and pasta/vegetable dishes or chicken/pasta dishes; omit the olives and cheese and ask for dressing or sauce on the side. Also, fresh grilled fish, minestrone soup, and plain bread are nice selections.

OLIVE GARDEN - Although at this printing they do not offer a "Lite" menu, there are still healthy choices. Order their beautiful salad bowl without the dressing or on the side. Ask for plain bread sticks, without added butter. Minestrone soup is a nice selection and plain spaghetti with tomato or marinara sauce is a much better choice than the higher fat lasagna and other pasta with cheese and heavy sauces. They do offer some pasta/vegetable dishes with chicken breast but they contain olive oil and/or butter.

PIZZA HUT - The salad bar offers green salad with a few vegetables, cottage cheese, and canned fruit. A few locations have tried serving whole wheat pizza crusts; make requests to the manager. The pizza lowest in fat and calories is a medium cheese Pan Pizza. Two slices have 18 grams of fat and 492 calories. This is a little over the 30% mark; I still suggest the no cheese version. Try it, you might be pleasantly surprised. Bread sticks can be ordered without added fat, but still seem to have quite a bit of fat in them.

RODOLFO'S - DALLAS, ARLINGTON, and FORT WORTH - What a pleasure to dine here. Rodolfo Sperandeo of the Dallas restaurant was so kind to visit with me and share his recipe for "Spinach Ricotta Dumplings"✔ found in the cookbook. He is the founder of the Ital-Lite cuisine offered in the Rodolfo's restaurants. They offer a complete menu for the health-conscious customer including the calorie, cholesterol, fat, and sodium count per serving. These recipes meet the dietary guidelines set by the American Heart Association. A few favorites, other than the dumplings include Lasagna Vegetarian, Pasta, Chicken, Fish, or Veal with a choice of at least ten low-fat sauces.

SHOWBIZ PIZZA - You can even eat healthy when you take the kids out for a day of fun. They offer a beautiful salad bar with fresh fruits and vegetables and fat free salad dressing. Order the bread sticks plain (be specific - dry, no butter or oil); I've discovered my kids would much rather have the bread sticks than pizza - GREAT!

ORIENTAL CUISINE:

Choose vegetable dishes prepared without oil or fat, and dishes containing chicken breast and fish or shellfish prepared without fat. (Be careful of sauces; ask how they are prepared.)

Steamed rice is best. Some fried rice is lower in fat than others; ask them to prepare it as low-fat as possible if you choose it over the steamed rice. Vegetable soup is usually acceptable (avoid the crispy fried Chinese noodles). Choose items that are not fried; if sodium intake is a concern, avoid soy sauce. For dessert have a Fortune Cookie.

AUGUST MOON CHINESE RESTAURANT - They offer lite vegetarian entrees which are low in calories, fat and sodium; you may add chicken breast, scallops, or shrimp to some. They also offer steamed whole fish. Order it without the sauce or with sauce on the side.

CHIN'S CHINESE RESTAURANT - ARLINGTON, TEXAS - They offer 4 delicious "Diet Plates" and will prepare them without any added fat if you ask them. Choose from Jumbo Shrimps, Chicken, and Beef all served with mixed Chinese vegetables and one main dish with vegetables only.

LOTUS - They offer fresh peel-and-eat shrimp and a beautiful buffet-style salad and fruit bar almost every day.

MEXICAN RESTAURANTS:

Ask the waiter to bring corn tortillas, instead of fried chips, with salsa. Corn tortillas only contain about 50 calories with less than a gram of fat, where one serving of tortilla chips can contain approximately 150 calories with over half of the calories coming from fat. Tortilla soup can be a good choice if it is made with broth and vegetables; omit cheese, chips, avocados, or sour cream. Order plain beans as opposed to refried beans.

Unfortunately, Mexican rice is sometimes full of added fat and may not be a healthy choice. Be sure to ask how it is prepared. Fajitas made from grilled skinless chicken breast or shrimp are usually good choices providing no added fat is used in cooking; usually it's what you put on them that makes them unhealthy. Guacamole, sour cream, and cheese are the culprits. Fold flour or corn tortillas around a combination of ingredients such as salsa, lettuce, diced tomatoes, green peppers, jalapeños, and onions; vegetable fajitas or soft tacos are great without the chicken or shrimp.

Taco salads are high in fat because of the hard shell. Choose salads with lean chicken, fish, and vegetables with the dressing on the side. Many Mexican restaurants now offer fresh grilled fish and plain baked potatoes.

LOW-FAT FOOD CHOICES

Use this list to help you make healthy food choices while eating out:

Breadsticks (without added fat if possible)
Broth-based soups (without cheese)
Salads
Baked Potatoes, dry (add your own seasonings)
Steamed Vegetables
Grilled, broiled, baked fish, skinless chicken breast, lean cuts of beef (eye of round, top round - see chart in Beef Helpful Hints Section).
Fruit salads
Spaghetti (Red or Marinara Sauce on the side)
Grilled chicken sandwiches on whole wheat bread without mayonnaise
All-Fruit drinks

FAST FOOD CHOICES

It is inevitable; we will at one time or another have to choose a fast food restaurant. However, even with busy schedules, it is possible to eat a healthy well-balanced meal. Surprisingly, there are more selections available than ever before and the choices are better and increasing every day.

The main drawback to eating the healthier fast foods is that a lot of it contains high levels of sodium and some of it tends to be expensive; some restaurants also use MSG. (Foods containing over 900 mg. of sodium per serving are noted with an *). I applaud the efforts, however, of these food chains because, even though the unhealthy choices are still available, they give us alternative choices we can live with, choices that should fit in with our healthy lifetime plan. I listed some choices that may be high in sugar simply to give you a choice if you are faced with a decision about what to eat or drink. For example, if you are hungry for something sweet, I would much rather see you have a Strawberry Breeze from Dairy Queen, for example, than a regular Heath Blizzard with 820 calories and 36 fat grams.

If you are faced with eating at a fast food restaurant and don't care for the menu, consider a different plan of action. Some restaurants will let you buy everything that goes on a burger except for the meat at a reduced price. Restaurants such as Dairy Queen will sometimes sell you a banana which is a great substitute for other high fat alternatives. If you can't seem to find anything appealing to go with your grilled chicken sandwich, for example, stop by a grocery or convenience food store for a bag of pretzels and a piece of fruit. I'm sure we will see more and more healthy choices; keep asking and be patient.

FAST FOOD RESTAURANTS:

On the following pages is a list of some of the better selections (30% fat or less unless otherwise specified) provided by many popular fast food restaurants. Some items may not be at all locations. Information on specific items including their fat and calorie count came from nutritional brochures from the companies - available at some locations or order through the company - and from the computer software "Health and Diet Pro." Salad counts and baked potatoes do not include dressing or added fat unless otherwise specified. Not all restaurants are mentioned, for obvious reasons; try other restaurants as well and check their nutritional booklets.

RESTAURANTS	CALORIES	FAT
ARBY'S		
Blueberry Muffin	200	6 g
Cinnamon Nut Danish	340	9 g
6 oz. Orange Juice	180	0 g
Side Salad	25	0 g
Plain Baked Potato	240	2 g
Chicken Noodle Soup*	99	2 g
Tomato Florentine Soup*	84	1 g
Light Roast Chicken Deluxe	253	5 g
" " Turkey Deluxe*	249	4 g
(leave off reduced fat and reduced calorie mayonnaise for even less fat and calories)		
Arby's Sauce	30	0 g
Chocolate Chip Cookie	130	4 g
BASKIN-ROBBINS		
½ C Fat Free Frozen Dairy Dessert	100	0 g
(with sugar cone)	60	1 g
(with Waffle cone)	140	2 g

RESTAURANTS	CALORIES	FAT
BASKIN-ROBBINS (CONTINUED)		
Small (5-oz.) Nonfat Frozen Yogurt		
Strawberry and Raspberry	125	0 g
Coconut	100	0 g
(About 20 Calories per oz.)		
1 Scoop Daiquiri Ice	140	0 g
½ C Light Strawberry Royal	110	3 g
1 Scoop Rainbow Sherbet	160	2 g
1 Scoop Red Raspberry Sorbet	140	0 g
½ C Chunky Banana Sugar Free Dairy Dessert	100	1 g
BURGER KING		
Bagel	272	6 g
6 oz. Orange Juice	183	0 g
Chunky Chicken Salad	142	4 g
Side Salad	25	0 g
1 packet croutons	31	1 g
BK Broiler Chicken Sandwich (no mayonnaise)	267	8 g
Bull's Eye Barbecue Sauce	30	0 g
Breyers Frozen Yogurt Average	125	3 g
CARL'S JR.		
Blueberry Muffin	340	9 g
Bran Muffin	310	7 g
1% Low fat Milk (10-oz.)	138	2 g
English Muffin (nutritional with (includes margarine; omit margarine for fat and calorie savings)	190	5 g
Santa Fe Chicken Sandwich* (omit mayonnaise if included)	540	13 g
Charbroiler BBQ Chicken Sandwich	310	6 g
Lite Baked Potato	290	1 g
CHICK-FIL-A		
Tossed Salad	21	0 g
Hearty Breast of Chicken Soup (small)	152	2.6 g
Grilled 'n Lites (1 skewer)	50	< 1 g
Chargrilled Chicken (no bun)	128	2.4 g

RESTAURANTS	CALORIES	FAT
Chargrilled Chicken Sandwich (with lettuce and tomato only)	258	4.8 g
Chick-n-Q Sandwich	206	6.8 g
Chicken Deluxe Sandwich with bun	368	8.6 g
Ice Dream	134	4.8 g
1 Slice lemon pie	329	5 g
DAIRY QUEEN		
Side Salad	25	0 g
Garden Salad		
Grilled Chicken Fillet Sandwich (omit reduced calorie and fat mayonnaise for greater fat and calorie savings)	300	8 g
BBQ Beef Sandwich	225	4 g
For a big calorie splurge - Banana Split (share with friends, omit nuts)	510	11 g
Regular Yogurt Cone	180	0 g
Regular Yogurt Cup	170	0 g
Large Yogurt Cone	260	0 g
Large Yogurt Cup	230	0 g
Small Strawberry Breeze	400	0 g
DOMINOS PIZZA		
2 slices (16-inch thin crust) cheese	375	10 g
2 slices (16-inch thin crust) ham	415	11 g
(Add vegetables to these for a more well-rounded meal; better yet add vegetables and omit cheese).		
DUNKIN' DONUTS		
Apple and Spice Muffin	300	8 g
Banana Nut Muffin	310	10 g
Bran Muffin with Raisins	310	9 g
Cranberry Nut Muffin	290	9 g
Oat Bran Muffin	330	11 g
Plain Bagel	240	1 g
Cinnamon-Raisin Bagel	250	2 g
Egg Bagel (only 15 mg. CHOL)	250	2 g
Onion Bagel	230	1 g

RESTAURANTS	CALORIES	FAT
HARDEE'S		
3 Pancakes	280	2 g
Syrup	120	0 g
(choose jam for a lower calorie choice without fat)		
Side Salad	20	0 g
Chicken and Pasta Salad	230	3 g
1 regular size bun	74	1 g
Grilled Chicken Sandwich	310	9 g
(omit mayonnaise for even fewer calories and fat)		
Regular Roast Beef Sandwich	350	11 g
(specify lean Roy Rogers beef; not available at all locations)		
Large Roast Beef Sandwich	373	12 g
(Roy Rogers Beef)		
Frozen Softserve Yogurt (Average)	165	4 g
Turkey Club*	390	16 g
(About 37% fat as is; omit bacon and mayonnaise for a more healthy choice.)		
I CAN'T BELIEVE IT'S YOGURT		
6 3/4 oz. Yoglacé	68	0 g
9 1/3 oz. Yoglacé	93	0 g
12 oz. Yoglacé	120	0 g
6 3/4 oz. Sugar-Free Nonfat	115	0 g
9 1/3 oz. Sugar-Free Nonfat	150	0 g
12 oz. Sugar-Free Nonfat	4	0 g
6 3/4 oz. Nonfat	135	0 g
9 1/3 oz. Nonfat	186	0 g
12 oz. Nonfat	240	0 g
JACK-IN-THE-BOX		
Sesame Breadsticks	70	2 g
Chicken Fajita Pita	292	8 g
(Omit cheese for a greater savings in fat and calories)		
Grilled Chicken Fillet*	408	17 g
(as served is higher than 30% fat; omit the mayonnaise and cheese to reduce fat and calories)		

RESTAURANTS	CALORIES	FAT
LONG JOHN SILVER'S		
Side Salad	11	0 g
1 packet Lite Italian Dressing	12	0 g
1 packet Ranch Dressing	90	2 g
Ocean Chef Salad	150	5 g
Seafood Salad	230	5 g
Rice Pilaf	210	2 g
Green Beans	30	0 g
Baked Chicken Sandwich (no sauce)*	320	8 g
Honey Mustard Sauce	45	0 g
1 Hushpuppy	70	2 g
3-piece fish (lemon crumb)	150	1 g
2-piece lemon crumb fish* (with rice and small salad without dressing	262	4 g
Baked Chicken (light-herb)	130	4 g
Roll	110	<1 g
McDONALD'S		
Apple, Grapefruit, and Orange Juice (6 oz. each)	180	0 g
1% low fat milk (8 oz.)	110	2 g
Cheerios (3/4 C)	80	1 g
Wheaties (3/4 C)	90	1 g
English Muffin with Margarine (omit margarine for fat and calorie savings)	170	5 g
Fat-Free Apple Bran Muffin	180	0 g
Fat-Free Blueberry Muffin	175	0 g
Hot Cakes with margarine and syrup (Eggs are listed 10th in a list of about 14 ingredients; omit margarine for greater fat and calorie savings)	410	9 g
Side Salad	30	1 g
Chunky Chicken Salad	150	4 g
McLean Deluxe (No cheese)	320	10 g
McGrilled Chicken Sandwich	390	12 g
Carrot and Celery Sticks (instead of fries)	37/14	0 g
Vanilla Frozen Yogurt Cone	105	1 g
Strawberry Frozen Yogurt Sundae (Hot Fudge and Caramel contain saturated fat)	210	1 g
Chocolate Lowfat Milkshake	320	2 g
Strawberry Lowfat Milkshake	320	1 g

RESTAURANTS	CALORIES	FAT
Vanilla Lowfat Milkshake	290	1 g

Note: For kids the better choice is a plain hamburger (255 calories, 9 grams of fat) as opposed to a 6-piece order of Chicken McNuggets (270 calories and 15 grams of fat, where half of the calories come from fat). Add a muffin or carrot and celery sticks instead of fries.

LITTLE CAESAR'S PIZZA

2 slices (4.4 oz.) Cheese pizza (about 32% of calories come from fat)	340	12 g

TACO BELL

Bean Burrito with red sauce (omit cheese for an even greater fat and calorie savings)	447	14 g
Fiesta Tostada (about 38% fat; omit the cheese for fat and calorie savings)	167	7 g

TCBY

5 oz. Sugar-Free Nonfat	100	0 g
7 oz. Sugar-Free Nonfat	140	0 g
9 oz. Sugar-Free Nonfat	180	0 g
13 oz. Sugar-Free Nonfat	260	0 g
27 oz. Sugar-Free Nonfat	540	0 g
5 oz. Nonfat	137	0 g
7 oz. Nonfat	192	0 g
9 oz. Nonfat	247	0 g
13 oz. Nonfat	357	0 g
27 oz. Nonfat	742	0 g

SUBWAY

Note: You can have more of a choice here; order your salad or sandwich exactly the way you want it. Nutritional information is based on 2-2½ oz. meat, 1 t oil, a slice of cheese, a few olive slices, and healthy vegetables such as onion, green pepper, tomato, pickle, and lettuce. To reduce fat and calories, omit oil, cheese and olives. If you omit the ingredients I suggested, other choices are available which are not listed like salads with lean roast beef, turkey breast or other varieties as in sandwiches listed.

Large Garden Salad	46	0 g
6-inch Ham Salad	360	11 g

RESTAURANTS	CALORIES	FAT
6-inch Ham and Cheese Sub	336	10 g
6-inch Roast Beef Sub	358	11 g
6-inch Turkey Breast Sub	336	9 g
6-inch Subway Club	346	10 g
6-inch Tuna Sandwich*	402	13 g
6-inch Seafood and Crab Sandwich*	388	12 g
6-inch Veggie and Cheese Sub	282	8 g
WENDY'S		
Salad Bar and SuperBar:		
Alfalfa Sprouts	8	0 g
½ C Broccoli	12	0 g
¼ C Carrots	12	0 g
½ C Cauliflower	14	0 g
1 oz. Chives	71	1 g
4 Slices Cucumber	2	0 g
Garbanzo Beans	46	1 g
1 oz. Green Peas	21	0 g
¼ C Green Peppers	10	0 g
1 C Lettuce	8	0 g
½ C Mushrooms	4	0 g
Onions	2	0 g
1 oz. Tomatoes	6	0 g
¼ C Turkey Ham	35	1 g
¼ C 3-Bean Salad	60	0 g
2 oz. Fettucini	190	3 g
2 oz. Pasta Medley	60	2 g
¼ C Pasta Salad	35	0 g
2 oz. Rotini	90	2 g
2 oz. Alfredo Sauce	35	1 g
2 oz. Picanté Sauce	18	0 g
2 oz. Spaghetti Sauce	28	0 g
2 oz. Spaghetti Sauce with Meat	60	2 g
Plain Flour Tortilla	110	3 g
2 oz. Spanish Rice	70	1 g
1 oz. Applesauce	22	0 g
1 oz. Bananas	26	0 g
2 oz. Cantaloupe or Honeydew	20	0 g
2 oz. Oranges	26	0 g
2 peach slices in syrup	31	0 g
½ C Pineapple Chunks	60	0 g
2 oz. Strawberries	17	0 g

RESTAURANTS	CALORIES	FAT
¼ C Watermelon	18	0 g
Other items not on salad bar:		
Plain Baked Potato	270	0 g
2 Breadsticks	30	1 g
(low fat, but contain palm oil)		
Garden Salad	70	2 g
(omit imitation cheese for reduced fat and calories)		
9 oz. Chili	220	7 g
Grilled Chicken Sandwich	320	9 g
Jr. Hamburger	260	9 g
(Just over 30% fat mark, but a better choice for kids than Crispy Chicken Nuggets - over 60% calories from fat)		

CONVENIENCE FOOD STORES:

Fresh Fruit and Vegetables
All-fruit juices
Pretzels
Hostess Lite Cupcakes and Lite Twinkies
Honey Maid Graham Crackers
Fig Newtons
Lean skinless turkey or chicken breast lunchmeat
Bread
Skim Milk
Applesauce
Popsickles
(Some have places to order sandwiches just the way you like them)

EATING OUT - SPECIAL CHALLENGES

Of course the best way to avoid the high fat foods found at most sporting events, amusement parks, movies, and other entertainment places is to eat before you go or take something with you. Some amusement parks, for example, will allow you to bring a picnic; you can eat their own picnic grounds. Or, you can put a few low-fat snacks in a "fanny pack", snap it around you and you're ready to go. Of course, this is not always possible; you may not have the time or perhaps you just want to eat with everyone else. Believe it or not, it can be done!

Eating healthy while on vacation can be just as easy as eating out has been described in the previous paragraphs. The biggest challenge is to yourself. You can choose to stay with your new eating plan, have a few special treats balanced within your daily or weekly fat budget, continue exercising, and come back from your trip without extra pounds and feeling great. On the other hand, you can choose to ignore your diet all-together and come back regretting what you've done and feeling guilty. Whatever you decide is up to you; however, you really have so many delicious choices, there's no way you should feel deprived. See the box at the end of this section for healthy eating ideas while on vacation.

Some of the suggestions below contain a lot of sugar; however, I am trying to show you how to make choices. I would much rather you have a snow cone than a real chocolate ice cream bar! Also, remember, sometimes it's not what you order that has most of the fat - it's what you put on it or what you eat with it that adds all the fat! (Refer to the tips at the first part on "General Tips on Eating Out").

AMUSEMENT PARKS:

Frozen nonfat yogurt or soft-serve ice cream
Popsicles
Snow-Cones
Soft Pretzels - without butter or oil or salt
Thin crust cheese pizza
In some restaurants within parks - Grilled chicken sandwiches without mayonnaise or cheese, spaghetti with plain tomato sauce, plain salads or baked potato - add your own low fat toppings.
Diet Drinks, Iced Tea, Fruit Juice

SPORTING EVENTS:

Frozen nonfat yogurt or soft-serve ice cream
Soft Pretzels - without butter or oil or salt
Diet Drinks
Grilled Chicken Sandwich without mayonnaise

MOVIES:

If your theater allows it, take your own air-popped popcorn, pretzels or fruit into the theater with you. If not, some choices are:
Soft pretzels (omit the oil or butter and salt)
A small amount of hard candy or fruit candy (containing no fat but lots of sugar; definitely use in moderation - at least it is a better choice than a chocolate candy bar containing high levels of saturated fat as well as sugar).

CONCERTS AND OTHER ENTERTAINMENT PLACES OR EVENTS:

Fresh fruit or fruit smoothies
Baked potatoes
Salads
Grilled Chicken Sandwich (without mayonnaise)
Fresh raw or cooked vegetables with dip (leave off their dip and use your own low-fat)
Thin crust cheese pizza
Soft Pretzels (without butter, oil, or salt)
Corn on the Cob (without the butter)
Breadsticks (without the butter)

VACATIONS

Use the following ideas, and you will come back from vacation feeling guilt-free and looking great:

- Continue to use the suggestions for restaurant dining.
- When traveling by air, you can call ahead and request a low fat meal in some cases.
- Many cruise lines now have "heart healthy" menus available.
- Many hotels have exercise facilities on the premises. If not, check with the front desk; they should be able to direct you to an exercise facility close by.
- Walking is still a great way to exercise while out of town. Take a lap or two around the mall - but no shopping until you're through.
- Keep some low fat snacks in your room so you're not tempted to hit the vending machine if you get hungry.
- Take advantage of the swimming pool when weather permits; swimming is great exercise.
- The beach is a great place to exercise; running or walking in the shallow surf in the sand is great for the lower body.
- Active vacations centered around skiing, rafting, hiking, scuba diving, etc. are good choices.
- When possible, forget the elevator and take the stairs. Use safety precautions.

Notes and Extra Recipes:

Notes and Extra Recipes:

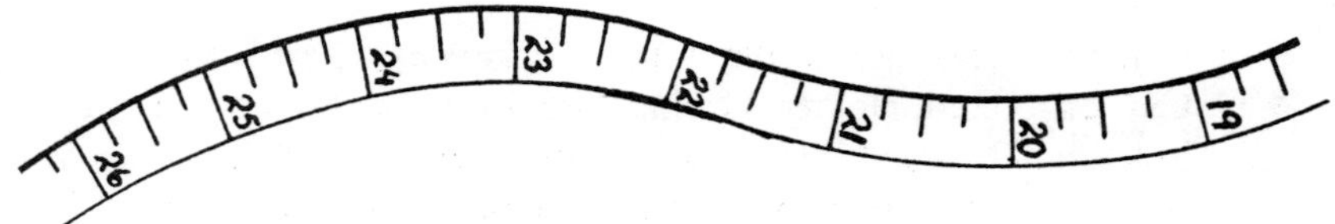

PARTY FOODS & BEVERAGES

PARTY FOODS

Time Savers (Finger Foods):

- Wrap melon balls with thin-sliced Healthy Choice ham; secure with toothpick.
- Fill celery pieces with nonfat ricotta cheese plus crushed pineapple; low-fat chicken, tuna, ham, or egg salad; or nonfat pimiento cheese.
- Alternate any 3 of the following on a toothpick: pickle chips; green, yellow, or red pepper slices; nonfat cubed cheese; onion slices; cooked lean ham or boneless skinless chicken breast cubes; mushrooms; low-fat meatballs; cucumber slices; pickled okra; fruit chunks; baby corn; cherry tomatoes; artichoke hearts; cooked shrimp; scallops or salmon; chunks of low-fat or nonfat cake; marshmallows.
- Wrap whole water chestnuts with thin-sliced Healthy Choice ham or chicken.
- Coat whole dill pickles with Healthy Choice Fat Free cream cheese; encircle with thin slice of Healthy Choice ham; chill and slice into pieces.
- Serve fruit and nonfat cheese on a tray with nonfat crackers.
- Place boiled shrimp on toothpicks and serve with red sauce.
- Thin-sliced smoked salmon topped with cracked pepper on melba rounds makes a great appetizer.
- Serve thin-sliced lean meats with nonfat spreads and cheeses on thin-sliced low-fat party rolls or breads.
- Pour quiche recipe into small muffin tins for mini quiches.
- Make mini pizzas or nachos with pita bread cut into small triangles. Top each piece with nonfat sauce, sliced vegetables, spices, and nonfat grated cheese.

- Many people enjoy sardines and crackers as a first course.
- Cut uncooked Hearty Grains biscuits in half and roll into individual balls; place in sprayed miniature muffin tins or on a sprayed baking sheet. Make an impression in the center of each ball and bake until done. Fill with your favorite low-fat filling. For example: unsweetened jam or jelly; low-fat tuna, chicken, or ham salad; low-fat pimiento cheese; or any of the pizza, pasta, or potato toppings, etc.

Time Savers (Spreads For Nonfat Crackers, "Pita or Bagel Chips,"✔ or Vegetables):

- Mix 4 oz. each Healthy Choice Fat Free cream cheese and nonfat ricotta cheese; 1 can chunk chicken breast in water; ½ t each almond extract and Worcestershire; ½ t garlic salt plus; and 1 can sliced water chestnuts.
- Blend 4 oz. Healthy Choice Fat Free cream cheese, 2 oz. nonfat ricotta cheese, ½ C Egg Beaters, 1 t each lemon and onion juice, and salt (optional). Spoon on toasted nonfat bread squares; sprinkle with chutney. Bake at 450° on sprayed cookie sheet.
- Mix 12 oz. nonfat ricotta cheese and 4 oz. Healthy Choice Fat Free cream cheese with 1 package lite taco or chili seasoning and ¼ C picanté sauce. Serve on low-fat tortilla chips.

Time Savers (Hot and Cold Dips):

- 1 C "Nonfat Yogurt Cheese"✔ with 1 C picanté sauce.
- "Mock Sour Cream"✔ plus Beau Monde Seasoning and garlic powder.
- "Nonfat Yogurt Cheese"✔ plus your favorite low-fat dry soup mix.
- Combine 1 can Health Valley Fat-Free chili, 1 C Healthy Choice Fat Free cream cheese, and ½ C chunky picanté sauce. Serve hot.
- Drain 3 (7-oz.) cans minced clams, reserving ½ C liquid. Mix clams, reserved liquid, 8 oz. each nonfat ricotta cheese and Healthy Choice Fat Free cream cheese, ¼ t Tabasco, and 2 T each Worcestershire, chives, and lemon juice. Place in hollowed-out round loaf of bread; cover with foil and bake at 250° for 3 hours.

Time Savers (Miscellaneous):

- Cubed Healthy Choice hot dogs cooked in nonfat B-B-Q sauce are an easy appetizer.
- Press Pillsbury Soft breadsticks into a 9 X 13-inch baking sheet

to form a crust. Season 1 (15-oz.) carton fat free ricotta cheese with favorite seasoning and spread on dough. Fold dough over cheese; seal. Bake as directed on breadstick package.

Helpful Hints:

- Serve dip in a hollowed out cabbage or bread.
- Place finger foods on toothpicks; press each pick into a head of cabbage or a whole pineapple to serve.
- Serve fresh cut up vegetables for dippers as well as low fat crackers or rice crackers.
- When purchasing party trays, stay away from high fat and high sodium meats such as sausages, pepperoni, and bologna. Choose lean chunks of meat and nonfat cheeses, fresh cut fruits, and vegetables.
- To stuff celery, eggs or any food with a filling, place filling in a strong ziploc bag and seal. Cut a small hole in one corner of the bag; squeeze out and fill.

BEVERAGES

Time Savers (Blender Drinks):

- Mix 4 C orange juice, 4 bananas, and 10 ice cubes.
- Blend 1 C each 1% or less buttermilk and chunk frozen fruit with ice cubes and artificial sweetener to taste.
- Mix 2 C unsweetened juice, 2 C fresh or frozen fruit, 1 C vanilla nonfat yogurt, and artificial sweetener to taste.
- Mock Daiquiri - 1 C each frozen unsweetened strawberries and crushed ice; 3 T unsweetened pineapple juice concentrate; 1 t fresh lemon juice.

Time Savers (Other Beverages):

- Add 1 scoop coffee nonfat frozen yogurt to 1 C lite sugar-free hot chocolate.
- Squeeze the juice of 1 large slice of lemon or lime into 1 tall glass of ice water.
- Squeeze juice from lemons, limes, or oranges into a glass; add artificial sweetener and ice. Water may be added if necessary.
- For a Mimosa - Mix 1 part champagne to 1 part orange juice.
- Lemonade Tea - Mix 1 part sugar-free lemonade to 1 part unsweetened iced tea.
- For a refreshing beverage mix 2 parts sparkling water or club soda to 1 part unsweetened fruit juice.
- Quick Punch - Mix a 2 liter bottle of Diet Cherry 7-Up with the juice of 3 limes.

- Add a sprig of fresh mint to brewed apricot iced tea.
- Egg Nog : Whip 1 chilled (13-oz.) can evaporated skim milk with ½ C each skim milk and Egg Beaters. Add 1 t each rum flavoring and vanilla plus artificial sweetener to taste. Chill and serve.
- Serve hot or over ice a mixture of: 4 C skim milk; 1 C each strong coffee and evaporated skim milk; sweetener to taste.
- Great beverages to keep on hand are: unsweetened peach, pear, or apricot nectar; low-fat buttermilk; fortified skim milk; tomato juice; vegetable juice; carrot juice; 1 part each unsweetened fruit juice and water; milk shakes made with fresh fruit and skim milk; club soda with lime; cranberry juice diluted with water; hot or cold herb tea; hot or cold flavored or plain coffee.

Helpful Hints:

- Freeze leftover fruit juices in decorative molds; float in punch bowl.
- To clear up cloudy tea, add a little boiling water.
- Drink juice that is not made from concentrate if possible; it contains less natural sugar.

HORS D'OEUVRES

CHEESE PHYLLO ROLLS

2 C (8 oz.) grated Healthy Choice fat free mozzarella cheese
½ of a (4-oz.) carton Healthy Choice fat free garlic and herb cream cheese spread, softened
2 T Butter Buds liquid
9 sheets frozen phyllo dough pastry, thawed
Butter flavor Pam no stick cooking spray
Paprika or chili powder for garnish

1. In a food processor, combine the first 3 ingredients; process until smooth. Set aside.
2. Coat a pastry board or wax paper with Pam. Place 1 sheet of thawed dough on board. (Always keep remaining phyllo dough covered.) Spray phyllo with Pam, place another sheet of dough on top, spray, and repeat layer one more time. This makes a total of 3 sprayed layers. Slice layered dough vertically into 5 equal slices, then, cut each strip in half to make 10 total pieces. Repeat step #2 two more times using remaining phyllo. There will be 30 pieces in all.
3. Spoon about 1 T cheese mixture at the bottom of each phyllo strip. Roll up like a jellyroll; seal edges and place seam side down on a baking sheet coated with Pam. Sprinkle each with a little paprika or chili powder and bake at 375° for about 20 - 25 minutes or until golden brown. Serve warm.

Serves: 30

Per Serving: 0.18 g Fat, 20 Calories, 1 % Fat, 3.13 g Protein, 1.2 g Carb, 104 mg Sodium, 1.6 mg Cholesterol

TORTILLA ROLL-UPS

(Do the day before!)

2 (8-oz.) cartons Healthy Choice Fat Free cream cheese
2 C "Nonfat Yogurt Cheese"✔
1 small onion, chopped
5 finely chopped jalapeño peppers (seeds removed)
2 T picanté sauce plus extra for dipping
3 dashes garlic salt (optional)
30 (7-inch) flour tortillas, no lard, softened in microwave

1. Mix all ingredients, except tortillas. (Mixture may appear to be a little runny.) Spread each tortilla with about 1 T of mixture; roll and place seam-side down in large non-metal dish. Place a damp cloth over tortillas; chill overnight.
2. Cut into bite-size pieces and serve with picanté sauce.

Serves: 60

Per Serving: 0.5 g Fat, 48 Calories, 9 % Fat, 2.8 g Protein, 8.2 g Carb, 50 mg Sodium, 1.58 mg Cholesterol

SPICY HAMBURGER CHEESE BALLS

1 lb. Healthy Choice ground beef
¼ t EACH garlic salt, nutmeg, and ginger
½ t EACH black pepper, marjoram, cayenne pepper, and oregano
1 t EACH sage, basil, thyme, cumin, and chili powder
1 C Truly Lite Fat Free ricotta cheese
¼ C shredded Healthy Choice Fat Free Cheddar cheese
8 oz. Healthy Choice Fat Free cheese singles, diced
2 C "Best Baker's Mix"✔
1 package Butter Buds

1. Mix all ingredients; form into balls. Bake at 325° on sprayed baking sheet for 10-12 minutes or until brown. Do not over bake.

Serves: 60

Per Serving: 0.27 g Fat, 17 Calories, 14 % Fat, 1.6 g Protein, 0.8 g Carb, 90.5 mg Sodium, 4.6 mg Cholesterol

CHEESE SQUARES
(Quick Fix)

4 oz. Healthy Choice Fat Free cream cheese
½ C (2 oz.) EACH Healthy Choice Fat Free Cheddar cheese and Healthy Choice Fat Free mozzarella cheese
½ C liquid Butter Buds
2 egg whites at room temperature, stiffly beaten
1 (1½-lb.) loaf sliced French bread

1. Place first 3 ingredients in microwave-safe bowl; cook until melted, stirring occasionally. Remove from heat; fold in egg whites.
2. Cut bread slices into squares and coat with cheese mixture. Place squares on sprayed cookie sheet and bake at 400° for 10 minutes. (May freeze before baking.)

Serves: 36

Per Serving: 0.39 g Fat, 45 Calories, 8 % Fat, 2.8 g Protein, 7.3 g Carb, 137 mg Sodium, 1.1 mg Cholesterol

CRISPY QUESADILLAS
(Quick Fix)

16 oz. Truly Lite Fat Free ricotta cheese
¾ C grated Healthy Choice Fat Free mozarella cheese
5 Healthy Choice Fat Free cheese singles, diced
2 T minced fresh onion
10 (7-inch) flour tortillas
Butter Flavor Pam no stick cooking spray
Mild chunky picanté sauce

1. In a medium bowl combine first 4 ingredients. This mixture will keep in a closed container for up to a week. When ready to use, spread 2 T cheese mixture on half of each tortilla. Fold tortillas in half and spray both sides with Pam. Spray baking dish and place quesadillas inside. Bake at 375°-400° until crisp. Serve with "Great Guacamolé,"✔ "Nonfat Yogurt Cheese,"✔ and picanté sauce.

Note: You may add 2 slices of boneless, skinless chicken or turkey breast (about 2 oz.) to each tortilla. Bake as directed.

Serves: 10

Per Serving: 1 g Fat, 114 Calories, 1 % Fat, 6.5 g Protein, 18.5 g Carb, 298 mg Sodium, 3.3 mg Cholesterol

MARGARET'S FAMOUS HAM BALL

1½ lbs. Healthy Choice cooked ham, finely ground
¾ C EACH Kraft Free mayonnaise and ½ minced fresh onion
½ C fat free cracker crumbs, about 10 - 12 crackers (adjust as needed to desired consistency)
1 t Worcestershire sauce
¼ t EACH powdered mustard and curry
8 oz. Healthy Choice Fat Free cream cheese, softened and whipped

1. Mix all ingredients, except cream cheese. Line a small bowl with plastic wrap, overlapping the sides. Place ham mixture into bowl and press into a ball. Chill well.
2. When ready, lift ham ball out of bowl using plastic wrap and place on serving tray. Remove wrap and "ice" with cream cheese. Garnish with parsley and paprika.

Serves: 20

Note: May make these in small individual balls.

Per Serving: 1.2 g Fat, 68 Calories, 16 % Fat, 13.8 g Protein, 6.2 g Carb, 463 mg Sodium, 17 mg Cholesterol

BAKED GREEN CHILES
(Quick Fix)

½ C Truly Lite Fat Free ricotta cheese
3 T grated Healthy Choice Fat Free Cheddar cheese
⅔ C dry "Basic Bread Crumbs"✔ or fat free cracker crumbs
2 egg whites, slightly beaten
6 whole green chiles, fresh or canned
Pam no stick cooking spray

1. Spray broiler pan with Pam, place in oven; turn oven to broil.
2. Mix cheese together in a small bowl; fill each chile carefully.
3. Dip filled chile into egg whites and roll in bread crumbs. Broil on preheated pan until golden, about 4-6 minutes. Serve with picanté sauce if desired.

Serves: 6 (**Note:** This also makes a great side dish)

Per Serving: 0 g Fat, 29 Calories, 1 % Fat, 5.3 g Protein, 1.5 g Carb, 117.6 mg Sodium, 0.37 mg Cholesterol

PULL-A-PART PARTY BREAD
(Quick Fix)

4 oz. Healthy Choice Fat Free cream cheese
2 packages Butter Buds plus ¼ C hot water
3 slices Healthy Choice Fat Free cheese singles
¼ C (1 oz.) grated Healthy Choice Fat Free mozzarella cheese
1 t EACH minced onion and cracked pepper
¼ C chopped fresh basil or 1½ t dried basil
1 T Parmesan cheese
2 oz. coarsely chopped Healthy Choice cooked ham
1 (1-lb.) loaf Italian or sour dough bread
Butter flavor Pam no stick cooking spray

1. Preheat oven to 450°.
2. Mix all ingredients well, except bread, in a medium bowl.
3. Slice bread diagonally into 1-inch slices, but do not cut all the way through. Stop about ¼- inch from the bottom.
4. Using half of the ham mixture, spread about 1 T between each slice. Turn bread around so ends are reversed and repeat slicing as in step #2 creating diamond patterns or cross patterns on top of bread. Spread the remaining ham mixture 1 T at a time between each slice.
5. Spray cookie sheet with Pam, place loaf on sheet, and place a loose foil tent over the bread. Bake about 10 minutes or until heated through and crust is crisp.

Serves: 16

Per Serving: 0.2 g Fat, 104 Calories, 2 % Fat, 7 g Protein, 24.5 g Carb, 436 mg Sodium, 3.2 mg Cholesterol

ISLANDS OF FRUIT
(Easy Prep)

1 (8-oz.) carton Healthy Choice fat free cream cheese
1 t grated orange rind
½ t ginger
2 T orange juice or apricot nectar
4 dozen Nabisco Garden Crisp vegetable crackers
½ C fresh blueberries
1 C EACH green grapes, red grapes, kiwi, and pineapple
1½ C strawberries

1. Mix together the first 4 ingredients; spread 1 t cream cheese mixture on each cracker. Slice grapes in half; slice remaining fruit except blueberries into bite-size pieces and arrange on top of cream cheese mixture.

Serves: 48

Per Serving: 0.11 g Fat, 15 Calories, 6 % Fat, 1 g Protein, 2.5 g Carb, 43 mg Sodium, 0.9 mg Cholesterol

CRAB PUFFS
(Easy Prep)

1 (6-oz.) can crabmeat, drained
½ C (2 oz.) grated Healthy Choice fat free mozzarella cheese
⅓ C green onion including tops, chopped
1 t EACH dry mustard and Worcestershire sauce
1½ C water
1 package dry Butter Buds
¼ t salt (optional)
1 C flour
1 C Egg Beaters

1. Mix together the first 5 ingredients; set aside.
2. Boil water, Butter Buds, and salt in saucepan. Reduce heat, gradually add flour. Stir vigorously until mixture forms a ball. Remove from heat; cool 10 minutes.
3. Stir in Egg Beaters, beating with a wooden spoon. When smooth, add crab mixture.
4. Drop heaping teaspoonfuls onto sprayed baking sheet. Bake at 400° for 15 minutes. Reduce to 350° and bake 10 more minutes. (Freezes well.)

Serves: 48

Per Serving: 0.08 g Fat, 18 Calories, 4 % Fat, 1.7 g Protein, 2 g Carb, 42 mg Sodium, 3.6 mg Cholesterol

PASTA CRUNCH
(Quick Fix)

1 chicken bouillon cube
1 C (4 oz.) dry salad macaroni
1 C (4 oz.) dry small shell macaroni
1 C (1.5 oz.) dry egg noodles substitute or egg noodles made without the yolk
Pam no stick cooking spray
1 C (1.5 oz.) small 3-ring pretzels
1 C bite size shredded wheat cereal
¼ C EACH Worcestershire sauce and Butter Buds liquid
2 T "Ross's Special Seasoning"✔
Dash hot pepper sauce or to taste

1. Bring water to boil in a medium saucepan. Add bouillon cube and stir to dissolve. Add pasta to boiling water; reduce heat and simmer 4 - 5 minutes. Drain well.
2. Place cooked pasta in a large microwave-safe bowl that has been coated with Pam. Stir seasoning into Worcestershire and Butter Buds liquid; pour into bowl, add remaining ingredients and mix well, coating evenly.
3. Cook uncovered on high in microwave about 5 minutes stirring halfway through cooking time. Stir again after the 5 minutes, return to microwave and cook about 8 - 10 minutes more stirring about every 2 - 3 minutes. Remove from oven, cool and serve. Store in an airtight container. **Note:** Try using different cereals and experiment with your favorite seasonings.

Makes: 10 (½ C) servings

Per Serving: 1.7 g Fat, 165 Calories, 10 % Fat, 4.7 g Protein, 32.5 g Carb, 734 mg Sodium, 0 mg Cholesterol

LAYERED MOUNTAIN NACHOS

(Pretty and very easy)

1 bag Guiltless Gourmet low-fat baked tortilla chips
1 can Old El Paso vegetarian refried beans
1 C chopped fresh tomatoes
2 C shredded lettuce
1 recipe "Great Guacamole"✔
½ C "Nonfat Yogurt Cheese"✔
½ C (2 oz.) EACH Healthy Choice Fat Free mozzarella, Cheddar, and cheese singles

1. On a large round serving platter, arrange 1 layer of chips extending to edges of plate. Randomly drop spoonfuls of beans and guacamole on top of chips. Sprinkle bits of lettuce, tomatoes and shredded cheese onto this layer.
2. Repeat layers, moving chips closer in away from the edge of the plate a little each time a new layer is created, eventually forming a mountain shape.
3. Garnish with yogurt cheese and picanté if desired.

Serves: 24

Note: These may be served hot. Heat in 400° oven but do not add lettuce, tomatoes, guacamole, or yogurt cheese until after they are heated through, about 2-3 minutes.

Per Serving: 0.7 g Fat, 67 Calories, 3 % Fat, 2.87 g Protein, 11.2 g Carb, 275 mg Sodium, 1 mg Cholesterol

PITA CHIPS

(Quick Fix)

1 (6 count) bag, any flavor, pita pocket bread
Pam butter flavor no stick cooking spray
Cinnamon/sugar, Garlic salt, or favorite seasonings

1. Separate each pita and cut into wedges. (About 16 per pita.)
2. Place each wedge on sprayed cookie sheet, coat each pita with Pam, and sprinkle with desired seasoning. Bake at 350° for 6-10 minutes or until crisp. Store in sealed container. Great with picante sauce.

Serves: 12 (8 or wedges per serving)

Per Serving: 1 g Fat, 80 Calories, 11 % Fat, 1.5 g Protein, 15 g Carb, 125 mg Sodium, 0 mg Cholesterol

BAKED CHEESE
(Easy Prep)

1 (15-oz.) container Truly Lite Fat Free ricotta cheese
2 t garlic salt or any of your favorite seasoning

1. Using a yogurt strainer or cheese cloth as in the recipe for "Nonfat Yogurt Cheese"✔, follow directions and strain ricotta overnight.
2. Combine ricotta and seasoning, form into a ball, and bake in a 400° oven in a small baking dish for 45 minutes or 1 hour or until cheese is lightly browned.
3. Cool and drain any excess liquid if necessary. Chill well before serving. (May serve warm if desired).

Variation: Wrap with thawed phyllo sheets, twist top to secure, and bake.
Serves: 15

Per Serving: 0 g Fat, 20 Calories, 0 % Fat, 4 g Protein, 2 g Carb, 15 mg Sodium, 3 mg Cholesterol

GREAT POTATO SKINS
(Easy Prep; may also use the microwave in step #1)

4 medium-size baking potatoes
Butter flavor Pam no stick cooking spray
"Nonfat Yogurt Cheese"✔, fat free cheese, seasoned salt (optional)
Bac-Os, chives, picanté sauce, or low fat toppings

1. Spray potatoes evenly with Pam. Pierce once with a fork and bake at 400° for 1 hour. Cool slightly.
2. Cut potatoes in half lengthwise, scoop out pulp, leaving a ¼-inch shell. Save pulp for mashed potatoes or other recipes.
3. Cut each shell in half lengthwise, then crosswise. Dust each piece lightly with flour, spray both sides with Pam and bake in 425°- 450° oven about 15 minutes or until crisp. Serve with toppings. May omit flour if desired.

Makes: 32 (1 piece, without toppings)

Per Serving: 0 g Fat, 18 Calories, 1 % Fat, 0.5 g Protein, 4.1 g Carb, 3.5 mg Sodium, 1 mg Cholesterol

BAGEL CHIPS
(Quick Fix)

1 package (6-count) bagels (2-oz. each), any flavor, sliced ⅛-inch thick
Pam butter flavor no stick cooking spray
Garlic powder or salt (optional), chili powder, or any nonfat seasoning

1. Put each bagel piece in a single layer on sprayed cookie sheet. Coat each piece with Pam and sprinkle with spices.
2. Bake in 350° oven for 8-10 minutes or until crisp.

Serves: 6

Per Serving: 1.0 g Fat, 160 Calories, 6 % Fat, 7 g Protein, 31 g Carb, 320 mg Sodium, 0 mg Cholesterol

CORPUS CHRISTI CANAPÉS

1 (6 count) package sour dough English muffins, halved
1 (7-oz) can crabmeat
½ t salt (optional)
½ t garlic powder
¼ C hot water mixed with 1 package dry Butter Buds
7 Healthy Choice Fat Free cheese singles
1½ t Kraft Free mayonnaise

1. Preheat oven to 375°. Mix cheese, water and Butter Buds and melt in microwave oven, about 60 seconds. Remove from microwave and add crabmeat, garlic powder, mayonnaise and salt. Spread on muffins and put in freezer. When frozen, cut each muffin half in fourths. Place on cookie sheet; bake at 375° for 15 minutes

Yields 48 canapés

Per Serving: 0.3 g Fat, 32 Calories, 8 % Fat, 2.3 g Protein, 4.54 g Carb, 193 mg Sodium, 6.5 mg Cholesterol

SPICY HAM BALLS

1½ lbs. Healthy Choice ham, ground
1 C "Basic Bread Crumbs"✔, finely ground
2 egg whites
½ C skim milk
1 C brown sugar
1 t dry mustard
1 C water
½ C vinegar

1. Combine first 3 ingredients and form into balls. (About 1 T per ball)
2. Place balls in oblong sprayed dish. Mix remaining ingredients; stir until sugar dissolves. Pour over ham balls. Bake at 350° for 1 hour; baste often.

Serves: 40

Per Serving: 0.3 g Fat, 40 Calories, 7 % Fat, 3.2 g Protein, 5.4 g Carb, 180 mg Sodium, 9 mg Cholesterol

RICOTTA BREAD
(Quick Fix)

1 (14-oz.) loaf unsliced French bread
¼ C hot water plus 1 package Butter Buds
1½ C (6 oz.) Truly Lite Fat Free ricotta cheese
6 slices Healthy Choice Fat Free cheese slices
¼ C (1 oz.) Healthy Choice Fat Free Cheddar or mozzarella cheese, grated
½ C finely chopped onion
½ t garlic salt (optional)
Pam no stick cooking spray

1. Place bread on Pam-coated cookie sheet. Slice bread diagonally into ½-inch slices, not cutting all the way through. Drizzle the Butter Buds mixture over bread and set aside.
2. Combine remaining ingredients; place in microwave and heat until cheeses melt. Stir.
3. Spread cheese mixture between bread slices and on top. Broil about 6- inches from heat until heated through.

Serves: 14

Per Serving: 0.7 g Fat, 115 Calories, 5 % Fat, 7.7 g Protein, 19.2 g Carb, 387 mg Sodium, 3.7 mg Cholesterol

DIPS

SPICY MEAT AND CHEESE DIP

(Quick Fix)

1 lb. Healthy Choice ground beef, cooked, rinsed, and drained
½ t garlic salt (optional)
½ package Butter Buds
10 - 12 oz. Healthy Choice Fat Free Pasteurized Process cheese
½ C Truly Lite Fat Free ricotta cheese (optional)
1 can Weight Watcher's cream of mushroom soup
1 can diced Rotel tomatoes and green chiles, drained
1 T cornstarch
Pam no stick cooking spray

1. In a microwave-safe bowl coated with Pam, cook all the ingredients except the meat, tomatoes, and cornstarch until the cheese melts. Stir in the cornstarch and then the tomatoes. Add the meat and heat through. Serve warm with baked tortilla chips or "Pita Chips."✔

Serves: 12

Per Serving: 1.5 g Fat, 77 Calories,
18 % Fat, 10.5 g Protein, 4.1 g Carb,
435 mg Sodium, 21 mg Cholesterol

SHRIMPLY DELICIOUS DIP

(Easy Prep)

2 (4½-oz.) cans shrimp, drained, rinsed and chopped
1 C celery, chopped fine
½ C green onion with tops, chopped
1 C Kraft Free mayonnaise
3 oz. Healthy Choice Fat Free cream cheese, softened
3 oz. "Mock Sour Cream"✔
1 t Worcestershire sauce
½ t lemon peel

1. Beat cream cheese, yogurt, and mayonnaise. Add remaining ingredients and mix well. Chill overnight.

Serves: 16

Per Serving: 0.14 g Fat, 28 Calories,
4 % Fat, 3.6 g Protein, 3.1 g Carb,
158 mg Sodium, 26.8 mg Cholesterol

SALLY'S SPINACH DIP

1 envelope "Knorrs" vegetable soup mix
2 C "Mock Sour Cream"✓
1 (10-oz.) package frozen chopped spinach, thawed and drained
½ C (2 oz.) grated Healthy Choice Fat Free Cheddar cheese
1 can water chestnuts, drained and minced
¼ t garlic powder

1. Combine all ingredients and chill. Serve with pita or bagel chips or fresh vegetables.

Serves: 12

Per Serving: 0.25 g Fat, 26 Calories, 7 % Fat, 2.5 g Protein, 3.6 g Carb, 350 mg Sodium, 0.83 mg Cholesterol

HOT CRAB DIP
(Quick Fix)

8 oz. EACH Healthy Choice Fat Free cream cheese
3 T Kraft Free mayonnaise
1 package Butter Buds
1 t Dijon or creole mustard
2 T dry white wine
1 (7¾-oz.) can crab meat, rinsed, drained, and flaked

1. Combine first four ingredients in a microwave-safe bowl. Heat until softened; mix well. Add wine and crab meat; heat through.

Serves: 8

Per Serving: 0.45 g Fat, 67 Calories, 6 % Fat, 10.2 g Protein, 4.1 g Carb, 408 mg Sodium, 31 mg Cholesterol

CLAM DIP

1 C EACH "Nonfat Yogurt Cheese"✓ and "Mock Sour Cream"✓
1 (7 to 8-oz.) can minced clams, well drained
1 t EACH Worcestershire sauce and Creole mustard
2 t chopped green onion
2-3 dashes hot pepper sauce

1. Mix all ingredients together and chill.

Serves: 8

Per Serving: 0.3 g Fat, 33 Calories, 8 % Fat, 3.6 g Protein, 4 g Carb, 57 mg Sodium, 16 mg Cholesterol

NEW YEAR'S CELEBRATION DIP

2 C black-eyed peas with no oil
1 (15-oz.) can Health Valley spicy Fat Free vegetarian chili
¼ C chunky style picanté sauce or to taste
1 (4-oz.) can chopped green chiles
2 C (8 oz.) grated Healthy Choice fat free cheddar cheese
4 oz. Healthy Choice cheese slices
1 t ground cumin
½ t oregano
¼ t EACH cilantro and garlic powder
Dash red pepper
Salt to taste (optional)

1. Combine all ingredients in a food processor or blender; mix until smooth. Pour into a baking dish that has been sprayed with Pam; bake at 350° for about 35 - 45 minutes. Serve warm with Guiltless Gourmet no oil tortilla chips or "Pita Chips or Bagel Chips"✔.

Makes: about 20 (¼ C) servings

Per Serving: 0.27 g Fat, 64 Calories, 4 % Fat, 6.5 g Protein, 7.8 g Carb, 211 mg Sodium, 2.25 mg Cholesterol

LISA'S FAVORITE HOT BROCCOLI DIP
(Quick Fix)

1 C chopped celery
½ C chopped onion
¼ C hot water mixed with 1 package Butter Buds
1 (10-oz.) package frozen chopped broccoli, thawed
1 (4-oz.) jar chopped mushrooms
¼ t garlic salt (optional)
1 (10¾-oz.) can Weight Watcher's cream of mushroom soup
1 can chopped water chestnuts (optional)

1. Sauté celery and onion in Butter Buds mixture. Add remaining ingredients and heat through.

Serves: 10

Per Serving: 0.46 g Fat, 35 Calories, 11 % Fat, 2.1 g Protein, 6.3 g Carb, 219 mg Sodium, 0 mg Cholesterol

8 LAYER CHALUPA DIP

1 can Old El Paso vegetarian refried beans
1 package lite Taco seasoning mix
3 oz. Healthy Choice Fat Free cheese singles, shredded
1 recipe "Great Guacamole"✔, prepared
2 small tomatoes, chopped
¼ C chopped onion (optional)
1 small can chopped green chiles
8 oz. "Nonfat Yogurt Cheese"✔ plus 1 T cornstarch
½ C (2 oz.) EACH shredded Healthy Choice Fat Free mozzarella cheese and cheese singles

1. Mix beans with taco mix; Layer above ingredients in order listed in an oven-proof serving dish.
2. Place in 300° oven or heat slowly in microwave until heated through. Serve with baked tortilla chips or "Pita Chips"✔. (May be served at room temperature.)

Serves: 16

Per Serving: 0.2 g Fat, 65 Calories, 2 % Fat, 6.4 g Protein, 6 g Carb, 401 mg Sodium, 4 mg Cholesterol

SUSAN'S CHEESE DIP
(Quick Fix)

8 oz. Healthy Choice Fat Free Fat Free cream cheese
¼ C EACH skim milk and Kraft Free mayonnaise
¼ C "Nonfat Yogurt Cheese"✔
¼ C Healthy Choice Fat Free grated Cheddar cheese
½ C Healthy Choice Fat Free grated mozzarella cheese
¼ C chopped green onions including tops
2 dashes EACH onion and garlic salt

1. Mix the first 3 ingredients until smooth.
2. Add remaining ingredients and chill.

Makes: 12 (¼ C) servings

Per Serving: 0 g Fat, 37 Calories, 0 % Fat, 5.1 g Protein, 3.5 g Carb, 222 mg Sodium, 4.75 mg Cholesterol

BROCCOLI GARLIC-CHEESE DIP
(Easy Prep)

2 (10-oz.) packages frozen chopped broccoli
½ C Butter Buds liquid
1 C chopped onion
1 can Weight Watcher's cream of mushroom soup
4 oz. Healthy Choice Fat Free garlic and herb cream cheese
4 oz. Healthy Choice Fat Free pasteurized process cheese

1. Cook broccoli according to directions on package; drain well.
2. Sauté onion in Butter Buds liquid in a large saucepan until crisp tender. Add soup, cheeses, and hot pepper sauce. Stir and heat until cheese is melted. Add broccoli/onion mixture and heat through. Serve warm with "Pita Chips or Bagel Chips"✔. Add a dash of hot pepper sauce if desired.

Makes: about 20 (¼ C servings)

Per Serving: 0.22 g Fat, 40 Calories, 5 % Fat, 5 g Protein, 4.5 g Carb, 244 mg Sodium, 4.0 mg Cholesterol

CUCUMBER DIP
(Easy Prep)

½ C (2 oz.) Healthy Choice Fat Free cream cheese
¼ C Truly Lite Fat Free ricotta cheese
2 C "Nonfat Yogurt Cheese"✔
⅔ C chopped green onion, including tops
½ chopped cucumber
1 ¼ t Worcestershire sauce
½ t EACH chili powder and salt (optional)

1. Mix together, chill and serve.

Serves: 12

Per Serving: 0 g Fat, 38 Calories, 0 % Fat, 5.08 g Protein, 4.8 g Carb, 122 mg Sodium, 3.5 mg Cholesterol

BEAN DIP OLÉ
(Quick Fix)

1 can Old El Paso vegetarian refried beans
2 T picanté sauce (no oil)
¼ t cilantro

1. Mix all ingredients. Serve hot or cold with "Pita Chips"✔.

Serves: 10

Per Serving: 0.1 g Fat, 7.2 Calories, 12 % Fat, 0.6 g Protein, 1.5 g Carb, 59 mg Sodium, 0 mg Cholesterol

GREAT GUACAMOLE
(Try it!! You won't believe it!)

1 (10-oz.) package frozen asparagus spears, cooked
¾ C non-chunky picanté sauce
½ C diced fresh tomatoes
1 t oregano
1½ t cumin
2 T Healthy Choice Fat Free cream cheese
1¼ t cilantro
⅛ t garlic powder
Dash garlic salt and chili powder, or to taste
1 package dry Butter Buds

1. Blend all ingredients in blender or food processor until smooth. Chill and serve.

Serves: 8

Per Serving: 0 g Fat, 54 Calories, 0 % Fat, 5.1 g Protein, 8.1 g Carb, 469 mg Sodium, 0 mg Cholesterol

EASY SPINACH ONION DIP
(Easy Prep)

2 C "Nonfat Yogurt Cheese"✔
1 package dry onion soup mix
1 (10-oz.) package frozen chopped spinach, thawed, squeezed and well-drained
Dash Tabasco sauce
¼ t garlic powder

1. Mix all ingredients together and chill.

Makes 10 (¼ C) servings.

Per Serving: 0.35 g Fat, 35 Calories, 9 % Fat, 4.2 g Protein, 7.5 g Carb, 529 mg Sodium, 0 mg Cholesterol

CHEESY ONION DIP

1 envelope dry onion soup mix
1 C (4 oz.) grated Healthy Choice Fat Free mozzarella cheese
1 C (4 oz.) EACH Healthy Choice Fat Free cream cheese and Truly Lite Fat Free ricotta cheese
¾ C evaporated skim milk

1. Beat first 3 ingredients at medium speed of electric mixer or in food processor until smooth. Slowly add milk; mix.

Serves: 10

Per Serving: 0.32 g Fat, 55 Calories, 2 % Fat, 7.8 g Protein, 4.67 g Carb, 553 mg Sodium, 5.9 mg Cholesterol

ZIPPY SPINACH DIP
(Easy Prep)

1 (10-oz) package frozen spinach
½ C chopped green onions
½ C chopped parsley
1 C Kraft Free mayonnaise
1 C "Nonfat Yogurt Cheese"✔
Juice of 1 lemon
½ t dillweed
1 t salt (optional)
1 t Beaumonde seasoning

1. Cook spinach and drain well (you can even pat it dry with a paper towel).
2. Combine all ingredients and mix well. Refrigerate.
3. Serve with "Pita Chips"✔, vegetables, or low-fat crackers.

Makes: About 16 (¼ C) servings

Per Serving: 0.15 g Fat, 18 Calories, 7 % Fat, 1.5 g Protein, 3 g Carb, 29 mg Sodium, 0 mg Cholesterol

CREAMY ARTICHOKE DIP

1 (14-oz.) can artichoke hearts, drained and chopped
1 C Kraft Free mayonnaise
1 (3-oz.) can chopped green chiles, drained
¾ C Truly Lite Fat Free ricotta cheese
¼ C Healthy Choice Fat Free Cheddar cheese, grated

1. Mix ingredients well and place in a 1-quart baking dish. Bake at 350° for about 30 minutes. Serve with baked tortilla chips, "Bagel Chips or Pita Chips."✔

Serves: 10

Per Serving: 0.7 g Fat, 65 Calories, 9 % Fat, 3.78 g Protein, 11.1 g Carb, 206 mg Sodium, 1.98 mg Cholesterol

EVA LOU'S CUCUMBER DIP
(Quick Fix)

2 (8-oz) cartons Healthy Choice Fat Free cream cheese
1 cucumber, grated, including rind (let drain)
1 C Kraft Free mayonnaise
½ t Worcestershire sauce
Dash garlic salt
½ T onion juice

1. Combine cream cheese, mayonnaise and remaining ingredients in mixer, then add well-drained cucumber. Delicious with "Pita Chips"* or fresh vegetable sticks.

Makes: About 16 (¼ C) servings

Per Serving: 0 g Fat, 36 Calories, 0 % Fat, 5 g Protein, 3.5 g Carb, 275 mg Sodium, 5 mg Cholesterol

FAT-FREE QUESO DIP
(Quick Fix)

1½ - 2 cans Rotel tomatoes and green chiles
12-oz. Healthy Choice Fat Free Pasteurized Process cheese
1 C (4 oz.) shredded Healthy Choice Fat Free mozarella cheese
1 C picanté sauce
¼ C evaporated skim milk
Dash garlic salt
1 package dry Butter Buds

1. Place all ingredients in a large microwave-safe bowl. Microwave until cheese is melted, stirring frequently.

Serves: 16 (about ¼ C each)

Per Serving: 0.06 g Fat, 54 Calories, 1 % Fat, 7 g Protein, 4.3 g Carb, 521 mg Sodium, 5.12 mg Cholesterol

CREAMY FRUIT DIP
(Easy Prep)

1 C "Mock Sour Cream"✔
1 T instant orange breakfast drink
1 T sugar or sugar substitute to taste

1. Combine all ingredients. Chill 1 hour. Serve with fruit.

Serves: 4

Per Serving: 0 g Fat, 10 Calories, 0 % Fat, 0.1 g Protein, 2 g Carb, 63 mg Sodium, 0 mg Cholesterol

CHEESE DIP FOR FRUIT
(Easy Prep)

1 C Truly Lite Fat Free ricotta cheese
8 oz. Healthy Choice Fat Free cream cheese
2 T fresh lemon juice
3-5 packages sugar substitute to taste

1. Puree all ingredients in food processor until smooth. Chill; serve with fruit.

Serves: 8

Per Serving: 0 g Fat, 41 Calories, 0 % Fat, 7 g Protein, 3.3 g Carb, 187 mg Sodium, 6.5 mg Cholesterol

BEVERAGES

GRANDADDY ROUSE'S SYLLABUB
(Quick Fix)

1 medium size lemon
½ gallon frozen nonfat vanilla yogurt
1 C EACH Port and Madeira wine or 2 C grape juice for a non-alcoholic punch
Dash nutmeg

1. Combine both wines. Peel lemon into one continuous curl. Soak peel in wine about 5 minutes.
2. Place yogurt in a medium size punch bowl to soften. Discard lemon peel; whisk wines into yogurt. Stir until combined. Serve in punch cups with a dash of nutmeg.

Note: If a sweeter punch is desired, add sugar or sugar substitute to taste.
Serves: 12

Per Serving: 0 g Fat, 61 Calories, o % Fat, 50 g Protein, 9.5 g Carb, 57 mg Sodium, 3.7 mg Cholesterol

SKINNY SHAKE
(Quick Fix)

1 C skim milk or ⅓ C nonfat dry milk
1 C fresh or (no sugar added) frozen fruit
1 t vanilla
Ice cubes
Sugar substitute to taste

1. Blend in blender until smooth, adding ice cubes until of desired consistency.

Serves: 2 (Based on 1 C strawberries)

Per Serving: 0 g Fat, 80 Calories, 0 % Fat, 3.5 g Protein, 15 g Carb, 122 mg Sodium, 0 mg Cholesterol

SLEEPYTIME COCOA
(Quick Fix)

¾ C sugar or artificial sweetener to taste
⅓ C cocoa
½ C instant decaffeinated coffee powder
1 C instant nonfat nondairy creamer

1. Blend all ingredients and store in airtight container.
2. For one serving, use 4 tsp. mix to 6 oz. hot water.

Serves: 12

Per Serving: 0 g Fat, 48 Calories, 0 % Fat, 0 g Protein, 6 g Carb, 6.2 mg Sodium, 0 mg Cholesterol

ALMOST JULIUS
(Quick Fix)

1 quart orange juice
1 C nonfat vanilla frozen yogurt
1 (12-oz.) can diet cream soda

1. Pour 1 C juice into each of four large glasses. Top with ¼ C of yogurt. Top each glass with ¼ C soda; stir.

Serves: 4

Per Serving: 0 g Fat, 135 Calories, 0 % Fat, 3.6 g Protein, 30 g Carb, 16 mg Sodium, 2.75 mg Cholesterol

BLACK COW
(Quick Fix)

½ pint chocolate nonfat frozen yogurt
16 oz. diet root beer

1. Scoop yogurt into tall glass. Fill glass with root beer.

Serves: 2

Per Serving: 0 g Fat, 55 Calories, 0 % Fat, 3 g Protein, 24 g Carb, 28 mg Sodium, 3 mg Cholesterol

COOL ALMOND COFFEE
(Quick Fix)

6½ C freshly brewed strong coffee or instant decaffeinated coffee
¼ C sugar (or serve sugar substitute individually)
1½ C skim milk
2 t almond extract

1. Combine coffee and sugar; stir until well-blended. Cool slightly.
2. Stir in milk and almond extract. Chill well.
3. Pour coffee over lots of ice to serve.

Makes: 8 (1 C Servings)

Per Serving: 0 g Fat, 23 Calories, 0 % Fat, 2 g Protein, 6 g Carb, 115 mg Sodium, 0 mg Cholesterol

SHERRI LOU'S SUGAR-FREE SPICED TEA
(Quick Fix)

2 C dry instant tea with lemon and Nutrasweet
1 small plastic tub of Tang (sugar-free)
2 t cinnamon
1 t cloves

1. Mix; use 1 t per 1 cup hot water.

Serves: 1 (1 C serving)

Per Serving: 0 g Fat, <2 Calories, 0 % Fat, 0.5 g Protein, 0 g Carb, <10 mg Sodium, 0 mg Cholesterol

PARTY PUNCH

3 C EACH water and unsweetened pineapple juice
1¼ C sugar
1 (6-oz.) can frozen orange juice concentrate
2 T lemon juice
1¼ C mashed bananas
9 C chilled diet ginger ale

1. Combine water and sugar in saucepan or microwave. Boil 3 minutes. Remove from heat; add juices and bananas. Freeze firm.
2. To serve, place frozen mixture in punch bowl, pour ginger ale over, and stir.

Serves: 30 (½ C each)

Note: Banana mixture does not have to be frozen. Just chill all after cooking and serve.

Per Serving: 0 g Fat, 63 Calories,
0 % Fat, 0.2 g Protein, 15.9 g Carb,
4 mg Sodium, 0 mg Cholesterol

FROSTY PEACH SODA
(Quick Fix)

2 C non-fat peach frozen yogurt, or your favorite flavor
12 oz. club soda

1. Divide yogurt between 2 tall glasses. Fill each glass with club soda. Serve.

Serves: 2

Per Serving: 0 g Fat, 63 Calories,
0 % Fat, 6.5 Protein, 8.5 g Carb,
57 mg Sodium, 9 mg Cholesterol

PINK PUNCH
(Easy Prep)

4 C unsweetened orange juice
2 C unsweetened pineapple juice
1 (48-oz.) bottle cranberry juice
2 C club soda plus 2 C diet 7-Up
Ice ring if desired

1. Mix together juices. Chill. Add sodas just before serving. Pour over ice ring.

Serves: 32 (½ C each)

Per Serving: 0 g Fat, 49 Calories,
0 % Fat, 10 g Protein, 12 g Carb,
0 mg Sodium, 0 mg Cholesterol

LILLIAN'S MARGARITAS
(Quick Fix)

½-⅔ C sugar
6 oz. fresh lemon juice
6 oz. tequila
22 ice cubes

1. Place all ingredients in blender and blend until ice is crushed. Serve in glasses with salt around rim if desired.

Serves: 8

Per Serving: 0 g Fat, 176 Calories, 0 % Fat, 0 g Protein, 17 g Carb, 0 mg Sodium, 0 mg Cholesterol

RAVE REVIEWS HOT CRANBERRY PUNCH
(Quick Fix)

1 (48-oz.) container cranberry juice cocktail
1 C water
⅓ C packed brown sugar
¾ t ground cloves
½ t EACH ground allspice and ground cinnamon
¼ t nutmeg
1 (46-oz.) can unsweetened pineapple juice

1. Combine ingredients in a large pan. Bring to a boil, reduce heat and simmer 5 minutes.

Serves: 20

Per Serving: 0 g Fat, 157 Calories, 0 % Fat, 0.5 g Protein, 39.9 g Carb, 4.5 mg Sodium, 0 mg Cholesterol

MERRY MARY'S
(Good with or without the alcohol)

1 (12-oz.) bottle ketchup
1 pint lemon juice
3 t EACH salt (optional), pepper, and celery seed
¼ C Worcestershire sauce
2 dashes hot pepper sauce
2 (48-oz.) cans tomato juice
⅓ quart gin (optional)

1. Mix all ingredients well. Chill 12-24 hours before serving. Serve in a tall glass with a celery stalk.

Serves: 20 (about 6 oz. each)

Per Serving: (with alcohol)
0.15 g Fat, 227 Calories, 1 % Fat, 5 g Protein, 34.8 g Carb, 1421 mg Sodium, 0 mg Cholesterol
Per Serving: (without alcohol)
0.15 g Fat, 147 Calories, 1 % Fat, 5 g Protein, 34.8 g Carb, 1421 mg Sodium, 0 mg Cholesterol

Notes and Extra Recipes:

Notes and Extra Recipes:

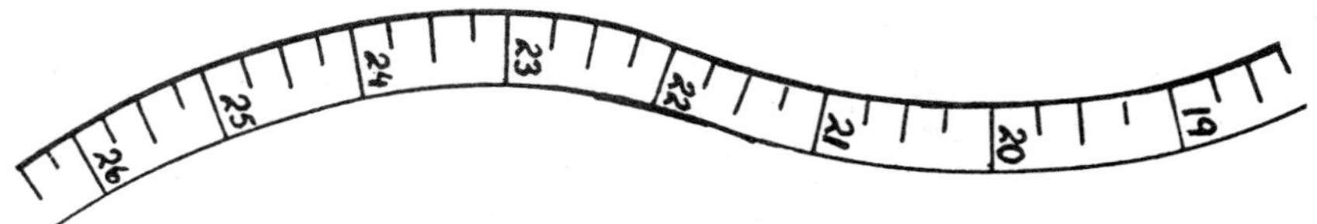

SOUPS & SALADS

Soups, stews, chili, etc. and salads can be a lovely addition to a meal or they can be served as the main dish. If you are not much of a vegetable eater, try getting part of your daily requirement in soups and salads. Warm soups are a great appetite depressor as well.

SOUPS, STEWS & CHILI

Time Savers:

- Drop bouillon cubes into boiling water; add your favorite vegetables, pasta, rice, and/or beans. Add lean chicken if desired.
- Stir two nonfat soups together for an interesting taste.
- Bouillon plus chopped green onion.
- Egg Drop - Mix until smooth: 1 T cornstarch plus 3 T cold water. Stir into 1 quart boiling "Defatted Chicken Broth"✔. Add ½ C green onions plus 1 t low sodium soy sauce. Beat 4 egg whites until foamy; drizzle into broth; stir. Add ½ t cooking sherry and serve.
- Mock Won Ton: Combine ½ C chopped green onions plus uncooked lasagna noodles broken into 1½-inch squares; small pieces of cooked Healthy Choice Ground beef or thin strips of lean ham; and 1 t low sodium soy sauce. Add to 1 quart boiling "Defatted Chicken Broth"✔. Cook until noodles are tender.
- For quick bean chili - Heat 1 (16-oz.) can pinto beans with 1 C chunky picanté sauce plus 1 T fresh chopped cilantro.

Helpful Hints:

- Freeze leftover soup using ice cube trays or small bread pans. Once frozen, pour into plastic bags and return to freezer.
- A large variety of beans mixed together and cooked makes a great main dish starter, but it also makes a great gift, uncooked. Pour equal quantities of dried barley pearls, black-eyed peas, black beans, Great Northern beans, kidney beans, lentils, lima beans, navy beans, pinto beans, red beans, yellow and green

split peas, soy beans, and/or any other beans or peas into a large container. Place 2 C of bean mixture in a glass jar or other see-through container, decorate with a ribbon, and attach a recipe for "Country Market Soup"✔.

- Instant potato flakes make a great thickener for soup.

SALADS & SALAD DRESSINGS

Time Savers For Vegetable, Rice, Pasta, Bean, and Main Dish Salads:

- Stir nonfat mayonnaise, chopped celery, and green onion into cooked brown rice. Season to taste; chill.
- Mix 1 can each kidney, wax, and green beans with chopped onion and green pepper. Stir in ⅔ C vinegar plus ⅓ C corn syrup (may use artificial sweetener instead).
- Mix ¾ C nonfat mayonnaise; ¼ C evaporated skim milk; 1 t vinegar; 2 packages Equal; and salt and pepper to taste. Pour over 2-3 C each broccoli and cauliflower florets.
- Mix ½ C evaporated skim milk plus 1-2 packages Equal plus 3 T vinegar and salt to taste. Pour over salad greens; chill.
- Marinate 6 C thin-sliced cucumbers and 1 thin-sliced onion in 1¼ C water and vinegar to taste, plus 4-6 packs Equal and ½ t each celery seed, garlic, onion, and celery salt.
- One large package spiral noodles, cooked, plus 4 oz. Weight Watcher's lean roast beef; ½ C each chopped green pepper and purple onion; ⅓ C nonfat mozzarella cheese; ½ C nonfat Italian dressing; and 2 T Parmesan.
- Mix torn lettuce with cooked spaghetti, water chestnuts, plain artichoke hearts, and nonfat croutons. Top with "Cucumber Dip"✔ (dilute with a little evaporated skim milk and some diced cooked chicken breast if desired).
- Great Spaghetti Salad - Mix 8 C cooked spaghetti with 1 C Healthy Choice spaghetti sauce, ⅔ C "Cucumber Dip"✔, 1⅓ C chunky-style picanté sauce, and 2 T poppy seeds. Chill.
- Prepare box of Taboule salad as directed on the box; omit the oil and use water and extra lemon juice instead. Add chopped celery, water chestnuts, and diced tomatoes or picanté sauce.
- Prepare 1 box long grain and wild rice without margarine or butter. Mix cooked rice with 1 can drained chopped water chestnuts, and ½ C each cooked green peas, picanté sauce and nonfat mayonnaise.
- Mix 1 C diced cooked chicken breast with ½ C each diced celery and evaporated skim milk; 1 C fat free mayonnaise; and ½ C each diced apricots, pineapple or apple. Season to taste.

Time Savers For Fruit and Gelatin Salads:

- 1 C each pineapple, lite fruit cocktail, nonfat cottage cheese, "Nonfat Yogurt Cheese"✔, marshmallows, and Grape Nuts.
- Cut fresh pineapple in half lengthwise. Scoop out pineapple. Fill shell with cut pineapple and other assorted fruits. Top with nonfat sherbet or sorbet.
- Prepare pineapple as in previous step. Fill with low-fat chicken, ham, or tuna salad made with pineapple.

Time Savers For Salad Dressings:

- Mix 1 C each 1% fat or less buttermilk and nonfat cottage cheese with 1-2 T lemon or lime juice, 1 t each dried basil and chives, 1 T minced fresh onion, ½ t garlic powder and salt and pepper to taste.
- Puree 1 C frozen asparagus, cooked and drained, with ½ C "Mock Sour Cream"✔, and 1 t chili powder; season to taste.
- When starting to learn how to eat low-fat, try mixing 1 T low-fat salad dressing with ½ C nonfat plain yogurt and season to taste. Gradually back off on the low-fat and go to no fat.
- Puree 3 C cooked white beans with ⅓ C red wine vinegar, ½ C partially cooked Egg Beaters, ½ t salt or lite salt, 1 t Accent, 2 t chopped chives, 1-2 T each Creole mustard and chopped shallots, and a pinch of course ground pepper. Add evaporated skim milk to desired consistency. Serve over salads.

Helpful Hints For Salads:

- To remove excess water from salad greens, place washed greens in A clean pillow case, secure end with rubber band, and place in washer on spin cycle for 2 minutes. Turn inside out to remove.
- Keep torn salad greens in crisper in refrigerator. Buy vegetables that need little preparation (sliced mushrooms, shredded carrots, broccoli and cauliflower florets, cherry tomatoes). Toss vegetables with salad; make enough for tomorrow night.
- In a hurry? Buy prepackaged salad in the produce section of your supermarket. It costs more, but it's a great time saver.
- As mentioned in the "Eating Out The Low Fat Way"✔ section, order salad dressings on the side at restaurants and ask for any low or no fat selections. Dip your bite of salad into the dressing instead of pouring the dressing on the salad. You'll be surprised at how much dressing you have left.
- Instead of dressing, order lemon juice or red wine vinegar and cracked pepper for your salad.

SOUPS, STEWS & CHILI

VEGETARIAN CHILI

(Easy Prep)

1 C rice cooked in 3 C boiling water until tender, drained (may use barley)
1 C EACH chopped onions and celery
⅔ C green pepper, chopped
1 t garlic salt (optional)
1 T EACH cumin, chili powder, and cilantro
3 C boiling water plus 2 chicken bouillon cubes and 1 beef bouillon cube
1 medium can EACH kidney beans, black beans, and corn, drained
1 medium can stewed tomatoes
Pam no stick cooking spray

1. Coat a large saucepan with Pam. Pour about 3 T broth mixture in pan. Sauté onions, celery, and green pepper until tender. Stir in cooked rice and remaining ingredients. Bring to a boil, reduce heat, and simmer about 30 minutes. Serve with cornbread.

Serves: 8

Per Serving: 0.25 g Fat, 101 Calories, 2 % Fat, 5.1 g Protein, 28.5 g Carb, 237 mg Sodium, 0 mg Cholesterol

POTATO SOUP

(Quick Fix)

2 large potatoes, peeled and sliced
2 medium onions, diced
2 stalks celery with leaves, diced
3 chicken bouillon cubes
1 package Butter Buds
¼ C skim milk (or enough for desired consistency)
Dash sugar and dill
Celery salt (optional) and pepper to taste

1. Place the first 4 ingredients in a medium saucepan, cover with water and boil until potatoes are tender. Drain well and puree.
2. Return potatoes to pan; add Butter Buds, enough milk to make desired consistency, and remaining seasonings. Simmer and serve.

Serves: 8

Per Serving: 0 g Fat, 58 Calories, 0 % Fat, 1.6 g Protein, 12.2 g Carb, 433 mg Sodium, 0 mg Cholesterol

POTATO-ONION SOUP

¼ C Butter Buds liquid
1 large onion, chopped
1 bunch green onions with tops, chopped
2 large red potatoes, peeled and cubed
2 quarts water plus 4 chicken bouillon cubes
1 t salt (optional)
1 package Butter Buds
½ C evaporated skim milk
Dash sugar or sugar substitute

1. In a large Dutch oven, sauté onions in Butter Buds liquid about 3 minutes or until crisp-tender. Add remaining ingredients except milk and sugar. Bring to a boil; reduce heat and simmer until potatoes are tender. Cool.
2. In a blender or food processor, puree soup until smooth. Return to pan, add milk and sugar; heat but do not boil.

Serves: 8

Per Serving: 0.07 g Fat, 46 Calories, 1 % Fat, 1.5 g Protein, 8.8 g Carb, 568 mg Sodium, 0.56 mg Cholesterol

FRENCH ONION SOUP
(Quick Fix-Microwave)

1 medium onion, sliced thin
2 T liquid Butter Buds
2 t flour
3½ C "Defatted Beef Broth"
½ C water plus 2 T dry white wine
1 t Worcestershire sauce
4 (1-inch thick) slices French bread, toasted
1 t garlic salt (optional)
½ C (2 oz.) Healthy Choice Fat Free mozzarella cheese plus 1 t grated Parmesan

1. Place onion slices in a microwaveable bowl with Butter Buds. Cover and cook on high about 8 minutes; stir in flour, cover and cook 1 more minute.
2. Add remaining liquid ingredients. Cover and cook until mixture boils.Spoon equal amounts of soup into 4 microwave-safe bowls. Place 1 slice of bread into each bowl. Sprinkle each serving equally with garlic salt and cheeses. Cook on high until cheese melts, about 30 second. Serve hot.

Serves: 4

Per Serving: 1.2 g Fat, 155 Calories, 7 % Fat, 8.5 g Protein, 24 g Carb, 375 mg Sodium, 3 mg Cholesterol

QUICK SOUP

1 can Healthy Choice minestrone soup
1 C cooked vermicelli
1½ C pinto beans, undrained
½ C green beans, drained
Pinch garlic powder
⅛ t dry leaf marjoram
1 T picanté sauce, or to taste
1 T ketchup

1. Mix all ingredients and heat through.

Serves: 4 (1¼ C each)

Per Serving: 1.15 g Fat, 177 Calories 6% Fat, 8.7 g Protein, 34 g Carb, 269 mg Sodium, 0 mg Cholesterol

TORTILLA SOUP

(Quick Fix)

6 C "Defatted Chicken Broth"✔
1 large tomato, chopped
1 EACH medium onion and zucchini, chopped
1 large carrot, peeled and sliced
1 can kidney beans, drained
1 handful fresh cilantro
8 oz. cooked boneless, skinless chicken breasts, cubed
1 package Guiltless Gourmet baked tortilla chips
1 t EACH ground cumin and chili powder
Salt (optional) and pepper to taste

1. Place all ingredients except tortilla chips in a large soup pan and simmer for about 20 minutes. To serve, break 4 tortilla chips into bite-size pieces and place into soup bowl. Top with soup and serve.

Serves: 10 (about 1½ C each)

Variation: To make the soup go farther, add 1 C cooked rice and another can of beans or use your imagination.

Per Serving: 1 g Fat, 144 Calories, 6 % Fat, 12.5 g Protein, 31.5 g Carb, 220 mg Sodium, 14.6 mg Cholesterol

BASIC CREAM SOUP BASE

2 T Butter Buds liquid
2 T flour
2 C skim milk
2 C evaporated skim milk
½ t minced onion
Salt (optional) and pepper to taste

1. In a 2 quart saucepan, blend together the flour and Butter Buds over medium heat; add milk and evaporated milk slowly. Stir until thick.

Cream of Spinach: Add 1 (10-oz.) package frozen chopped spinach (cooked and pureed) plus ¼ t nutmeg and a dash of cayenne pepper.

Cream of Mushroom: Sauté ½-lb. diced fresh mushrooms in ¼ C Butter Buds liquid until tender. Add mushrooms and liquid to cream base. Thicken if needed with flour/water paste.

Cream of Celery: Add 2 C chopped celery sautéd in 2 T Butter Buds liquid until tender; add to cream base.

Cream of Potato: Add 2 C chopped cooked potatoes that have been pureed to soup base, or add instant mashed potatoes to desired consistency.

Cream of Chicken: Use basic cream soup recipe only substitute 1 C chicken broth for 1 C of skim milk. Add ½ C finely diced cooked chicken breast and a dash of poultry seasoning.

Cream of Broccoli: Prepare as in Cream of Spinach soup only use 1 (10-oz.) package frozen chopped broccoli. It is not necessary to pureé.

Cream of Cheese: Add 1 C (4 oz.) grated nonfat mozzarella or cheddar cheese to soup base. Stir in a dash of mace and nutmeg.

Each recipe: approximately 6 (¾ C servings)

Per Serving: 0 g Fat, 72 Calories,
0 % Fat, 5.83 g Protein, 16.3 g Carb,
121 mg Sodium, 2.5 mg Cholesterol

DEFATTED BEEF BROTH
(Quick Fix)

1 beef bouillon cube
OR
1 C canned beef broth

1. Prepare as directed on the beef bouillon cube package using the cubes and water. Canned broth may be used but you must defat it by placing it in the refrigerator for fat to come to the top, or by using a defatting cup.

Serving size: 1 C

Per Serving: 0 g Fat, 16 Calories, 0 % Fat, 1.3 g Protein, 2.3 g Carb, 86 mg Sodium, 5 mg Cholesterol

DEFATTED CHICKEN BROTH
There are several ways to do this - choose the one best for you!

1 (3 - 4-lb.) chicken washed and rinsed
½ C EACH chopped celery, onion, and carrot
½ bayleaf
Pinch thyme
Season to taste

1. Place chicken in a large soup pot, cover with water and simmer for 1 or 2 hours until chicken is tender.
2. Remove chicken and remaining ingredients with a slotted spoon. Set in refrigerator for fat to solidify. Remove fat and use as needed in recipes. Freezes well.

Variation #1: Use a defatting cup found in kitchen stores to remove fat without having to refrigerate.

Variation #2: My favorite way is to use bouillon cubes or granules dissolved in water for a quick fix, however the sodium count is higher.

Serving size: 1 C

Per Serving: 0.2 g Fat, 16 Calories, 11 % Fat, 1.3 g Protein, 2.3 g Carb, 86 mg Sodium, 5 mg Cholesterol

JULIO AND LUIS' BLACK BEAN SOUP

2 C dried black beans
4 oz. Healthy Choice ham, chopped
1 C EACH chopped onion, celery, and carrot
3 cloves garlic, minced
¼ t thyme
Pinch mace
2 bay leaves
1 t dry mustard
1 T Worcestershire sauce
2 - 3 T cooking sherry or to taste
4 T nonfat plain yogurt

1. Sort and rinse beans; cover with water and soak overnight.
2. Drain beans and place in a large pot; cover with about 2 quarts water. Add the next 8 ingredients and bring to a boil. Reduce heat and simmer very slowly for 3½-4 hours or until beans are tender; add water if necessary.
3. Remove ¾ of soup to blender; pureé and return to pot. Soup should be thick and creamy. Add sherry to taste if desired and heat through. If soup is too thick, add a little water. Top each serving with 1 T yogurt and serve.

Serves: 4

Per Serving: 0.5 g Fat, 153 Calories, 3 % Fat, 13.4 g Protein, 34.75 g Carb, 300 mg Sodium, 15 mg Cholesterol

CAMERON'S FAVORITE HAMBURGER SOUP
(Easy Prep)

1 lb. Healthy Choice ground beef or ground turkey breast
1 (8-oz.) can tomato paste
2 C V-8 juice
Water
¼ C chopped onion
2 stalks celery, chopped
6 small potatoes, cubed
1 large carrot, cubed
1 C fresh broccoli
1 (10-oz.) package frozen corn
2 shakes minced garlic
2 T soup greens
¼ C red wine

1. Cook ground beef or turkey breast until done; rinse and drain. Place in a large soup pot and add tomato paste, V-8 juice and water to desired consistency. Mix well.
2. Add remaining ingredients and simmer until vegetables are tender.

Makes: about 10 (1½ C) servings

Per Serving: 1.8 g Fat, 236 Calories, 7 % Fat, 24 g Protein, 32 g Carb, 689 mg Sodium, 43 mg Cholesterol

CREAMY SPLIT-PEA SOUP

¼ C water plus 1 package Butter Buds
1 medium onion, chopped
2 stalks celery with tops, finely chopped
2 lbs. or 4 C dry split peas, rinsed and drained
1 quart water plus 3 quarts "Defatted Chicken Broth"
1 beef bouillon cube
3 T bacon-flavor Molly McButter
¼ t EACH celery and garlic salt plus 1 minced clove garlic
⅛ t EACH basil and black pepper
2 EACH medium carrots and potatoes, peeled and cut into chunks

1. In a large Dutch oven, sauté onion and celery in Butter Buds mixture about 3 minutes. Add remaining ingredients except carrots and potatoes. Bring to a boil; reduce heat, and simmer uncovered about 30 minutes.
2. Add remaining ingredients to pot; cook 30 minutes more until vegetables are tender, not mushy. Cool to lukewarm.
3. With a large slotted spoon, dip out carrots and potatoes; place them into a food processor or blender. Add about 1 C of soup liquid to blender. Blend together, pulsing to achieve a semi-chunky consistency, like that of cooked rice. Return mixture to soup pot. Stir and serve.

Serves: 16 (1 C each)

Per Serving: 0.2 g Fat, 87 Calories, 3 % Fat, 4.6 g Protein, 17 g Carb, 187 mg Sodium, 0 mg Cholesterol

MY MOM'S BEST CHICKEN SOUP
(Quick Fix)

4 oz. boneless skinless chicken breast, diced
8 C "Defatted Chicken Broth"✔
2 medium carrots, peeled and julienned
2 medium celery stalks with tops, sliced
½ C uncooked rice (noodles may be used)

1. Bring broth to boil in a 3 quart cooking pot; add vegetables, reduce heat and simmer until tender. Add chicken and rice; simmer until tender. Add salt (optional) and pepper to taste.

Makes: about 10 (1 C servings)

Per Serving: 1.1 g Fat, 67 Calories, 15 % Fat, 5.3 g Protein, 8 g Carb, 352 mg Sodium, 5.6 mg Cholesterol

MINESTRONE SOUP

Olive oil flavored Pam no stick cooking spray
½ C EACH chopped onion and celery
2 cloves garlic, minced
10 C water plus 4 chicken bouillon cubes
1 (14-oz.) can chopped tomatoes
½ (10-oz.) package frozen chopped spinach; thaw and drain
1 (15-oz.) can kidney beans
1 C EACH chopped carrots, potato, and zucchini
1 t EACH oregano and basil
¾ C uncooked shell macaroni
Salt (optional) and pepper to taste

1. Spray a large pan with Pam; sauté onion, celery, and garlic 2-3 minutes, adding a little of the water if needed.
2. Add remaining ingredients, except macaroni and bring to a boil. Reduce heat and simmer until vegetables are tender, about 15 minutes.
3. Add macaroni and cook about 8 minutes. Serve with nonfat breadsticks.

Serves: 14

Per Serving: 0.4 g Fat, 107 Calories, 3 % Fat, 6 g Protein, 20.6 g Carb, 357 mg Sodium, 0 mg Cholesterol

COUNTRY MARKET SOUP
(Easy Prep)

2 cups mixed dry peas and beans, washed, sorted, and drained
3 quarts water
1 (11.5-oz.) can V-8 juice
1 (16-oz.) can stewed tomatoes
1 chicken bouillon cube
3 T Bac-Os
2 T parsley
1 C EACH chopped onion and celery
2 cloves garlic

1. Boil bean mixture gently in remaining ingredients 3-4 hours, adding water if necessary. Stir occasionally. Add salt (optional) and pepper if desired. Serve with rice and cornbread.

Serves: 16

Per Serving: 0.21 g Fat, 34 Calories, 6 % Fat, 1.75 g Protein, 6.7 g Carb, 208 mg Sodium, 0 mg Cholesterol

SHRIMP AND OKRA GUMBO

1 medium-large onion, chopped
½ C chopped green pepper
1 package Butter Buds plus ¼ C hot water
1 (28-oz.) can stewed tomatoes
1 t EACH salt (optional) and sugar
¾ t thyme
2 chicken bouillon cubes plus 1 C water
½ C uncooked rice
1 small can corn, drained
1 (10-oz.) package frozen sliced okra
Dash hot pepper sauce and black pepper
6 oz. cooked medium-size shrimp

1. Coat a large saucepan with Pam. Place first 3 ingredients in pan and sauté vegetables until crisp-tender. Add remaining ingredients and simmer 2 hours.

Serves: 8 (about 1½ C each)

Per Serving: 0.43 g Fat, 145 Calories, 3 % Fat, 8.25 g Protein, 27.2 g Carb, 380 mg Sodium, 41.5 mg Cholesterol

HOLLY'S FAVORITE RECYCLED SOUP
(Easy Prep)

Some suggestions for ingredients are: Edible freezable leftovers from the refrigerator such as mixed vegetables, juice from canned or fresh cooked vegetables, broth, liquid and beans from can or fresh cooked, bits of onions, celery and other vegetables, leftover soups, etc.

1. This is a good way to use some of your leftovers from your refrigerator or your everyday cooking to make a delicious soup. Keep a large freezer-safe container in the freezer. Accumulate the ingredients over a period of time and store in this container. Instead of discarding the juice from cooked vegetables or other things you cook, pour them into the container in the freezer.
2. When the container is full, thaw and place the leftovers in a large Dutch oven or crockpot. Add cooked chicken, beans, macaroni, potatoes, rice, or any favorites that would make a good soup. Simmer until heated through.

Serves: a crowd

JUNE'S ORIGINAL LASAGNA SOUP
(Easy Prep)

1 lb. Healthy Choice ground beef, cooked, rinsed, and drained
2 (27-oz.) cans Hunts Chunky Style spaghetti sauce
2 (27-oz.) cans water
1 t beef bouillon crystals
2 chicken bouillon cubes
8 oz. dry lasagna noodles, uncooked and broken into 3" pieces
3 C frozen Stillwell low sodium Italian Mix vegetables
2 cans red kidney beans, undrained
1 (6-oz.) package Zebbie's Quick Sauteed Mushroom Seasoning
½ C Truly Lite Fat Free ricotta cheese
1 recipe "Easy Eggplant"✔

1. Prepare half the recipe for "Easy Eggplant"✔ and set aside. You will need only 1 C for soup.
2. In a 4 quart pot, mix together the first 5 ingredients; bring to a boil. Add noodles and remaining ingredients, including eggplant; reduce heat and simmer until noodles are tender. Stir occasionally to keep ingredients from sticking to bottom of pan.

Serves: 16

Per Serving: 1.5 g Fat, 180 Calories, 8 % Fat, 9.3 g Protein, 31 g Carb, 574 mg Sodium, 0 mg Cholesterol

HEARTY CLAM CHOWDER

2 T Bacon flavor Molly McButter plus 2 - 3 T water
1 C chopped onion
2 C water, divided
1 T cornstarch
8 oz. clam juice
2 medium potatoes, peeled and cut into small cubes
2 (7-oz.) cans minced clams
1 (12-oz.) can evaporated skim milk
1 C skim milk
1 T dried chives

1. Sauté onion in Molly McButter liquid until crisp-tender; add 1 C water mixed with 1 T cornstarch. Stir until smooth.
2. Add remaining 1 C water, clam juice, and potatoes; bring to a boil. Reduce heat and simmer until potatoes are tender, about 10 minutes.
3. Add evaporated milk, skim milk, and 1 T dried chives. Cook over low heat until soup is heated through; do not boil. Season to taste. If a thicker soup is desired, add a few tablespoons of instant mashed potatoes to hot soup. Add more liquid for a thinner soup.

Makes: about 8 (1¼ - 1½ C) servings

Per Serving: 0.62 g Fat, 149 Calories, 4 % Fat, 11.5 g Protein, 21.8 g Carb, 180 mg Sodium, 12 mg Cholesterol

TACO SOUP

1 lb. Healthy Choice ground beef, cooked, drained, and rinsed
1 small onion, chopped
1 (4-oz.) can chopped green chiles
1 t salt (optional)
1 package lite taco seasoning
1 package lite ranch dressing mix
1 (14½-oz.) can hominy, undrained
3 (14½-oz.) can stewed tomatoes
1 (15-oz.) can kidney beans, undrained
1 (15-oz.) can pinto beans, undrained
1½ C water

1. Mix cooked beef and remaining ingredients in a large pan. Simmer about 30 minutes.

Serves: 15

Note: This easy recipe came to me through the "Heart Watcher's" group in Waxahachie, Texas. They meet once a month to discuss healthy eating and ways to stay fit. What an inspiration they are!

Per Serving: 0.51 g Fat, 169 Calories, 3 % Fat, 10 g Protein, 33.6 g Carb, 152 mg Sodium, 3.6 mg Cholesterol

JACK'S FAVORITE BEEF STEW

¼ C all-purpose flour
¼ t pepper
¼ t dried thyme, crushed
1 lb. top round steak, cubed
1 package dry Butter Buds
1 C "Defatted Beef Broth"✔
½ C red wine
3 medium potatoes, cubed and peeled if desired
2 C (1-lb.) cubed carrots
2 C chopped onions
2 C sliced mushrooms
1 C sliced celery
2 bay leaves
1 C English peas or frozen peas, drained

1. Combine flour, salt, pepper, and thyme in a plastic bag. Add meat and shake to coat.
2. Spray a large saucepan or Dutch oven with Pam. Heat pan and add meat; brown meat quickly, adding a little of the beef broth if necessary. Drain off any fat. Add remaining broth, wine, and Butter Buds. Cover and simmer over low heat about 15 to 20 minutes.
3. Add remaining ingredients except peas. Cover and cook over medium heat about an hour, or until vegetables and meat are tender.
4. Add peas; cook uncovered about 5 minutes or until peas are heated through. Remove bay leaves before serving.

Serves: 8

Per Serving: 2.3 g Fat, 331 Calories, 0.06 % Fat, 45.1 g Protein, 33 g Carb, 437 mg Sodium, 66 mg Cholesterol

EASY TEXAS CHILI

(Easy Prep)

2 lbs. Healthy Choice ground beef, cooked, drained, and rinsed
2 medium onions, chopped
2 large cloves garlic, minced
1 (16-oz.) can tomato sauce
½ t cumin
2 jalapeno peppers, seeded and chopped
1 envelope McCormick/Schilling chili seasoning mix
Salt (optional) and pepper to taste
3 T cornmeal
1 (15-oz.) can pinto beans

1. Sauté onions, garlic, and peppers in sprayed saucepan in a little water until crisp/tender. Add cooked beef, tomato sauce, chili mix, cumin, salt, and pepper.
2. Stir in cornmeal and beans; simmer 30 minutes adding water to desired consistency.

Serves: 8

Note: May use ground turkey breast plus 2 beef bouillon cubes instead of beef.

Per Serving: 4.5 g Fat, 208 Calories, 19 % Fat, 25 g Protein, 18.3 g Carb, 688 mg Sodium, 55 mg Cholesterol

BROCCOLI CHEESE SOUP

(Quick Fix)

3 chicken bouillon cubes
2½ C water
2 C broccoli, chopped
¾ C chopped onion
2 T EACH flour and cornstarch plus 1½ C skim milk, blended
2 packages Butter Buds
6 oz. Healthy Choice Fat Free cheese singles, shredded
3 oz. Healthy Choice Fat Free Cheddar cheese, shredded
1 t Worcestershire sauce
Salt (optional) and pepper to taste

1. Boil water and add bouillon, broccoli, and onion. Return to boil; slowly whisk in flour mixture and remaining ingredients. Stir until cheese melts and soup thickens.

Serves: 6

Per Serving: 0 g Fat, 134 Calories, 0 % Fat, 15.8 g Protein, 12.5 g Carb, 1005 mg Sodium, 13.6 mg Cholesterol

BAKED POTATO SOUP
(Quick Fix)

1 large baking potato
1 can Weight Watcher's cream of mushroom soup mixed with ¾ can of water
1 chicken bouillon cube
¼ t ginger
1 package Butter Buds
2 slices (1½ oz.) Healthy Choice Fat Free cheese singles
½ t EACH garlic salt and chives
1 C instant mashed potato flakes
2 T Truly Lite Fat Free ricotta cheese
2 T Bac-Os artificial bacon bits
2 t nonfat plain yogurt or "Nonfat Yogurt Cheese"✔

1. Cook potato with skin on, cut into chunks, and set aside.
2. Combine the next 9 ingredients in a medium saucepan. Bring to a boil; reduce heat and simmer until heated through. Add potato chunks. Stir well.
3. To serve, spoon equal amounts of soup into bowls and top with yogurt and Bac-Os if desired. Salt (optional) and pepper to taste.

Serves: 3

Per Serving: 2 g Fat, 158 Calories,
11 % Fat, 9 g Protein, 23.6 g Carb,
1284 mg Sodium, 3.1 mg Cholesterol

CHUNKY TURKEY CHILI
(Quick Fix)

2 (4-oz.) boneless skinless chicken breasts
1 medium onion, chopped
1 (4-oz.) can chopped green chiles
½ t EACH chili powder and ground cumin
¼ t EACH basil and cinnamon
1 C frozen corn, thawed
1 can EACH black beans and pinto beans, mashed
2 T fresh cilantro
2 C "Defatted Chicken Broth"✔
Pam no stick cooking spray

1. Place chicken in small microwave-safe dish; cover halfway with water. Microwave chicken until tender. Drain and cut into chunks.
2. Spray a large pot with Pam. Sauté onion in a little broth until crisp-tender. Stir in green chiles and chicken; add remaining ingredients. Heat chili to boiling; reduce heat, and simmer 15 minutes.

Serves: 6

Per Serving: 0.8 g Fat, 227 Calories, 3 % Fat, 20 g Protein, 33 g Carb, 25.5 mg Sodium, 24 mg Cholesterol

VEGETABLE CHOWDER
(Quick Fix)

2 C "Defatted Chicken Broth"✔
1 C chopped onions
½ t garlic salt (optional)
1 package Butter Buds
1 C diced zucchini
½ C diced carrots, pureed
3 C fresh or fresh frozen corn, (1½ C pureed)
¼ C green onions including tops
¼ C evaporated skim milk
1 t cornstarch
Salt (optional) and pepper to taste
1-2 T fresh cilantro

1. In a large saucepan, sauté onions in 3 T broth, dry Butter Buds, and garlic salt until onions are crisp-tender.
2. Stir in remaining ingredients except cilantro. Simmer until vegetables are tender. Remove from heat; stir in cilantro.

Serves: 6

Per Serving: 0.5 g Fat, 97 Calories, 5 % Fat, 3.8 g Protein, 22 g Carb, 125 mg Sodium, 0 mg Cholesterol

MY MOM'S BEST HOMEMADE VEGETABLE SOUP

½ lb. cubed lean top round steak

½ C water
1 chicken bouillon cube
1 medium onion, chopped
1 bunch celery hearts with tops, chopped
2 t Worcestershire sauce

2 (13½-oz.) cans tomato sauce, no oil, plus 2 sauce cans water
3 (11½-oz.) cans V-8 juice

1 medium potato, peeled and cut into chunks
3 medium carrots, peeled and cut into chunks
½ C frozen corn
2 C frozen mixed vegetables

½ C rice
½ of a (7-oz.) package "bite-size" spaghetti

1 can pinto beans, drained
¼ C small sprigs fresh cilantro, or to taste

1. Cook steak, drain, and set aside.
2. In a large stew pot coated with Pam combine the ½ C water, bouillon cube, onion, celery hearts and worcestershire sauce. Sauté 3-5 minutes over medium heat. Add water if needed.
3. Add meat and tomato sauce, 2 cans water and V-8 juice. Bring to a boil.
4. Add potatoes, carrots, corn and mixed vegetables to pot; return to a boil and cook 10 minutes stirring occasionally.
5. Add rice and spaghetti to boiling soup and cook until tender, stirring frequently; add salt (optional) and pepper to taste.
6. Add pinto beans and cilantro. Simmer and serve.

Serves: 16

Note: Better each day. Freeze without potatoes

Per Serving: 1.3 g Fat, 125 Calories, 9 % Fat, 9.1 g Protein, 26 g Carb, 625 mg Sodium, 10.9 mg Cholesterol

MAIN DISH SALADS

LIGHT AND HEARTY CHEF SALAD
(Easy Prep)

1 head lettuce washed and torn into bite-size pieces
1 package fresh spinach washed thoroughly, stems removed, and torn into bite-size pieces
1 large green pepper sliced into rings
½ large purple onion sliced into rings
8 cherry tomatoes
1 can sliced water chestnuts, drained
1 C sliced fresh mushrooms
1 medium cucumber, sliced
1 C water packed artichoke hearts, chopped and drained
3 hard boiled eggs, yolk discarded, and cut into wedges
4 oz. Healthy Choice Fat Free mozzarella cheese, cubed
4 oz. EACH Healthy Choice smoked turkey breast and cooked ham cut into strips
1 C kidney beans, drained
1 C "Crunchy Croutons"✔

1. In a large salad bowl mix lettuce and spinach; toss in remaining ingredients except croutons. Divide salad evenly for 8 servings, sprinkle croutons on top, and serve with your choice of nonfat salad dressing, lemon juice or picanté sauce to taste.

Serves: 4

Per Serving: 2 g Fat, 277 Calories, 6% Fat, 30 g Protein, 33.75 Carb, 727 mg Sodium, 78 mg Cholesterol

SPINACH PASTA SALAD
(Easy Prep)

6 C fresh spinach
Salt to taste (optional)
¼ t nutmeg
1 cucumber, sliced (optional)
3 C cooked mixed vegetable pasta (about 6 oz. dry)
2 oz. feta cheese, crumbled into small pieces
¼ C Truly Lite Fat Free ricotta cheese
¼ C green onion, chopped
6 cherry tomatoes, cut in half
1 can sliced water chestnuts, drained
⅓ C nonfat Italian salad dressing

1. Wash spinach thoroughly, pat dry, and remove stems. Tear into pieces.
2. Toss spinach with salt and nutmeg; place in salad bowl. Arrange cucumber slices around edge of bowl for an added touch.
3. Mix all remaining ingredients together and spoon on spinach.

Serves: 8

Per Serving: 2.1 g Fat, 133 Calories, 14 % Fat, 7 g Protein, 23.3 g Carb, 180 mg Sodium, 8 mg Cholesterol

HONOLULU CHICKEN SALAD

4 C (about 12 oz.) diced cooked chicken breast
2 C diced celery
1 (20-oz.) can pineapple chunks, drained
½ t coconut extract
1 C seedless grapes
2½ C cold cooked rice
1 C EACH Kraft Free mayonnaise and Truly Lite Fat Free ricotta
2 t curry powder
1½ t salt (optional)
¼ t pepper
2 t grated onion

1. Combine first 6 ingredients in a large bowl; mix well. Blend remaining ingredients and pour over chicken. Toss lightly.
2. Chill and serve on lettuce leaves.

Serves 15.

Per Serving: 1 g Fat, 159 Calories, 5 % Fat, 7.8 g Protein, 30.2 g Carb, 361 mg Sodium, 15.4 mg Cholesterol

JEFF'S FAVORITE TURKEY BEAN SALAD

6 oz. cooked hickory smoked Louis Rich whole boneless, skinless, turkey breast, cubed
1 (15-oz.) can EACH pinto, black, navy, and kidney beans
½ large red bell pepper, chopped
½ C EACH diced green onions with tops and celery
3 oz. EACH Healthy Choice Fat Free mozzarella cheese and cheese singles, cubed
1 C chunky picanté sauce plus 2 T lime juice and ¼ C fresh chopped cilantro

1. Line a medium salad bowl with lettuce leaves.
2. Mix all ingredients and spoon on top of lettuce. Chill.

Serves: 10

Per Serving: 1.3 g Fat, 291 Calories, 4 % Fat, 23.2 g Protein, 47.6 g Carb, 233.4 mg Sodium, 17.3 mg Cholesterol

CAROL'S CORNBREAD SALAD

(Quick Fix and the flavor get's better each day.)

½ recipe "Stephanie's Favorite Cornbread"✓
1 EACH medium onion and green pepper, chopped
2 medium tomatoes, diced; or 1 can stewed tomatoes, drained; or 1 C picanté sauce
1 C Kraft Free mayonnaise, or enough to moisten
½ package Butter Buds
Bac-Os (optional)

1. Prepare cornbread as directed in recipe. Cool and crumble.
2. Add remaining ingredients; chill. Bac-Os (1 t) may be added to each serving.

Serves: 16

Per Serving: 0.13 g Fat, 53 Calories, 2 % Fat, 2.5 g Protein, 8.9 g Carb, 118 mg Sodium, 0 mg Cholesterol

GREEN & WHITE SALAD

1 head lettuce, washed and torn into pieces
1 C diced celery
4 hard cooked eggs, yolks discarded, whites sliced
1 (10-oz.) package frozen green peas
½ C diced green pepper
1 medium onion, diced (optional)
4 t Bac-Os artificial bacon bits
1 small can sliced water chestnuts
2 C Kraft Free mayonnaise
1 to 2 T sugar (optional)
1 C (4 oz.) grated Healthy Choice Fat Free mozzarella cheese
Lettuce leaves

1. Layer first 8 ingredients in a deep clear glass dish.
2. Combine mayonnaise and sugar; spread over top, seal edges.
3. Sprinkle with cheese. Cover; refrigerate 8 to 12 hours.

Serves: 12

Variation: Place a layer of cooked vermicelli on bottom of dish and layer as above.

Per Serving: 0.39 g Fat, 108 Calories, 3 % Fat, 11.2 g Protein, 18.2 g Carb, 653 mg Sodium, 3.75 mg Cholesterol

HULA SALAD
(Quick Fix)

½ C orange juice
1 t canola oil
2 T plus 1 t honey
¼ t EACH ground ginger and salt (optional)
Pinch pepper
12 oz. cooked skinless chicken breast, shredded
1 C fresh orange sections
4 C assorted torn lettuce leaves
1 C lite pineapple chunks, drained

1. Toss together the first 5 ingredients. Combine the last 4 ingredients and pour dressing over just before serving.

Serves: 8

Per Serving: 1.12 g Fat, 102 Calories, 9 % Fat, 11 g Protein, 9.8 g Carb, 24 mg Sodium, 27.3 mg Cholesterol

LAYERED PASTA SALAD
(Easy Prep)

5 C cooked or 1 (12-oz.) package pasta twirls
Butter or olive oil flavored Pam
½ head of lettuce, approximately 6 C
1½ C Kraft Free mayonnaise plus 2 t salt (optional), mixed well
1 can sliced water chestnuts, drained
1½ C frozen green peas
¼ C sweet purple onion, chopped fine (optional)
⅓ C chopped green pepper
½ C grated Healthy Choice Fat Free mozzarella cheese
3 oz. Healthy Choice Fat Free cheese singles, diced
Bac-Os

1. Cook pasta, rinse with cold water and drain well. Spray with Pam, toss and spray again.
2. Tear lettuce into bite-size pieces. In a deep glass bowl layer ⅓ each of lettuce, pasta, peas, onion, green pepper and water chestnuts. Repeat this layer 2 more times for a total of 3 layers.
3. "Ice" the top layer with the mayonnaise and salt mixture, sprinkle with the remaining cheeses, cover and chill.
4. If desired, serve salad and sprinkle 2 t bacon bits on top of each serving.

Serves: 10 (Including Bac-Os)

Per Serving: 0.3 g Fat, 143 Calories, 2 % Fat, 7.1 g Protein, 25.3 g Carb, 558 mg Sodium, 2.5 mg Cholesterol

PASTA PASTA SALAD
(Quick Fix)

4 C Rotini with vegetables, no fat, thawed (found at Sam's Club)
1 C cooked vermicelli
2 oz. Healthy Choice Fat Free mozarella cheese, cubed
½ C Kraft Free mayonnaise
¼ t garlic salt
1 t Bacon flavor Molly McButter

1. Mix together, chill and serve.

Makes 3 (2-C) servings

Per Serving: 0.8 g Fat, 175 Calories, 4 % Fat, 10 g Protein, 31 g Carb, 640 mg Sodium, 3.3 mg Cholesterol

SPINACH SALAD
(QUICK FIX)

1 C nonfat Italian dressing
1/2 C "Nonfat Yogurt Cheese"✔
1/2 t dry mustard
2 T sugar or sugar substitute equivalent
1/4 C chopped parsley
2 cloves garlic, minced
1 1/2 t salt (optional)
1 small sweet red onion
1 lb. fresh spinach
4 t Bac-Os artificial bacon bits
1/2 lb. mushrooms, sliced
6 hard-boiled eggs, yolks discarded
1/2 can water chestnuts
1/2 C artichoke hearts
1/2 C whole baby corn

1. Mix together the first 7 dressing ingredients; set aside.
2. Slice the onion into rings and place in salad bowl
3. Wash spinach well; drain. Tear spinach into bite-size pieces, discard stems, and put in salad bowl.
4. Chop egg whites, water chestnuts, and artichoke hearts. Place in bowl; add baby corn.
5. Pour dressing over salad; toss and serve.

Serves: 6

Per Serving: .5 g Fat, 131 Calories, 2 % Fat, 7 g Protein, 37 g Carb, 110 mg Sodium, 5 mg Cholesterol

MRS. NEAL'S CHICKEN ALMOND SALAD

1 small package sugar-free lime jello
1 C (4 oz.) diced boneless skin-less chicken breasts
1/2 C green grapes, cut in half
2 T slivered almonds
1/2 C Kraft Free mayonnaise plus a little extra for garnish
1/2 t salt (optional)
Cherries for garnish

1. Prepare jello and let stand in refrigerator until it begins to set.
2. Add remaining ingredients, place in serving dish, and chill until set. Garnish with mayonnaise and a cherry on top.

Serves: 8

Per Serving: 1.5 g Fat, 54 Calories, 25 % Fat, 1 g Protein, 4.8 g Carb, 197 mg Sodium, 9 mg Cholesterol

CRISPY TACO SHELL SALAD
(Quick Fix

1 Mission brand burrito size flour tortilla
Pinch each salt and cumin
Butter flavor Pam no stick cooking spray
¼ C Old El Paso vegetarian refried beans
2 C shredded lettuce
2 T pinto beans
¼ C chopped fresh tomatoes
3 T grated Healthy Choice Fat Free Cheddar Cheese
3 T prepared "Great Guacamole"*
1 T "Nonfat Yogurt Cheese"*
1 T picanté sauce

1. Preheat oven to 350°. Spray tortilla on both sides with Pam; sprinkle with salt and cumin. Press tortilla into a small 2½-inch deep 1½ quart casserole dish forming the tortilla into a bowl shape. Bake in oven about 5-10 minutes or until crisp.
2. Remove shell from oven and place on serving plate. Spread refried beans on inside bottom of tortilla shell. Top with remaining ingredients and serve with fresh fruit.

Note: For a party, make an extra large taco bowl by overlapping 2 burrito size tortillas. Place in 2 quart casserole and bake as directed. Notice the calories and fat grams saved by making it yourself - commercially prepared taco salad with shell = approximately 941 calories and 61 grams of fat!)

Variations: Chicken: Add 2 oz. cooked and shredded boneless, skinless chicken breast to above recipe. Beef: Mix 1 t chili powder with 2 oz. cooked, rinsed, and drained Healthy Choice ground beef; add to original recipe.

Serves: 1

Per Serving: 6.5 Fat, 325 Calories,
18 % Fat, 23 g Protein, 66 g Carb,
803 mg Sodium, 50 mg Cholesterol

SIDE SALADS & SALAD DRESSINGS

CHICKEN & ORANGE SALAD

2 T finely chopped green onions
Juice of ½ lime (or 2 T)
1 t salt (optional)
6 oz. cubed cooked chicken breast
1 C cooked green peas
¼ C EACH finely chopped carrots, celery and water chestnuts
1 C Kraft Free mayonnaise or salad dressing
Juice of ½ orange (about 3 T)
½ t ground cinnamon
¼ t freshly ground pepper
Lettuce leaves
3 oranges, pared and sectioned

1. Sprinkle onions with lime juice (and salt, if desired). Cover and refrigerate.
2. Mix remaining ingredients except lettuce and oranges. Cover and refrigerate at least 1 hour. Spoon salad mixture onto lettuce leaves; garnish with oranges and onions.
3. Spoon salad mixture onto lettuce leaves; garnish with oranges and onions.

Serves: 6

Per Serving: 1.8 g Fat, 143 Calories, 11 % Fat, 11.3 g Protein, 21.36 g Carb, 90 mg Sodium, 18 mg Cholesterol

FRUIT MEDLEY

¾ C sugar
3 bananas, mashed
2 C "Mock Sour Cream"✔
1 (8-oz.) can peaches, drained
1 (6-oz.) can crushed pineapple with juice
¾ C canned cherries, ¼ C juice reserved

1. Mix all ingredients until smooth. Pour into an 8-C mold.
2. Freeze 3 hours. Invert on a chilled plate, rub with a hot towel, and remove from mold. Let stand 20 minutes.

Serves: 8

Per Serving: 0 g Fat, 160 Calories, 0 % Fat, 0.57 g Protein, 41 g Carb, 0.9 mg Sodium, 0 mg Cholesterol

GREEN PEA SALAD

1 (16-oz.) can small English peas, drained
Scant ¼ C sweet purple onion, finely chopped
½ C celery, chopped
2 hard boiled eggs, yolk discarded, whites chopped
2 oz. EACH Healthy Choice Fat Free Cheddar cheese, and Healthy Choice Fat Free cheese singles, cubed
¼ C Kraft Free mayonnaise
Juice of ½ orange (about 3 T)
½ t ground cinnamon
¼ t freshly ground pepper
Lettuce leaves
3 oranges, pared and sectioned

1. Mix all ingredients. Chill and serve.

Serves: 4

Per Serving: 0.02 g Fat, 90 Calories, 0.2 % Fat, 11.3 g Protein, 10 g Carb, 691 mg Sodium, 5 mg Cholesterol

HEAVENLY AMBROSIA

1 (10½-oz.) can lite mandarin oranges
1 (8¼-oz.) can lite chunk pineapple, drained
2 firm medium bananas, peeled and sliced
1 C miniature marshmallows
½ t coconut extract
1 C seedless grapes
½ C Grape Nuts dusted with flour
1 recipe "Nonfat Whipped Cream"✔, prepared as directed
1 T grated orange peel

1. Drain oranges, reserving 1 T juice. Mix together with the next 6 ingredients.
2. Fold orange peel and reserved juice into whipped cream. Fold in fruit mixture, then mandarin oranges.

Serves: 6

Per Serving: 0.3 g Fat, 146 Calories, 2 % Fat, 1.9 g Protein, 36.6 g Carb, 48.3 mg Sodium, 0.33 mg Cholesterol

FRESH GREEN SALAD
(Easy Prep)

Lettuce Base: Romaine, Bib, Boston, Butter Head, Curly Leaf, Endive, Red Tip, Spinach, Iceberg,
Vegetables: carrots, zucchini, cabbage, radishes, celery, onions, scallions, mushrooms, tomatoes, raw green beans, broccoli, cauliflower, alfalfa sprouts, cucumbers, yellow squash, jicama, green, red, and yellow bell peppers, asparagus
Condiments: Artichokes packed in water, water chestnuts, Greek peppers, cherry peppers, baby corn packed in water, canned green beans, kidney, pinto, garbanzo, white beans, chopped fresh cilantro, banana peppers, nonfat cheese, "Crunchy Croutons"✔, chopped pickles, pickled okra.

1. Choose any 2 or 3 lettuce base greens. Add up to 5 vegetables which have been chopped, sliced, or shredded. Top with a small amount of any 2-4 condiments. Sprinkle with crushed black pepper. Lightly squeeze fresh lemon juice on top. Toss and serve.

Serves: 4 (depending on amount of base used)

Note: May also serve with nonfat salad dressings.

Per Serving: 0 g Fat, 45 Calories, 0 % Fat, 4 g Protein, 5 g Carb, 35 mg Sodium, 0 mg Cholesterol

SOOKIE'S SLAW

½ medium cabbage, chopped
4 medium carrots, peeled and grated
1 C raisins, softened in warm water, drained
½ C Kraft Free mayonnaise or to taste
1 T sugar or 2 packages Equal

1. Mix well all ingredients and chill. Keeps well one week.

Serves: 8

Per Serving: 0 g Fat, 90 Calories, 0 % Fat, 1.3 g Protein, 23.2 g Carb, 216 mg Sodium, 0 mg Cholesterol

GRANMA DEE'S JELLO

1 large package sugar-free strawberry jello
2 C boiling water
1 small can unsweetened crushed pineapple,drain, reserve juice
2 medium carrots, peeled and grated
2 C "Nonfat Yogurt Cheese"✔ (may use Kraft Free mayonnaise)
¼ t cinnamon
Pam no stick cooking spray

1. Dissolve jello in boiling water in a medium bowl. Measure reserved pineapple juice with water to make 1 cup. Add to jello.
2. Pour ½ of jello mixture into another bowl; chill until slightly firm. Set remaining jello aside.
3. When chilled mixture is ready, add pineapple and carrots; place in jello mold that has been coated with Pam and chill 15-20 minutes.
4. Mix remaining jello mixture with yogurt cheese and cinnamon; pour over chilled jello in mold. Chill until firm. To serve, set mold in a small amount of warm water to loosen sides. Lay lettuce leaves on top of mold; lay serving platter on top of leaves. Invert quickly, holding on to mold and platter.

Serves: 10

Variation: Add a thin layer of sliced fruit, bananas, kiwi, strawberries, etc., before pouring on remaining jello mixture in step #4. Add shredded zucchini instead of, or in addition to, carrots.

Per Serving: 0 g Fat, 46 Calories,
0 % Fat, 1 g Protein, 10.8 g Carb,
0 mg Sodium, 0 mg Cholesterol

STRAWBERRY SALAD SUPREME

2 envelopes unflavored gelatin
1 C reconstituted frozen lemonade
2 C diet ginger ale
¾ C Kraft Free mayonnaise
¼ C maraschino cherry juice
¼ t salt (optional)
¾ t almond extract
1 C sliced strawberries
¼ C Grape Nuts, dusted with flour
8 maraschino cherries, cut in half

1. Sprinkle gelatin over lemonade in a small saucepan. Let stand 1 minute. Heat over low heat, stirring constantly until gelatin is dissolved. Pour into large bowl, add next 5 ingredients, and beat until smooth. Chill this mixture until the consistency of unbeaten egg white.
3. When ready, fold in strawberries, Grape Nuts, and cherries. Pour into 5 cup mold or dish and refrigerate until firm.

Serves: 10

Per Serving: 0.9 g Fat, 82 Calories, 10 % Fat, 1.5 g Protein, 19.4 g Carb, 252 mg Sodium, 0 mg Cholesterol

FRANCES' APRICOT JELLO SALAD
(Easy Prep)

2 (4-serving size) packages sugar-free apricot jello
2 small jars apricot baby food
⅔ C EACH sugar and water
1 (15½-oz.) can crushed pineapple in its own juice, drained
8 oz. Healthy Choice Fat Free cream cheese
1 (12-oz.) can evaporated skim milk
½ C Grape Nuts cereal

1. Boil the jello, water, and sugar together until dissolved. Remove from heat; add baby food and pineapple. Cool.
2. Beat cream cheese and milk until smooth; add to jello. Fold in Grape Nuts, pour into dish and chill until firm.

Serves: 16

Per Serving: 0.5 g Fat, 126 Calories, 3 % Fat, 4.6 g Protein, 27.1 g Carb, 148 mg Sodium, 4.3 mg Cholesterol

ORANGE PINEAPPLE SALAD

2 (3-oz.) packages sugar-free orange jello
2 C miniature marshmallows
2 C EACH boiling water and diet orange soda
1 (8-oz.) can lite crushed pineapple; drain, reserve juice
2 medium bananas, mashed
½ C sugar or sugar substitute equivalent
2 T flour
¼ C Egg Beaters
2 C prepared "Nonfat Whipping Cream"✔

1. Dissolve first 2 ingredients in the 2 C water. Stir in soda; let cool.
2. Add pineapple and bananas to jello mixture. Pour into a 9 x 13-inch dish; chill until firm.
3. Combine sugar, flour, and egg substitute in saucepan. Add water to reserved pineapple juice to make 1 C liquid; gradually stir into sugar mixture. Cook and stir until smooth and thick. Cool completely. Fold in whipped cream; spread over firm jello.

Serves: 15

Per Serving: 0 g Fat, 72 Calories, 0 % Fat, 0.8 g Protein, 18.2 g Carb, 15 mg Sodium, 0 mg Cholesterol

CRANBERRY SALAD

1½ C crushed pineapple
Hot water
1 (3-oz.) package raspberry gelatin
1 lb whole berry cranberry sauce
1 (11-oz.) can lite mandarin oranges, drained
½ C Grape Nuts
2 T frozen orange juice, undiluted
1 C prepared "Nonfat Whipped Cream"✔

1. Drain pineapple reserving juice. Measure juice and enough hot water to make 1¼ cups liquid. Bring to a boil, add gelatin and stir until it is dissolved. Chill until it begins to set.
2. Stir in pineapple, cranberry sauce, mandarin oranges, Grape Nuts, and orange juice. Fold in whipped cream.
3. Pour all into an 8 cup mold and chill in refrigerator until firm.

Serves: 8

Per Serving: 0 g Fat, 171 Calories, 0 % Fat, 2 g Protein, 40.8 g Carb, 36 mg Sodium, 0 mg Cholesterol

STRAWBERRY JELLO SALAD

2 large boxes sugar-free strawberry jello
2½ C plus 2 T boiling water
1 envelope unflavored gelatin
1 (10-oz.) box unsweetened frozen strawberries (thawed)
1 large can crushed pineapple, undrained
Scant ½ t cinnamon
2 mashed bananas
½ C Grape Nuts cereal dusted with flour
2 C "Nonfat Yogurt Cheese"✔

1. Mix jello and gelatin with boiling water in a large bowl and stir to dissolve.
2. In another bowl, blend together strawberries and remaining ingredients except yogurt cheese. Add to jello.
3. Pour ½ of mixture into a 9 x 13-inch dish. Let mixture gel.
4. Spread yogurt cheese evenly on top. Pour remaining mixture over yogurt cheese and chill until firm.

Serves: 16

Per Serving: 0 g Fat, 58 Calories, 0 % Fat, 1.5 g Protein, 11.5 g Carb, 30 mg Sodium, 0 mg Cholesterol

LILLIAN'S CRANBERRY SALAD

1 lb. cranberries, washed and drained
2 medium oranges, peeled and seeded
2 C chopped celery
2 C sugar
2 small packages sugar-free orange Jello
2½ C hot water
1 C Grape Nuts dusted with flour (see Note)

1. Grind cranberries, oranges, and celery in food processor. Add sugar; let stand. Dissolve jello in hot water. Chill until it begins to set. Fold Grape Nuts and cranberry mixture into jello. Chill overnight.

Serves: 12

Note: The original recipe calls for 2 C chopped pecans instead of the Grape Nuts; using cereal reduces the fat content.

Per Serving: 0 g Fat, 173 Calories, 0 % Fat, 0.9 g Protein, 43 g Carb, 88 mg Sodium, 0 mg Cholesterol

ANNIVERSARY APRICOT SALAD
(Easy Prep)

1 small package apricot jello
1 C boiling water
⅔ C cold water
⅓ C evaporated skim milk
1 ½ C chopped apricots
1 (8-oz.) carton sugarfree nonfat strawberry banana yogurt or vanilla yogurt

1. Dissolve the jello in boiling water; stir in cold water and evaporated milk. Chill until slightly set; fold in apricots. Ice the top of the jello with yogurt. Chill until set. This can double as a light dessert.

Serves: 8

Per Serving: 0.5 g Fat, 76 Calories, 6 % Fat, 2.5 g Protein, 16.6 g Carb, 25 mg Sodium, 2 mg Cholesterol

LAYERED CRANBERRY SALAD
(Pretty and very good)

4 envelopes unflavored gelatin
¾ C sugar
1½ C boiling water
1 C diet Ginger Ale
1½ C fresh cranberries, ground
3 T sugar
½ C plus 2 T boiling water
1½ C "Nonfat Yogurt Cheese"✔
1½ C nonfat lemon or pineapple sherbet,
¾ C Grape Nuts cereal

1. Dissolve 2 envelopes gelatin and ¾ cup sugar in 1½ C boiling water. Stir in Ginger Ale and cranberries. Pour into a sprayed 8-cup mold. Chill.
2. Combine remaining 2 envelopes gelatin and 3 T sugar in a bowl. Add remaining boiling water and stir until gelatin is dissolved. Add yogurt cheese and sherbet; beat until blended and allow to cool.
3. Fold in cereal; pour over cranberry layer and chill.

Serves: 12

Per Serving: 0 g Fat, 125 Calories, 0 % Fat, 3.9 g Protein, 23.4 g Carb, 60 mg Sodium, 3 mg Cholesterol

CREAMY CRUNCHY POTATO SALAD

3 medium size baking potatoes peeled and cubed (about 6 C cooked)
3 hard boiled eggs, yolks discarded
1½ C chopped celery
¾ - 1 C Kraft Free mayonnaise
1½ T Kraft Free Ranch dressing
3 T Healthy Choice fat free cream cheese, softened
Scant ½ t prepared mustard
1 t celery salt or celery seed

1. Place potatoes in a 2 quart saucepan, cover with water and boil 5 - 10 minutes until potatoes are tender, not mushy.
2. Chop egg whites and celery; set aside. Combine remaining ingredients and mix well. Stir in egg whites, celery, and cooked potatoes. Chill and serve.

Makes: 8 (¾ C) servings

Per Serving: 0 g Fat, 60 Calories, 0 % Fat, 4 g Protein, 13.2 g Carb, 38 mg Sodium, 0 mg Cholesterol

COCKTAIL FRUIT SALAD
(Easy Prep)

2 C nonfat frozen vanilla yogurt or dairy dessert
3 T Fat Free salad dressing
2 (16-oz.) cans lite fruit cocktail, drained

1. Combine salad dressing with yogurt and add to fruit cocktail; stir with spoon.
2. Pour into a 13 x 9 x 2-inch container. Freeze. (Will keep several weeks in freezer).
3. About 10 minutes before serving, remove from freezer, cut in squares and place on lettuce leaf.

Serves: 12

Per Serving: 0 g Fat, 143 Calories, 0 % Fat, 1.75 g Protein, 35.5 g Carb, 65 mg Sodium, 1.5 mg Cholesterol

APRICOT SALAD
(Easy Prep)

1 (16-oz.) can lite apricot halves, drained, liquid reserved
1 small package instant sugar free vanilla pudding
1 (20-oz.) can unsweetened pineapple chunks in water, drained
1 (22-oz.) can lite mandarin oranges, drained
¾ C grated Healthy Choice Fat Free Cheddar cheese
10 cherries, chopped
¼ C Grape Nuts

1. Dice apricots and set aside.
2. Mix ½ C reserved liquid and pudding mix in serving dish. Chill until thick.
3. Combine fruits, cheese, and Grape nuts. Pour over pudding mixture and mix well. Chill and serve.

Serves: 10

Per Serving: 0 g Fat, 165 Calories, 0 % Fat, 2.97 g Protein, 38 g Carb, 94 mg Sodium, 1.5 mg Cholesterol

EIGHT HOUR FRUIT SALAD

1 (16-oz.) can lite fruit cocktail, drained
2 C miniature marshmallows
1 C "Nonfat Yogurt Cheese"✔
½ t coconut extract
Pinch salt (optional)
1 t lemon peel
Equal to taste (if desired)

1. Mix and refrigerate 8 hours before serving.

Serves: 8

Note: You don't have to wait 8 hours but the flavor is better.

Per Serving: 0 g Fat, 61 Calories, 0 % Fat, 1.2 g Protein, 12.7 g Carb, 7.8 mg Sodium, 0 mg Cholesterol

ORANGE CONGEALED SALAD
(Easy Prep)

1 large package sugar-free orange jello
2½ C hot water
1 small can unsweetened crushed pineapple, drained
1 small can frozen orange juice
1 small package sugar-free instant lemon pudding
1 C skim milk
1½ C prepared Betty Crocker Fluffy White Frosting mix

1. Mix together the first 4 ingredients; chill until firm.
2. Mix together the remaining ingredients except oranges. Spoon over top of chilled jello. Garnish with mandarin oranges, if desired.

Serves: 12

Per Serving: 0 g Fat, 60 Calories, 0 % Fat, 1.8 g Protein, 13.9 g Carb, 23 mg Sodium, 0.4 mg Cholesterol

APPLE PEAR SALAD
(Quick Fix)

2 medium red Golden Delicious apples, peeled and cubed
1 medium pear, cut into chunks
2 (½-oz.) packages raisins
2 T chopped dates
3 T Kraft Free mayonnaise

1. Mix all ingredients and serve. Chill first if desired.

Serves: 4

Per Serving: 0.75 g Fat, 139 Calories, 5 % Fat, 0 g Protein, 34.5 g Carb, 144 mg Sodium, 0 mg Cholesterol

PINEAPPLE CARROT TOSS
(Easy Prep)

1 (8¾-oz.) can pineapple tidbits, drained
2 C shredded carrots
½ C raisins
1 C Kraft Free mayonnaise, or to taste

1. Mix the first 3 ingredients; chill. Just before serving, add mayonnaise.

Serves: 6

Per Serving: 0 g Fat, 148 Calories, 0 % Fat, 1 g Protein, 38 g Carb, 521 mg Sodium, 0 mg Cholesterol

CREAMY FRUIT SALAD

1 C prepared "Nonfat Whipped Cream"✔
1 C "Nonfat Yogurt Cheese"✔
½ C sugar
1 (8-oz.) can pineapple chunks, drained
1 (8-oz.) jar cherries, drained
3 bananas, sliced
½ C Grape Nuts

1. Combine all ingredients; blend well. Chill 30 minutes.

Serves: 12

Per Serving: 0 g Fat, 134 Calories, 0 % Fat, 1.5 g Protein, 32.9 g Carb, 40.6 mg Sodium, 0 mg Cholesterol

CONGEALED SPINACH SALAD
(Easy Prep)

1 (3-oz.) package sugar-free lemon jello
¾ C boiling water
1 T vinegar
⅓ C EACH chopped celery and onion
¼ C chopped green pepper
1 C frozen chopped spinach, thawed and drained
1 C EACH Kraft Free mayonnaise and nonfat cottage cheese

1. Dissolve jello in water. Add remaining ingredients and chill.

Serves: 6

Per Serving: 0.5 g Fat, 66 Calories, 7 % Fat, 6 g Protein, 10 g Carb, 421 mg Sodium, 1.6 mg Cholesterol

ADAM'S APPLE SALAD
(Quick Fix)

2 "Red Delicious" apples tossed with 2 t lemon juice
½ C celery, chopped
2 T Grape Nuts cereal
⅓ C Kraft Free mayonnaise
¼ C raisins
Dash of cinnamon

1. Peel apples and cut into chunks.
2. Mix rest of ingredients and add apples.
3. Chill and serve.

Serves: 6

Per Serving: 0 g Fat, 62 Calories, 0 % Fat, 0.36 g Protein, 15.8 g Carb, 200 mg Sodium, 0 mg Cholesterol

BROCCOLI-CAULIFLOWER SALAD
(Easy Prep)

1½ pounds broccoli
1 medium cauliflower, cut into flowerettes
1 red onion, sliced
½ C sliced celery
1 (2-oz.) jar diced pimento, drained
¾ C Kraft Free mayonnaise or salad dressing
2 T Kraft Free Ranch dressing
Artificial sweetener or sugar to taste
1 t dry mustard
¼ t salt (optional)
⅛ t pepper
2 T Butter Buds liquid
Lettuce leaves

1. Remove broccoli leaves and cut off tough ends of stalks; discard. Wash thoroughly and cut into 1-inch pieces. Combine broccoli, cauliflower, and next 3 ingredients in a large bowl.
2. Combine mayonnaise and next 5 ingredients; spoon over vegetables, tossing to coat. Cover and chill. Serve salad with a slotted spoon on lettuce-lined plates.

Serves: 10

Per Serving: 0 g Fat, 57 Calories, 0 % Fat, 3.9 g Protein, 12 g Carb, 318 mg Sodium, 0 mg Cholesterol

SHOE PEG VEGETABLE SALAD

(Quick Fix and good for "the munchies")

1 medium can shoe peg corn, drained
1 small can sweet peas, drained
1 can cut green beans, drained
1 C chopped onions
1½ C chopped celery
½ C EACH white vinegar and light corn syrup
1 or 2 packages Equal or to taste

1. Mix all vegetables in a bowl. Combine vinegar and corn syrup; stir into vegetables. Add sweetener and chill well.

Serves: 12

Note: To reduce the sugar more, use only ¼ C corn syrup.

Per Serving: 0.2 g Fat, 51 Calories, 4 % Fat, 1.6 g Protein, 10.9 g Carb, 70 mg Sodium, 0 mg Cholesterol

LIME-PINEAPPLE SALAD

1 (6-oz.) package sugar-free lime flavored gelatin
2 C minus 3 T boiling water
1 (8-oz.) can unsweetened crushed pineapple
8 oz. Healthy Choice Fat Free cream cheese, softened
½ C Grape Nuts

1. Dissolve gelatin in water.
2. Drain pineapple; reserve juice. Add water to reserved juice to make 1½ cups liquid. Stir liquid into the gelatin. Chill until partially set.
3. Combine pineapple, cream cheese, and Grape Nuts; mix well. Stir into gelatin. Pour into an oblong dish and chill about 12 hours. Serve on lettuce.

Serves: 10

Per Serving: 0 g Fat, 77 Calories, 0 % Fat, 4.6 g Protein, 13.3 g Carb, 192 mg Sodium, 4 mg Cholesterol

FROZEN FRUIT SALAD

(Easy Prep)

1 quart nonfat frozen vanilla yogurt, softened
1 pint "Nonfat Yogurt Cheese"✔
1½ C sugar
½ C Grape Nuts
4 T lemon juice
1 (20-oz.) can crushed pineapple in its own juice, drained
5 Large bananas, diced
1 C maraschino cherries, chopped

1. Mix all ingredients and pour into 2 glass oblong dishes.
2. Freeze firm and cut into squares to serve.

Serves: 36

Per Serving: 0 g Fat, 94 Calories, 0 % Fat, 1.8 g Protein, 22 g Carb, 20.2 mg Sodium, 10 mg Cholesterol

ORIENTAL SALAD

1 (11-oz.) can lite mandarin oranges
1 (15¼-oz.) can lite pineapple chunks
1 (3-oz.) package orange jello
½ of 8-oz. can sliced water chestnuts, drained
½ t almond extract
½ C Kraft Free mayonnaise
1 T chopped candied ginger
½ t lemon juice

1. Drain all fruit; reserve juice. Add water to reserved juice to make 1¾ C liquid. Bring liquid to boil in saucepan; stir in jello until dissolved.
2. Add fruit, water chestnuts, and almond flavoring to pan; stir. Pour into dish; chill until firm.
3. Mix remaining ingredients; spoon on top of jello.

Serves: 8

Per Serving: 0 g Fat, 115 Calories, 0 % Fat, 0.5 g Protein, 19.2 g Carb, 191 mg Sodium, 0 mg Cholesterol

FROZEN STRAWBERRY SALAD

¼ C honey
8 oz. Healthy Choice Fat Free Fat Free cream cheese
½ C nonfat vanilla frozen yogurt
1 (10-oz.) package frozen unsweetened strawberries, partially thawed
1 C bananas, finely chopped
2 C miniature marshmallows

1. Gradually add honey to cream cheese and beat until smooth.
2. Fold in frozen yogurt and remaining ingredients.
3. Pour into 9 x 12-inch pan or 16 muffin cups. Freeze firm.

Serves: 16

Per Serving: 0.15 g Fat, 65 Calories, 2 % Fat, 3.1 g Protein, 13.6 g Carb, 93 mg Sodium, 2.7 mg Cholesterol

BLUE CHEESE DRESSING

(Easy Prep)

¾ oz. blue cheese, crumbled
2 T EACH Kraft Free mayonnaise and nonfat cottage cheese
¼ C 1% buttermilk
1 T lemon juice
⅛ t EACH dill weed, garlic powder, and white pepper
¼ C nonfat plain yogurt

1. Combine all ingredients in a blender or food processor. Blend until smooth. Chill.

Serves: 4

Per Serving: 1.7 g Fat, 52 Calories, 29.4 % Fat, 10 g Protein, 2 g Carb, 124 mg Sodium, 4.3 mg Cholesterol

SUZI'S SHERRY DRESSING

½ C sherry
1 C apricot-pineapple preserves
2 T lemon juice
½ t EACH herb pepper seasoning, onion salt, and ground ginger

1. Combine all ingredients and chill overnight. Serve with chilled fruit.

Serves: 24 (1 T each)

Per Serving: 0 g Fat, 49 Calories, 0 % Fat, 0 g Protein, 7 g Carb, 0 mg Sodium, 0 mg Cholesterol

FRESH FRUIT SALAD WITH POPPY SEED DRESSING
(Quick Fix)

1 small pineapple
2 C honeydew melon
2 C cantaloupe
2 C watermelon
1 C green grapes
1 C red grapes
2 C sliced strawberries
1 peach
Lemon juice
1 recipe "Poppy Seed Dressing"✔ (optional)

1. Cut fruit into chunks. Squeeze lemon juice over fruit; toss together in a large bowl. Chill and serve with poppy seed dressing if desired.

Serves: 6 (without dressing)
Variation: Add any of your favorite fruit.

Per Serving: 0.31 g Fat, 143 Calorie 2 % Fat, 1.6 g Protein, 32.5 g Carb, 25 mg Sodium, 0 mg Cholesterol

FAT-FREE POPPY SEED DRESSING
(Easy Prep)

1 t EACH unflavored gelatin and dry apricot jello
2 C unsweetened pineapple juice
2½ T honey
½ t dry mustard
1 t onion juice
1 T poppy seeds
Dash EACH lime juice & salt (optional)

1. Place gelatin, jello and pineapple juice in saucepan; let stand 1 minute. Cook over medium heat, stirring constantly, 2-3 minutes until it dissolves. Whisk in remaining ingredients and chill at least 5 hours. Serve over fresh fruit.

Makes about 2¼ C or 36 T (nutritional analysis by T)

Per Serving: 0 g Fat, 13 Calories, 0 % Fat, 0.1 g Protein, 3.2 g Carb, 0 mg Sodium, 0 mg Cholesterol

CREAMY HOUSE DRESSING

¼ C Butter Buds liquid
4½ t basil vinegar
½ t salt (optional)
½ t fresh basil, chopped
½ t minced onion
6 oz. Healthy Choice Fat Free cream cheese, softened
1 head lettuce, washed and drained well

1. Combine all ingredients except the lettuce in a food processor or blender; mix well. Slowly add torn pieces of lettuce a little at a time until all lettuce is used (about 2 C). Chill well and serve over salads or as a dip for fresh vegetables.

Makes: about 6 (¼ C) servings

Per Serving: 0 g Fat, 60 Calories, 0 % Fat, 4 g Protein, 13,2 g Carb, 38 mg Sodium, 0 mg Cholesterol

Notes and Extra Recipes:

Notes and Extra Recipes:

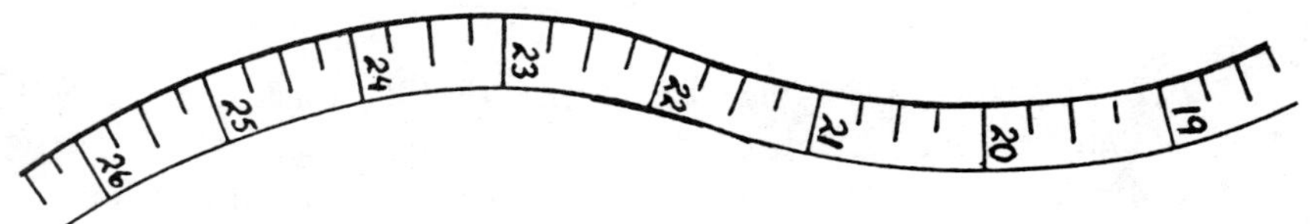

MAIN DISHES

Main dish refers to what you might build your meal around. However, it does not necessarily mean that the majority of the meal is made up of meat, poultry, or fish. Dishes made from pasta, beans and rice, fat free cheeses, fat free cream, ricotta, or cottage cheese, egg whites or Egg Beaters, or combinations of these make a great beginning to a meal. Then add a salad, fruit, or whatever you enjoy. Most of the meal should be made up of complex carbohydrates which include vegetables, potatoes, rice and grains, pasta, fruit, and breads. The average adult requires only about 2 servings (4 oz. total) of protein derived from the fat free cheeses and cheese products and egg products mentioned above, as well as from lean beef, boneless, skinless chicken breasts, lean fish and shellfish each day. Protein should make up only about 15 - 20% of your daily caloric intake. For an adult consuming 2000 calories, 15% - 20% = 300-600 calories. To figure this, multiply .15 X 2000 or .20 X 2000. Do the same for your personal caloric intake.

BEEF

A word about beef: With the new choices we have, beef is no longer a forbidden food. The new Healthy Choice ground beef found in most grocery store freezers or meat sections has 4 grams of fat per 4-oz. serving, with only one of those fat grams coming from saturated fat. (You should consume no more than 10% or less of your daily calories from saturated fat). Each 130 calorie serving of Healthy Choice ground beef contains 7% saturated fat and total fat percentage is only 28%. This beef product has 11% added ingredients of beef stock, hydrolyzed oat flour and salt to replace the fat and add flavor and juiciness. Now we can enjoy hamburgers and other favorites without the guilt. You may also choose from other cuts of beef. (See chart below.) Please limit yourself to 2-3 times per week.

Time Savers:

- Mix ½ lb. cooked Healthy Choice ground beef with 1 can pinto beans, 1 small chopped onion, ½ t chili powder, and 1 C nonfat cheese; place in baking dish. Top with 1 C crushed Guiltless Gourmet baked tortilla chips. Cover and bake 20 minutes at 350°.

- Mix ½ lb. Healthy Choice ground beef with 4 C Healthy Choice spaghetti sauce, 10 oz. cooked spaghetti, 2 C grated fat free mozzarella cheese, and 1 C nonfat ricotta cheese. Bake at 350° for 30 minutes.
- Try cooking meatloaf recipes in small muffin or bread tins; cut the baking time in half.
- Unroll 1 can Hearty Grains biscuits and separate. Roll out into one rectangular-shaped piece of dough. Cook 1 lb. Healthy Choice ground beef mixed with sausage seasoning. Try the seasoning in the recipe for "Hamburger Cheese Balls"✔. (Cook meat half way, then rinse and drain.) Sprinkle over the dough. Roll up like jellyroll starting at short end. Wrap in wax paper and freeze. To cook, cut into ½-inch slices, place on cookie sheet and bake at 350° for 15 minutes.
- Cheeseburger Roll-Up (Kid's Favorite): Using Pillsbury Hot Roll Mix, prepare as for Thick Crust Pizza, omitting the oil (do not prick holes in dough). Spread dough in oblong pan. Spread a thin layer of your favorite hamburger spread (ketchup, mustard, fat free mayonnaise) over the dough. Sprinkle cooked Healthy Choice ground beef over half of the dough. Top beef with shredded fat free Cheddar cheese and your favorite diced hamburger toppings. Fold the other half of the dough carefully over the beef and press to seal. Bake as directed for pizza.
- Using the "Jalapeño Corn Bread"✔ recipe: Substitute skim milk for buttermilk and add ½ lb. cooked, drained, and rinsed Healthy Choice ground beef (about 1¼ C) to recipe. Bake as directed.
- Chimichangas: Shred leftover lean roast or chicken breast, place about ¼ C (1 oz.) each meat and fat free Cheddar cheese inside a 10-inch flour tortilla and roll up. Coat entire tortilla with Butter flavor Pam; bake in a 375° oven until crisp. Serve with "Great Guacamole"✔, picanté sauce, "Quick Cheese Sauce"✔ nonfat plain yogurt, or "Nonfat Yogurt Cheese"✔.

Helpful Hints:

- When buying beef, choose the leanest cuts. In the chart below, the leanest cuts are listed first and are based on approximate 3 oz. cooked serving.*

Top Round	153 calories	4.2 grams of fat
Eye of Round	143 calories	4.2 grams of fat
Top Sirloin	165 calories	6.1 grams of fat
Round Tip	157 calories	5.9 grams of fat

Top Loin strip steak	176 calories	8.0 grams of fat
Tenderloin Steak	179 calories	8.5 grams of fat

*(These numbers based on USDA Handbook 8-13 1990 Rev., USRDA National Research Council 1989, 19th Edition.)

You may notice that some of these meats are higher priced per pound than those with more fat. However, I encourage you to notice how much fat you will have to trim off of the fattier cuts of beef. By the time you have trimmed the fat from a cheaper cut of meat, you can buy an eye of round roast, for example, and really get a better deal for about the same price.

- Top round steak, as well as the leaner cuts, can be great for stir-frying, grilling or broiling if it is marinated. Try using a more acidic marinade like 7-Up or lime juice; add low sodium soy or teriyaki sauce to it for a different flavor. Marinate 30 minutes - 1 hour; grill, but watch closely.
- Trim meat of all visible fat before cooking.
- 4 oz. uncooked beef = 3 oz. cooked
- 1 lb. cooked, rinsed, and drained Healthy Choice ground beef = about 2½ C.
- When using ground beef, choose Healthy Choice ground beef. Microwave in a colander suspended over a bowl. Remove from oven and rinse beef under hot running water; drain well.

POULTRY

A little information regarding turkey and chicken: Skinless, white meat chicken or turkey can be a great low-fat replacement for beef; it contains about ⅓ less fat than dark meat. Remember, if you want to purchase ground chicken or ground turkey, you will probably need to buy boneless, skinless chicken or turkey breasts and have the butcher grind them for you. You can also do it yourself in a food processor or meat grinder. Buying white meat with skin, then removing the skin before grinding, is a less expensive route. Be aware of the commercially prepared packaged ground turkey. Most people are unaware of just how much fat it contains. A 3-oz. serving of ground turkey usually contains about 12-13 grams of fat. Ground white meat, however, usually has about 140 calories and 3 grams of fat in a 3-oz. serving (obviously a better choice). Watch for special prices on ground turkey or chicken breast and stock up.

Time Savers:

- Cook chicken breasts in microwave with bouillon cubes and Molly McButter 5-8 minutes or until done.

- Mix 2 C cooked cornbread, 1 can Weight Watcher's cream of mushroom soup, ½ C "Defatted Chicken Broth,"✔ 1 C diced cooked chicken breast, and ¼ C each chopped green pepper and onion. Bake at 350° for about 30 minutes.
- Place 8 oz. cooked, cubed boneless skinless chicken breast in casserole; top with a mixture of 1 C plain nonfat yogurt, 2 cans Weight Watcher's cream of mushroom soup, 1 T cornstarch. Sprinkle top with 28 crushed Garden Crisp crackers and 2 T poppy seeds. Pour ½ C Butter Buds liquid over the top; bake at 350° 30 minutes.
- Top 4 boneless skinless chicken breasts with mixture of ¾ C fat free Italian salad dressing or any flavor, 1 package dry onion soup mix and 1 C apricot preserves. Cover; bake at 325° for 30 minutes.
- Mix together 1 can Healthy Choice chicken with rice soup, 1 can Weight Watcher's cream of mushroom soup, 1½ C cubed cooked boneless skinless chicken breast, 1 small can evaporated skim milk, and 1 can drained and diced water chestnuts. Top with bread crumbs and bake at 350° for about 30 minutes or until heated through.
- Sauté 4 boneless skinless chicken breasts in 2 T each "Defatted Chicken Broth"✔ and red wine vinegar plus 1 t chili powder. Stir in 4 oz. green chilies; cook 3-4 minutes. Remove chicken from liquid; stir in 2 T evaporated skim milk plus 1 package dry Butter Buds and pinch cilantro. Heat and serve over chicken.
- Pound 4 boneless skinless chicken breasts between wax paper to flatten. Top each breast with 1 thin slice each Healthy Choice ham and fat free mozzarella cheese. Roll up (chicken side out) and secure with a toothpick. Dip each roll in a mixture of ¼ C evaporated skim milk and ½ t each mustard and fat free mayonnaise. Roll in seasoned nonfat bread crumbs, cover, and bake on a sprayed cookie sheet at 350° for 20 minutes; uncover, spray with Pam and bake 5-10 more minutes.

Helpful Hints:

- Remember to buy uncooked ground turkey breast or ground chicken breast as opposed to regular ground turkey or chicken. Over half of the calories in regular ground turkey or chicken come from fat.
- Do not overcook ground turkey breast; try adding a little defatted chicken or beef broth for added flavor.
- To save money, you can buy chicken breasts with the skin on. Before cooking or grinding, pull the skin off. An easy way is to grasp the skin with a paper towel, pull it off, and discard.

- Thaw frozen chicken quickly (about 15 minutes) in cold water with a little lime or lemon juice; change the water frequently. Cook immediately.
- To cook a moist thawed unstuffed turkey follow these tips: (Note: Try to avoid self-basting turkeys or chickens; saturated fats and other oils are usually used as the basting product.) After freeing the legs and tail, remove the neck piece and giblets from cavities; rinse turkey well inside and out; pat dry. Tuck legs back under if desired. Wrap turkey in foil that has been sprayed with Pam no stick cooking spray or lightly greased with canola oil. Place breast-side up in a shallow roasting pan; insert meat thermometer through the foil into center of thigh muscle, making sure thermometer bulb does not touch the bone. Roast at 450° (see approximate cooking times and suggested servings below); open foil for the last 30 minutes of cooking to brown.

8- to 10-lb. turkey	1¼-1¾ hours	Serves: 8-10
10- to 12-lb. turkey	1¾-2¼ hours	Serves: 10-12
12- to 16-lb. turkey	2¼-3 hours	Serves: 16-21
16- to 20-lb. turkey	3-3½ hours	Serves: 21-26
20- to 24-lb. turkey	3½-4 hours	Serves: 26-32

Thermometer should register from 180° - 185° when testing for doneness; when thigh is pierced, juices should be clear.

- To bake a turkey breast only (including the bone): Place thawed turkey, skin side up on a rack in a shallow roasting pan. Coat with Pam no stick cooking spray or brush with a little canola oil. Place meat thermometer in center next to but not touching the bone. Bake uncovered at 325° and cover loosely with a foil tent if it begins to brown too quickly:

2- to 4-lb. breast	1½-2 hours	Serves: 6-12
4- to 6-lb. breast	1½-2½ hours	Serves: 12-18
6- to 8-lb. breast	2-2½ hours	Serves: 18-24

Thermometer should register 170° when testing for doneness; be careful not to overcook the breast.

SEAFOOD

In the swim with fish: Today, more people are eating fish. It is one of the best sources of protein and has a reputation for helping reduce the risk of heart attack because of the Omega-3 component contained in fish oil which is thought to reduce cholesterol levels in the body. Even when consuming the higher fat fish, the health benefits are evident. When choosing fresh or frozen fish, select fish with flesh that is firm and elastic or, when touched, the flesh returns to its original position. Inquire about the freshness of the fish, how it should be stored, and how long it should remain in your refrigerator or freezer before you cook it. Purchase canned fish or shellfish packed in water or its own juice, not oil.

Time Savers:

- For boiled shrimp, drop 2 lbs. shrimp into 2 quarts salty boiling water; boil 3-5 minutes. Chill, peel, and eat. For a little different flavor, add 1 T lemon juice ½ package crab boil, and 1 t dried minced onion to the water.
- Dip catfish fillets in beaten egg white, roll in instant mashed potato flakes. Fry quickly in skillet coated with Pam, turning frequently, or bake at 375° for 7-8 minutes or until brown.
- Coat 4 (4-oz.) orange roughy fish fillets with a mixture of 4 T cornmeal, 2 T Parmesan cheese, and a dash each garlic powder and cayenne. Broil on sprayed broiler until done.
- Cut lean ½-inch steaks into 1-inch cubes. Marinate in low sodium soy sauce and Madeira wine from 30 minutes to overnight (in refrigerator) if desired. Place on skewers with fresh cubed vegetables and broil until tender about 4 - 5 minutes per side.
- Bake at 450° 8-10 minutes, or grill/broil 4-5 minutes per side, 1 lb. fresh or frozen lean fish or boneless skinless chicken breasts: Spray dry fish or chicken with Olive Oil flavored Pam; coat with a mixture of 1 C nonfat bread crumbs, 2 T Parmesan, ½ t dry tarragon, and a dash cayenne.
- To poach fresh salmon, place 8 oz. salmon in microwave-safe dish; cover with ¼ C "Defatted Chicken Broth"✔. Cover and cook on high 3-4 minutes. Let stand 2 minutes; cool, remove bones, skin, and serve.

Helpful Hints:

- Listed below are names of types of seafood to help in your selection of fish. Some fish contain more fat than others. The National Fisheries Institute rates fish as lean (less than 2.5% fat), medium-fat (2.5%-5%), and fatty fish (over 5% fat). However, fish is lower in cholesterol than beef or poultry and should be eaten frequently. Even the fish high in fat are good choices because of the health benefits. One benefit is that people who include fish at least 2 times a week get the bonus of the Omega-3 component found in fish oil which has been shown to reduce blood cholesterol and triglycerides and help prevent blood clots that can cause strokes and heart attacks.

According to the USDA, some extra lean fish (1 fat gram or less per 3.5 oz. serving) are:

Abalone	Alaskan King Crab	Cod
Flounder	Grouper	Haddock
Lobster, northern	Pike, northern	Pollock
Scallops	Sole, Dover	

Some choices in the lean category (1-3 grams of fat per serving) are:

Clams	Crab, blue	Crayfish
Halibut	Monkfish	Oysters
Perch, ocean	Pike, walleye	Red Snapper
Shrimp	Squid	

Some medium-fat fish (3-6 grams of fat per serving) include:

Bass, freshwater	Bluefish	Catfish, Channel
Croaker, Atlantic	Lox/smoked Salmon	Salmon, Coho
Shark		
Sturgeon	Swordfish	
Trout, rainbow	Tuna	Whitefish

Choices of some fatty fish (6-10 grams of fat per serving) include:

Mackerel, Spanish	Orange Roughy	Pompano
Salmon (Atlantic and sockeye)		

Some very fatty fish (over 10 fat grams per serving) are:

Herring, smoked	Mackerel, Atlantic	Sablefish
Salmon, Chinook	Sardines	Shad

- ½ lb. cooked and shelled shrimp or 1 (4½ oz.) can = 1 C chopped, cooked shrimp.
- Shrimp with the shell on is twice the weight of the cooked shrimp without the shell.

OTHER MAIN DISHES

Time Savers:

- Fresh cooked beans mixed with white or brown rice is a great main dish.
- Serve steamed zucchini, yellow squash, broccoli, onion, and mushrooms over cooked spaghetti. Mix together and heat a mixture of ½ C each evaporated skim milk and Butter Buds liquid, 2 T each fat free ricotta and Parmesan cheese, and ½ C fat free mozzarella cheese. Serve over pasta and vegetables.
- Sauté ½ C each chopped onion and sliced mushrooms, and a clove garlic in 1-2 T "Defatted Chicken Broth"✔ until tender; blend in 1¼ T flour and ½ each dried oregano, basil, and pepper. Stir in 1 C each evaporated skim milk and skim milk; cook and stir until thick. Add 1½ C drained white beans. Serve over your favorite pasta.
- Try substituting spaghetti squash for all or part of the pasta in some recipes.
- Stuff 12 large cooked manicotti shells with a mixture of: 2 C cooked diced zucchini, 1½ C nonfat cottage cheese, 2 T dry Butter Buds, 1 C fat free mozzarella or Cheddar cheese. Place in a sprayed casserole dish and top with 1 C Healthy Choice spaghetti sauce. Bake covered at 350° for 20 minutes; uncover, sprinkle with ½ C fat free mozzarella or Cheddar cheese and bake 5-10 minutes.
- Stir a little garlic and herb or plain Healthy Choice fat free cream cheese into scrambled Egg Beaters.

Grilling Beef, Poultry and Seafood:

- Start grill about 30 minutes before you wish to begin cooking. You should be able to apply these tips for broiling as well. (Vegetable cooking spray used on the grill before lighting the fire can prevent fish and other foods from sticking to the grill surface.) Be safe: follow all safety instructions in relation to the grill, charcoal, lighter fluid, etc. Never leave children unattended when these items are around.
- The coals are considered to be medium/hot when you are able to hold your hand over the coals at cooking height for about 4 seconds. (350°-400°)
- The coals are considered to be hot when the coals are gray and you are able to hold your hand over them for about 2 seconds. (400°-450°)
- The coals are considered to be extremely hot when the coals have a glow with a little gray ash around the edges. (450°-500°)
- After marinating lean beef, grill over medium coals for 10-15 minutes or to desired doneness, turning once.
- Boneless, skinless chicken breast, after marinating, can be grilled over hot coals for 5-8 minutes or to desired doneness, turning once.
- Shellfish, after marinating, can be grilled over hot coals for 4-8 minutes, turning once.
- Fish can be grilled over hot coals; the general rule is 10 minutes per inch of thickness. Turn only once halfway through cooking time and baste frequently with marinade. Fish is done usually when it's not transparent or has a dull (not shiny) look.
- When marinating, remember to refrigerate the meat and marinade if marinating for over an hour. Discard marinade after using; do not reuse.

BEEF

BEEF RICE CASSEROLE

1 lb. Healthy Choice ground beef, cooked, drained and rinsed
1 medium onion, diced
1 small green pepper, diced
1 C chopped celery
1 t sage
½ t mace
1 C uncooked vermicelli, broken into small pieces
1 C uncooked rice
3 T slivered almonds for garnish, (optional)
6 C "Defatted Chicken Broth"✔

1. In a large skillet, saute´ vegetables in a little water until crisp-tender. Add beef and seasonings; set aside.
2. Bring broth to a boil and stir into beef mixture.
3. Add vermicelli and rice, pour into a sprayed oblong dish, and bake at 350° for 1 hour. Garnish; salt (optional) and pepper to taste.

Serves: 8

Per Serving: 3.3 g Fat, 197 Calories, 15 % Fat, 13.7 g Protein, 27.6 g Carb, 144 mg Sodium, 27.5 mg Cholesterol

BEEF NOODLE SUPPER
(Quick Fix)

1 lb. Healthy Choice ground beef, cooked, drained, and rinsed
½ C EACH chopped onion and green pepper
1 (12-oz.) can V-8 juice
2 C cooked noodles, drained
½ C (2 oz.) grated Healthy Choice Fat Free mozzarella cheese

1. Place cooked beef, onion, and green pepper in a large skillet that has been coated with Pam. Saute´ quickly 1-2 minutes, add V-8 juice and simmer about 5 minutes.
2. Mix beef mixture with noodles, place in a sprayed casserole, and bake 15 minutes at 350°; sprinkle with cheese and bake until cheese melts.

Serves: 6

Per Serving: 3 g Fat, 181 Calories, 15 % Fat, 20 g Protein, 18.6 g Carb, 502 mg Sodium, 38.3 mg Cholesterol

ROSS'S FAVORITE CHICKEN FRIED STEAK AND GRAVY

16 oz. (½-inch thick) top round steak cut into 4 equal serving pieces
½ C lime juice
4 t "Ross's Special Seasoning,"✔ divided
2 t Worcestershire sauce, divided
2 egg whites at room temperature
¼ C cornstarch
1 C Grape Nuts
1 C boiling water plus 2 chicken bouillon cubes
Pam no stick cooking spray
1 recipe "Chicken Fried Gravy"✔

1. One hour before cooking, dip each steak in lime juice. Sprinkle one side of each steak with ½ t of "Ross's Special Seasoning"✔ and place seasoned side down on plate. Pour ½ t Worcestershire sauce on top of each steak and sprinkle each with ½ t of remaining seasoning. Marinate one hour; if marinating longer, refrigerate.
2. Beat egg whites until foamy; add cornstarch and beat until stiff. Spray a large skillet with Pam and heat until hot but not smoking. Dip steak into egg whites, then Grape Nuts; coat evenly.
3. Place steak carefully in skillet and brown on both sides, adding broth a little at a time to keep from burning. Cook to desired doneness, about 2-3 minutes per side.

Serves: 4

Per Serving: 4.3 g Fat, 307 Calories, 13 % Fat, 37.5 g Protein, 34.5 g Carb, 697 mg Sodium, 93 mg Cholesterol

MEXICAN LASAGNA

- **1¼ t EACH coriander and chili powder**
- **1 T cumin**
- **2 cloves minced garlic**
- **1 C EACH chopped onion and green pepper**
- **2 (16-oz.) cans tomatoes, finely chopped**
- **2 (16-oz.) cans pinto beans, no lard, drained (puree 1 can)**
- **1 (4-oz.) can chopped green chiles**
- **1 (8-oz.) can tomato sauce**
- **1 can Weight Watcher's cream of mushroom soup**
- **¼ lb. Healthy Choice ground beef, cooked, drained, & rinsed**
- **1 C nonfat cottage cheese**
- **4 oz. EACH Healthy Choice Fat Free cheese singles (diced) & Healthy Choice Fat Free Cheddar cheese (grated), divided**
- **1 (8-oz.) box lasagna noodles, uncooked**

1. Sauté onion, garlic, and green pepper in 2 T water until crisp-tender. Add spices, tomatoes, green chiles, tomato sauce, soup and ½ C water. Simmer at least 20 minutes. Add beef to sauce.
2. Preheat oven to 375°. Spray oblong casserole with Pam. Mix cheese together. Layer ⅓ each of sauce, noodles, cottage cheese, beans, and 6 oz. of cheese. Repeat layers, ending with sauce.
3. Cover with foil; bake 55 minutes. Uncover, sprinkle with remaining 2 oz. cheese, and bake 5 more minutes. Let stand 5 minutes before serving.

Serves: 10

Per Serving: 2.1 g Fat, 314 Calories, 6 % Fat, 24 g Protein, 51.6 g Carb, 873 mg Sodium, 10 mg Cholesterol

BEST BAKED LASAGNA

(This is easy; no need to precook the lasagna noodles)

2⅓ C plus ¼ C Healthy Choice spaghetti sauce
1½ C hot tap water
⅔ C Weight Watcher's cream of mushroom soup
¾ C Hunts Chunky Style spaghetti sauce
1 (15-oz.) carton Truly Lite Fat Free ricotta cheese
8 oz. Healthy Choice Fat Free cream cheese or nonfat cottage cheese
1 package dry Butter Buds
⅛ t garlic powder
Pinch thyme
Scant t oregano
¼ t garlic salt
4 C (16 oz.) Healthy Choice Fat Free mozzarella cheese
½ lb. Healthy Choice ground beef, cooked, drained and rinsed (optional)
1 (12-oz) package lasagna noodles (about 15), uncooked
2 t grated Parmesan cheese

1. In a large bowl mix together all ingredients except the noodles, Pam, and Parmesan cheese. Set aside.
2. Coat a large oblong casserole dish with Pam. Spread about ¾ C of sauce in bottom of dish. Lay 3 lasagna noodles on sauce in the middle of the dish, allowing room for the noodles to expand. Spread another layer of sauce, then noodles, and repeat, creating 5 layers ending with sauce. Cover with foil and bake in 375° oven for about 1 hour. Uncover, sprinkle with Parmesan cheese and let stand 10 minutes before serving.

Serves: 12

Variation: You may substitute 8 oz. of ground turkey breast for beef or 1 C of sliced vegetables. If you like meat and vegetables, add chopped vegetables to meat sauce.

Note: If you like more of a tomato taste, top each serving of lasagna with a little of the Hunts or Healthy Choice spaghetti sauce.

Per Serving: 0.75 g Fat, 93 Calories,
7 % Fat, 13 g Protein, 7.3 g Carb,
565 mg Sodium, o.24 mg Cholesterol

HAMBURGER STEAK
(Quick Fix)

1 lb. Healthy Choice ground beef
1 T EACH minced onion and Worcestershire sauce
¼ t garlic salt
¼ C Egg Beaters
⅓ C "Basic Bread Crumbs"✔
1 can Weight Watcher's cream of mushroom soup, divided
Pam no stick cooking spray

1. Combine first 5 ingredients plus½ of soup in a medium-size bowl. Mix and form into 5 patties.
2. Coat a large skillet with Pam and heat. Place patties in pan and brown quickly and evenly on both sides, turning once. Drain off any fat.
3. Add remaining soup to skillet; cover and simmer slowly about 15 minutes or until cooked through. Turn once during cooking time.

Serves: 5

Variation: Replace Worcestershire with white wine Worcestershire and add ¼ C ketchup.

Per Serving: 3.6 g Fat, 127 Calories, 26 % Fat, 18.6 g Protein, 4.4 g Carb, 458 mg Sodium, 44 mg Cholesterol

VEGETABLE LASAGNA

1 recipe "Easy Baked Lasagna"✔
2 C sliced zucchini, spinach or broccoli

1. Prepare lasagna as instructed in "Easy Baked Lasagna"✔ recipe; but, replace meat with sliced vegetables. Bake as directed.

Serves: 12

Per Serving: 0.3 g Fat, 53 Calories, 5 % Fat, 7.3 g Protein, 4.8 g Carb, 282 mg Sodium, 12.1 mg Cholesterol

BEST OVEN HASH

½ lb. Healthy Choice ground beef, cooked, drained and rinsed
1 C coarsely ground cooked potatoes
¼ C coarsely ground onion
¼ C fresh snipped parsley
2 t Worcestershire sauce
⅔ C evaporated skim milk
Salt (optional) and pepper to taste
¼ C "Basic Bread Crumbs", finely ground
Pam no stick cooking spray

1. Coarsely grind the beef and mix with the next 6 ingredients.
2. Coat a 1 quart casserole with Pam, pour mixture into dish, top with bread crumbs and bake at 350 for 30 minutes.

Serves: 4

Per Serving: 0.7 g Fat, 128 Calories, 5 % Fat, 13 g Protein, 14 g Carb, 47.8 mg Sodium, 28.7 mg Cholesterol

NANNY'S TAMALE PIE

1 recipe "Easy Texas Chili,"✔ doubled, prepared✔
1 C cornmeal
1 t salt (optional)
1 C cold water
3 C boiling water
Butter flavor Pam no stick cooking spray

1. Combine cornmeal, salt, and cold water. Gradually pour into boiling water, stirring constantly. Return to boil and continue to stir about 1 minute. Reduce heat, cover, and cook over low heat about 5 minutes, stirring frequently.
2. Place cooked chili in sprayed deep casserole dish. Top with cornmeal mush. Spray top with Pam; bake at 400° for 30-40 minutes until bubbly and crusty on top.

Serves: 16

Per Serving: 2.7 g Fat, 185 Calories, 13 % Fat, 29.2 g Protein, 18 g Carb, 323 mg Sodium, 23 mg Cholesterol

BURGUNDY MEATBALLS
(Quick Fix)

1 lb. Healthy Choice ground beef
¼ C EACH chopped onion and finely chopped water chestnuts
½ C dry "Basic Bread Crumbs"✔
¼ C skim milk
1 t EACH salt (optional), parsley, and coriander
½ t Worcestershire sauce
⅛ t pepper
2 egg whites, slightly beaten
⅓ C water plus 4 T cornstarch
1½ C water plus 2 beef bouillon cubes
⅓ C Burgundy wine
2 T low sodium soy sauce
1 t brown sugar
Dash garlic powder
Pam no stick cooking spray

1. Mix the first 8 ingredients; shape into 1" balls. Place meat on a baking sheet coated with Pam and bake at 400° about 10 minutes.
2. Heat remaining ingredients in a large saucepan. Spoon meatballs into pan; heat in sauce thoroughly, about 10 minutes. Serve meatballs and sauce over cooked noodles or rice.

Serves: 6

Per Serving: 2.6 g Fat, 110 Calories, 21 % Fat, 15.3 g Protein, 4 g Carb, 482 mg Sodium, 36 mg Cholesterol

EASY ENCHILADA STACK-UP

18 corn tortillas
18 T or 1 C plus 2 T Old El Paso vegetarian refried beans
18 T or 1 C plus 2 T Healthy Choice ground beef, cooked rinsed and drained (may use ground or diced chicken breast instead)
6 T minced cooked onion, divided
3½ C "Enchilada Sâlsa"✔
4 ½ slices Healthy Choice Fat Free Cheddar cheese
Pam no stick cooking spray
Diced fresh tomatoes, "Great Guacamole"✔, "Nonfat Yogurt Cheese"✔ for garnish

1. Coat a large oblong baking dish with Pam. Pour 1 C sauce in bottom of dish. Place 6 tortillas on top of sauce. They will overlap. Cut each cheese slice into quarters. Tear each 4th into small pieces.
2. Spread 1 T beans over EACH tortilla; top with 1 T ground beef, 1 t minced onion, and ¼ of diced cheese slice. Pour about ½ C salsa over entire layer. Repeat layers twice for a total of 3 layers, only pour 1 C salsa over top or last layer of casserole. Bake at 350° for 15 minutes or until heated through. To serve, top with diced tomatoes, "Great Guacamole"✔, and "Nonfat Yogurt Cheese"✔ if desired.

Serves: 9

Per Serving: 1 g Fat, 91 Calories, 10 % Fat, 7 g Protein, 15.76 g Carbs, 139 mg Sodium, 2.9 mg Cholesterol

CHEESE BLANKET CONCOCTION
(Easy Prep)

2 lbs. Healthy Choice ground beef, cooked, rinsed, and drained
1 (15-oz.) can pinto beans, undrained
1 small can sliced mushrooms, drained
1 (15-oz.) can corn, drained
1 (8-oz.) can tomato sauce
1 (6-oz.) can tomato paste
½ C EACH chopped onion and green pepper
1 C cooked macaroni noodles
9 slices (6 oz.) Healthy Choice Fat Free cheese slices

1. Place all ingredients, except noodles and cheese, in a large skillet. Simmer until vegetables are tender, about 5 minutes.
2. Stir in noodles. Cover entire surface of mixture with whole cheese slices, forming a blanket; allow to melt. Serve.

Note: Feel free to substitute your favorite vegetable or grain for any of the items above to make your own concoction.
Serves: 10 (about 1 C each)

Per Serving: 3.8 g Fat, 255 Calories, 13 % Fat, 26.5 g Protein, 31 g Carbs, 560 mg Sodium, 47 mg Cholesterol

LITE MEATBALLS
(Easy Prep)

1 lb. Healthy Choice ground beef
¼ C dry oatmeal
Scant ¼ C Egg Beaters
1 T dried parsley
1 chicken bouillon cube dissolved in ½ C boiling water
1 scant T minced onion
1 t Worcestershire sauce
2 slices Wonder Lite Fat Free reduced calorie bread
½ C ketchup
Pam no stick cooking spray

1. Combine all ingredients except ketchup, mixing well. Form into balls and place on a cookie sheet that has been coated with Pam. Cover with foil and bake about 5 minutes at 350°.
2. Uncover, dot each meatball with ketchup, and bake uncovered about 10 more minutes. Do not overbake.

Makes: 50

Per Serving: 0.33 g Fat, 17 Calories, 17 % Fat, 1.9 g Protein, 1.4 g Carbs, 71 mg Sodium, 4.4 mg Cholesterol

WAXAHACHIE CASSEROLE

1 lb. Healthy Choice ground beef, cooked, drained, and rinsed
1 clove garlic, pressed
Salt (optional) and pepper to taste
1 (12-oz.) can vegetable cocktail juice
1 (5-oz.) package noodles, cooked
1 bunch green onions, chopped with tops
1 C "Nonfat Yogurt Cheese"✔
1 T cornstarch
6 oz. Healthy Choice Fat Free cream cheese, softened
4 oz. EACH Healthy Choice mozzarella cheese and Healthy Choice Fat Free cheese singles
Pam no stick cooking spray

1. Stir meat, garlic, salt and pepper, and juice together in large pan. Simmer 5 minutes.
2. Combine noodles, onions, yogurt, cornstarch and cream cheese; mix well. Spread into a sprayed 2-quart casserole; top cheese. Spread meat mixture on top. Bake at 350° for 20 minutes. Freezes well.

Serves: 8

Per Serving: 2.2 g Fat, 171 Calories, 12 % Fat, 22 g Protein, 12.6 g Carb, 767 mg Sodium, 36 mg Cholesterol

CROCK POT STEAK
(Easy Prep)

1½ lbs. top round steak, cut into serving pieces
1 can Weight Watcher's cream of mushroom soup
1 medium can whole peeled tomatoes
½ t EACH salt (optional), pepper, and garlic powder
1 T Worcestershire sauce

1. Place steak in microwave and cook about 2 minutes. Drain well. Place in bottom of Pam-sprayed crock pot and sprinkle with seasonings. Add soup, tomatoes, and Worcestershire.
2. Cover and cook on low for about 3-4 hours. Serve over rice.

Serves: 8

Per Serving: 4.4 g Fat, 185 Calories, 21 % Fat, 25 g Protein, 3.6 g Carb, 269 mg Sodium, 70 mg Cholesterol

SUNDAY ROAST AND VEGETABLES

1 (4- to 5-lb.) eye of round beef roast, trimmed of all visible fat
½ C EACH Butter Buds liquid and defatted beef bouillon
¼ C Worcestershire sauce
¼ C "Ross's Special Seasoning"✔, divided
Olive oil flavored Pam no stick cooking spray
4 large baking potatoes cut into thirds
2 large onions sliced into chunks
4 large carrots, sliced into sticks
2 T dry Butter Buds
Salt (optional) and pepper to taste

1. Spray a roasting rack and roasting pan with Pam. Place the rack in the pan. Set aside.
2. 1 hour before cooking, coat the roast thoroughly with Butter Buds liquid and beef bouillon. Rub 2 T of the special seasoning into the roast; spoon on the Worcestershire sauce, coating evenly. Rub in remaining seasoning. Marinate 1 hour. Place in refrigerator if marinating longer than an hour.
3. Place roast on rack and bake at 325° for 45-55 minutes. Remove from oven; pour off any fat.
4. Arrange potatoes around roast on rack; some may have to be placed in roasting pan if rack becomes too full. Pour 1½-2 C water into roasting pan; cover roast and potatoes with foil and bake at 325° for approximately 30 minutes. Remove foil, add onions and carrots, recover, and bake 45 minutes more or until vegetables are tender and roast is cooked to desired doneness. If cooking roast longer, remove vegetables so they will not become mushy. Sprinkle vegetables with Butter Buds and serve with roast.

Serves: 12 (3 oz. beef, 1 potato chunk, ⅓ large carrot, 1/6 of 1 onion)

Per Serving: 3.75 g Fat, 363 Calories, 9 % Fat, 43.9 g Protein, 16.5 g Carbs, 250 mg Sodium, 122 mg Cholesterol

KATHY'S SKILLET BEEF BAKE

(Quick Fix)

1 medium onion, sliced
3 T "Defatted Beef Broth"✔
1 can Weight Watcher's cream of mushroom soup
½ C skim milk
1 t Worcestershire sauce
8 oz. cubed lean top round steak
1 C cubed potatoes, boiled crisp tender
½ C canned or fresh cooked cut green beans, drained
1 (9-oz.) can Pillsbury Hearty Grains biscuits

1. In a large oven-proof skillet, cook onion and beef in broth until lightly browned; drain well. Blend in soup, milk, and Worcestershire; add vegetables. Simmer over low heat about 10 minutes, stirring often. Top with biscuits; bake at 450° for 10 minutes or until browned.

Serves: 4

Per Serving: 1.5 g Fat, 340 Calories, 4 % Fat, 18.5 g Protein, 15 g Carb, 122 mg Sodium, 0 mg Cholesterol

MELT-IN-YOUR-MOUTH EYE OF ROUND ROAST

1 eye of round roast, trimmed of all visible fat
Cracked pepper
Pam no stick cooking spray

1. Preheat oven to 500°. Coat a roasting pan with Pam; place roast in pan and cover with cracked pepper. Bake uncovered for about 35 minutes. Turn oven off; DO NOT OPEN THE DOOR! Let beef stay in oven another 35 minutes for medium rare. Add 5 minutes to the first cooking time for medium and 5 minutes to the end cooking time. Adjust cooking time up 5 minutes each time according to how you like your beef cooked.

Serving size: 3 oz. cooked

Per Serving: 4.2 g Fat, 165 Calories, 23 % Fat, 24 g Protein, 0 g Carbs, 54 mg Sodium, 70 mg Cholesterol

BROCCOLI BEEF

¾ lb. top round steak, cut into strips
1 T orange juice concentrate, undiluted
2 T low sodium soy sauce
1 T plus 1 t nonfat Italian salad dressing
1 t cornstarch
1 minced clove garlic
1 T fresh ginger, grated
½ C "Defatted Beef Bouillon"✔
1 lb. fresh broccoli, trimmed and cut into 2-inch pieces (3-4 C)
½ C EACH sliced mushrooms and green onions including tops
4 oz. fettucine cooked until almost done; drain and spray with butter flavor Pam

1. Marinade beef 15 minutes at room temperature in the orange juice, soy sauce, salad dressing, cornstarch, and garlic.
2. Remove beef with slotted spoon to microwave dish and cook 2-3 minutes until beef is almost cooked through.
3. In a large skillet sprayed with Pam, heat ¼ C broth, ginger, and garlic. Add broccoli, cover and simmer 5 minutes. (May add more broth if necessary.)
4. Uncover, and add beef, onions, and mushrooms. Stir-fry until beef and vegetables are tender. Serve over fettucine.

Serves: 4

Per Serving: 4.25 g Fat, 256 Calories, 15 % Fat, 30.7 g Protein, 17.7 g Carb, 72.5 mg Sodium, 70 mg Cholesterol

SUPER MEATLOAF
(Easy Prep)

2 lbs. Healthy Choice ground beef
1 can condensed tomato soup
1 C EACH crushed corn flakes and Nabisco fat free cracker crumbs
½ C chopped onion
1 T Worcestershire sauce
2 egg whites, slightly beaten
1 t salt (optional)
Dash pepper
Pam no stick cooking spray
1 (6-oz.) can tomato paste

1. Combine all ingredients except tomato paste in a medium size bowl. Spray a large loaf pan with Pam; pour meat mixture in pan and bake in 350° oven for about 45 minutes. Remove from oven, top with tomato paste, and bake an additional 15 minutes or until done. Do not overbake.

Mexican Variation: Substitute 1 can Rotel tomatoes and green chiles for tomato soup; add 1 t cumin and a pinch each cilantro and garlic powder. Top tomato paste with grated nonfat cheddar cheese the last 5 minutes of baking if desired.

Bar-B-Que Variation: Substitute 1¼ C fat free Bar-B-Que sauce for tomato soup; omit Worcestershire sauce. Top with more B-B-Q sauce instead of tomato paste.

Italian Variation: Substitute 1¼ C Healthy Choice spaghetti sauce for tomato soup; omit Worcestershire and add 1 t oregano. Top with Hunts Chunky style spaghetti sauce instead of tomato paste.

Serves: 8

Per Serving: 4 g Fat, 208 Calories, 18 % Fat, 23 g Protein, 13 g Carb, 578 mg Sodium, 55 mg Cholesterol

BEEF "SOUR CREAM" ENCHILADAS
(Quick Fix)

1 lb. Healthy Choice ground beef, browned, rinsed and drained
1 C "Nonfat Yogurt Cheese"✔
2 T cornstarch
2 cans Weight Watcher's cream of mushroom soup
1 small can chopped green chiles
1 C (4 oz.) Healthy Choice Fat Free cheese singles, shredded
1 t EACH garlic salt and chili powder
½ C (2 oz.) EACH Healthy Choice Fat Free Cheddar and Healthy Choice Fat Free mozzarella cheese
12 flour tortillas, softened
Pam no stick cooking spray

1. Mix together the first 5 ingredients.
2. Place about 2 large tablespoons of meat mixture on each tortilla; roll up place in casserole, sprayed with Pam. Mix remaining meat mixture with remaining ingredients; spread on top of tortillas. Bake at 400° about 15-20 minutes.

Serves: 12

Per Serving: 1.9 g Fat, 173 Calories, 10 % Fat, 16.9 g Protein, 20.3 g Carb, 528 mg Sodium, 21.6 mg Cholesterol

BEEF TIPS WITH RICE

(Easy Prep)

¼ C Butter Buds liquid
½ C all-purpose flour
1 t salt (optional)
½ t pepper
1½ lbs. lean top round steak, cut into 2 x ½-inch strips
2 C "Defatted Beef Broth"✔
½ C EACH evaporated skim milk and skim milk
4 C hot cooked rice
Pam no stick cooking spray

1. Combine flour, salt, and pepper. Dredge beef strips in mixture; brown in Butter Buds liquid in a sprayed skillet.
2. Add bouillon; cover and simmer 30-45 minutes or until beef is very tender. Add milk, cover, and simmer 30 minutes. Serve over rice.

Serves: 8 (3 oz. beef; ½ C rice)

Per Serving: 4.3 g Fat, 227 Calories, 17 % Fat, 32 g Protein, 5 g Carb, 216 mg Sodium, 78 mg Cholesterol

VEAL SCALLOPINI

(Quick Fix)

¾ C yellow cornmeal
½ lb. veal scallopini, pounded thin, sliced
½ C 1% fat buttermilk
¼ C "Defatted Beef Broth"✔
¾ package Butter Buds plus 2 T hot water; mix and reserve 1 t
¼ C lemon juice
Dash cilantro
Pam no stick cooking spray

1. Dip veal in buttermilk, then in cornmeal; shake excess.
2. Spray skillet with Pam; pour in 2 T of broth plus Butter Buds mixture. Add veal to skillet; sauté over medium heat about 2 minutes on each side or until brown (add more broth if necessary). Do not overcook. When cooked, remove veal from pan and set aside.
3. Pour off any liquid left in pan. Place reserved Butter Buds mixture, lemon juice, and cilantro into skillet. Cook 1 minute over medium heat. Pour sauce over each serving.

Serves: 3

Per Serving: 5 g Fat, 284 Calories, 16 % Fat, 31 g Protein, 28 g Carb, 293 mg Sodium, 111 mg Cholesterol

HEALTHY HAMBURGER STROGANOFF

(Easy Prep)

1 lb. Healthy Choice ground beef
½ C minced onion
1 clove garlic,minced
¼ C Butter Buds liquid
2 T flour
1 t salt (optional)
¼ t pepper
1 lb. fresh mushrooms, sliced or 1 (8-oz.) can sliced mushrooms, drained
1 (10½ oz.) can Weight Watcher's cream of chicken soup, undiluted
1 C plain nonfat yogurt plus 1 T cornstarch
Parsley

1. Cook meat, drain and rinse.
2. Sauté onion and garlic in Butter Buds over medium heat. Stir in meat. Mix in flour, salt, pepper and mushrooms; cook 5 minutes. Stir in soup. Simmer, uncovered, 10 minutes. Stir in yogurt-cornstarch mixture. Heat through. Garnish with parsley.

Serves: 6

Per Serving: 3.3 g Fat, 180 Calories, 24 % Fat, 20.5 g Protein, 1.3 g Carb, 538 mg Sodium, 15.6 mg Cholesterol

POULTRY

HOMEMADE CHICKEN AND DUMPLINGS

6 (4-oz.) boneless skinless chicken breasts
4 quarts "Defatted Chicken Broth"✔
1 medium onion, minced
2 stalks celery, minced
½ bay leaf
Dash of cayenne pepper and garlic powder
Salt (optional) and pepper to taste
½ C cool water plus ¼ C flour (more if needed)
1 recipe "Dumplings #1,"✔ "Quick Dumplings,"✔ or "Quick Biscuit Dumplings"✔

1. Place all soup ingredients except flour/water mixture in a large soup pot and bring to a boil. Reduce heat and simmer until chicken is tender.
2. Remove chicken, and bay leaf with a slotted spoon. Cut chicken into bite size pieces, discard bay leaf, and return chicken to broth.
3. Mix together the flour and water, stirring to make a smooth paste. Bring pan liquid to a slow boil; drizzle in paste and stir constantly until slightly thickened. (Add more paste if needed.) Make dumplings and proceed as dumpling recipes suggest.

Serves: 8 (nutr. without Dumpling)

Per Serving: 2.2 g Fat, 144 Calories, 14 % Fat, 21.6 g Protein, 4.6 g Carbs, 59 mg Sodium, 55 mg Cholesterol

DUMPLINGS #1

2 C cake flour
1 heaping T baking powder
½ t EACH salt (optional) and white pepper
1 t crushed parsley
¼ C Egg Beaters
½ C evaporated skim milk plus ¼ C skim milk

1. Sift together the flour, baking powder, salt, and pepper; slowly stir in remaining ingredients, adding more milk if necessary. Batter should be stiff. Bring broth just to a boil. With a ¼ C measure, drop dumpling batter into broth. Do not crowd the pan; dumplings must have room to expand. Immediately reduce broth to a simmer; do not boil dumplings. Cover tightly and simmer 8-10 minutes. Dumplings are done when a toothpick inserted in center comes out clean.

Makes: 8 large dumplings

Per Serving: 0.3 g Fat, 100 Calories, 3 % Fat, 3.1 g Protein, 20.5 g Carbs, 145 mg Sodium, 0.7 mg Cholesterol

QUICK DUMPLINGS

8 (fajita size) (no lard) flour tortillas
½ C evaporated skim milk
½ C flour plus 1 package dry Butter Buds

1. Cut each tortilla into quarters and dip in milk; then, coat with flour. Drop into boiling broth, reduce heat and simmer until tender about 3-5 minutes.

Serves: 8

Per Serving: 0.11 g Fat, 37 Calories, 3 % Fat, 1.2 g Protein, 7.2 g Carbs, 93 mg Sodium, 0.5 mg Cholesterol

EASY BISCUIT DUMPLINGS

1 can Pillsbury Hearty Grains biscuits or 1 can Pillsbury breadsticks

1. Cut each biscuit or breadstick into fourths. Bring broth to a boil; drop dough pieces into broth. Simmer covered 15-18 minutes or until tender.

Serves: 8

Per Serving: 2 g Fat, 80 Calories, 22 % Fat, 0 g Protein, 15 g Carbs, 0 mg Sodium, 0 mg Cholesterol

PARTY CHICKEN
(Easy Prep)

8 (4-oz.) boneless, skinless, chicken breasts
4 (1-oz.) slices Healthy Choice ham
4 oz. Weight Watcher's roast beef, shredded
1 can Weight Watcher's cream of mushroom soup
1 C "Nonfat Yogurt Cheese"✔ plus 1 T cornstarch

1. Wrap each chicken breast with ½ of a slice of ham. Spray an oblong casserole dish with Pam and place shredded beef in a single layer in bottom of dish. Arrange chicken on top of beef.
2. Mix soup with yogurt cheese; pour mixture over chicken. You may refrigerate or immediately bake uncovered at 275° for about 1 hour. Serve over rice.

Serves: 8

Per Serving: 4.75 g Fat, 255 Calories, 17 % Fat, 32 g Protein, 5 g Carb, 216 mg Sodium, 78 mg Cholesterol

RANCHER'S CHICKEN

12 corn tortillas
¼ C "Defatted Chicken Broth"✔
4 (4-oz.) boneless skinless chicken breasts, cooked and cubed
1 C EACH chopped onion and green pepper
1 t chili powder
2 C (8 oz.) grated Healthy Choice Fat Free Cheddar cheese, divided
½ t garlic salt (optional)
1 T cornstarch
2 cans Weight Watchers cream of mushroom soup
1 can Rotel tomatoes and green chiles

1. Soften tortillas in broth and place in Pam-coated casserole dish; cover sides and bottom of dish.
2. Mix remaining broth with chicken and 1 C cheese. Place over tortillas.
3. Combine remaining ingredients except cheese; Spoon over chicken. Bake at 375° for 20 minutes. Sprinkle with remaining cheese and bake 10 more minutes.

Serves: 10

Per Serving: 4.2 g Fat, 223 Calories, 17 % Fat, 22.4 g Protein, 22.7 g Carb, 559 mg Sodium, 332 mg Cholesterol

CHICKEN SUPREME
(Do the day before)

6 (4-oz.) boneless skinless chicken breasts
2 C "Nonfat Yogurt Cheese"✔ plus 2 T cornstarch
4 t Worcestershire sauce
2 t EACH salt (optional) and paprika
½ t pepper
1 ¾ C "Basic Bread Crumbs"✔
1 C Butter Buds liquid

1. Rinse chicken; pat dry. Mix yogurt and seasonings; pour over chicken coating well. Cover and chill overnight.
2. Preheat oven to 350°. Remove chicken and coat each piece evenly with bread crumbs. Arrange on flat pan coated with Pam. Spoon half the Butter Buds mixture over chicken and bake uncovered 25 minutes. Spoon rest of Butter Buds mixture over chicken and bake 10 more minutes. DO NOT OVER BAKE.

Serves: 6

Per Serving: 3.16 g Fat, 255 Calories, 10 % Fat, 37.6 g Protein, 19.6 g Carb, 173 mg Sodium, 85 mg Cholesterol

EASY CHICKEN PARMESAN
(Easy Prep)

4 (4-oz.) boneless, skinless chicken breasts
2 C "Basic Bread Crumbs"✔
¼ C Egg Beaters
Olive Oil flavor Pam no stick cooking spray
2 oz. Healthy Choice Fat Free mozzarella cheese, grated
2 oz. Truly Lite Fat Free ricotta cheese
1⅓ C Healthy Choice spaghetti sauce

1. Dip each chicken breast in Egg Beaters, then coat with bread crumbs.
2. Spray a large skillet with Pam and heat. Quickly brown chicken breasts on both sides, about 3-5 minutes total.
3. Coat baking dish with Pam. Place chicken in pan; top each breast with ⅓ C of spaghetti sauce.
4. Combine mozzarella and ricotta cheeses. Place an equal amount of cheese on each chicken breast.
5. Cover and bake for 20 minutes at 375°.
6. Remove chicken from oven. Sprinkle with remaining bread crumbs and bake uncovered for 5-10 more minutes or until browned.

Serves: 4

Per Serving: 4 g Fat, 256 Calories, 14 % Fat, 28.8 Protein, 10.6 Carb, 805 mg Sodium, 65 Cholesterol

STIR-FRIED GARDEN CHICKEN

¾ lb. skinless, boneless chicken breast, sliced into strips
⅓ C orange juice
¼ t grated orange peel
¼ C reduced sodium soy sauce
1 t cornstarch
3 C broccoli florets, cooked, drained, and diced
1 chicken bouillon cube plus ½ C boiling water
1 t grated fresh ginger
8 oz. dry whole wheat spaghetti, cooked

1. Marinate chicken in the next 4 ingredients for 15 minutes.
2. Heat 2 T of chicken bouillon mixture in a sprayed skillet. Add ginger; spoon in marinade and chicken. Cook until tender, about 5 minutes over med-high heat. Stir in broccoli; mix well and heat through. Serve over spaghetti.

Serves: 4

Per Serving: 2.5 g Fat, 360 Calories, 6 % Fat, 30.9 g Protein, 50.3 g Carb, 750 mg Sodium, 55 mg Cholesterol

CHICKEN & VEGETABLES
(Quick Fix)

4 (4-oz.) boneless, skinless chicken breasts
½ C "Defatted Chicken Broth"✔
½ C white wine
Butter flavor Pam no stick cooking spray
2 C EACH broccoli and cauliflower florets
1 recipe "Quick Cheese Sauce"✔

1. Coat a large skillet with Pam. Place chicken in skillet, add broth and wine. Simmer 10 minutes, add vegetables and cook 10-15 minutes or until chicken is done and vegetables are tender.

Serves: 4

Variation: Use your own favorite vegetables and another sauce if desired.

Per Serving: 2.3 g Fat, 269 Calories, 7 % Fat, 54.7 g Protein, 7.2 g Carb, 371 mg Sodium, 59.7 mg Cholesterol

LITE CHICKEN TETRAZZINI
(Quick Fix)

4 (4-oz.) boneless skinless chicken breasts, cooked and cubed
2 C "Nonfat Yogurt cheese"✔
2 T cornstarch
2 cans Weight Watcher's cream of mushroom soup
8 mushrooms, sliced
½ C "Defatted Chicken Broth"✔ plus 1 package dry Butter Buds
1 (7-oz.) package spaghetti, cooked
¼ C white wine
2 oz. fresh grated Parmesan cheese

1. Sauté mushrooms in broth mixture; combine with remaining ingredients except Parmesan.
2. Pour all ingredients in glass dish; sprinkle with cheese and bake at 350° for 30 minutes.

Serves: 8

Per Serving: 4 g Fat, 182 Calories, 20 % Fat, 18.8 g Protein, 13.7 g Carb, 474 mg Sodium, 44 mg Cholesterol

TURKEY TACO CASSEROLE

(Quick Fix)

1 can diced Rotel tomatoes and green chiles
1 can Weight Watcher's cream of mushroom soup
1 (15-oz.) can Health Valley mild Fat Free vegetarian chili
1 (15-oz.) can evaporated skim milk
1 lb. ground turkey breast
1 T "Defatted Beef Broth"✔
1 can pinto beans, undrained
2 C (8 oz.) EACH Healthy Choice Fat Free cheddar cheese
2 C (8 oz.) Healthy Choice Fat Free cheese singles, diced
15 (7-inch) corn tortillas
1 onion, chopped
Pam no stick cooking spray

1. In the microwave or skillet, cook turkey and onion in beef broth until almost done. Heat remaining ingredients except tortillas until cheese is melted; add to turkey mixture.
2. Spray a large casserole with Pam. Beginning with tortillas, layer 1/3 tortillas and 1/3 turkey-cheese mixture in dish. Repeat layers two more times. Bake at 350° for 15 - 20 minutes or until heated through.

Serves: 10

Per Serving: 2.4 g Fat, 367 Calories, 6 % Fat, 35 g Protein, 43 g Carb, 1129 mg Sodium, 41 mg Cholesterol

CRANBERRY CHICKEN MARINARA

4 (4-oz.) boneless skinless chicken breasts, uncooked
1 (.75-oz.) package Marinara pasta sauce blend
1 can Weight Watcher's cream of mushroom soup
½ C cranberry juice
2 chicken bouillon cubes
8 oz. spinach pasta, cooked in boiling water until done (Rinse with cold water and set aside.

1. Place chicken in a microwaveable dish and add bouillon cubes and about ⅓ C water.
2. Microwave, covered, for about 5 minutes on high. Turn chicken over, add sauce mix and cranberry juice and continue cooking until done, about 3 - 5 more minutes (Do not overcook).
3. Remove chicken dish from oven and place chicken pieces on a serving platter, reserving liquid.
4. Add cream of mushroom soup to liquid remaining in dish and stir.
5. Place noodles on plate, top with chicken, then sauce, and serve.

Serves: 4

Per Serving: 5 g Fat, 196 Calories, 22 % Fat, 11.2 g Protein, 20 g Carb, 1027 mg Sodium, 16 mg Cholesterol

TERIYAKI CHICKEN

1 C low sodium soy sauce
½ C Butter Buds liquid
1 heaping (¼ t) minced garlic
1 T grated fresh gingerroot
2 T cooking sherry
6 (4-oz.) boneless skinless chicken breasts

1. Mix first 5 ingredients and set aside. Place chicken in a single layer in a non-metal dish, pour 1st mixture over chicken and marinate 2-6 hours in the refrigerator.
2. Remove and bake at 350° for about 30 minutes.

Serves: 6

Per Serving: 3.5 Fat, 160 Calories, 20 % Fat, 20 g Protein, 7.4 g Carb 644 mg Sodium, 10 mg Cholesterol

CHICKEN-SPINACH ENCHILADAS

4 (4-oz.) boneless, skinless chicken breasts
1 medium onion, chopped
¼ t cumin
¼ C fresh cilantro, chopped or broken into pieces
1 (10-oz.) package fresh-frozen chopped spinach, cooked and well-drained
½ t lemon juice
1 package Butter Buds
2 C "Nonfat Yogurt Cheese"✔
¼ t paprika
12 flour tortillas (you may use corn tortillas)
1 C Truly Lite Fat Free ricotta cheese
½ C grated Healthy Choice Fat Free mozzarella cheese
½ C Healthy Choice Fat Free cheese singles, shredded
1 sliced jalapeño pepper (optional)
2 C boiling water plus 2 bouillon cubes, to make broth
Pam no stick cooking spray

1. Cook the first 4 ingredients on stovetop or in microwave until chicken is tender and cooked through (about 5-8 minutes in microwave). Set aside and let cool. Drain liquid. Chop finely.
2. Mix the well-drained spinach with the lemon juice, paprika and Butter Buds; add to chicken, mixing well.
3. Dip each tortilla into the chicken broth and fill with chicken/spinach mixture (about 2 T per tortilla).
4. Roll up and place seam-side down in long casserole dish that has been sprayed with Pam.
5. In microwave-safe bowl, mix yogurt cheese, ricotta and 4 T of broth. Heat gently for only about 10-15 seconds, just to soften cheeses. Pour over enchiladas.
6. Bake uncovered at 325° for approximately 25 minutes. Top with remaining two cheeses and return to oven for about 5 more minutes or until cheese melts.

Serves: 12

Per Serving: 3.6 g Fat, 179 Calories, 18 % Fat, 13.5 g Protein, 19.5 g Carb, 437 mg Sodium, 19 mg Cholesterol

CRISPY CHICKEN
(Easy Prep)

4 (4-oz.) boneless, skinless chicken breasts
½ C lemon juice
2 T reduced sodium soy sauce
¼ C 1% or less fat buttermilk
2 beaten egg whites
1 C crispy rice cereal, crushed
Pam no stick cooking spray

1. Marinate chicken in the next 2 ingredients 20-30 minutes. Drain and pat dry.
2. Mix buttermilk with egg whites. Coat chicken pieces with buttermilk mixture, roll in cereal, and place on sprayed broiler pan.
3. Bake uncovered at 400° for about 30 minutes. This may also be done in strips or chunks, though cooking time will be shorter.

Serves: 4

Per Serving: 3 g Fat, 205 Calories, 13 % Fat, 31.5 g Protein, 7.17 g Carb, 184 mg Sodium, 73.5 mg Cholesterol

CHICKEN SHAKESPEARE
(Easy Prep)

6 (4-oz.) boneless skinless chicken breasts
1 package onion soup mix
1 medium can frozen orange juice concentrate
Pam no stick cooking spray

1. Place chicken in sprayed casserole dish. Pour soup mix over chicken; top with concentrate.
2. Bake covered 20 minutes at 350°; uncover and continue baking 10-15 more minutes.

Serves: 6

Per Serving: 3.2 g Fat, 244 Calories, 12 % Fat, 28.8 g Protein, 0.7 g Carb, 527 mg Sodium, 73 mg Cholesterol

QUICK CHICKEN SPAGHETTI
(Easy Prep)

½ C EACH chopped green onions (with tops), celery and green pepper
¼ C "Defatted Chicken Broth"✔ plus 1 package Butter Buds
1 can Weight Watcher's cream of mushroom soup
1 small can sliced mushrooms, drained
4 (4-oz.) cooked boneless, skinless chicken breasts, cubed
1 (1-lb.) package spaghetti, cooked about 6 minutes, drain
½ C (2 oz.) EACH Healthy Choice Fat Free cheese singles and mozzarella cheese
1 t chili powder
Salt (optional) and pepper to taste
Pam no stick cooking spray

1. Sauté onion, celery and green pepper in broth and Butter Buds about 2 minutes. Add remaining ingredients; mix well.
2. Pour into a Pam-coated casserole; bake at 350° for 20 minutes.

Serves: 8

Per Serving: 1.8 g Fat, 199 Calories, 8 % Fat, 21 g Protein, 20 g Carb, 368 mg Sodium, 39 mg Cholesterol

EASY YOGURT CHICKEN

4 (4-oz.) boneless, skinless chicken breasts
1 can Weight Watcher's cream of mushroom soup
½ soup can cranberry juice (may use apple, orange or pineapple juice)
1 C plain nonfat yogurt
1 T cornstarch
1 t minced onion
1 C sliced fresh mushrooms
Pam no stick cooking spray

1. Place chicken in baking dish coated with Pam. Stir together soup, juice, yogurt, cornstarch and onion. Spoon over chicken pieces, coating evenly.
2. Arrange mushrooms on top of sauce. Cover and bake in 350° oven for 25-30 minutes or until done.

Serves: 4

Per Serving: 2.5 g Fat, 175 Calories, 13 % Fat, 23 g Protein, 26.5 g Carb, 350 mg Sodium, 38.7 mg Cholesterol

CHICKEN CACCIATORE
(Quick Fix)

4 (4-oz.) boneless, skinless chicken breasts, cubed
¾ C chopped onion
¼ C "Defatted Chicken Broth"✔
½ medium green pepper, cut into strips
½ t basil
½ t oregano
Parsley
2 C Healthy Choice spaghetti sauce
1¼ C water
1½ C instant rice, uncooked
1 small can chopped water chestnuts

1. In a large skillet, sauté chicken and onions in chicken broth, using a few tablespoons at a time when needed. Stir until both are light brown.
2. Stir in next 6 ingredients and bring to a boil. Stir in rice and water chestnuts; remove from heat. Cover and let stand until water is absorbed, about 8 minutes.

Serves: 4

Per Serving: 3.5 g Fat, 331 Calories, 9 % Fat, 34 g Protein, 67 g Carb, 73 mg Sodium, 3 mg Cholesterol

GREAT GUACAMOLE CHICKEN

- **1 recipe "Great Guacamole"✔**
- **4 (4-oz.) boneless skinless chicken breasts**
- **2 T flour**
- **1 t EACH cumin, cilantro, and garlic salt (optional)**
- **¼ C Egg Beaters**
- **1 T water**
- **⅓ C cornmeal**
- **3 T "Defatted Chicken Broth"✔**
- **2 oz. EACH Healthy Choice Fat Free Fat Free cheese singles and Healthy Choice Fat Free Cheddar cheese, shredded**
- **½ C "Nonfat Yogurt Cheese"✔, divided**
- **¼ C EACH green onion and sweet red pepper, chopped**

1. Pound chicken pieces to about ¼" thick and set aside.
2. Mix flour and spices; coat each chicken breast entirely.
3. Mix egg substitute and water in a small bowl and cornmeal in another. Coat chicken in egg, then in cornmeal and place in a heated skillet that had been coated with Pam.
4. Brown chicken quickly, about 1-2 minutes on each side. Add chicken broth gradually to keep chicken from burning.
5. Remove chicken to square sprayed baking pan. Place 2 T guacamole on each piece, top with equal amounts of cheese, and bake at 350° for about 15 minutes. Garnish with yogurt cheese, onion and red pepper.

Serves: 4

Per Serving: 3.25 g Fat, 265 Calories, 11 % Fat, 37.5 g Protein, 12.8 g Carb, 472 mg Sodium, 78 mg Cholesterol

CHICKEN A LA KING IN A HURRY

- **¼ C EACH minced green pepper and onion**
- **1-2 T "Defatted Chicken Broth"✔**
- **1 can Weight Watcher's cream of mushroom soup**
- **2 T skim milk**
- **Dash cooking sherry (optional)**
- **¼ C diced pimentos**
- **2 (6-oz.) cans chicken breast, rinsed and drained**

1. Combine all ingredients; heat until warm and season to taste. Serve over non fat reduced calorie toasted bread, rice, or pasta.

Serves: 6

Per Serving: 1.3 g Fat, 107 Calories, 28 % Fat, 13 g Protein, 3.7 g Carbs, 262 mg Sodium, 31.3 mg Cholesterol

BEST BAR-B-Q CHICKEN
(Quick Fix)

6 (4-oz.) boneless skinless chicken breasts
1 C "Lite and Easy Bar-B-Q"✔ sauce or your favorite no-oil Bar-B-Q sauce
1 T "Ross's Special Seasoning"✔
Pam no stick cooking spray

1. Line a 13 X 9-inch dish with foil; spray with Pam. Dip chicken in sauce and place on foil. Rub ½ t seasoning into each chicken breast. Pour remaining sauce over chicken and seal foil. Bake in 400 ° oven for 18-25 minutes. Do not overcook.

Note: For an added treat, place sliced onions and green pepper in foil with the chicken and bake.

Serves: 6

Per Serving: 3 g Fat, 165 Calories,
16 % Fat, 28 g Protein, 0 g Carbs,
60 mg Sodium, 73 mg Cholesterol

CHICKEN PIE
(Easy Prep)

1 "Hearty Grains Pie Crust"✔ prepared
8 oz. cooked boneless skinless chicken breast, cubed
4 C "Lite White Sauce"✔ prepared
¼ t poultry seasoning
1 C cooked mixed vegetables or 1 C vegetables of your choice
Pam no stick cooking spray

1. Prepare pie crust (filled version). Prepare sauce.
2. Mix vegetables and seasoning with sauce. Pour into crust. Bake in 350° oven until pie is heated through and crust is lightly browned. If crust browns too fast, place foil tent over crust.

Serves: 6

Note: You may wish to reserve a little of the crust and make strips of dough on top of the pie for a prettier pie.

Per Serving: 4 g Fat, 206 Calories,
17 % Fat, 12.5 g Protein, 21 g Carbs,
25 mg Sodium, 29 mg Cholesterol

CHICKEN FINGERS
(Easy Prep)

2 lbs. boneless, skinless chicken breasts
½ C EACH lemon and lime juice
4 T soy sauce
½ t salt (optional)
1½ C flour
1 t pepper
½ t paprika
½ t garlic salt (optional)
Butter flavor Pam no stick cooking spray

1. Cut chicken into strips. Place in shallow dish. Pour next 3 ingredients over chicken. Cover and marinate 30 minutes.
2. Combine flour, pepper, paprika and salt. Coat drained chicken pieces with flour mixture.
3. Coat baking pan with Pam and place chicken pieces in pan. Spray chicken pieces with Pam and bake at 350° until tender, about 15-25 minutes. Do not overcook.

Serves: 10

Per Serving: 1.8 g Fat, 160 Calories, 10 % Fat, 22 g Protein, 19.4 g Carb, 108 mg Sodium, 63 mg Cholesterol

FRANCES FOLEY'S CROCKPOT CHICKEN
(Easy Prep)

1 (3-lb.) boneless skinless whole chicken or turkey breast
1 can Weight Watcher's cream of mushroom soup
½ C McCormick/Schilling gravy mix
Pam no stick cooking spray

1. Place chicken in sprayed crockpot; top with soup, then gravy mix, and cook covered on low for 4-6 hours.

Serves: 12 (4 oz. each)

Per Serving: 3.2 g Fat, 171 Calories, 17 % Fat, 21 g Protein, 1.16 g Carb, 109 mg Sodium, 14.08 mg Cholesterol

CRUNCHY OVEN-FRIED CHICKEN

12 (4-oz.) boneless, skinless chicken breasts
1 recipe "Ross's Special Seasoning,"✔ prepared
1 recipe "Ross's Chicken on the Grill,"✔ (triple the ingredients)
4 egg whites at room temperature
¼ C plus 2 T cornstarch
2 C Grape Nuts cereal
Pam no stick cooking spray

1. Prepare chicken breasts through step #2 in "Ross's Chicken on the Grill."✔ Let stand 1 hour; refrigerate if marinating longer.
2. Beat egg whites until foamy; gradually add in cornstarch and beat until stiff peaks form.
3. Dip chicken in egg white mixture, roll in Grape Nuts, place on a cookie sheet sprayed with Pam, and bake at 400° for 20-25 minutes. Do not overbake.

Serves: 12

Variation: May do chicken nuggets or chicken strips by cutting chicken up accordingly. Bake at 400° for 12-15 minutes. Do not overbake.

Per Serving: 2.5 g Fat, 220 Calories, 10 % Fat, 40 g Protein, 10 g Carb, 90 mg Sodium, 40.75 mg Cholesterol

CLUB CHICKEN CASSEROLE

¼ C Butter Buds liquid
¼ C flour
1 ⅔ C evaporated skim milk
1 C "Defatted Chicken Broth"✔
½ C water
3 C cooked rice
12 oz. cooked chicken breast, diced
1 (3-oz.) can sliced mushrooms, drained
⅓ C chopped green pepper
¼ C chopped canned pimento
1½ t salt (optional)

1. Blend Butter Buds with flour in saucepan. Add milk, broth, and water. Cook quickly, stirring constantly until thick and bubbly. Add rice, chicken, and remaining ingredients.
2. Pour into sprayed casserole and bake uncovered in 350 degree oven for 30-40 minutes until heated through.

Serves: 8

Per Serving: 2.75 g Fat, 223 Calories, 11 % Fat, 15.5 g Protein, 33 g Carb, 349 mg Sodium, 29 mg Cholesterol

MEXICAN CHICKEN WITH RICE

12 oz. boneless skinless chicken breasts, sliced into strips
2-4 T Butter Buds liquid
1½ C cooked uncooked rice
1 C chopped onion
2 cloves garlic, minced
3 C water plus 3 chicken bouillon cubes
1 (8-oz.) can diced tomatoes, undrained
½ t EACH cumin and cilantro
1 C frozen green peas
Salt (optional) and pepper to taste

1. Sauté chicken in 2 T Butter Buds liquid in non-stick skillet until brown on both sides. Remove from pan. Add rice, onion, and garlic to skillet and sauté until rice is golden, adding remaining 2 T of broth if needed.
2. Add water and bouillon cubes, tomatoes, seasonings, and spices. Stir; bring to a boil. Place chicken pieces on top of rice mixture. Cover and simmer 25-30 minutes or until rice is tender. Stir in peas and cook about 5 more minutes.

Serves: 6

Per Serving: 1.6 g Fat, 189 Calories, 7 % Fat, 17.1 g Protein, 22 g Carbs, 762 mg Sodium, 36.5 mg Cholesterol

CHICKEN ABERNATHY

1 can Weight Watcher's cream of mushroom soup
1 (14½-oz.) can skim evaporated milk
1 C "Defatted Chicken Broth"✔
1 T cornstarch
½ C water
3 C cooked long grain rice
2½ C (8 oz.) diced cooked chicken breast
1 (3-oz.) can sliced mushrooms, drained
⅓ C chopped green pepper
¼ C chopped pimiento, drained
1½ t salt (optional)
Pam no stick cooking spray

1. Combine first 5 ingredients; cook until bubbly, stirring constantly. Add remaining ingredients.
2. Pour into a 2-quart casserole that has been coated with cooking spray.
3. Bake uncovered at 350° for 30 minutes or until heated through.

Serves: 8-10

Per Serving: 3.1 g Fat, 172 Calories, 16 % Fat, 11 g Protein, 23.8 g Carb, 437 mg Sodium, 15.7 mg Cholesterol

CHICKEN AND RICE

2 cans Weight Watcher's cream of mushroom soup
1 package broccoli Lipton Cup-A-Soup
1¾ C water
½ C unsweetened apple juice or dry white wine
1 C uncooked rice
4 (4-oz.) boneless, skinless chicken breasts

1. Mix together first five ingredients; place in a sprayed oblong casserole dish. Arrange chicken on top.
2. Bake at 350° for 25-30 minutes; remove chicken. Continue baking rice 20-30 minutes more or until rice is done.

Serves: 6

Per Serving: 2.8 g Fat, 205 Calories, 12 % Fat, 18.3 g Protein, 47 g Carb, 147 mg Sodium, 49 mg Cholesterol

JAN'S CHICKEN ENCHILADAS

12 oz. cooked boneless, skinless chicken breasts, cubed
¼ C chopped green onion with tops
2 cans Weight Watcher's cream of mushroom soup
2 C "Nonfat Yogurt Cheese"✔
2 T cornstarch
1 can green chiles
⅓ C "Defatted Chicken Broth"
1 ¾ C (7 oz.) EACH grated Healthy Choice Fat Free mozzarella cheese and cheese singles
½ C (2 oz.) Healthy Choice Fat Free Cheddar cheese
24 corn tortillas, softened
Pam no stick cooking spray

1. Combine all ingredients except tortillas. Spoon about 2-3 T of chicken mixture into each tortilla and roll up.
2. Place seam-side down in a sprayed baking dish; top with remaining sauce and bake at 350° for 30 minutes.

Serves: 12

Per Serving: 3 g Fat, 210 Calories, 13 % Fat, 21 g Protein, 37.5 g Carb, 946 mg Sodium, 22 mg Cholesterol

CHICKEN IN A BISCUIT
(Quick Fix)

1 (9-oz.) can Hearty Grains refrigerated biscuits
½ of an (8-oz.) carton Healthy Choice Fat Free cream cheese, softened
¼ C Butter Buds liquid
½ t salt (optional)
¼ t pepper
1½ C (6 oz.) boneless skinless cooked chicken breast, chopped
Butter flavor Pam no stick cooking spray

1. Separate each biscuit creating 2 biscuits from 1. Roll out each biscuit piece to about ⅛-inch thickness, about 4-5 inches in diameter. Set aside.
2. Combine remaining ingredients. Place equal amounts of chicken filling on each of 8 biscuits; top with remaining biscuit, press together and seal well. Spray each with Pam and place in a 13 X 9-inch baking dish that has been coated with Pam. Bake at 350° for about 20 minutes or until browned.

Serves: 8

Per Serving: 2.2 1 g Fat, 148 Calories, 8 % Fat, 7.7 g Protein, 16.2 g Carbs, 122 mg Sodium, 41 mg Cholesterol

CREAMY WHITE WINE CHICKEN

4 (4-oz.) boneless, skinless chicken breasts
2 T dry Butter Buds
¼ C white wine
1½ C "Lite White Sauce,"✔ prepared
1 C sliced fresh mushrooms
½ C water chestnuts, diced
Pam no stick cooking spray

1. Spray medium casserole dish with Pam. Place chicken in dish. Combine remaining ingredients; pour over chicken. Cover and cook about 25 minutes at 350°. Uncover and bake about 5-10 minutes longer.

Serves: 4

Per Serving: 4.5 g Fat, 236 Calories, 17 % Fat, 33 g Protein, 6.75 g Carb, 502 mg Sodium, 73 mg Cholesterol

COMPANY TURKEY LOAF

(A great main dish for company or your family!)

2 lb. skinless ground turkey or chicken breast
1 C EACH chopped onion and green pepper
1 small can pimentos or 1/3 C diced red bell pepper
Scant 3/4 C Egg Beaters
1 (6-oz.) can tomato paste
1/2 can Weight Watcher's cream of mushroom soup
3 chicken bouillon cubes plus 2 beef bouillon cubes
2 3/4 C boiling water
2 C cooked rice (may use brown rice)
2 C "Basic Bread Crumbs"✔
1 t celery salt or celery seed
Pam no stick cooking spray

1. Dissolve the bouillon cubes in the boiling water. In a large bowl, combine bouillon with remaining ingredients; mix well.
2. Coat one large loaf pan or 2 medium loaf pans with Pam. Pour turkey mixture into pan and bake at 350° for 1 hour and 30 minutes or until turkey is cooked through. Do not overcook.
3. Remove from oven and let stand about 10 minutes. If desired, serve with remaining cream of mushroom soup, more tomato paste, or "Easy Chicken Gravy"✔. Simply warm gravy or sauce and spoon over individual servings.

Note: Try baking mini chicken loaves in sprayed muffin tins. The cooking time will be much shorter and they make great take-along lunches or snacks.

Serves: 14

Per Serving: 1.3 g Fat, 119 Calories, 9.8 % Fat, 13.2 g Protein, 12 g Carbs, 518 mg Sodium, 25 mg Cholesterol

FAMILY SUPPER

(Quick Fix)

2 C (8 oz.) cooked boneless skinless chicken breast, cubed
2 C cooked brown or white rice
1 medium green pepper, chopped
1 can Weight Watcher's cream of mushroom soup
1 C evaporated skim milk
Pam no stick cooking spray

1. Spray a baking dish with Pam. Combine the first 3 ingredients and place in dish. Mix soup and milk; pour over chicken mixture. Bake at 350° 20-30 minutes until heated through.

Serves: 4

Per Serving: 0.17 g Fat, 246 Calories, 0.6 % Fat, 19.2 g Protein, 32 g Carbs, 750 mg Sodium, 38 mg Cholesterol

JAMBALAYA FOR JAMES

2 T "Defatted Chicken Broth"*
4 C chopped onion
1½ C chopped green pepper
1 C diced green onion tops
1 T minced parsley
3 cloves garlic, minced
1 lb. boneless skinless chicken breasts, sliced
1 (14 oz.) package Healthy Choice smoked sausage sliced into 1-inch cubes
¼ t each basil and cayenne
2 t chili powder (or to taste)
Salt and pepper to taste
1 or 2 whole bay leaves, crushed
1/8 t each mace and cloves
2 C "Defatted Chicken Broth"*
1 C water
1½ C long grain rice
Pam no stick cooking spray

1. Spray a large stew pot with Pam. Heat broth until hot; add the next 5 ingredients. Reduce heat and saute' until vegetables are browned, about 10 minutes.
2. Add the chicken, sausage, and seasonings; mix until combined well. Add the broth and water; stir in rice and bring to a boil. Cover and simmer slowly over low heat about 35 minutes stirring occasionally.
3. Remove lid, turn heat to medium and cook about 10 more minutes stirring frequently.

Serves: 8

Per Serving: 3.3 g Fat, 253 Calories, 12 % Fat, 29.6 g Protein, 26 g Carb 346 mg Sodium, 63 mg Cholesterol

SEAFOOD

MARINATED MAHI MAHI

(Easy and delicious)

½ C low sodium soy sauce
½ C plus 2 T Sherry wine
1 ¾ C unsweetened pineapple juice
¼ C red wine vinegar
¼ C plus 2 T sugar
½ t granulated garlic
6 (4-oz.) mahi mahi fish fillets

1. Mix all ingredients and marinate fish for 1 hour. Refrigerate if marinating for more than an hour.
2. Grill or bake 10 minutes per inch of thickness. If less than an inch, adjust time accordingly.

Serves: 6

Per Serving: 0.83 g Fat, 210 Calories, 3 % Fat, 20.8 g Protein, 14.8 g Carbs, 95 mg Sodium, 65 mg Cholesterol

FRIDAY SHRIMP FRY

(Quick Fix)

1 lb. large butterfly shrimp, peeled, with tails
3 egg whites
¼ C cornstarch
Salt (optional) and pepper to taste
½ C Premium Fat Free cracker crumbs
Pam no stick cooking spray

1. Beat egg whites until foamy; add cornstarch and beat until stiff but not dry. Season shrimp, dip in egg whites, roll in cracker crumbs, then back in egg whites. Place on baking sheet that has been coated with Pam and bake at 400° 10-15 minutes.

Serves: 4

Per Serving: 1.0 g Fat, 160 Calories, 6 % Fat, 25.2 g Protein, 4.5 g Carbs, 101 mg Sodium, 215 mg Cholesterol

SEAFOOD SUPREME

10 lasagna noodles, cooked
1 lb. fresh medium-size shrimp in shell
1 large onion, chopped
4 oz. Healthy Choice Fat Free cream cheese
1 C nonfat cottage cheese
2 egg whites
½ t EACH oregano, basil and salt (optional)
1 (10-oz.) package frozen chopped spinach, thawed and drained
⅓ C evaporated skim milk
1 can Weight Watcher's cream of mushroom soup plus 1 T cornstarch
1 lb. flounder or other mild fish, cut into bite-size pieces
1 lb. crabmeat
2 T EACH lemon juice and grated Parmesan cheese
4 T dry "Basic Bread Crumbs"✓
1 pkg. Butter Buds mixed with 2 T hot water
½ C (2 oz.) EACH Healthy Choice Fat Free mozzarella cheese and Truly Lite Fat Free ricotta cheese

1. Cover shrimp with water. Boil for 1 minute. Rinse with cold water, drain, peel, and de-vein.
2. Coat a 9 x 13-inch dish with Pam. Drain noodles, spray them with Pam; place 5 noodles in dish.
3. Coat a skillet with Pam; sauté onion until transparent, adding water if necessary. Add the cream cheese, cottage cheese, egg whites, and spices; cook until blended. Stir in well-drained spinach. Pour skillet mixture over noodles.
4. Mix cornstarch, soup, seafood, milk and lemon juice; spoon over spinach layer. Top with remaining noodles.
5. Combine Parmesan cheese, bread crumbs, and Butter Buds mixture; sprinkle over top of casserole. Bake at 350° for 45 minutes. Top with cheeses and bake 5 more minutes. Let stand 10 minutes before serving.

Serves: 12

Per Serving: 1.3 g Fat, 189 Calories, 6 % Fat, 31.5 g Protein, 13 g Carb, 354 mg Sodium, 86.7 mg Cholesterol

SPANISH FISH
(Quick Fix)

4 (4-oz.) cod or flounder fish fillets
1 can Rotel tomatoes and green chilies
½ C chopped onion
1 T Butter Buds liquid
⅓ C lemon juice
Pam no stick cooking spray

1. Place fish in an oblong baking dish that has been coated with Pam. Combine remaining ingredients and pour over fish. Bake in 475° oven for 8-10 minutes.

Serves: 4

Per Serving: 1 g Fat, 144 Calories, 6 % Fat, 20.5 g Protein, 3.5 g Carbs, 204 mg Sodium, 41 mg Cholesterol

OVEN FRIED CATFISH
(Quick Fix and the kids will love it!)

4 (4-oz.) catfish fillets
½ C flour
¼ C Egg Beaters
1 C finely crushed cornflakes or nonfat cracker crumbs
¼ t salt (optional)
Butter flavor Pam no stick cooking spray

1. Coat each fillet with flour; shake off excess but make sure fish is completely coated. Mix Egg Beaters with salt; dip each fillet into Egg Beaters mixture and roll in cornflakes, covering completely.
2. Coat a flat baking pan with Pam; place fish on pan. Coat each fillet with Pam and bake at 450° for 10 minutes for every inch of fish thickness. Adjust cooking time as needed.

Serves: 4

Variation: Coat fish with Pam, roll in Fat Free cracker crumbs and bake.

Per Serving: 1.1 g Fat, 207 Calories, 5 % Fat, 23.2 g Protein, 16.2 g Carbs, 15 mg Sodium, 41 mg Cholesterol

UNCLE BOB'S FAVORITE ORANGE ROUGHY
(Quick Fix)

4 (4-oz.) orange roughy fillets
1 C "Mock Sour Cream"✔
1 C "Basic Bread Crumbs"✔
Butter flavored Pam no stick cooking spray

1. Spray a broiler pan with Pam. Coat each fillet with Mock Sour Cream; press bread crumbs into sour cream. Place fillets on pan and broil 3-5 minutes or until tender and flakes easily with a fork. (May microwave.)

Serves: 4

Per Serving: 1.25 g Fat, 185 Calories, 6 % Fat, 22 g Protein, 11.25 g Carbs, 69 mg Sodium, 41 mg Cholesterol

NANA'S SALMON PATTIES
(Quick Fix)

1 (1-lb.) can pink or red salmon
4 egg whites
⅔ C oat bran cereal
1 medium onion, finely minced
1 T finely chopped parsley
1 T fresh lemon juice
Pam no stick cooking spray

1. Mix all ingredients; form into patties.
2. Coat a skillet with Pam and "fry" until crisp.

Great with mashed potatoes and a dash of ketchup.

Serves: 8

Per Serving: 2.8 g Fat, 129 Calories, 19 % Fat, 18.5 g Protein, 3.6 g Carb, 71 mg Sodium, 17 mg Cholesterol

DEE'S SWORDFISH
(Easy Prep)

1 lb. swordfish steaks, cut into 4 equal pieces
2 T hot water plus 1 package dry Butter Buds
½ C Kraft Free mayonnaise
Pam no stick cooking spray

1. Coat the grill or broiler pan with Pam. Spread the Butter Buds mixture carefully on each steak, coating evenly. Coat each steak thoroughly with mayonnaise on both sides and cook over hot coals for about 4-6 minutes per side.

Serves: 4

Per Serving: 1 g Fat, 161 Calories, 5 % Fat, 20 g Protein, 8 g Carbs, 619 mg Sodium, 41 mg Cholesterol

CHEESE CRUNCH FISH
(Quick Fix)

4 (4-oz.) flounder fillets
¼ C Kraft Free mayonnaise
2 oz. cheese flavored Crispy Rice Bites, crushed
Butter flavor Pam no stick cooking spray

1. Coat a baking sheet with Pam. Coat each fillet with mayonnaise and press rice bites into fillets, covering completely.
2. Place fillets on baking sheet and bake at 450° 10-15 minutes or until fish flakes easily with a fork.

Serves: 4

Per Serving: 1.25 g Fat, 197 Calories, 6 % Fat, 21 g Protein, 14 g Carbs, 351 mg Sodium, 41 mg Cholesterol

PERFECT PINK SALMON
(Quick Fix)

1 t grated orange peel
1 T EACH grapefruit juice and orange juice
½ t ginger
¼ t EACH salt (optional) and pepper
1 T hot water plus 2 T dry Butter Buds
1 lb. pink salmon, cut into 4 equal pieces
Pam no stick cooking spray

1. Combine the first 5 ingredients; pour over salmon, turning to coat. Spray a shallow pan with Pam, place salmon on pan, and drizzle sauce over each. Broil or grill 4-6 inches from heat for 8-10 minutes.

Serves: 4

Per Serving: 3.4 g Fat, 231 Calories, 13 % Fat, 30 g Protein, 4.25 g Carbs, 405 mg Sodium, 55 mg Cholesterol

SHRIMP AND FETA CHEESE

1 (10-oz.) package cooked fettucini or vermicelli, drain
¼ C EACH diced onion and zucchini
1 lb. medium-size shrimp, peeled and deveined
Olive oil flavored Pam no stick cooking spray
⅓ C hot water plus 2 packages Butter Buds
Pinch crushed red pepper flakes
2 oz. feta cheese
4 oz. Truly Lite Fat Free ricotta cheese, crumbled
1 medium can Italian tomatoes, cut into chunks, undrained
½ t EACH garlic salt, white pepper, basil, and parsley
¼ C Blush wine

1. In a large skillet coated with Pam, sauté onions, zucchini, shrimp, and red pepper in 3 T Butter Buds liquid 2 minutes. Shrimp will be slightly pink. Remove shrimp and vegetables to medium bowl; gently fold in all cheese.
2. In same skillet, place remaining Butter Buds liquid; add remaining ingredients, except pasta, and simmer over low heat 10 minutes.
3. Spray an oblong casserole with Pam; place shrimp mixture in dish. Pour tomato mixture over shrimp and bake uncovered at 375° for 15 minutes. To serve, spoon equal amounts of cooked pasta on each plate; top with shrimp mixture.

Serves: 6

Per Serving: 3.16 g Fat, 210 Calories, 13 % Fat, 21 g Protein, 20.8 g Carb, 463 mg Sodium, 150 mg Cholesterol

FLOUNDER ALMONDINE
(Quick Fix)

1 lb. flounder fillets, or other fish fillets
2 t EACH Butter Buds liquid and lemon juice
⅛ t almond flavoring
½ C "Mock Sour Cream"✔ or Kraft Free mayonnaise
Salt (optional) and pepper to taste
½ C crushed Nabisco Garden Crisps crackers
3 T Butter Buds liquid
1 T slivered almonds, (optional)
Pam no stick cooking spray

1. Place fish fillets in a medium casserole dish that has been sprayed with Pam. Mix the next 4 ingredients and spread over fish.
2. Mix the crushed crackers with the 3 T Butter Buds liquid and spoon on top of fish, pressing crumbs into fish. Sprinkle with almonds if desired.
3. Bake at 400° oven for about 12-15 minutes or until fish flakes easily with a fork.

Serves: 4

Per Serving: 2.2 g Fat, 166 Calories, 12 % Fat, 20 g Protein, 7 g Carbs, 48 mg Sodium, 41 mg Cholesterol

CITRUS BAKED HALIBUT
(Easy Prep)

4 (4-oz.) halibut steaks or any lean fish
¼ C minced fresh onion
1 T dry Butter Buds
½ t garlic powder
1 T fresh cilantro
Salt (optional) and pepper to taste
¼ C orange juice plus 1 t EACH lemon and lime juice

1. Pat fish dry with a paper towel. Coat a baking dish with Pam; place fish steaks in dish. Mix together the onion with remaining ingredients except the juices. Place onion mixture in microwave; heat and stir until onion is crisp-tender.
2. Spoon onion mixture evenly over fish; slowly pour juice mixture over fish. Cover and bake at 425° for about 15-18 minutes or until fish flakes easily with a fork.

Serves: 4

Per Serving: 1 g Fat, 148 Calories, 6 % Fat, 20 g Protein, 4.75 g Carbs, 240 mg Sodium, 41 mg Cholesterol

AUNT MAGGIE'S SHRIMP CASSEROLE
(A family favorite)

2½ lbs. shrimp
1 T lemon juice
1 package dry Butter Buds
2 C cooked rice
½ C cooking sherry
⅛ t almond extract
3 T Butter Buds liquid
¼ C EACH minced green pepper and onion
1 (10-oz.) can tomato soup
1 C evaporated skim milk
1 t salt (optional)
⅛ t EACH white pepper and mace
Dash cayenne pepper
2 T slivered almonds (optional)
Pam no stick cooking spray

1. Bring water to boil in a large saucepan; place shrimp in water and return to a boil. Boil shrimp for 5 minutes. When cooked, remove from heat and let stand until cool. Preheat oven to 350°.
2. Sauté green pepper and onion in Butter Buds liquid until crisp tender. Stir in sherry, almond extract, salt, pepper, mace, and tomato soup. Set aside.
3. Drain cooled shrimp; place in a 2 quart casserole that has been sprayed with Pam. Sprinkle with the lemon juice, dry Butter Buds, and cooked rice. Pour green pepper/onion mixture over shrimp mixture and toss. Pour evaporated milk over the top and bake for 1 hour at 350°.

Serves: 10

Per Serving: 1.7 g Fat, 220 Calories,
7 % Fat, 22.1 g Protein, 17.6 g Carbs,
30 mg Sodium, 191 mg Cholesterol

FISH FILLETS ACAPULCO
(Quick Fix)

1 can Rotel tomatoes and green chiles
1 can Weight Watcher's cream of mushroom soup
1½ lb. scrod or haddock fillets.

1. Stir together the first 2 ingredients; spoon half of mixture over fillets. Bake at 350° for 20 minutes or until flaky. Serve with rice. Top rice and fish with remaining soup mixture.

Serves: 8

Per Serving: 0.86 Fat, 94 Calories,
8 % Fat, 16.7 Protein, 4 Carb
358 mg Sodium, 48.8 Cholesterol

LITE FLOUNDER FILLETS
(Quick Fix)

½ C Kraft Free mayonnaise
¼ C minced fresh onion
1 T lemon juice
¼ t dill
Dash red pepper
2 egg whites stiffly beaten, not dry
¼ t EACH salt (optional) and pepper
4 (4-oz.) flounder fillets
Pam no stick cooking spray

1. Combine the 1st 5 ingredients; set aside. Beat egg whites and fold into the 1st mixture. Set aside.
2. Coat a shallow pan with Pam. Pat fillets dry with a paper towel and arrange on baking sheet. Spray fillets with Pam and sprinkle with salt and pepper. Broil fish about 3 inches from heat for about 6-8 minutes or until almost done. Spread sauce evenly over each fillet and broil about 2-3 more minutes or until brown and puffy. Serve immediately.

Serves: 4

Per Serving: 1 g Fat, 139 Calories, 6 % Fat, 21.5 g Protein, 1.8 g Carbs, 117 mg Sodium, 41 mg Cholesterol

QUICK FLOUNDER PARMESAN

1 lb. flounder fillets or other fish
½ of a (26-oz.)jar Healthy Choice spaghetti sauce with mushrooms
1 C (4 oz.) shredded Healthy Choice Fat Free mozzarella cheese
2 t Parmesan cheese
Olive oil flavored Pam no stick cooking spray

1. Spray an oblong baking dish with Pam. Place fillets in dish and spoon sauce over each. Bake at 375° for about 15 minutes or until fish flakes easily with a fork. Top with cheeses and bake an additional 5 minutes or until cheese is melted.

Serves: 4

Per Serving: 1.2 g Fat, 200 Calories, 5 % Fat, 30.7 g Protein, 7.3 g Carbs, 364 mg Sodium, 63 mg Cholesterol

SIMPLE SCALLOPS
(Quick Fix)

1 lb. bay or sea scallops
½ C flour
¼ t EACH dried basil and salt (optional)
¼ C Egg Beaters plus 1 egg white
1 T plus 1 t skim milk or 1% Buttermilk
1 T Kraft Free mayonnaise
1 C "Basic Bread Crumbs"✔, prepared
3 T lemon juice
Pam no stick cooking spray
3 T Butter Buds liquid

1. Dry scallops between paper towels. Mix the flour together with the salt and basil. Mix the Egg Beaters with the egg white, milk, and mayonnaise.
2. Coat each scallop evenly with flour mixture; shake off any excess. Dip scallops in egg mixture, then in bread crumbs, coating well. Set aside to dry for about 10-15 minutes.
3. Coat a large nonstick skillet or broiler pan with Pam. Place scallops in heated skillet and sauté for 5-8 minutes or until done. Add liquid Butter Buds if needed. Cook the same amount of time in broiler at 400°, turning frequently. Sprinkle lemon juice over all, stir once, and remove from heat.

Serves: 4

Per Serving: 0.97 g Fat, 191 Calories, 4 % Fat, 22.7 g Protein, 15.6 g Carbs, 114 mg Sodium, 0.02 mg Cholesterol

PASTA, BEAN, COMBINATION & OTHER MAIN DISHES

CONFETTI SPAGHETTI

8 oz. spaghetti, cook 7 minutes, drain; rinse with cold water
1 EACH medium yellow and zucchini squash
1 large carrot
1 small onion
½ C "Defatted Chicken Broth"✔
1 package dry Butter Buds
2 cloves garlic, minced
1 T parsley
½ t basil
½-1 package Equal
¼ C (1 oz.) Parmesan cheese

1. Peel yellow squash, carrot and onion. Julienne these vegetables and zucchini to resemble spaghetti.
2. Heat 2 T broth in skillet. Add garlic and carrot; sauté 5 minutes. Add remaining vegetables and spaghetti. Stir in Butter Buds, and spices; cook 5 minutes. Stir in Equal. Sprinkle with cheese and serve.

Serves: 4

Variation: For a tomato taste - add ¾ C stewed tomatoes. For a creamier dish - add ½ C nonfat cottage cheese

Per Serving: 2.3 g Fat, 148 Calories, 14 % Fat, 6.7 g Protein, 25 g Carb, 224 mg Sodium, 7.5 mg Cholesterol

EASY BRUNCH CASSEROLE

8 slices Wonder Lite Fat Free reduced calorie bread
1¼ C Egg Beaters
¾ C EACH skim milk and evaporated skim milk
4 slices Healthy Choice Fat Free cheese slices
6 oz. Healthy Choice cooked ham, sliced or cubed
½ C chopped green pepper
¼ C minced onion
½ C Healthy Choice Fat Free Cheddar cheese, grated
Salt (optional) and pepper to taste

1. Coat a square baking dish with Pam. Line the bottom of the pan with 4 pieces of bread, top with 4 cheese slices, and sprinkle with half of the ham.
2. Mix Egg Beaters with milks, green pepper, onion, and seasoning and pour half of the mixture over ham. Lay remaining bread slices over Egg Beaters, sprinkle with grated cheese, remaining ham and remaining egg mixture. Bake at 325° for about 40-50 minutes or until set. Let stand about 10 minutes before serving.

Serves: 6

Per Serving: 2.6 g Fat, 236 Calories, 10 % Fat, 25 g Protein, 22.6 g Carbs, 771 mg Sodium, 24.5 mg Cholesterol

ROSS'S CHICKEN OR FAJITAS ON THE GRILL
(Easy Prep)

4 (4-oz.) boneless skinless chicken breasts
½ C Butter Buds liquid
2 t Worcestershire sauce, divided
4 t "Ross's Special Seasoning"✔, divided

1. 1 hour before grilling dip each chicken breast in Butter Buds liquid. Sprinkle one side of each chicken breast with ½ t "Ross's Special Seasoning"✔ and place seasoned side down on a plate. Pour ½ t Worcestershire on top of each chicken piece, and sprinkle each with ½ t of remaining seasoning. Marinate 1 hour. If marinating longer, place chicken in refrigerator.
2. Grill chicken slowly over medium/hot coals, turning frequently to prevent burning, until chicken is tender but not overcooked.

For Fajitas: Slice chicken into strips after cooking and serve with flour tortillas, grilled onions, tomatoes, lettuce, non-fat cheese, "Great Guacamole"✔, "Non-fat Yogurt Cheese"✔, picanté sauce, etc. toppings.

Serves: 4 (Plain chicken breast)

1 Chicken fajita = 1 oz. cooked chicken breast, and 1 (7-inch) flour tortilla = 3 Fat g, 120 Calories

Per Serving: 3.25 g Fat, 171 Calories,
17 % Fat, 28 g Protein, 1 g Carbs,
145 mg Sodium, 73 mg Cholesterol

BEEF FAJITAS
(Easy Prep)

1 lb. top round steak
½ C Butter Buds liquid
2 t Worcestershire sauce
4 t "Ross's Special Seasoning"✔

1. Pound meat with mallet to tenderize. Prepare meat according to directions in "Ross's Chicken or Fajitas on the Grill"✔ and cook as directed.

Serves: 4 (3 oz. each, cooked)
1 Fajita = 1.5 oz. beef and 1 (7-inch) flour tortilla

Per Serving: 3.5 g Fat, 220 Calories, 14 % Fat, 31 g Protein, 1 g Carbs, 155 mg Sodium, 91 mg Cholesterol

HAM AND ASPARAGUS ROLL-UPS WITH RICE

8 oz. Healthy Choice Fat Free pasteurized process cheese spread
4 T Butter Buds
4 T flour
1 t salt (optional)
⅛ t pepper
¼-½ C skim milk
Paprika
1 (10-oz.) package frozen asparagus, cooked
8 (1-oz.) slices Healthy Choice ham
2 C cooked rice
Season to taste

1. To make cheese sauce, melt the cheese spread in microwave, stirring frequently. Heat Butter Buds in pan, blend in the flour and seasoning. Remove from heat and slowly stir in the cheese spread. Return to the heat and cook until the sauce begins to thicken, stirring constantly. Add skim milk if needed for desired consistency.
2. To make the rolls, roll a thin slice of ham around 2 or 3 stalks of cooked asparagus; fasten with a wooden pick.
3. Put cooked rice in a shallow baking dish coated with Pam. Place ham and asparagus rolls on top of rice. Pour the cheese sauce over each roll. Sprinkle with a little paprika.
4. Bake 12-15 minutes at 400° until heated through.

Serves: 4 (2 rolls each serving) plus ½ C rice each

Per Serving: 0.12 g Fat, 315 Calories, 6 % Fat, 27 g Protein, 38 g Carb, 1581 mg Sodium, 40 mg Cholesterol

HIS AND HERS GRILLED KABOBS

(Easy Prep but, do ahead)

½ lb. EACH top round steak and boneless skinless chicken breast
¼ C reduced sodium soy sauce
¼ C 7-Up
2 T EACH lemon juice and Butter Buds liquid
¼ t garlic powder
½ t pepper
Pam no stick cooking spray

1. Trim any fat from meat and cut into 1-inch cubes. Place in a shallow non-metal baking dish. Combine remaining ingredients, mix well, and pour over meat. Cover and marinate 2-4 hours, stirring occasionally. (The longer you marinate the better.)
2. Remove meat from marinade; reserve marinade. Thread chicken and beef on different skewers and brush with marinade. (Add vegetables to skewers if desired.) Coat grill with Pam. Grill meat over medium hot coals for about 12-15 minutes or to desired doneness. Turn and baste when necessary, but do not overcook.

Makes: 2 (4-oz.) beef servings and 2 (4-oz.) chicken servings

Per Serving: 2.5 g Fat, 207 Calories,
3 % Fat, 31.5 g Protein, 0.8 g Carbs,
90 mg Sodium, 88 mg Cholesterol

TACO PUFF PIE

(An Easy Prep with many variations and very pretty to serve. It's a sure winner with everyone!)

1 box Pillsbury hot roll mix
1-1½ C thick and chunky picanté sauce
¾ C Old El Paso vegetarian refried beans
¾ C (3 oz.) EACH Healthy Choice Fat Free Cheddar and mozzarella cheese
½ lb. (about 1¼ C) Healthy Choice ground beef cooked, rinsed, and drained
Butter Flavor Pam no stick cooking spray
Chili powder

1. Prepare crust according to pizza recipe for 1 thick crust following directions on box and omitting oil. After letting the dough rise for 15 minutes as directed on the box, uncover the dough and spray lightly with Pam. With your fingers, start in the center of pan and gently press dough out toward the rim of the pan making a dough border all the way around.
2. Spread picanté sauce over crust to about 1 inch from the rim. Spread beans evenly over sauce; sprinkle cheese over beans and top with cooked beef. Gently stretch and pull the dough border from the edge of the pan into the center of the pan, bringing all sides together in the middle. Press dough together to seal and brush lightly with a little water. Sprinkle a generous amount of chili powder completely over pie. Place in 425° oven and bake for about 15-25 minutes or until golden brown.

Note: See dessert "Time Savers" section for a sweet version of puff pie.
Serves: 8

Per Serving: 1.1 g Fat, 272 Calories, 4 % Fat, 18.2 g Protein, 44.6 g Carbs, 533 mg Sodium, 17.5 mg Cholesterol

PIZZA PUFF PIE

1 box Pillsbury Hot Roll Mix
1 C Healthy Choice spaghetti sauce
¼ C EACH chopped green pepper and mushrooms
1 C (4 oz.) Healthy Choice Fat Free mozzarella cheese
½ lb. Healthy Choice cooked ground beef

1. Prepare crust as directed for Taco Puff Pie; For filling, combine remaining ingredients; pour into crust. Sprinkle paprika over crust and bake at 425° for 15-25 minutes.

Serves: 8

Per Serving: 1.1 g Fat, 259 Calories, 4 % Fat, 16.1 g Protein, 44 g Carbs, 406 mg Sodium, 65 mg Cholesterol

SEAFOOD PUFF PIE

1 box Pillsbury Hot Roll Mix
½ recipe "Seafood and Chicken Sauce,"✔ using only seafood

Prepare crust as directed for Taco Puff Pie. Add filling; bake at 425° for 15-25 minutes.

Serves: 8

Per Serving: 0.8 g Fat, 259 Calories, 3 % Fat, 13.6 g Protein, 45.7 g Carbs, 431 mg Sodium, 18 mg Cholesterol

BAR-B-QUE PUFF PIE

1 box Pillsbury Hot Roll Mix
1¼ C "Lite and Easy Bar-B-Que Sauce,"✔ divided
½ C EACH cooked pinto beans and diced onion
1 lb. cooked boneless, skinless chicken breast, cubed

1. Prepare crust as directed for Taco Puff Pie. Combine remaining ingredients, using 1 C bar-b-que sauce; pour into crust. Drizzle ¼ C bar-b-que sauce over top before folding crust over. Bake at 425° for 15-25 minutes.

Serves: 8

Per Serving: 1.5 g Fat, 299 Calories, 4 % Fat, 21 g Protein, 45.25 g Carbs, 431 mg Sodium, 36 mg Cholesterol

CHICKEN PUFF PIE

1 box Pillsbury Hot Roll Mix
1 C "Lite White Sauce"✔
½ C cooked, cubed potatoes
½ C EACH diced mushrooms and carrots
¼ C green peas
½ lb. cooked boneless, skinless chicken breast, cubed or ground.

1. Prepare crust as directed for Taco Puff Pie. For filling, combine remaining ingredients; pour into crust. Bake at 425° for 15-25 minutes.

Serves: 8

Per Serving: 0.8 g Fat, 259 Calories, 3 % Fat, 13.6 g Protein, 45.7 g Carbs, 431 mg Sodium, 18 mg Cholesterol

VEGETARIAN PUFF PIE

1 box Pillsbury Hot Roll Mix
1 C "Lite White Sauce"✔
¼ C EACH shredded zucchini and carrots
¼ C EACH diced broccoli, mushrooms and tomatoes
½ C cooked pinto beans
1 C Healthy Choice Fat Free mozzarella cheese

1. Prepare crust as directed for "Taco Puff Pie"✔ For filling, combine remaining ingredients; pour into crust. Bake at 425° for 15-25 minutes.

Serves: 8

Per Serving: 0 g Fat, 222 Calories, 0 % Fat, 8.5 g Protein, 45.25 g Carbs, 438 mg Sodium, 0.6 mg Cholesterol

FATHER'S SUNDAY NIGHT SUPPER
(Quick Fix)

1 (10-oz.) can tomato soup
1 C (4 oz.) grated Healthy Choice Fat Free mozzarella cheese
¼ C Egg Beaters
Scant ½ t Worcestershire sauce (optional)
4 slices nonfat reduced calorie bread, toasted

1. Combine soup and cheese in a microwave safe dish; cook on high about 3-5 minutes, stirring frequently until cheese is melted. Drizzle in Egg Beaters and Worcestershire; mix well. Season to taste and serve over toasted bread.

Serves: 4

Per Serving: 0.67 g Fat, 148 [illegible]
4 % Fat, 11.2 g Protein, [illegible]
135 mg Sodium, 5 mg [illegible]

QUICK THICK PIZZA CRUST
(Easy Prep)

1 package Butter Buds
1 C wheat flour
2 C white flour
1 T baking powder
12 oz. lite beer at room temperature (see note)
¼ t garlic powder
½ t salt (optional)
Pam no stick cooking spray
"Pizza Toppers"✔

1. Mix all ingredients and spread on a large sprayed pizza pan or deep cookie sheet.
2. Dust hands with flour; dough will be sticky.
3. Bake crust for about 10 minutes at 425°.
4. Top with your favorite "Pizza Toppers"✔ and bake for about 15-20 minutes more.

Serves: 12 (without toppings - see Pizza Toppers)

Note: To get beer to room temperature in a hurry, microwave about 30 seconds, stir and microwave again if necessary.

Per Serving: 0.2 g Fat, 136 Calories, 1 % Fat, 3.4 g Protein, 40 g Carb, 140 mg Sodium, 0 mg Cholesterol

PIZZA, PASTA, AND BAKED POTATO TOPPERS

This is a list of several toppers. No nutritional analysis is given simply because it depends on the quantity and variety of ingredients used; however, they are all low fat choices. Mix and match to create your favorite combinations.

1. Chopped or sliced green and red bell peppers, onions, drained artichoke hearts, broccoli, tomatoes, zucchini water chestnuts, mushrooms, drained or undrained canned vegetables.
2. Cooked, drained, and rinsed Healthy Choice ground beef, cooked diced chicken breast, Healthy Choice ham, Hormel Canadian Bacon, cooked shrimp, scallops, or lean fish.
3. Healthy Choice Fat Free cheddar, mozzarella, and cheese singles, Truly Lite fat free ricotta cheese, nonfat cottage cheese, 2 - 4 t Parmesan cheese (too much can add up to too many calories and fat grams.)
4. See index for "Taco Puff Pie"✔. These variations make great toppers.
5. Check index for sauces and foods like "Mock Sour Cream"*, "Nonfat Yogurt Cheese"*, "Quick Cheese Sauce"*, "Great Guacamole"*, etc; these make great finishing touches.
6. All flavors liquid or dry Butter Buds, Bacon flavor Molly McButter, 2 - 3 t Bac-Os imitation bacon bits, fat free salad dressings or mayonnaise.
7. Healthy Choice soups or other low-fat soups, "Defatted Chicken or Beef Broth"✔, cooked beans, picanté sauce, Healthy Choice spaghetti sauce, Health Valley spicy vegetable chili.
8. Frozen lowfat vegetable medleys - see grocery section.

POPEYE'S MEATLOAF

1½ lb. Healthy Choice ground beef
½ lb. ground turkey breast
1 small onion, finely chopped
½ C coarsely shredded carrot
⅓ C instant mashed potatoes flakes
⅓ C "Non-fat Yogurt Cheese"✔
¼ t nutmeg
½ t garlic salt (optional)
2 egg whites
½ (10-oz.) package frozen spinach, thawed and well drained
¼ t cumin
½ C (2 oz.) grated Healthy Choice Fat Free mozzarella cheese
2 T skim milk
1 can tomato soup
Pam no stick cooking spray

1. Combine the first 9 ingredients in a large bowl. Coat a loaf pan with Pam; pour ½ of meat mixture in bottom of pan. With a spoon, make a small indentation in the center of the meat mixture for filling; leave a 2" space at ends.
2. Combine the spinach, cumin, cheese, and milk; spoon into indentation and top with remaining meat mixture.
3. Bake at 350° for 45 minutes to 1 hour. Remove loaf, spoon soup over top, and bake 5-10 more minutes.

Serves: 10

Per Serving: 3 g Fat, 150 Calories, 18 % Fat, 21 g Protein, 9.3 g Carb, 437 mg Sodium, 39 mg Cholesterol

VEGI-CHEESE ENCHILADAS

16 corn tortillas
½ C minced fresh onion
1 C Old El Paso vegetarian refried beans, divided
1 C diced or shredded cooked potato
1 C (4 oz.) grated Healthy Choice Fat Free Cheddar cheese
4 slices Healthy Choice Fat Free cheese slices
3-3½ C prepared "Enchilada Salsa"✔
½ C (2 oz.) grated Healthy Choice Fat Free Cheddar cheese
Pam no stick cooking spray

1. Warm tortillas, about 3 at a time, between two paper towels in microwave for 20-30 seconds. Coat a large oblong baking dish with Pam. Slice each of the 4 cheese slices into quarters.
2. For each warm tortilla, spread 1 T refried beans down the center; top with 1 T each potato and Cheddar cheese, ½ T minced onion, and ¼ of a cheese slice. Roll up and place seam-side down in sprayed casserole.
3. Top with "Enchilada Salsa"✔, sprinkle with ½ C fat free Cheddar cheese, and bake at 350° for 12-15 minutes or until heated through.

Serves: 16

Per Serving: 1.08 g Fat, 120 Calories, 8 % Fat, 8 g Protein, 19 g Carbs, 240 mg Sodium, 2.9 mg Cholesterol

MEAT OR CHICKEN ENCHILADAS

½ lb. Healthy Choice ground beef, cooked rinsed and drained OR ½ lb. ground cooked chicken breast
1 recipe "Vegi-Cheese Enchiladas"✔

1. Prepare tortillas as in "Vegi-Cheese Enchiladas"✔. Substitute 1 heaping T ground beef or ground chicken for potatoes. Roll and bake as directed.

Serves: 16

1 Beef Enchilada: 1.58 g Fat, 136 Calories, 10 % Fat, 10.6 g Protein, 19.25 g Carbs, 270 mg Sodium, 9.7 mg Cholesterol

1 Chicken Enchilada: 1.29 g Fat, 133 Calories, 9 % Fat, 13.8 g Protein, 19 g Carbs, 265 mg Sodium, 8.9 mg Cholesterol

VERSATILE TEX-MEX TACOS

(This Easy Prep can be made with beans, chicken breast, Healthy Choice ground beef and/or vegetables - or be creative and use a combination of these)

Corn tortillas
1 recipe "Vegetarian Taco Filling,"✔ "Chicken Taco Filling,"✔ or "Beef Taco Filling"✔
Butter flavor Pam no stick cooking spray

Crisp Taco Shells or Chalupa Shells:

1. Warm corn tortillas between two paper towels in microwave about 3 at a time, to soften, for about 20 seconds.
2. Coat both sides of warm tortillas with Pam. Lay tortillas over the sides of a sprayed casserole dish, forming each tortilla into the shape of a taco shell, or lay warm tortillas in bottom of baking dish, fold gently in half, and place an oblong piece of foil inside shell to hold shell apart. For Chalupas, lay tortillas flat on a cookie sheet. Bake in a 350°-375° oven for 25-30 minutes or until crisp but not burned. Remove, fill with your choice of taco filling, and serve immediately.

Soft Taco Shells:

1. Warm corn tortillas as in Step #1 of "Crisp Taco Shells. Fill and serve immediately.

CHICKEN TACO FILLING

Same as "Vegetarian Taco Filling;"✔ replace beans with 2 T shredded boneless, skinless cooked chicken breast.

1. Spread chicken in or on taco shells; Add remaining ingredients and serve.

Makes: 1 taco including shell

Per Serving: 1.5 g Fat, 192 Calories, 7 % Fat, 8.8 g Protein, 15 g Carbs, 460 mg Sodium, 2.3 mg Cholesterol

BEEF TACO FILLING

Same as "Vegetarian Taco Filling;"✔ replace beans with 2 T cooked Healthy Choice ground beef.

1. Spread beef in or on taco shells; Add remaining ingredients and serve.

Makes: 1 taco including shell

Per Serving: 2 g Fat, 192 Calories, 9 % Fat, 9.8 g Protein, 15 g Carbs, 460 mg Sodium, 8.2 mg Cholesterol

VEGETARIAN TACO FILLING
(Quick Fix)

2 T vegetarian refried beans (Old El Paso) or 2 T pinto beans
1-2 T chunky style picanté sauce
1 T chopped tomatoes
2 T grated Healthy Choice Fat Free Cheddar cheese or cheese singles
Shredded lettuce
1 T "Great Guacamole"✔ prepared
1 t plain nonfat yogurt (optional)

1. Spread beans in or on taco shells; top with picanté sauce, cheese, lettuce, guacamole, and yogurt, if desired. Top each with 2 T guacamole, 1 t nonfat yogurt and shredded lettuce.

Makes: 1 taco including shell

Per Serving: 1.1 g Fat, 184 Calories, 5 % Fat, 8.8 g Protein, 27.2 g Carbs, 275 mg Sodium, 2.6 mg Cholesterol

PASTA-BEAN CASSEROLE
(Easy Prep)

1 medium fresh tomato, chopped
3½ C (8 oz.) "Pasta Perfect" Rotini with vegetables (4-lb. bag in freezer section at Sam's Wholesale)
¼ C Butter Buds liquid
1-2 T cornstarch
1 T minced onion
1 C EACH skim milk and evaporated skim milk
4 oz. Healthy Choice Fat Free cheese singles
½ C (2 oz.) EACH grated Healthy Choice Fat Free mozzarella cheese and Truly Lite Fat Free ricotta cheese
1 small can chopped green chiles

1. Preheat oven to 350° and coat a 2-quart casserole with Pam. Thaw pasta mix according to quick directions.
2. In a large skillet, heat Butter Buds liquid; sprinkle with cornstarch, stirring constantly. Stir in milk; heat until mixture boils and thickens. Add shredded cheeses and minced onion.
3. When cheese is melted, add drained pasta mixture and remaining ingredients. Pour into casserole dish, cover, and bake 20 minutes. Uncover and bake another 5-10 minutes. Add salt (optional) and pepper to taste.

Serves: 4

Per Serving: 1.5 g Fat, 326 Calories, 4 % Fat, 20.7 g Protein, 55 g Carb, 327 mg Sodium, 6.5 mg Cholesterol

ITALIAN VEGETABLE LASAGNA

1 lb. uncooked lasagna noodles
Olive oil flavored Pam no stick cooking spray
2 C grated or thin-sliced mixed vegetables (zucchini, carrots, broccoli, etc.)
1 medium onion, diced
1 (26-oz.) jar Healthy Choice spaghetti sauce with mushrooms
1 C water
¼ t EACH mace, ground pepper and dill
4 T Butter Buds liquid
3 T all-purpose flour
3 C skim milk plus 2 chicken bouillon cubes
1 t garlic salt
Pinch nutmeg
¼ C Truly Lite Fat Free ricotta cheese plus 1 T grated Parmesan cheese
3 C (12 oz.) grated Healthy Choice mozzarella cheese

1. Boil lasagna noodles about 4 minutes. Drain; lay on wax paper and spray noodles lightly with Pam.
2. Spray a large saucepan with Pam. Sauté onion about 2 minutes, adding a little water if necessary. Add vegetables, spaghetti sauce, water, mace, and pepper. Simmer 5 minutes. Set aside.
3. Make cheese sauce by heating Butter Buds liquid in a medium saucepan. Whisk in flour and cook about 2 minutes; do not brown. Slowly whisk in milk, bouillon and spices; bring to a boil. Reduce heat and simmer 5 minutes or until thick, stirring frequently. Remove from heat; stir in ricotta and Parmesan cheeses. (If sauce is too thin, mix 1 T each flour and cornstarch in a cup; add enough water to make a paste. Stir into boiling sauce; cook until thick.)
4. Coat a 13 X 9-inch casserole dish with Pam. Evenly pour about ¼ C of vegetable sauce into pan. Place a layer of noodles on top; dot noodles with a little cheese sauce and sprinkle a little mozzarella on top. Repeat layers until all ingredients are used up.
5. Cover dish with a sheet of foil that has been coated with Pam. Place dish on a cookie sheet and bake in 375° oven for about one hour. Freezes well.

Serves: 8

Per Serving: 0.97 g Fat, 281 Calories, 3 % Fat, 23.3 g Protein, 41 g Carb, 1123 mg Sodium, 10.8 mg Cholesterol

VEGGIE BURGER

- **¼ C bulgur plus 1 C boiling water, set aside 30 minutes**
- **1 small onion, minced**
- **3 cloves garlic, minced**
- **10 sprigs parsley, minced**
- **½ C Egg Beaters**
- **3 C cooked garbanzo beans**
- **2 T nonfat plain yogurt**
- **1 t EACH salt (optional) and cumin**
- **½ t EACH pepper and cayenne pepper**
- **½ C "Basic Bread Crumbs"✔**

1. Drain bulgur. Blend in food processor with remaining ingredients except bread crumbs. Puree to a smooth paste.
2. Shape ½ C mixture into patties. Coat with bread crumbs and chill about 1 hour.
3. To grill, spray grill with Pam. Cook over medium hot coals about 3-4 minutes on each side. To cook in skillet, coat pan with Pam. Sauté patties over medium high heat the same amount of time. Serve on low-fat hamburger buns.

Serves: 8

Per Serving: 0 g Fat, 103 Calories, 0 % Fat, 6.4 g Protein, 18 g Carb, 375 mg Sodium, 0 mg Cholesterol

LITE QUICHE

(An Easy Prep whether you make it with or without meat)

1 recipe "Basic Pie Crust"✔, unbaked
4 oz. Healthy Choice ham, shredded (see note)
2 T EACH chopped onion and green pepper
1 (4-oz.) can sliced mushrooms, drained
2 C (8 oz.) shredded Healthy Choice Fat Free mozzarella cheese
1 C EACH evaporated skim milk and skim milk
1¼ C Egg Beaters
¼ t dry mustard
2 T Bacon flavored Molly McButter

1. Prepare pastry and place in a 9-inch pie plate. Follow crust instructions for filled crust.
2. Sprinkle ham, vegetables and cheese in bottom of pie crust. Beat remaining ingredients together and pour on top of cheese. Set aside 10 minutes. Preheat oven to 350°.
3. Bake for 40-45 minutes or until set. Remove from oven; set aside for 10 minutes and serve.

Serves: 6

Note: For a meatless quiche, substitute 1 C chopped or shredded vegetables for ham. May also substitute chicken, seafood, or Healthy Choice ground beef for ham.

Per Serving: 0.66 g Fat, 113 Calories, 6 % Fat, 10.8 g Protein, 13.1 g Carbs, 341 mg Sodium, 20 mg Cholesterol

LAZY DAY CHILI SURPRISE

(Quick Fix and also makes a great pasta or baked potato topping)

1 (15-oz.) can pinto beans without oil
1 (15-oz.) can Health Valley Fat Free Spicy Vegetarian Chili with beans
½ of (10-oz.) can diced Rotel tomatoes and green chiles
1 (8-oz.) can tomatoes
2 C (8 oz.) grated Healthy Choice Fat Free Cheddar cheese
1 C evaporated skim milk
1 bag Guiltless Gourmet No Oil baked tortilla chips
Jalapeño peppers (optional)

1. Combine 1st 5 ingredients in medium saucepan; simmer 15-20 minutes. Stir in evaporated milk and heat through.
2. Place ½ serving (½ oz. or about 12 chips) tortilla chips on each serving plate. Pour 1 C of chili mixture on top of chips. Serve with or without jalapeño peppers.

Serves: 6

Per Serving: 0.7 g Fat, 277 Calories, 2 % Fat, 24.8 g Protein, 42.4 g Carbs, 994 mg Sodium, 5 mg Cholesterol

SUZANNE'S BREAKFAST TORTILLAS

(Quick Fix)

1 can Rotel chopped tomatoes and green chiles, drained
1¼ C Egg Beaters plus 3 egg whites, slightly beaten
4.5 oz. Healthy Choice Fat Free cheese singles, diced
Salt (optional) and pepper to taste
8 flour tortillas, softened
Pam no stick cooking spray

1. Heat a large skillet sprayed with Pam. Add all ingredients except tortillas. Stir until smooth and cooked through.
2. Spoon equal amounts into tortillas, roll-up, and serve (corn tortillas may be used).

Serves: 8

Per Serving: 1 g Fat, 134 Calories, 7 % Fat, 9.8 g Protein, 13.5 g Carb, 375 mg Sodium, 3.5 mg Cholesterol

CHEESY LAYERED PASTA
(Easy Prep)

1½ C Healthy Choice spaghetti sauce, divided
½ of a 12 oz. package garden pasta spirals, cooked
2 C dry spaghetti or vermicelli noodles, cooked
1 C EACH grated zucchini and carrot
¼ C evaporated skim milk
¼ t garlic powder
½ t EACH basil and oregano
½ t garlic salt (optional)
½ (10-oz.) can stewed tomatoes
½ package dry Butter Buds
1 (15-oz.) carton nonfat ricotta cheese
1 (6-oz.) package Healthy Choice Fat Free mozzarella cheese
4 t Parmesan cheese
Pam no stick cooking spray

1. Spread ½ C spaghetti sauce in bottom of an oblong casserole that has been sprayed with Pam. Combine the cooked pasta; layer ½ the pasta on top of the sauce. Sprinkle the vegetables on top of the pasta.
2. Process the evaporated milk with the next 7 ingredients and spread ½ of this mixture over vegetables. Top with remaining pasta and cheese sauce.
3. Pour remaining 1 C spaghetti sauce over entire casserole, sprinkle with Parmesan cheese and bake covered at 350° for about 15-20 minutes or until heated through.

Serves: 10

Per Serving: 0.73 g Fat, 192 Calories, 3 % Fat, 16.6 g Protein, 31.1 g Carbs, 50 mg Sodium, 24.2 mg Cholesterol

Notes and Extra Recipes:

Notes and Extra Recipes:

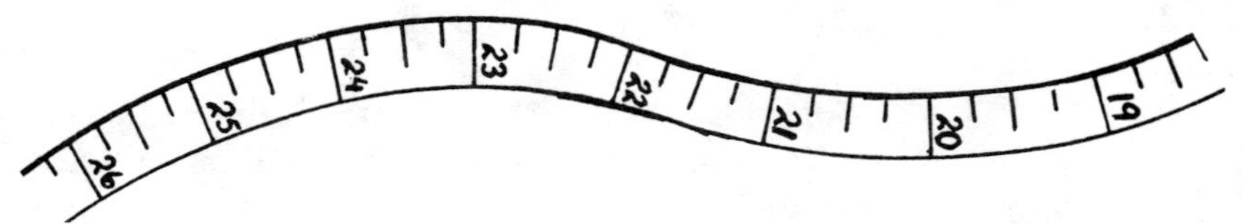

VEGETABLES & OTHER SIDE DISHES

Vegetables and side dishes are a great way to begin planning your meal. Dark green leafy, deep yellow, white, etc. vegetables such as spinach, broccoli, yellow squash, carrots, and others; and, starchy vegetables such as corn, green peas, and potatoes or any other types should be eaten every day. Allow 3-5 servings; a serving size is ½ C cooked or 1 C raw vegetables or 1 C leafy raw vegetables. Pasta, grains, cereal, rice, grits, etc. are excellent additions to a meal, however, the best way to use them is for a main dish. Allow 6-11 servings of pasta and grains per day. A serving size is ½ C cooked pasta, rice, grits or 1 oz. ready-to-eat cereal. Make sure you select plain or vegetable pasta that does not contain whole eggs; be careful not to choose filled pasta containing cheese or other fat. These pastas, whole grains, vegetables, etc. are all complex carbohydrates as are breads; most of your daily caloric intake should come from these.

Time Savers:

- Tater Tots: Mix 1½ t each Smartbeat margarine and "Defatted Chicken Broth"✔ with 1 C cooked white or brown rice; ¾ C each cooked nonfat mashed potatoes and "Basic Bread Crumbs"✔; 1 T tomato paste; and 2 T Parmesan cheese. Add more broth if needed. Form into balls; spray with butter flavor Pam. Bake 20 minutes at 350°.
- Toss cooked noodles and broccoli florets with "Defatted Chicken Broth"✔ and garlic.
- Bake at 350° - 2 cans cream corn, 1 C cooked rice, 1 small jar chopped pimientos, 2 T minced onion, ½ C chopped green pepper, and ¼ C Egg Beaters.
- Place in baking dish: 1 (14-oz.) drained can water-packed artichoke hearts and 1 (28-oz.) drained can chopped tomatoes. Sprinkle with 1 T minced onion, 2 T Butter Buds and 1 T Parmesan cheese. Bake 12 minutes at 325°.
- Cook and drain 1 package frozen chopped spinach. Heat with

⅓ C "Nonfat Yogurt Cheese,"✔ 1 t cornstarch, 1 drained small jar sliced mushrooms, and 1 T each minced onion and evaporated skim milk.

- Replace the water you use in cooking vegetables, pasta, rice and other packaged or boxed foods with defatted chicken, vegetable or beef broth.
- Cut fresh asparagus into thin diagonal slices. Coat skillet with butter flavor Pam and sauté asparagus in Butter Buds until crisp-tender adding a pinch of sugar, salt, pepper, fresh tarragon and parsley. Stir in ½-1 t white wine vinegar and 2 T Grape Nuts.
- Wash fresh spinach, remove stems. Cook on medium-high heat until wilted. Add lemon juice and bacon flavor Molly McButter.
- Toss 1 lb. fresh trimmed snow peas with Butter Buds, onion, basil, and salt. Microwave 3-6 minutes until crisp-tender.
- Heat brussels sprouts in Butter Buds with 1 t ginger.
- Place 1½ lb. fresh trimmed green beans, sliced onion, 6-8 small red potatoes, and bacon flavored Molly McButter in large pan. Cover with "Defatted Chicken Broth"✔, bring to boil. Turn down, cover, and simmer 30 minutes.
- Simmer 2 C sliced onion in nonfat B-B-Q sauce for 5 minutes.
- Arrange 4 medium potatoes sliced ½" thick on sprayed foil. Drizzle with ½ C Butter Buds liquid and 2 packages dry onion soup mix. Wrap and grill over med/hot coals 45 min.-1 hour.
- Try previous recipe with other vegetables. May prepare in oven.
- Heat together 1 drained can each corn, lima beans, and pinto beans plus 1 can undrained zucchini and tomatoes. Add 2 T ketchup; season to taste.
- Spread 6 C fresh cubed vegetables on sprayed foil. Coat with a mixture of ¼ C "Defatted Beef Broth"✔ and 1 T brown sugar. Wrap and grill over medium/hot coals 15 minutes.
- Quick Fried Rice - Sauté ½ C each green onions with tops and frozen green peas in ¼ C "Defatted Chicken Broth"✔. Add 2 egg whites, 3 C cooked rice and 2 T low sodium soy sauce. Heat through.
- Place fat free cheese or fat free cream cheese on cooked vegetables. Heat in microwave until cheese melts.
- In a large skillet, add frozen vegetables, cooked brown rice, ½ C sliced mushrooms plus a dash of wine, and "Defatted Chicken Broth"✔ to cubed chicken breast.
- Creamy Garlic Grits: Mix 4 C hot cooked grits with 8 oz. Healthy Choice Fat Free garlic and herb cream cheese plus 4 oz. Healthy Choice Fat Free pasteurized process cheese spread Add enough Butter Buds Liquid to desired consistency.

- Sauté 1 lb. sliced okra in ½ C Butter Buds liquid over high heat until tender; season with salt (optional), pepper, and lime juice.
- Cut 1 lb. peeled eggplant into cubes. Soak in refrigerator overnight; drain well and pat dry. Cook on stove until tender. Mix 1 C "Basic Bread Crumbs"✔ with ¾ C evaporated skim milk. Set aside. Sauté ¼ C each diced onion and celery in ¼ C Butter Buds. Mix bread crumb mixture with drained eggplant, ½ C Egg Beaters, salt and pepper to taste, and ¼ t sage; add to vegetables. Pour into sprayed casserole and bake at 350° for 30 minutes; top with grated nonfat Cheddar or mozzarella cheese and bake until melted.
- Sauté 2 C each sliced mushrooms and onions in a mixture of: ¼ C Butter Buds liquid, ½ C lemon juice, and a dash of Worcestershire sauce. Season to taste.
- Cover torn fresh cabbage with water. Boil until tender; drain well. Remove to plate and mash; add salt (optional) and pepper to taste and a little sugar if desired. Kids love it like this.
- Cut acorn squash in half; place in microwave-safe dish with 2-4 T water. Sprinkle with dry Butter Buds, cinnamon, and sugar or artificial sweetener. Cook about 4-6 minutes.
- Mix about 4 C cooked vermicelli with 2 C nonfat cottage cheese, ¼ C Egg Beaters, ⅓ C "Basic Bread Crumbs"✔, and ¼ C Butter Buds liquid. Microwave until hot. Season to taste.
- Mix 1 (16-oz.) can corn with ½ carton of Healthy Choice Fat Free cream cheese, ¼ C evaporated skim milk, and 1 (4-oz.) can chopped green chiles. Season to taste; bake at 350° for 20 minutes.
- Boil 2 lbs. fresh washed and dried spinach, stems removed, in 4 quarts of water until tender. Drain well and pat dry. Puree with 1 package dry Butter Buds, 1 small cooked onion, a dash of nutmeg, and 2-3 T evaporated skim milk; set aside. Place 6 thawed sheets of phyllo dough on wax paper; brush with liquid Butter buds, sprinkle with a little Parmesan cheese and stack one on top of the other. Cut entire stack in half forming 12 squares. Spoon equal amounts of spinach puree into the center of each square and gather phyllo together at the top and in the center and twist. Place each little pouch on a sprayed cookie sheet and bake at 425° for about 5 minutes.
- Sauté green beans, minced onion, 1 t basil, sliced mushrooms, and salt (optional) and pepper in "Defatted Chicken Broth"✔.
- Skillet French Fries: Julienne potatoes with skins on. Spray a nonstick skillet with Pam and fry potatoes until brown on one side. Turn potatoes and brown other side. Cover for a few minutes until done. Season with salt (optional) and pepper to

taste. May also add chopped onion to potatoes.

Helpful Hints:

- Add 1 t ground ginger to beans when cooking to help prevent discomfort. Also try "Beano," a product found in health food stores and some drug and grocery stores. Two or 3 stalks of cut-up celery and a dash of baking soda sometimes helps also.
- Remember that calorie counts are high in beans, but there is basically no fat. Beans tend to fill you up and stay with you; they are also a good source of fiber.
- 1 C dried beans = 3 C cooked beans.
- Vegetables and side dishes also make great main dishes.
- 2 oz. dry pasta = about 1¼ C cooked.
- Many times (read the labels for hidden fats or fatty ingredients) you may use packaged vegetable entrees or side dishes found in the grocery store. Simply omit the fat the package suggests you use when cooking or use Butter Buds equivalent.
- Season fresh vegetables with lemon juice and fresh herbs and spices. Experiment!
- Vegetables cooked with the skin on have more nutrients. Instead of peeling some vegetables, use a stiff vegetable brush; scrub vegetables thus leaving the skin intact.
- Keep large bags of frozen mixed vegetables on hand. Mix and match for a nice variety. These can be used for stir-fry also.
- Serve spaghetti squash dishes in the hollowed out spaghetti squash shell. Prepare and put back in shell.
- Experiment with your pasta recipes. Use different types of pasta in different dishes. For example, in lasagna recipe, replace lasagna noodles with any pasta you have on hand. Pour all ingredients into large baking dish; stir well and bake as directed.
- Don't forget to save leftover vegetable juices, vegetables, or any other "goodies" to be used in "Holly's Favorite Recycled Soup"✔.
- They'll think you've been cooking all day - place an onion in the oven to bake for a heavenly smell.
- Freeze cooked pasta up to 2 months; place in colander under warm running water to thaw.
- About eggplant - 1 lb. eggplant = about 3 C diced. To use eggplant in recipes containing a thick base, get rid of moisture by salting sliced eggplant and stacking slices on top of each other. Place slices between two plates; place a heavy weight on top to help squeeze out moisture.

VEGETABLES & POTATOES

JUST PLAIN OL' COOKED VEGGIES #1
(Quick Fix)

Vegetables cooked in 1 C "Defatted Beef Broth"✓:
10 oz. brussels sprouts plus garlic salt and pepper; OR 1 package spinach plus cayenne pepper, nutmeg, and tabasco; OR 1 package any type greens plus pepper, garlic salt,½ t vinegar; OR 1 lb. fresh green beans plus 1 jar EACH pimientos and mushrooms; OR 1 small head cabbage plus Butter Buds and black pepper; OR 1 bunch broccoli plus garlic powder & lemon pepper

1. Choose 1 or more of vegetables and seasonings listed on left.
2. Wash and clean vegetable of choice. Slice, quarter, or cook entire vegetable until tender in broth, stirring in suggested seasonings.

Microwave Directions:

1. Wash and clean vegetable of choice. Slice, quarter or cook whole the vegetables in ½ C of broth. Place in covered microwave-safe dish, and cook on high 5-8 minutes; stir twice during cooking.

Butter Buds and onion may be added to any of the vegetables.

Serves: 4-10 depending on size of vegetable

Per Serving: 0 g Fat, 35 Calories, 0 % Fat, 2.3 g Protein, 7 g Carb, 29 mg Sodium, 0 mg Cholesterol

BEER BRUSSELS SPROUTS

2 (10-oz.) package frozen brussels sprouts
1 can lite beer
1 package Butter Buds
½ t salt (optional)

1. Bring vegetables to a boil in the beer. Cover; reduce heat and simmer until tender, about 10 minutes. Drain and toss with Butter Buds and salt.

Serves: 8

Per Serving: 0 g Fat, 48 Calories, 0 % Fat, 3.2 g Protein, 8.3 g Carb, 101 mg Sodium, 0 mg Cholesterol

JUST PLAIN OL' COOKED VEGGIES #2
(Quick Fix)

Vegetables cooked in 1 C "Defatted Chicken Broth"✔:
1 head cauliflower plus parsley and basil; OR Yellow and zucchini squash plus oregano, thyme, and basil; OR Asparagus plus a pinch of salt (optional) and fresh squeezed lemon juice; OR carrots plus lemon pepper and garlic powder; OR Corn plus Butter Buds, black pepper, red pepper and green chiles; OR Red potatoes plus parsley and Butter Buds; OR Beets plus 2 T flour mixed with ¼ C water; OR Rutabaga turnip plus Equal, Butter Buds, salt (optional) and pepper OR Onions plus Butter Buds and pepper

1. Choose 1 or more of vegetables and seasonings listed on left.
2. Wash and clean vegetable of choice. Slice, quarter or cook whole the vegetable in broth and stir in suggested seasonings. Cook until tender.

Microwave Directions:

1. Wash and clean vegetable of choice. Slice, quarter or cook whole the vegetables in ½ C of broth. Place in microwave-safe dish, cover, and cook on high 5-8 minutes; stir twice during cooking.

Butter Buds and onion may be added to any of the vegetables.

Serves: 4-10 depending on size of vegetable

Per Serving: 0 g Fat, 35 Calories, 0 % Fat, 2.3 g Protein, 7 g Carb, 29 mg Sodium, 0 mg Cholesterol

HONEY-GLAZED CARROTS
(Quick Fix)

8 medium carrots, peeled, trimmed and cut lengthwise into 2- or 3-inch strips
¼ C EACH honey, Butter Buds liquid, and Grape Nuts

1. Cook carrots just until tender. Drain. Add remaining ingredients and cook over medium heat; toss occasionally until lightly glazed.

Serves: 8

Per Serving: 0 g Fat, 62 Calories, 0 % Fat, 0.91 g Protein, 15.2 g Carb, 72 mg Sodium, 0 mg Cholesterol

CRISPY ONION RINGS

(Do ahead but worth it!)

1 C self-rising flour plus 1 T sugar
1 C white wine or lite beer
½ C EACH evaporated skim milk & water (mixed)
¼ C flour
2 large sweet onions, cut into ⅛" - ¼" slices and separated into rings
1 egg white at room temperature
Pam no stick cooking spray

1. Blend together self-rising flour, sugar, and wine. Place in refrigerator for at least 3 hours (may be left overnight). Mixture should be thick like pancake batter.
2. Thirty minutes before cooking, place onion rings in evaporated milk and water and set aside. Drain onions and pat dry; dust with flour.
3. Beat egg white until stiff; fold into batter. Dip onion rings into batter, place on a Pam-coated cookie sheet and bake in preheated 450° oven until crisp.

Serves: 4

Variation: Try same batter with different vegetables, like zucchini or mushrooms.

Per Serving: 0.5 g Fat, 224 Calories, 2 % Fat, 8 g Protein, 41.5 g Carb, 393 mg Sodium, 2.5 mg Cholesterol

EASY EGGPLANT

1 medium eggplant, peeled and diced
1 t salt (optional)
1 medium onion, sliced
1 package Butter Buds
Salt (optional) and pepper to taste

1. Cover vegetables with water; add salt and bring to boil. Simmer for about 20 minutes. Drain and toss with seasoning.

Serves: 8

Per Serving: 0 g Fat, 15 Calories, 0 % Fat, 0.43 g Protein, 3.2 g Carb, 86 mg Sodium, 0 mg Cholesterol

MASHED POTATO BAKE

4 large baking potatoes, peeled, cubed, and boiled until tender
4 oz. Healthy Choice Fat Free cream cheese, softened
¾ C EACH nonfat cottage cheese and "Nonfat Yogurt Cheese"✔
1 T cornstarch
⅛ t ground pepper
1 t salt (optional)
1 package Butter Buds
2 oz. Healthy Choice Fat Free Cheddar cheese, grated
2 t Bac-Os artificial bacon bits

1. Drain potatoes; mash in a large bowl. Add remaining ingredients, except bacon bits, mixing well.
2. Pour mixture into a sprayed casserole dish. Sprinkle with bacon bits; bake at 350° for 20 minutes or until heated.

Serves: 8

Note: Use leftovers for potato pancakes. Chill potatoes. Form into patties and "fry" in a Pam-coated skillet until brown.

Per Serving: 0.25 g Fat, 162 Calories, 1 % Fat, 16 g Protein, 22.3 g Carb, 597 mg Sodium, 12 mg Cholesterol

POTATO CROQUETTES

4 C cooked mashed potatoes plus 1 package Butter Buds
½ C Egg Beaters
3 T EACH 1% fat buttermilk and chopped onion
Salt (optional) and pepper to taste
2 oz. American Grains Exotic Pepper and Cheese flavor rice bites

1. Crush rice bites into crumbs; set aside. Combine remaining ingredients and form into 8 patties. Coat with crumbs.
2. Place patties on sprayed cookie sheet and refrigerate until firm, up to 24 hrs.
3. Coat each patty with butter-flavor Pam and bake at 375° for 20-25 minutes or until golden.

Serves: 8

Per Serving: 0.9 g Fat, 118 Calories, 7 % Fat, 4 g Protein, 23.6 g Carb, 162.5 mg Sodium, 0 mg Cholesterol

MEME'S FAMOUS CARROTS
(Quick Fix)

8 medium-size carrots; peel, quarter, and cut diagonally into 3-inch sticks
1 package Butter Buds
1 package Equal or sugar substitute equivalent

1. Place carrots in medium saucepan; barely cover with water. Boil slowly until crisp-tender, about 10 minutes. Drain juice; reserve for "Holly's Favorite Recycled Soup"✔ at a later time.
2. Add remaining ingredients; salt and pepper to taste. Toss and serve. Salt brings out the sweetness in carrots.

Serves: 4

Per Serving: 0 g Fat, 72 Calories, 0 % Fat, 2 g Protein, 16 g Carb, 236 mg Sodium, 0 mg Cholesterol

BAKED YELLOW SQUASH

1¾ lbs. yellow crookneck squash, peeled, trimmed and cut into bite-size chunks
1 medium onion, chopped fine
½ t mace
1 package Butter Buds
1 C "Basic Bread Crumbs"✔, divided
1½ T sugar
4 beaten egg whites or ½ C Egg Beaters
Salt (optional) and pepper to taste
Dash nutmeg

1. Boil squash with onion just until tender, not mushy. DRAIN WELL and press in colander to remove most of the water.
2. Mix Butter Buds, ½ of bread crumbs, and remaining ingredients. Add squash and pour in dish coated with Pam. Top with rest of bread crumbs; cover and bake 20 minutes at 350°.

Serves: 8

Per Serving: 0 g Fat, 88 Calories, 0 % Fat, 6.2 g Protein, 16.2 g Carb, 112.5 mg Sodium, 0 mg Cholesterol

GRILLED VEGETABLE KABOBS
(Easy Prep)

1 EACH medium zucchini and yellow squash
1 (14-oz.) can artichoke hearts packed in water, drained
16 fresh whole mushrooms
1 large onion cut into bite-size wedges
1 large tomato cut into bite-size wedges
½ EACH small green and red pepper, sliced
1 C Butter Buds liquid
½ C "Defatted Chicken Broth"✓
1 large clove garlic, crushed
½ t EACH basil and dill
½ t EACH salt (optional) and pepper

1. Slice squash into to 1½-inch chunks. Marinate all vegetables in a mixture of the last 5 ingredients about 30 minutes to 2 hours, turning vegetables occasionally.
2. Using 16 skewers, thread equal amounts of vegetables on each skewer. Grill over coals for about 4 minutes, basting with marinade; turn and grill on other side 3-5 minutes or until vegetables are done, continuing to baste with marinade.

Serves: 8 (2 skewers each)

Per Serving: 0 g Fat, 40 Calories, 0 % Fat, 3.3 g Protein, 7.6 g Carb, 13 mg Sodium, 0 mg Cholesterol

SPINACH BAKE
(Easy Prep)

1 small onion, chopped
3 (10-oz.) packages frozen chopped spinach, thawed and drained
½ C Egg Beaters
1 T plus 1 t lemon juice
Scant ½ t cumin
2 packages Butter Buds
3 T flour
1 t salt (optional)
1 T sugar (optional)
1 (12-oz.) can evaporated skim milk
Pam no stick cooking spray

1. Sauté onion in a little water until almost tender.
2. Mix all ingredients (make sure spinach is well drained) with the onion; bake in sprayed medium casserole for 30 minutes at 425°.

Serves: 12

Per Serving: 0.85 g Fat, 74 Calories, 10 % Fat, 6.9 g Protein, 11.9 g Carb, 227 mg Sodium, 2.2 mg Cholesterol

AUNT JODIE'S FAVORITE SWEET POTATOES

3 C cooked mashed sweet potatoes
⅓ - ⅔ C sugar
1 t salt (optional)
½ C Egg Beaters
¼ C skim milk
⅓ C evaporated skim milk
1 package Butter Buds
1 t vanilla
1 C brown sugar
⅓ C flour
½ C Grape Nuts cereal
⅓ C hot water plus 2 packages Butter Buds
Butter flavor Pam no stick cooking spray

1. Mix together the first 8 ingredients. Place in an oblong casserole that has been coated with Pam.
2. Combine remaining ingredients in a small bowl. Sprinkle over potato mixture and bake at 350° for 30 minutes.

Serves: 12

Per Serving: 0.16 g Fat, 171 Calories, 0.9 % Fat, 2.3 g Protein, 39.5 g Carb, 238 mg Sodium, 35 mg Cholesterol

MARGARET'S VEGETABLE MEDLEY
(Quick Fix)

1 large zucchini squash, cubed (about 6 C)
1 large onion, chopped (about 2 C)
½ C baby lima beans, drained
1 C corn, drained
½ C V-8 juice or 1 small can stewed tomatoes
2 shakes Schilling Parsley Patch Salt-Free Herb and Spice Blend plus 5 shakes Morton's Nature's Seasoning

1. In a large skillet simmer zucchini and onion in a small amount of V-8 juice or tomatoes until tender but firm.
2. Add lima beans and corn; cook 5 minutes. Stir in seasonings and serve.

Serves: 10 (1 C each)

Per Serving: 0.4 g Fat, 87 Calories, 4 % Fat, 3.8 g Protein, 18.7 g Carb, 39 mg Sodium, 0 mg Cholesterol

ZUCCHINI BOATS
(Easy Prep)

2 medium-size zucchini squash, cooked until tender, not mushy
1 package Butter Buds
½ C nonfat cottage cheese
1 oz. EACH Healthy Choice mozzarella cheese & Healthy Choice Cheddar cheese, grated
2 T instant mashed potato flakes
Salt (optional) and pepper to taste

1. Cool squash and slice oblong in half. Scoop out pulp to about ¼-inch of shell.
2. Mix pulp with remaining ingredients and spoon back into shells. Bake at 350° until heated, about 10 minutes.

Serves: 4

Per Serving: 0.25 g Fat, 70 Calories, 3 % Fat, 8.5 g Protein, 8 g Carb, 421 mg Sodium, 3.7 mg Cholesterol

HASH BROWN CASSEROLE
(Easy Prep)

1 (20-oz.) bag Simply Potatoes (in refrigerator section)
8 slices (6 oz.) diced Healthy Choice fat free cheese slices
⅓ C chopped onion
1 can Weight Watcher's cream of mushroom soup
1 C nonfat plain yogurt plus 1 T cornstarch
1 t salt (optional)
¼ t pepper
¾ C Butter Buds liquid. divided
1 ¾ C crushed cornflakes, divided
Pam no stick cooking spray

1. Coat a large baking dish with Pam. Mix ¼ C cornflakes, ½ C Butter Buds and remaining ingredients together; place in dish. Mix remaining 1 ½ C cornflakes and ¼ C Butter Buds. Sprinkle over top of casserole and bake at 350° for 35-40 minutes.

Makes: approximately 14 (½ C) servings

Per Serving: 0.87 g Fat, 81 Calories, 10 % Fat, 4.6 g Protein, 11.6 g Carb, 93 mg Sodium, 2.7 mg Cholesterol

SCALLOPED POTATOES

6 medium new potatoes, sliced and peeled if desired
3 green onions with tops, chopped
1½ C (6 oz.) Healthy Choice Fat Free cheddar cheese, divided
½ C Butter Buds liquid
2 t flour
Salt (optional) and pepper to taste
8 oz. Healthy Choice Fat Free pasteurized process cheese spread
¾ C EACH skim milk and evaporated skim milk

1. Mix the flour, salt and pepper together. Coat a 3 quart casserole dish with Pam. Place half of the potatoes in a single layer in the bottom of the dish. Sprinkle with ½ the flour mixture, ½ C cheddar cheese, and ½ the onions. Repeat layer once more in that order.
2. Heat together the cheese spread and milks; pour over potatoes and bake at 350° for about 30 minutes or until potatoes are tender. Five minutes before removing from oven, top with remaining ½ C cheddar cheese and bake.

Serves: 12

Per Serving: 0.09 g Fat, 137 Calories, 1 % Fat, 10.8 g Protein, 22 g Carb, 301 mg Sodium, 6.7 mg Cholesterol

HOLIDAY ASPARAGUS

2 (10-oz.) packages frozen chopped asparagus, thawed
1 can Weight Watcher's cream of mushroom soup plus 1 T cornstarch
1 package Butter Buds
1 t Worcestershire sauce
¼ t EACH salt (optional) and pepper
1 can sliced water chestnuts, drained
2 hard-boiled eggs, yolks discarded, whites sliced

1. Drain asparagus well; set aside. Combine and set aside the next 4 ingredients.
2. Coat an 8-inch square baking dish with butter-flavored Pam. Layer in order: half of the asparagus, water chestnuts egg whites and soup mixture. Repeat layers; chill in refrigerator 20 minutes.
3. Remove and bake uncovered at 350° for 25-30 minutes.

Serves: 8

Per Serving: 0.2 g Fat, 47 Calories, 4 % Fat, 5 g Protein, 6.8 g Carb, 254 mg Sodium, 0 mg Cholesterol

SKILLET STIR-FRY VEGETABLES

2 chicken bouillon cubes
1 head cauliflower broken into bite-size pieces
1 bundle broccoli broken into bite-size pieces
1 large carrot, diced
2 medium zucchini, sliced, or 1 EACH zucchini and yellow squash
1 medium onion, cut into bite size pieces
1 C sliced fresh mushrooms
1 can sliced water chestnuts, drained
Pinch minced clove garlic
2 t dry Butter Buds
1 t low sodium soy sauce
½ t salt (optional)
¼ t pepper
Pinch thyme
Pam no stick cooking spray

1. Dissolve bouillon in 1 C boiling water; set aside. Coat a large skillet with Pam. Place cauliflower, broccoli, and carrot in skillet with about ¼ C of the broth; cook 10 minutes over medium-high heat stirring occasionally. Add more broth when needed.
2. Add squash and remaining vegetables and seasonings; stir-fry until vegetables are tender, adding more chicken broth when needed. Sometimes I add a pinch of sugar or ½ packet of Equal near the end of cooking time.

Note: (May use pre-packaged frozen cut-up stir-fry vegetables.)
Makes: 10 (1 C) servings

Per Serving: 0 g Fat, 60 Calories, 0 % Fat, 4.2 g Protein, 11.5 g Carb, 257 mg Sodium, 0 mg Cholesterol

SPINACH-ARTICHOKE CASSEROLE

2 (10-oz.) packages frozen spinach
1 can water-packed artichoke hearts
½ C nonfat cottage cheese
Salt (optional) and pepper to taste
½ t garlic powder
1 C Corn flake crumbs
Pam no stick cooking spray

1. Cook spinach according to directions. Drain well.
2. Add the drained artichokes, cottage cheese, garlic, salt, and pepper. Place in a casserole dish sprayed with Pam. Top with corn flakes. Bake at 325° for 20-30 minutes.

Serves: 6

Per Serving: 0.16 g Fat, 44 Calories, 3 % Fat, 4.6 g Protein, 6.5 g Carb, 145 mg Sodium, 0.87 mg Cholesterol

RODOLFO'S SPINACH RICOTTA DUMPLINGS

(Given to me by Rodolfo Sperandeo of Rodolfo's Restaurant in Dallas - a pioneer in "lite" cooking! Also offered at Rodolfo's in Arlington.)

4 - 4½ lbs. fresh spinach or 3 lbs. frozen chopped spinach
1 medium onion, finely chopped
1 C Truly Lite Fat Free ricotta cheese (Rodolfo's recipe calls for part-skim ricotta)
1 C Parmesan cheese, grated
1 T fresh garlic puree
Pinch EACH of black pepper and oregano
3 cubes chicken bouillon dissolved in as little water as possible
Nutmeg, to taste (optional)
1¼ C soft bread crumbs
6 egg whites
3 C "Rodolfo's Marinara Sauce"✔
16 oz. dry linguini

1. When using fresh spinach, wash carefully and chop. If using frozen, defrost and squeeze out all excess water.
2. Place spinach in large bowl and add all ingredients except marinara sauce. Mix well with a large spoon and adjust bread crumbs and egg white as necessary to achieve cohesive mixture. Chill well, to improve consistency.
3. Roll into balls about 1½-inches in diameter.
4. Arrange dumplings in a shallow baking pan, not touching each other and bake in 325°- 350° oven. Set a pan of hot water on a lower shelf to steam dumplings and prevent drying out.
5. Bake 10-15 minutes or until lightly golden.

Note: The dumplings may be served immediately over cooked pasta with marinara sauce. However, for moister dumplings, cool them slightly, drop into marinara sauce and let sit for an hour or more so they absorb some of the tomato juices. Reheat before serving.

Serves: 8 (Each with 1 - 1¼ C pasta)

Per Serving: 4 g Fat, 342 Calories, 10 % Fat, 23.3 g Protein, 58.6 g Carb, 479 mg Sodium, 11 mg Cholesterol

TOSSED ITALIAN VEGETABLES
(Quick Fix)

1 package Butter Buds
¼ C "Defatted Chicken Broth"✔, divided
½ C chopped onion
½ C thin-sliced yellow squash
2 C thin-sliced zucchini
2 C chopped fresh tomatoes or Italian style canned tomatoes
1 garlic clove, minced
1 T dried basil
Garlic salt and pepper to taste
¼ C Truly Lite Fat Free ricotta cheese
Olive oil flavor Pam no stick cooking spray

1. Coat skillet with Pam. Mix all ingredients except ricotta cheese and simmer until vegetables are crisp-tender. Stir in ricotta; mix well and heat through.

Serves: 8 (about ½ C each)

Variation: Omit squash and use broccoli and cauliflower. Mexican variation: Use picanté sauce or Rotel tomatoes and green chiles in place of tomatoes. Use nonfat cheddar instead of ricotta and cilantro instead of basil.

Per Serving: 0 g Fat, 34 Calories,
0 % Fat, 2.3 g Protein, 6.8 g Carb,
217 mg Sodium, 0.37 mg Cholesterol

SKILLET POTATOES
(Quick Fix)

1 large baking potato, cut into ¼-inch thick circles
½ C chopped onion
1 chicken bouillon cube plus ½ C boiling water
1 t parsley plus garlic salt (optional) and pepper to taste

1. Coat bottom of large skillet with Pam. Pour 2 T of broth into skillet and heat; add potatoes. "Fry" potatoes turning occasionally, adding more broth as needed, until potatoes are tender, not mushy. Add onions half way through cooking time. Season with spices.

Serves: 2

Per Serving: 0 g Fat, 110 Calories,
0 % Fat, 3,5 g Protein, 25 g Carb,
461 mg Sodium, 0 mg Cholesterol

THREE LAYER ASPARAGUS CASSEROLE
(Quick Fix)

3 (10½-oz.) cans asparagus
½ C chopped onion
3 C nonfat plain yogurt plus 3 T cornstarch
3 C (12 oz.) Healthy Choice fat free mozzarella cheese
3 T Butter Buds liquid
1 C "Basic Bread Crumbs,"✔ divided into thirds
Season to taste
Pam no stick cooking spray

1. Layer 1 can asparagus in a baking dish coated with Pam. Sprinkle with ⅓ of the onion, ⅓ of the yogurt mixture, 1 C of cheese, 1 T of Butter Buds liquid, 1 C of bread crumbs, and the seasoning. Repeat layers 2 more times. Bake at 350° for about 20-30 minutes or until top is golden brown.

Serves: 10

Per Serving: 0 g Fat, 109 Calories, 0 % Fat, 15.4 g Protein, 9.95 g Carb, 570 mg Sodium, 0 mg Cholesterol

CALIFORNIA CASSEROLE

1 head cauliflower, cut into florets
1 (10-oz.) package frozen green peas, thawed
1 small onion, chopped
1 package Butter Buds plus ¼ C "Defatted Chicken Broth"✔
1½ C "Nonfat Yogurt Cheese"✔ plus 2 T cornstarch
½ t curry powder
1 t salt (optional)
2 T slivered almonds

1. Cook cauliflower until crisp tender; set aside.
2. Sauté onion in Butter Buds/broth mixture until crisp-tender. Slowly add yogurt cheese mixture, curry powder and salt; stir constantly until heated through.
3. Place cauliflower and peas in a sprayed 2 quart casserole; top with sauce and sprinkle with almonds if desired. Bake at 350° for 30 minutes.

Serves: 8

Per Serving: 0.38 g Fat, 87 Calories, 4 % Fat, 6 g Protein, 31 g Carb, 186 mg Sodium, 0 mg Cholesterol

SWEET POTATO SURPRISE

3 large or 6 medium sweet potatoes, peeled, and cubed
1 box Betty Crocker Fluffy White frosting mix, prepared, divided
1 t vanilla
1 t EACH almond extract, coconut extract and cinnamon
1 package Butter Buds

1. Boil potatoes until tender, about 20 minutes. Drain well.
2. Mix potatoes with 1½ C frosting and remaining ingredients. Spoon into sprayed oblong casserole. Bake uncovered at 350° about 15 minutes.

Serves: 12

Per Serving: 0 g Fat, 122 Calories, 0 % Fat, 2.3 g Protein, 27.6 g Carb, 98 mg Sodium, 0 mg Cholesterol

POTATO SCOOPS

3 large baking potatoes
1 package Butter Buds
¼ C evaporated skim milk
½ t garlic powder
Salt (optional) & pepper to taste
½ C (2 oz.) Healthy Choice Fat Free mozzarella cheese (grated)
½ C Truly Lite Fat Free ricotta cheese

1. Follow first two steps of "Potato Skin"✔ recipe.
2. After scooping out pulp, mash with Butter Buds, milk, seasonings and cheese.
3. Blend until smooth, restuff in potatoes. Heat at 350° until cheese is melted.

Serves: 6

Per Serving: 0 g Fat, 104 Calories, 0 % Fat, 6.6 g Protein, 19 g Carb, 223 mg Sodium, 3 mg Cholesterol

BIKINI POTATOES
(Easy Prep)

6 new potatoes (1½ x 2-inch diameter)
1 package Butter Buds
Butter flavor Pam no stick cooking spray
1 T parsley
Garlic and pepper to taste
4 t Bac-Os artificial bacon bits

1. Remove peeling from the center of each potato. Cover potatoes with water in a medium saucepan and boil until tender, about 20 minutes.
2. Drain potatoes and return to pan. Quickly sauté potatoes in remaining ingredients over hot burner (not necessary to turn burner on).

Serves: 2

Per Serving: 0 g Fat, 106 Calories, 0 % Fat, 0 g Protein, 23.3 g Carb, 4 mg Sodium, 0 mg Cholesterol

PEAS AND CORN
(Easy Prep)

2 C fresh shelled purple hull peas
1½ C fresh corn
½ C EACH chopped onion and celery including leaves
1 beef bouillon cube
1½ T fresh cilantro

1. Combine all ingredients except cilantro in a 2 quart pan on stove. Add about 2½ C water and bring to a boil. Reduce heat; simmer 60-70 minutes or until peas are tender, adding more water if necessary. Stir in cilantro and salt and pepper if desired and cook 5 minutes more.

Serves: 8

Per Serving: 0.18 g Fat, 98 Calories, 2 % Fat, 3.75 g Protein, 20.3 g Carb, 131 mg Sodium, 0 mg Cholesterol

SCRUMPTIOUS SAUERKRAUT

¼ C boiling water plus 1 chicken bouillon cube
1 package Butter Buds
½ C sliced onion
1 large can sauerkraut, drained well
2 T brown sugar or sugar substitute
3 whole cloves
1 large apple, peeled and grated
1 small carrot, peeled and grated

1. Sauté onions in broth and Butter Buds until onions are crisp-tender. Add remaining ingredients, heat through and serve.

Serves: 6

Per Serving: 0.16 g Fat, 53 Calories, 3 % Fat, 0.8 g Protein, 12.3 g Carb, 564 mg Sodium, 0 mg Cholesterol

CREAMY BROCCOLI
(Quick Fix)

1 bunch broccoli, cooked until tender; drain
1 C "Nonfat Yogurt Cheese"✔
1 T cornstarch
2 T brown sugar
1 t creole mustard

1. Combine last 4 ingredients; pour over broccoli and serve.

Serves: 6

Per Serving: 0 g Fat, 32 Calories, 0 % Fat, 2.1 g Protein, 6.6 g Carb, 5.3 mg Sodium, 0 mg Cholesterol

CREAMED POTATOES
(Easy Prep)

½ baking potato per person
Evaporated skim milk or fortified skim milk
⅓ package Butter Buds per person
Salt to taste (optional)
Lots of pepper

1. Peel potatoes and dice; boil until tender. With electric mixer, beat potatoes, milk and seasonings; add extra Butter Buds if needed.
3. For variety, per person, add 1 T "Nonfat Yogurt Cheese,"✔ 1 t Bac-Os, ½ slice Kraft Free cheese, paprika or other seasoning.

Serves: 1

Per Serving: 0.2 g Fat, 106 Calories, 2 % Fat, 3.8 g Protein, 21.7 g Carb, 237 mg Sodium, 2 mg Cholesterol

OVEN FRIED PATTYPAN
(Quick Fix)

2 medium pattypan squash
1 recipe "OVEN FRIED CATFISH"✔

1. Wash squash and cut it into ⅛-inch slices. Using the same batter ingredients in the catfish recipe, coat squash the same way and place in coated pan. Bake at 350° for about 8-12 minutes or until crisp. (You may also "fry" in nonstick skillet coated with Pam 5 - 10 minutes.)

Serves: 6

Per Serving: 0.85 g Fat, 123 Calories, 6 % Fat, 11.6 g Protein, 14.1 g Carb, 70 mg Sodium, 28.8 mg Cholesterol

OKRA AND TOMATOES

4 large tomatoes, peeled and chopped (may use canned)
3 C sliced okra, tops removed
2 C fresh corn
¼ C hot water plus 1 package Butter Buds
Pam no stick cooking spray

1. Stir all ingredients into a large Pam-coated skillet. Cover and simmer about 15 minutes until vegetables are tender, stirring occasionally. Season to taste.

Serves: 8

Per Serving: 0 g Fat, 71 Calories, 0 % Fat, 2.6 g Protein, 14.1 g Carb, 87 mg Sodium, 0 mg Cholesterol

BEANS, RICE & GRAINS

MEME'S QUICK-SIZZLE BEANS

(The way they're cooked is the secret!)

1 can cut "Blue Lake" green beans, drained
½ t garlic salt
1 package Butter Buds
1 t minced onion
Pam no stick cooking spray

1. Coat a medium-size saucepan with Pam. Heat pan to sizzling hot, but not smoking. Place the garlic salt, Butter Buds and onion in the green bean can on top of the beans.
2. When pan is ready, dump beans and seasonings quickly into pan and immediately put lid on; shake pan to coat beans. Reduce heat to low; cook beans 5 minutes, shaking occasionally.

Serves: 4

Per Serving: 0 g Fat, 20 Calories, 0 % Fat, 0.5 g Protein, 4.2 g Carb, 248 mg Sodium, 0 mg Cholesterol

QUICK HOPPIN' JOHN

(Easy Prep)

2 large cans black-eyed peas, no fat, or 2 (10-oz.) packages fresh frozen black-eyed peas, cooked and drained
4 C cooked rice
1 package Butter Buds plus 1 t bacon-flavor Molly McButter
Dash hot pepper sauce (optional)
Salt (optional) and pepper to taste

1. Combine rice and butter flavorings; stir well. Add peas and mix well. Serve with cornbread and green salad.

Serves: 8

Per Serving: 0 g Fat, 169 Calories, 0 % Fat, 4.5 g Protein, 35 g Carb, 817 mg Sodium, 0 mg Cholesterol

ROSS'S FAVORITE BLACK-EYED PEAS
(Easy Prep)

Fresh black-eyed peas
Fresh okra, tops removed

1. Cover peas with water; boil slowly 1½ hours, adding water when needed. When peas are tender, stir in okra and cook about 15 more minutes.

Servings: (½ C cooked peas plus 2 okra pieces)

Per Serving: 0.8 g Fat, 80 Calories, 9 % Fat, 3 g Protein, 15 g Carb, 65 mg Sodium, 0 mg Cholesterol

GREEN BEAN CASSEROLE
(Quick Fix)

2 cans Weight Watcher's cream of mushroom soup plus 2 T cornstarch
¼ C skim milk
½ C (2 oz.) Healthy Choice Fat Free mozzarella cheese, shredded plus ¼ C Truly Lite Fat Free ricotta cheese
1 package Butter Buds
3 cans cut green beans, drained
¼ C Grape Nuts, dusted with flour
½ C sliced water chestnuts, drained
¼ C "Basic Bread Crumbs"✔

1. Combine all ingredients except bread crumbs; stir well. Place in a sprayed 1½-quart casserole dish; top with bread crumbs. Spray crumbs with Pam and bake at 350° for 20-25 minutes.

Serves: 8

Per Serving: 1.5 g Fat, 81 Calories, 17 % Fat, 6 g Protein, 14.6 g Carb, 833 mg Sodium, 1.7 mg Cholesterol

GREAT BAKED BEANS

2 medium cans pinto or navy beans
¼ C brown sugar
½ t dry mustard
½ C ketchup
½ C EACH diced onion and green pepper
1 T bacon flavor Molly McButter
Pam no stick cooking spray

1. Combine all ingredients. Place in a 1 quart casserole and bake uncovered at 350° for about 1 hour.

Serves: 8

Per Serving: 0.43 g Fat, 133 Calories, 3 % Fat, 6.1 g Protein, 27 g Carb, 208 mg Sodium, 0 mg Cholesterol

BROCCOLI-CHEESE CORNBREAD

½ recipe "Stephanie's Favorite Cornbread"✔
1 medium onion, chopped
1 (10-oz.) package frozen chopped broccoli
½ C Egg Beaters
8 oz. nonfat cottage cheese
Butter flavor Pam no stick cooking spray
Paprika

1. Thaw broccoli in microwave; do not drain. Mix with remaining ingredients except cornbread. Set aside.
2. To prepare cornbread batter: Mix together the dry cornbread ingredients and make a well in the center. Mix the wet cornbread ingredients with the broccoli mixture and stir into the dry cornbread mixture. Mix just until combined. Do not overmix. Sprinkle paprika on top and bake at 350° for 35-45 minutes or until brown.

Serves: 16

Per Serving: 0.18 g Fat, 55 Calories, 3 % Fat, 7.6 g Protein, 7.6 g Carb, 128 mg Sodium, 3.56 mg Cholesterol

BROCCOLI RICE CASSEROLE

1 small onion, chopped
½ C chopped celery
¼ C hot water plus 1 chicken bouillon cube plus 1 package Butter Buds
2 (10-oz.) packages frozen chopped broccoli, cooked and drained
½ C chopped water chestnuts
1 can Weight Watcher's cream of mushroom soup
½ C evaporated skim milk
8 oz. shredded Healthy Choice Fat Free cheese singles
2 C cooked rice (may use brown rice if desired)
1 t garlic salt (optional)
Dash hot pepper sauce
Pam no stick cooking spray

1. Sauté onion and celery in Butter Buds/bouillon mixture in a large skillet until vegetables are crisp-tender. Add broccoli and remaining ingredients; mix well.
2. Pour into a sprayed casserole dish and bake at 350° for 30 minutes or until heated through.

Serves: 10

Per Serving: 0.8 g Fat, 128 Calories, 6 % Fat, 9.1 g Protein, 21.6 g Carb, 73 mg Sodium, 4.4 mg Cholesterol

CHEESE GRITS
(Easy Prep)

1 box Aunt Jemima enriched hominy grits
Butter Buds
Salt (optional) (or garlic salt if garlic grits are desired)
Healthy Choice Fat Free cheese singles

1. Decide how many servings of grits you will need and make according to directions on box. Add ⅓ package Butter Buds and 1 cheese slice per serving, and salt to taste. Mix until cheese melts.

Serves: 1

Note: If you wish to make as a casserole, prepare as above, add ½ C Egg Beaters (for 4 servings), pour into a casserole and bake at 350° for 20-30 minutes.

Per Serving: 0 g Fat, 138 Calories, 0 % Fat, 4.6 g Protein, 23 g Carb, 343 mg Sodium, 3.3 mg Cholesterol

FIESTA RICE

2 T Butter Buds liquid
½ C chopped onion
2 C cooked regular rice
1 C "Nonfat Yogurt Cheese"✔
½ C nonfat cottage cheese
Dash pepper
1 (7-oz.) can chopped green chiles (drained)
½ C (2 oz.) EACH shredded Healthy Choice Fat Free Cheddar and mozzarella cheese
Pam no stick cooking spray

1. Pour Butter Buds in large saucepan. Add onion and sauté until tender. Remove from heat and add next 5 ingredients.
2. Spoon half of rice mixture into 1-quart casserole sprayed with Pam. Top with green chiles and half of the cheese. Cover with remaining rice mixture. Bake at 375° uncovered for 20 minutes. Sprinkle with remaining cheese; bake an additional 5 minutes.

Serves: 10

Per Serving: 0.13 g Fat, 78 Calories, 2 % Fat, 7.1 g Protein, 11.8 g Carb, 282 mg Sodium, 2.3 mg Cholesterol

LAYERED BROWN RICE CASSEROLE

1 bunch chopped green onions with tops
½ C EACH chopped celery and carrots
½ C Butter Buds liquid
2 C uncooked brown rice
4½ C water plus 5 chicken bouillon cubes
½ C dry white wine
1 t garlic powder
1 T parsley
Salt (optional) and pepper to taste
1 C (4 oz.) grated Healthy Choice Fat Free mozzarella cheese
½ C Egg Beaters
½ t almond extract
1 C evaporated skim milk
½ frozen green peas

1. In a large saucepan, sauté onions, celery, and carrots in Butter Buds liquid until crisp-tender, about 3 minutes.
2. Add the next 6 ingredients to pan; bring to boil, reduce heat, cover, and simmer 35 minutes or until liquid is absorbed. Set aside.
3. Mix remaining ingredients except green peas in another bowl. Set aside.
4. Pour half the rice mixture into a sprayed 13 X 9" casserole dish; top with half the cheese mixture. Add green peas on top of cheese layer. Add remaining rice and cheese in that order. Bake at 350° for about 30 minutes.

Serves: 12

Per Serving: 0.16 g Fat, 123 Calories, 1 % Fat, 6.5 g Protein, 20.2 g Carb, 516 mg Sodium, 2.4 mg Cholesterol

AUNT JODIE'S CORNBREAD DRESSING

3 C bread cubes, toasted (see note)
5 C cooked cornbread, crumbled (using "Waxahachie Crunchy Cornbread"✔)
1 t poultry seasoning or to taste
1 t salt (optional)
Dash paprika
½ t pepper or to taste
1 C EACH finely chopped celery and onion
½ C Egg Beaters
2½ C "Defatted Chicken Broth"✔ (may need more)

1. Sauté onion and celery in a little of the chicken broth until tender. Mix bread cubes and cornbread and pour mixture over the bread.
2. Mix in egg, tossing lightly. Add broth, enough to look like the consistency of pudding, and mix well.
3. Bake 350° until brown, about 30 minutes.

Makes about 12 (½ C servings)

Note: For bread cubes, use your accumulated bread from the freezer (leftover heels, crusts, rolls, etc., for a variety of flavors).

Per Serving: 0.4 g Fat, 93 Calories, 4 % Fat, 2.75 g Protein, 15 g Carb, 18 mg Sodium, 0 mg Cholesterol

CREAMY DEVILED EGGS OR EGG SALAD
(Quick Fix)

9 hard boiled eggs
½ C Egg Beaters, cooked, scrambled, cooled, chilled
2 T Kraft Free mayonnaise
1 T evaporated skim milk
¾-1 t mustard
Pinch cayenne pepper
Pinch celery salt

1. Cut eggs in half; discard yolks. Place 12 egg halves in serving dish.
2. Chop and mix remaining egg whites and Egg Beaters together. Mix in remaining ingredients, adjusting mustard to your taste. Fill each egg half with about 2 heaping tsp of mixture.
3. For egg salad, chop all egg whites, use 1½ C Egg Beaters, 6 T mayonnaise, 3 T milk and 1 T mustard. Season to taste.

Serves: 12

Per Serving: 0.1 g Fat, 20.2 Calories, 7 % Fat, 3.5 g Protein, 1 g Carb, 92.8 mg Sodium, .01 mg Cholesterol

NORTH CAROLINA SPOON BREAD
(Easy Prep)

1 ½ C cornmeal plus ½ package dry Butter Buds
½ t salt (optional)
2 t baking powder
1 t sugar
3 C skim milk
¼ C Egg Beaters
2 T Butter Buds liquid
1 C evaporated skim milk
Pam no stick cooking spray

1. Preheat oven to 500°. Mix together the 1st 7 ingredients. Set aside. Spray a casserole dish with Pam. Two to three minutes before cooking place casserole in oven to heat.
2. Remove dish from oven, pour batter into dish. Place dish in oven and reduce heat to 450°. Bake for 15 - 20 minutes.
3. Heat evaporated milk; just as cooking is finished, remove casserole from oven and pour heated milk over mixture. Let stand 5-10 minutes.

Serves: 10

Variations: Serve as a side dish or top with vegetables or meat and a lite cream sauce for a main dish. Also makes an easy and delicious dressing for turkey. For a Texas flair, stir in jalapeños or green chilies.

Per Serving: 0.84 g Fat, 108 Calories, 7 % Fat, 5.4 g Protein, 19.7 g Carb, 166.9 mg Sodium, 24 mg Cholesterol

MILD MEXICAN RICE
(Quick Fix)

3⅓ C water
¾ t cumin
3 chicken bouillon cubes
½ package Butter Buds
3 T Pace picanté sauce
1½ C plus 2 T long grain rice

1. Place first 5 ingredients in a medium saucepan; bring to a boil and add rice.
2. Cover and simmer 20-25 minutes; remove from heat and let stand 5 minutes more.

Serves: 8

Per Serving: 0 g Fat, 50 Calories, 0 % Fat, 0.81 g Protein, 10.3 g Carb, 517 mg Sodium, 0 mg Cholesterol

GREEN CHILI RICE
(Easy Prep)

1 medium onion, chopped
¼ C "Defatted Chicken Broth"✔ plus 1 package Butter Buds
2 C nonfat cottage cheese
1 C "Nonfat Yogurt Cheese"✔
1 T cornstarch
½ t EACH cumin, pepper, salt (optional), and cilantro
1 (6-oz.) can plus 1 (4-oz.) can chopped green chiles
3 C cooked rice
½ C (2 oz.) EACH Healthy Choice Fat Free Cheddar cheese, and Healthy Choice Fat Free Fat Free cheese singles, shredded
Pam no stick cooking spray

1. Cook onion in broth and Butter Buds until tender.
2. Combine remaining ingredients in a large bowl; add onion mixture. Bake at 375° in sprayed dish 30 minutes.

Serves: 14

Per Serving: 0.3 g Fat, 87 Calories, 3 % Fat, 67 g Protein, 13.8 g Carb, 429 mg Sodium, 2.8 mg Cholesterol

OVEN BAKED VEGETABLES

Butternut, acorn, and spaghetti squash
Baking potatoes, sweet potatoes, corn on cob in husk

1. To prepare squash, cut in half and place cut side down on cookie sheet. Bake at 350° for 30-40 minutes or until tender when pricked with a fork. Season any of these with Butter Buds, cinnamon, honey, brown sugar, Equal, molasses, picanté sauce or your favorite seasoning - be creative!
2. For potatoes and corn, place on oven rack and bake at 400° for 1 to 1¼ hours, turning once. Season with Butter Buds, salt (optional), pepper, garlic, or favorite seasonings.

Serves: 1-4 depending on the vegetable

Notes and Extra Recipes:

Notes and Extra Recipes:

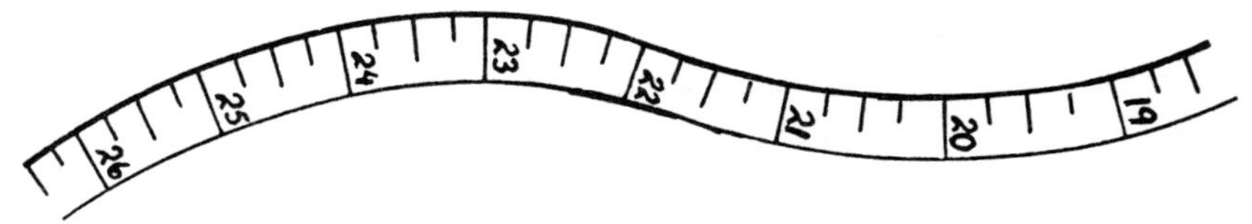

BREADS & ROLLS

We used to think of bread as a forbidden food. Now we know that it is a complex carbohydrate which is needed to fuel our bodies' energy. Approximately 60%-75% of our daily caloric intake should come from complex carbohydrates. Breads, along with vegetables, pasta, cereals, rice and grains, and fruits, are all complex carbohydrates. An average adult needs four servings from the bread and grains food group. One slice of bread is considered one serving.

Time Savers:

- Spread a little fat free Italian dressing on sour dough or French bread to make a quick garlic bread.
- Cheese Cornbread - Combine 1 C each cornmeal and all-purpose flour, 1 T baking powder, and 1 t salt (optional); add dry ingredients to a mixture of the following 5 ingredients just until combined: 1 C skim milk, 2 t melted Smart Beat margarine, 2 T unsweetened applesauce, ½ C Egg Beaters and 2 C nonfat grated Cheddar cheese. Bake at 425° for 12-15 minutes or until golden brown.
- Split Wonder Light low-fat hamburger or hot dog buns in half. Coat each with Butter flavor or Olive Oil flavor Pam, sprinkle with a little garlic powder and parsley and toast lightly. Prepare toast for breakfast or any other time the same way, but omit the garlic and parsley.
- For cinnamon toast, coat nonfat bread with Pam; sprinkle with a mixture of cinnamon and sugar. Toast lightly.
- DELICIOUS bagel doughnuts - Warm bagels; coat with Butter flavor Pam, roll in sugar, powdered sugar, cinnamon sugar, or drizzle with a glaze made from 1 C powdered sugar plus 2 T skim milk.
- Mix 1 C all-purpose flour and ½ C sugar; stir in (just until combined) a mixture of ½ C Egg Beaters, 1 C skim milk, and 1 t vanilla. Fill sprayed muffin cups ¾ full; bake at 450° for 20 minutes, then 350° for 15 minutes.
- Slice a loaf of sour dough or low-fat French bread; drizzle with

liquid Butter Buds and sprinkle with Parmesan cheese.

- Buy the long oval or rectangular shaped Afghan Bread at grocery; cut into strips for breadsticks, spray with Olive Oil or Butter Pam, sprinkle with a little garlic salt or garlic powder and toast or warm to desired doneness.

Helpful Hints:

- When measuring flour, make sure to spoon flour into measuring cup; do not pack.
- You may wish to substitute oat bran or ground oat flour for some of the all-purpose flour when baking breads or muffins. For every cup of flour, substitute ⅓ of it with oats. Example: 1 C all-purpose flour = ⅔ C all-purpose flour plus ⅓ C oats.
- Over-mixing breads and muffins will make them tough.
- Save money on bread by buying at the bread stores. Most accept coupons and have specials on certain days.
- Double bread or muffin recipes and freeze; they make great snacks or lunch box stuffers.
- To soften tortillas, steam over hot water or place 2 or 3 between paper towels and microwave for 20-30 seconds.
- When baking bread, make sure yeast is fresh. Test by adding a pinch of sugar as you dissolve yeast in water. Mixture should foam within 10 minutes or the yeast is dead.
- To test to see if bread dough has "doubled", press 2 fingers firmly into center of bread dough; if dents remain, then the bread has doubled.
- When recipe calls for "punching the dough down", place your fist firmly in center and fold in sides to press out bubbles.
- Try making square biscuits instead of round ones so you have no excess dough left to reroll.
- Dissolve yeast in very warm, not hot, water (105°-110°). If water is too hot it will kill the yeast.

BREADS & ROLLS

FABULOUS FOCACCIA BREAD

(Quick, Easy, and Delicious)

1 box Pillsbury Hot Roll Mix
Olive Oil Flavored Pam no stick cooking spray
Garlic Salt or Garlic Powder to taste
1 T Rosemary (Optional)

1. Mix contents of box and yeast packet in a large bowl; blend well. (Add Rosemary here if desired). Stir in 1¼ C hot water until dough pulls away from the sides of the bowl.
2. Turn dough out onto lightly floured surface. Spray dough and hands with Pam and shape into a ball; knead dough for about 5 minutes, or with a dough hook on mixer about 1 minute (until dough is smooth). Add a little extra flour if dough becomes too sticky.
3. Spray an oblong 2 - 3 inch deep baking pan with Pam; spritz hands and dough again and press dough evenly into pan. Cover and let rise in a draft free place about 15 minutes. Preheat oven to 425°.
4. Uncover dough; sprinkle with garlic salt or powder. Bake at lowest position in oven for 15 - 25 minutes or until golden brown. Remove from oven, cut into pieces and serve plain or dip in Healthy Choice spaghetti sauce.

Serves: 16

Per Serving: 1 g Fat, 108 Calories, 8 % Fat, 3 g Protein, 21 g Carb, 200 mg Sodium, 0 mg Cholesterol

GERMAN CINNAMON ROLLS

Batter ingredients:
½ C EACH evaporated skim milk and skim milk
1 package dry yeast
½ C Butter Buds liquid
¼ C sugar
1 t salt (optional)
¼ C Egg Beaters
3 C flour
Topping:
Butter Flavor Pam no stick cooking spray
½ C sugar plus 1½ t cinnamon
½ C evaporated skim milk
Icing: (optional)
1½ C powdered sugar
¼ C evaporated skim milk (more if needed for desired consistency)
¼ t vanilla extract

1. Scald milk on stove or in microwave, but do not boil. Cool milk in pan until lukewarm. Add yeast; mix well and let yeast soften 10 minutes.
2. Mix Butter Buds liquid, sugar, and salt until fluffy. Beat in egg substitute. Add yeast mixture and stir in flour, forming a soft dough. Knead until smooth and elastic. Place dough in a Pam-sprayed bowl, cover, and let rise to double in size, (about 1 hour).
3. Turn dough out onto lightly floured board and knead 1 minute. Roll out to ¼" thick and spray lightly with Pam. Sprinkle ½ of the cinnamon-sugar mixture onto the dough and roll up jelly-roll style (16"-18" long). Slice dough ½" thick and place rolls ½" apart in a Pam-sprayed baking pan. Spread evaporated milk evenly over rolls. Sprinkle with remaining cinnamon-sugar mixture, cover and let rise in warm place 30 minutes.
4. Bake at 350° for 20-25 minutes or until done. Drizzle with icing while warm if desired.

Serves: 32

Variation: For a fruit roll, try substituting unsweetened fruit, jam, or jelly for cinnamon-sugar mixture.

Per Serving: 0.12 g Fat, 80 Calories, 1 % Fat, 1.65 g Protein, 18.2 g Carb, 18 mg Sodium, 0.31 mg Cholesterol

STICKY FINGER ROLLS

1 recipe "German Cinnamon Rolls"✔
6 T EACH dark and light Karo syrup, divided
¾ C Grape Nuts cereal (optional)

1. Prepare "German Cinnamon Rolls"✔ through step #3.
2. Mix syrups together. Spread ½ C of syrup mixture on rolls, sprinkle Grape Nuts on if desired, and bake in 350° oven for 20-25 minutes or until done. Remove from oven, spread with remaining syrup and let stand 2-3 minutes.

Serves: 32 (without Grape Nuts) With Grape Nuts - 112 Calories, 0 Fat)

Per Serving: 0.12 g Fat, 102 Calories, 2 % Fat, 1.65 g Protein, 23.8 g Carb, 166 mg Sodium, 0 mg Cholesterol

CHEESE PULL-A-PART ROLLS

½ C water plus 2 packages Butter Buds
½ t salt (optional)
1¼ C flour
1 C Egg Beaters
½ C (2 oz.) EACH grated Healthy Choice Fat Free Cheddar and mozzarella cheeses
2 slices Healthy Choice Fat Free cheese singles, shredded
Butter flavor Pam no stick cooking spray
Flour

1. Heat Butter Buds, water, and salt in a saucepan until hot but not boiling. Remove from heat. Add flour all at once to hot mixture and stir vigorously until mixture forms a ball. Add Egg Beaters a little at a time, beating after each addition until egg is absorbed completely. Mix in cheese.
2. Spray a large cookie sheet with Pam and dust with flour. Drop batter by spoonfuls, 3 spoonfuls per roll to form a clover shape, on cookie sheet and bake at 450° for 10 minutes. Reduce heat to 325° and bake 10-15 more minutes.

Serves: 8

Per Serving: 0.18 g Fat, 118 Calories, 1 % Fat, 9.7 g Protein, 16.5 g Carb, 434 mg Sodium, 3.3 mg Cholesterol

NANA'S NEVER-FAIL HOT ROLLS

(We all beg Nana to bring her bread to family gatherings)

1 well-beaten egg white
½ C sugar
1 t salt (optional)
3 T Canola oil
1 Fleishman's Rapid Rise yeast cake
7 C sifted Gladiola all-purpose flour
Pam no stick cooking spray

1. Dissolve in 1 C hot water the sugar, salt, and shortening. Let cool to room temperature. Dissolve yeast in 1 C water (105°-115°) and add to sugar mixture.
2. Add ½ of the flour and egg white; stir. Mix in remaining flour to form smooth dough. Handle as little as possible. Place in sprayed pan to rise twice its size in a warm draft-free place.
3. Punch down. Place dough on a board lightly dusted with flour (no more than ¼ C) and knead about 1 minute.
4. Divide dough into 5 individual pieces, forming into 5 oblong loaves. Place into sprayed loaf pans. (You may divide into individual rolls and place in muffin tins). Allow to rise again in warm draft-free place until doubled.
5. Bake at 350° until golden brown. Spray butter-flavor Pam over each loaf or rolls; let cool. To freeze, wrap cooled loaves in a paper towel, then wrap in foil. Keeps well up to 6 months.

Serves: 50

Per Serving: 1 g Fat, 75 Calories, 2 % Fat, 1.8 g Protein, 14.3 g Carb, 1.46 mg Sodium, 0 mg Cholesterol

JALAPEÑO CORN BREAD

¼ C flour
1 C corn meal
1½ C (6 oz.) grated Healthy Choice Fat Free cheddar cheese
1 t baking soda
Dash garlic powder
½ C finely chopped onion
1 or 2 jalapeño peppers, seeded and chopped
¼ C Flour
1 C 1% buttermilk
½ C Egg Beaters
2 T Bacon flavor Molly McButter dissolved in ¼ C warm evaporated skim milk
1 C cream style corn
Pam no stick cooking spray

1. Combine first 7 ingredients; stir in remaining ingredients just until combined. Pour into a baking pan that has been coated with Pam and bake at 400° 25 - 30 minutes or until done.

Variation: For a main dish, add ½-lb. cooked, drained, and rinsed Healthy Choice ground beef or ½-lb. ground turkey breast.

Serves: 16

Per Serving: 0.71 g Fat, 85 Calories, 7 % Fat, 5.8 g Protein, 14 g Carb, 261 mg Sodium, 2.5 mg Cholesterol

WAXAHACHIE CRUNCHY CORNBREAD

(Easy Prep)

1½ C coarse-ground cornmeal
½ C flour
1 T sugar, (optional)
4 t baking powder
½ t salt (optional)
1¼ C skim milk
2 egg whites or ¼ C Egg Beaters
Pam no stick cooking spray

1. Combine dry ingredients. Add milk and egg whites; beat until almost smooth, about 1 minute.
2. Coat an 8-inch square pan with Pam and bake in a preheated 425° oven for 20-25 minutes.

Serves: 12

Variation: Add ½ - 1 (4-oz.) can chopped green chiles and 3 - 4 oz. grated fat free cheddar cheese to batter before baking.

Per Serving: 0.6 g Fat, 86 Calories, 7 % Fat, 3.2 g Protein, 17 g Carb, 21 mg Sodium, 0.5 mg Cholesterol

MARLANE'S FAVORITE HUSH PUPPIES

1 C EACH cornmeal and flour
2 T sugar
4 t baking powder
½ t EACH garlic powder and pepper
2 T Ultra Promise Fat Free margarine plus 1 T Butter Buds liquid
1 t hot pepper sauce plus salt to taste
¼ C white onions, chopped very fine
1 small jalapeno pepper, seeded and chopped fine
6 green onions, no tops, chopped very fine
¼ C Egg Beaters
¼ C evaporated skim milk or enough to form a stiff batter
Pam no stick cooking spray

1. Combine all ingredients; mix just until moist, adding enough milk to form a stiff batter. Form into balls and place into muffin tins or fill cornstick pans that have been coated with Pam and bake at 475° for 10 - 12 minutes or until golden brown. Brush with more liquid Butter Buds and serve.

Makes: 24 hush puppies or cornsticks

Per Serving: 0.34 g Fat, 38 Calories, 5 % Fat, 1.1 g Protein, 7.7 g Carb, 75 mg Sodium, 0 mg Cholesterol

APRICOT OAT-BRAN MUFFINS

(Easy Prep)

2 T lite corn syrup
1 banana, mashed
¼ C brown sugar
1 t vanilla
¾ C dried apricots
2 egg whites
1 C peeled apple, diced
¾ C raisins
2¼ C oat bran
1 T baking powder
2 C liquid (apricot nectar or apple juice
½ t cinnamon
Pam no stick cooking spray

1. Process apricots in a food processor until finely chopped. Stir in remaining ingredients.
2. Spoon into muffin tins sprayed with Pam. Bake in 400° oven for about 23 minutes. Do not overbake.

Serves: 12

Per Serving: 0.3 g Fat, 118 Calories, 2 % Fat, 1.75 g Protein, 28.1 g Carb, 153 mg Sodium, 0 mg Cholesterol

QUICK CAFE BISCUITS

1¼ - 1½ C self-rising flour plus 1 package dry Butter Buds
½ C plus 2 T evaporated skim milk
Pam no stick cooking spray

1. Combine flour and skim milk.
2. Roll out and cut into small biscuits and place dough on a pan sprayed with Pam and bake at 425° for 8-10 minutes.

Serves: 24

Per Serving: 0 g Fat, 29 Calories, 2 % Fat, 0.9 g Protein, 6 g Carb, 87 mg Sodium, 0.18 mg Cholesterol

YOGURT CHEESE-PEPPER BREAD

1 package dry yeast
¼ C warm water (105°-115°)
2⅓ C all-purpose flour, divided
2 T EACH sugar and Ultra Promise Fat Free margarine
1 t EACH salt (optional) & butter flavoring
¼ t EACH baking soda & garlic powder
½ t pepper
8 oz. "Nonfat Yogurt Cheese"✓
¼ C Egg Beaters
2 oz. EACH Healthy Choice Fat Free cheese singles, and Healthy Choice Fat Free mozzarella cheese
Butter flavor Pam no stick cooking spray

1. In a large bowl, dissolve yeast in water. Let stand 5 minutes.
2. Add 1½ C flour, sugar, salt, butter flavoring, soda, garlic powder, pepper, yogurt cheese, and Egg Beaters. Mix just until blended. Stir in remaining flour and cheese. Do not overmix!
3. Place dough in a large loaf pan coated with Pam. Cover; let rise in a warm draft-free place 1 hour. Dough does not double in bulk.
4. Bake at 350° for 35-40 minutes or until brown.

Serves: 12

Per Serving: 0.16 g Fat, 111 Calories, 1 % Fat, 6 g Protein, 20 g Carb, 127 mg Sodium, 1.6 mg Cholesterol

STEPHANIE'S FAVORITE CORNBREAD
(An "Easy Prep" cornbread with a cake-like texture)

2 C EACH cornmeal and flour
1 package Butter Buds
2 T baking powder
1½ t salt (optional)
2 T corn syrup
3 T unsweetened applesauce
½ C Egg Beaters
1 C 1% fat buttermilk
1 ¼ C plus 2 T skim milk
Pam no stick cooking spray

1. Mix well the first 4 ingredients. Add remaining ingredients and mix just until blended. Do not over-mix!
2. Spray muffin tins or pan with Pam and bake at 400° about 20 minutes or until done.

Serves: 24

Per Serving: 0.58 g Fat, 85 Calories, 6 % Fat, 2.3 g Protein, 17.4 g Carb, 128.8 mg Sodium, 0.44 mg Cholesterol

BLUEBERRY BRAN MUFFINS
(Easy Prep)

2 ⅔ C All Bran cereal
1 C unsweetened apple juice
½ C water
4 egg whites or 1 C Egg Beaters
1 T vanilla
1 C EACH white flour and whole wheat flour
⅓ C EACH brown sugar and white sugar
2 T baking powder
¾ t soda
1½ t cinnamon
2 heaping cups blueberries
Pam no stick cooking spray

1. Combine first 5 ingredients in a large bowl. Set aside for 5 minutes. Preheat oven to 325°.
2. Mix remaining ingredients except berries in another bowl. Add to first mixture; mix until just moist. Do not overmix. Fold in berries.
3. Pour into sprayed muffin tins and bake 30 minutes.

Serves: 16

Per Serving: 0.4 g Fat, 100 Calories, 3 % Fat, 3 g Protein, 28 g Carb, 189 mg Sodium, 0 mg Cholesterol

DOUGHNUT MUFFINS
(Quick Fix)

2 T light corn syrup
⅓ C sugar
⅓ C Egg Beaters
1½ t vanilla
⅔ C skim milk
2 C flour plus 1 package Butter Buds plus 1 T baking powder
1 t nutmeg plus ¼ t allspice, sifted together
½ C sugar plus 1½ t cinnamon
Butter flavor Pam no stick cooking spray

1. Beat together the first 3 ingredients. Stir in vanilla and milk. Gradually add the 4 sifted ingredients; mix just until blended. Do not over mix!
2. Coat muffin tins with Pam. Fill each ¾ full and bake in preheated 400° oven 12-15 minutes. Do not over bake!
3. Remove muffins from oven, spray immediately with Pam and roll each muffin in cinnamon-sugar mixture. Serve at once.

Serves: 18

Per Serving: 0.11 g Fat, 96 Calories, 1 % Fat, 2.1 g Protein, 21.7 g Carb, 109 mg Sodium, 0.16 mg Cholesterol

JOHNNY APPLESEED MUFFINS
(Easy Prep)

1 C "Nonfat Yogurt Cheese"✔
1 T cornstarch
½ C Egg Beaters
3 T EACH sugar and unsweetened applesauce
1½ C flour
1 t baking powder
¼ t EACH baking soda and allspice
1½ C Golden Delicious apple, peeled and finely chopped

1. Combine the first 4 listings. Set aside.
2. Combine dry ingredients; stir into wet mixture. Fold in the apples, spoon into sprayed muffin tins, and bake at 400° for about 20 minutes or until toothpick comes out clean.

Serves: 12

Per Serving: 0.25 g Fat, 100 Calories, 2 % Fat, 4.3 g Protein, 19.8 g Carb, 20.5 mg Sodium, 0 mg Cholesterol

MEMORABLE BANANA NUT BREAD
(Easy Prep)

1½ C flour
¾ C Egg Beaters
½ C light corn syrup
½-1 C sugar
1 heaping C bananas, mashed
1 t EACH vanilla, soda, and baking powder
¼ C 1% fat buttermilk
1 C Grape Nuts
Pam no stick cooking spray

1. Mix all ingredients; bake in large sprayed loaf pan at 350° for 50-60 minutes. Do not over-bake. Test for doneness with toothpick.

Serves: 16

Per Serving: 0.1 g Fat, 144 Calories, 0 % Fat, 2 g Protein, 34 g Carb, 84 mg Sodium, 0.18 mg Cholesterol

BEER BREAD
(Easy Prep)

3 C self-rising flour
3 T sugar
1 (12-oz.) can lite beer

1. Stir together all ingredients, pour into sprayed loaf pan, and bake at 350° for 1 hour or until done.

Serves: 10

Per Serving: 0.3 g Fat, 160 Calories, 2 % Fat, 3.7 g Protein, 32.8 g Carb, 406 mg Sodium, 0 mg Cholesterol

PUMPKIN SPICE BREAD
(Easy Prep)

3½ C flour
½ t baking powder
2 t baking soda
1 t EACH cinnamon, cloves and nutmeg
1½ C sugar
1¼ C Egg Beaters
2 C canned pumpkin
⅔ C liquid Butter Buds
¾ C Grape Nuts (optional)
⅔ C light corn syrup
Pam no stick cooking spray

1. Mix together dry ingredients. Add remaining ingredients and mix just until blended.
2. Pour into 2 8-inch loaf pans that have been coated with Pam and bake at 350° for about 30-40 minutes or until done.

Serves: 24

Per Serving: 0.25 g Fat, 140 Calories, 2 % Fat, 3.3 g Protein, 38.7 g Carb, 101 mg Sodium, 0 mg Cholesterol

STRAWBERRY BREAD
(Easy Prep)

1 package Butter Buds
3 C flour
1 t soda
1 T cinnamon
1¼ C sugar
¾ C Egg Beaters
1 C corn syrup
¼ C unsweetened applesauce
2 (10-oz.) packages frozen unsweetened strawberries
Red food coloring, optional, for a prettier bread

1. Combine all dry ingredients, mixing well. Add the egg substitute, corn syrup, and applesauce. Stir in the strawberries and pour into 2 (8") sprayed loaf pans.
2. Bake at 350° for 45-55 minutes or until done. Cool before serving.

Serves: 16

Per Serving: 0.2 g Fat, 194 Calories, 1 % Fat, 3.09 g Protein, 44 g Carb, 207 mg Sodium, 0 mg Cholesterol

BLUEBERRY ORANGE BREAD

1 package Butter Buds plus ¼ C hot water
3 T unsweetened applesauce
1 T grated orange peel
½ C orange juice
¼ C Egg Beaters
¾ C sugar
2 C all-purpose flour
1 t baking powder
¼ t baking soda
½ t salt (optional)
1 C fresh blueberries
1 t grated orange peel
2 T orange juice
2 T honey

1. Blend together and set aside the first 4 ingredients.
2. Beat the egg and sugar until fluffy.
3. Combine the flour baking powder, soda and salt; slowly add to the egg mixture along with juice mixture. Don't over mix.
4. Fold in blueberries. Pour into a sprayed and floured loaf pan and bake at 350° for 45 minutes or until done. Cool 10 minutes in pan, then move to wire rack.
5. Mix together the last 3 ingredients; spoon over hot bread.

Serves: 10

Per Serving: 0.3 g Fat, 175 Calories, 1 % Fat, 3 g Protein, 39.9 g Carb, 109 mg Sodium, 0 mg Cholesterol

CHEESY YEAST BREAD

1 C very hot water (near boiling stage)
1/4 C sugar
1 t salt (optional)
1 package yeast
1/4 C Egg Beaters, beaten with 1 t sugar
8 oz. grated Fat Free Healthy Choice cheddar cheese
2 T Ultra Promise Fat Free margarine, softened
4 C all-purpose flour
Butter flavor Pam no stick cooking spray

1. Mix together the first 3 ingredients; set aside until lukewarm.
2. Dissolve the yeast in 2 T warm tap water; add yeast mixture and egg mixture to first mixture.
3. Combine the cheese with the margarine; mix well and stir into yeast mixture. Add flour and mix until combined. Divide dough in half and place in two loaf pans that have been sprayed with Pam; let rise 1 - 1 1/2 times its original size. Bake in 350° oven for about 15 minutes.

Makes: 2 loaves or about 24 slices

Per Serving: 0.60 g Fat, 96 Calories, 5 % Fat, 5 g Protein, 16.8 g Carb, 102 mg Sodium, 1.6 mg Cholesterol

FAVORITE CHEESE BREAD

2 oz. Healthy Choice Fat Free cheese singles, diced
1 1/2 C (6 oz.) grated Healthy Choice Fat Free Cheddar cheese
1/2 C Egg Beaters
1 C evaporated skim milk
1 package yeast dissolved in 1/2 C very warm water
1/2 t EACH basil and mustard
2 T Ultra Promise Fat Free margarine
1 t butter flavoring
3 1/4 C "Best Baker's Mix"✔

1. Mix together all ingredients except baker's mix. Slowly add in baker's mix and mix just until blended.
2. Spoon into sprayed loaf pan, cover and let rise until double in size. Bake at 350° for 40-50 minutes. Do not overbake.

Serves: 18

Note: Makes 18 muffins or bread sticks (Bake about 25 minutes)

Per Serving: 0.1 g Fat, 108 Calories, 1 % Fat, 5.7 g Protein, 18 g Carb, 155 mg Sodium, 2.7 mg Cholesterol

CHEESE MUFFINS
(Quick Fix)

1 C wheat flour
1 C skim milk
¾ C Egg Beaters
1 package Butter Buds plus 3 T hot water
3 Healthy Choice Fat Free cheese singles
½ t salt (optional)
Butter flavored Pam no stick cooking spray

1. Beat all ingredients except cheese with a mixer until smooth.
2. Coat muffin tins with butter flavor Pam and place in a 450° oven until hot, about 2 minutes. Remove pan from oven.
3. Spoon about 1 heaping T of batter into each tin. Cut each cheese slice into 4 equal pieces. Place 1 cheese piece in center of each muffin cup on batter. Fill each tin to ¾ full with remaining batter and bake 20-25 minutes.

Serves: 12

Per Serving: 0 g Fat, 58 Calories, 1 % Fat, 3.4 g Protein, 10 g Carb, 179 mg Sodium, 1.6 mg Cholesterol

Notes and Extra Recipes:

Notes and Extra Recipes:

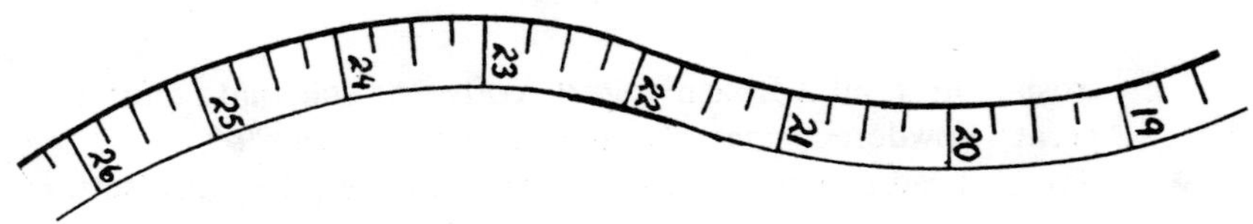

SWEET TREATS

Sweet treats are something most of us look forward to after a meal or perhaps for a snack. Choosing unsweetened fruit desserts is the best way to curb your sweet tooth and to be able to have dessert almost anytime. Recommended daily allowance of fruit is 4 servings; a serving is considered a whole medium-size piece of fruit, 1 C raw, ½ C cooked or canned fruit, ½ grapefruit, ¼ melon such as a cantaloupe, ¼ C dried fruit, or ½ C fruit juice. Sweetened desserts are not tabu as long as the fat grams are 30% or less of the caloric count per serving and do not contain saturated fat, but the key is moderation. Sweetened desserts are considered simple carbohydrates; you should limit your intake of refined sugar to no more than 10% of your total daily caloric intake. For someone eating 2000 calories a day, that adds up to 200 calories.

Time Savers For Sugar-free Desserts:

- Baked fruit - Place 5 C assorted unsweetened canned, drained fruits in sprayed baking dish. Pour a mixture of 1 C unsweetened apple juice + ¼ C Grape Nuts + ½-1 t each cinnamon and allspice. Bake at 325° for 35-40 minutes.
- Top cut up fresh or canned fruit with nonfat sugar-free frozen yogurt or pudding. Sprinkle nonfat sugar-free frozen or unfrozen yogurt with nonfat sugar-free crunchy cereal.
- Puree' strawberries; serve over peach, pear, or apricot halves.
- Slice fresh fruit into a bowl; top with ½ skim and ½ evaporated skim milk. Sprinkle with artificial sweetener if desired.
- Saute' sliced fruit in Butter Buds liquid, top with raisins and serve. Bake a large banana in skin at 400° for 12-15 minutes. Split one side of skin, stir in a little Butter Buds liquid, cinnamon, and artificial sweetener if desired.
- Alternate layers of different flavors of nonfat sugar-free yogurt in parfait glasses; top with fresh fruit.

Time Savers For Other Sweet Treats:

- Toss 3 C melon balls with ¼ C each Amaretto and Grape Nuts.
- Top baked lite brownies with one or more of the following:

fresh fruit, nonfat frozen yogurt (coffee or chocolate mint are great), powdered sugar, "Nonfat Whipped Cream"✔.

- Saute' sliced bananas in brown sugar, orange juice, and Butter Buds liquid.
- For baked apples: stuff cored apples with cinnamon, brown sugar, and raisins; drizzle with Butter Buds liquid. Bake at 350° for 35-45 minutes.
- Buttermilk Pie - Bake in unbaked pie shell at 350° until firm: 2 C sugar, 3 T flour, ½ C Butter Buds liquid, juice of 1 lemon, 1 T vanilla, Scant 1¼ C Egg Beaters, 1 C (1% fat) buttermilk.
- Lite Spice Cake - Stir into lite white or yellow cake mix: 2 t cinnamon, 1 t each vanilla, nutmeg, and cloves. Prepare according to lite cake mix directions and bake. (May add 1 C raisins if desired.) Frost cooled cake with a combination of prepared Betty Crocker Fluffy White frosting mix plus 1 t instant coffee granules and 1 t chocolate extract.
- Line a square baking dish with vanilla Teddy Grahams; place a layer of sliced bananas on top. Top bananas with 1 C nonfat raspberry frozen yogurt (softened), a small can drained crushed pineapple, ¼ C Grape Nuts, and another cup softened yogurt. Freeze. Garnish with "Nonfat Whipped Cream"✔ and cherries.
- Spray a 13 X 9 pan with Pam. Pour 1 can diced lite apricots in pan; top with dry Lite Spice Cake (as described in #6). Spoon 1 can lite apple pie filling on top of cake mix. Drizzle with ½ C liquid Butter Buds; sprinkle with ¼ C Grape Nuts. Bake at 375° for 45 minutes to 1 hour or until done. Experiment with other fruits, pie fillings, and lite cake mixes.
- Cover 1 C dried apricots with water and 1 t lemon juice in medium saucepan; simmer until tender. Drain, cool and process until smooth; add artificial sweetener to taste. Beat 4 egg whites at room temperature until stiff; fold in apricot puree'. Spoon into a Pam-coated dish and bake at 350° for about 30 minutes.
- Lime freeze - Mix and freeze in ice cream freezer: 3 C limeade, 1 C nonfat dry milk, grated rind of lime, and artificial sweetener to taste. May freeze in ice cube trays. Put in blender; blend until smooth and refreeze.
- Cherry-Cheese Pie - Beat together 4 oz. Healthy Choice Fat Free cream cheese with ⅓ C honey and ½ t vanilla; fold in 3 C "Nonfat Whipped Cream"✔. Pour into baked pie shell and chill. Spread 1 can lite cherry pie filling on top.
- Quick Dessert Sauce - Mix 2 T sugar with 1½ T cornstarch; add 1½ C fresh sliced peaches + ½ C sugar-free strawberry jelly. Microwave on high for about 5 minutes, stirring every minute until thickened. Stir in 1 C fresh blueberries or diced

strawberries and ¼ C Grape Nuts or fat free granola.

- Magnificent Mousse - Beat 4 egg whites at room temperature until stiff peaks form; fold in 3 C prepared Betty Crocker Fluffy White Frosting mix. Stir in 1 or more of the following: amaretto or coffee liqueur, peppermint, almond, vanilla, or maple extract, ¼ C cocoa, or any flavoring of your choice.
- For peach or apricot mousse - Boil 1½ C dried fruit in 1 C water, ½ C sugar, and a dash of lemon juice. Reduce heat and simmer until tender; cool and puree' apricots and water mixture. Fold into 3 C prepared frosting as in #13. Chill.
- Stir 1½ C grated carrots or zucchini into 1 box lite brownie mix or lite cake mix; add ¾ C each Egg Beaters and Grape Nuts, 1 C nonfat mayonnaise, ½ C sugar, and 1 t each cinnamon and vanilla. Stir just until moist, add more mayonnaise if needed. Bake at 350° for 45-55 min. Cool. Top with powdered sugar.
- Pour in an unbaked pie shell and bake for 35 minutes at 350° a mixture of 1 C nonfat plain yogurt, ½ C Egg Beaters, 1 C sugar, 2 T flour, 1 t each almond and coconut extract, and 1 (6-oz.) package dried apricots or peaches, chopped. Top with "Nonfat Whipped Cream"✔ to serve.
- Make "Mock Sweetened Condensed Milk"✔ - Mix, heat, and stir to dissolve ¾ C sugar and 2¼ C instant nonfat dry milk in ½ C water and ½ t vanilla.

Helpful Hints:

- Do not spray an angel food cake pan with Pam or grease; it rises better without it.
- Use sugar-free Jello to save on calories. Try omitting sugar in some recipes such as puddings or cobblers; after it has cooked add artificial sweetener, honey, or unsweetened fruit juices to individual servings.
- Instead of frosting a cake, place a large doily on cake, and sprinkle cake with powdered sugar; remove doily.
- To quickly bring egg whites to room temperature, place eggs in a bowl of warm water; cover and let stand for about 4 minutes. Separate egg white from yolk; discard yolk.
- One easy way to separate the egg white from the yolk is by cracking the egg into a very small funnel. The white will slide through; then, discard the yolk.
- Make sure egg whites are at room temperature before beating; they will have more volume.
- To reduce fat completely in "Nutty Graham Cracker Pie Crust"✔ replace graham crackers with Snack Wells Cinnamon Graham Crackers.

CAKES

I CAN'T WAIT CAKE

(You have to wait, but it's definitely worth it!)

Cake:
1 package lite yellow cake mix
1 package Butter Buds
Frosting:
2 C "Nonfat Yogurt Cheese"
2 C sugar
½ t EACH coconut and butter flavoring
1 t unflavored gelatin

1. Mix Butter Buds with cake mix and prepare according to directions. Bake in two round layers. Cool and freeze.
2. For frosting, combine all ingredients except gelatin.
3. Sprinkle gelatin over 2 T water in small saucepan; let stand 1 minute. Stir gelatin over medium heat until dissolved. Cool.
4. Stir gelatin into frosting mixture. Chill.
5. Remove cakes from freezer; slice each layer horizontally creating 4 layers.
6. Place 1 layer in bottom of cake dish; frost top. Repeat with remaining layers. Ice entire cake. Store in an airtight container if possible in refrigerator at least 3 days. Do not peek. For a more impressive cake, double the recipe, making it taller.

Serve: 16

Per Serving: 1.5 g Fat, 196 Calories, 7 % Fat, 5.4 g Protein, 58.3 g Carb, 275 mg Sodium, 0 mg Cholesterol

APRICOT CAKE

1 C Egg Beaters
½ C Kraft Free mayonnaise
½ C sugar
¼ C corn syrup
1 C apricot nectar
1 package lite yellow cake mix
1 t lemon juice
Pam no stick cooking spray

1. Mix all ingredients together until just combined. Bake in a sprayed and floured tube pan at 350° for about 45 minutes or until tooth pick inserted in center comes out clean.

Serves: 12

Per Serving: 1 g Fat, 157 Calories, 6 % Fat, 4.6 g Protein, 32.3 g Carb, 332 mg Sodium, 0 mg Cholesterol

QUICK GRAHAM CRACKER CAKE

(Quick Fix)

5 (2½ X 2½) Honey Maid Graham cracker squares
½ C strawberries
¼ t vanilla
¼ C prepared Betty Crocker Fluffy White frosting mix

1. Puree strawberries; fold in vanilla and prepared frosting.
2. Place 1 graham cracker square on a plate; spread about 1½ T of strawberry topping on cracker. Stack another cracker on top of the topping and spread with more topping. Repeat until all cracker are used. Ice entire stack with remaining frosting and serve. (May use any fruit of your choice.)

Serves: 1

Per Serving: 3 g Fat, 270 Calories, 10 % Fat, 4.5 g Protein, 55.5 g Carb, 292 mg Sodium, 0 mg Cholesterol

POUND CAKE DELIGHT

(Quick Fix)

1 (8-oz.) carton Healthy Choice Fat Free cream cheese, softened
½ t EACH vanilla and cinnamon
½ C nonfat chocolate pudding
1 box Betty Crocker Fluffy White Frosting mix, prepared
1 loaf Entenmann's nonfat plain or chocolate pound cake

1. Beat together the cream cheese, flavorings, and pudding. Fold in 1½ C of the frosting.
2. Split cake horizontally into 4 layers. Frost each layer, stacking as you go. Frost sides and top of cake. Chill.

Serves: 12

Per Serving: 0 g Fat, 155 Calories, 0 % Fat, 5.4 g Protein, 29 g Carb, 216 mg Sodium, 3.3 mg Cholesterol

CHEESECAKE TO DIE'T FOR

1 recipe "Nutty Graham Cracker Pie Crust"✔
1 C evaporated skim milk, chilled
1 C sugar
3 (8-oz.) containers Healthy Choice fat free cream cheese, softened
2 C prepared "Nonfat Yogurt Cheese"✔ plus 3 T cornstarch
½ C Truly Lite Fat Free ricotta cheese
1 C Egg Beaters, divided
¼ t lemon extract
2 t vanilla
Pam no stick cooking spray

1. Coat the sides and bottom of a large springform pan with Pam. Prepare graham cracker crust but, before you add the liquid to crust, crumb the sides of the springform pan. Dump remaining crumbs back into food processor; add liquid ingredients and press crust into the bottom of the pan to form the base of the cake. Set aside.
2. Preheat oven to 350°. In a large mixing bowl, place the sugar, cream cheese and ¼ of the Egg Beaters; mix thoroughly. Add remaining Egg Beaters a little at a time, mixing well. Add yogurt cheese mixture, ricotta cheese, and lemon and vanilla flavorings; mix until combined. Whip the evaporated milk until stiff; fold into cream cheese mixture and pour into pan.
3. Bake cheesecake 30 minutes at 350°. Turn oven off and leave cake in oven with the door closed for 1 hour. Take out and set on counter until COMPLETELY cool, about 3 - 5 hours. Store in refrigerator and serve with "Berry Puree"✔ or another of the fruit sauces or toppings if desired.

Serves: 16

Per Serving: 0.18 g Fat, 93 Calories, 1 % Fat, 5.5 g Protein, 16 g Carb, 139.6 mg Sodium, 3.62 mg Cholesterol

BEST BIRTHDAY CAKE EVER
(June's Favorite - Thanks Mom!)

1 Angel food cake, prepared✔
1 recipe "Nonfat Whipped Cream," prepared and divided✔
1 can lite pineapple pie filling or 2½ C "Basic Cream Pie Filling"✔
1 (16-oz.) can crushed pineapple, drained well

1. Cool cake completely and slice in ½ horizontally.
2. Place first layer on cake server, top with pie filling and about ⅓ of the whipped cream. Add top cake layer and ice cake with remaining whipped cream. Chill and serve.

Serves: 12

Per Serving: 0.3 g Fat, 136 Calories, 2 % Fat, 3.3 g Protein, 43.3 g Carb, 170 mg Sodium, 0 mg Cholesterol

LITE FRESH STRAWBERRY SHORTCAKE
(Easy Prep)

2 C all-purpose flour
½ C sugar
1 T baking powder
½ t cinnamon
¾ C evaporated skim milk
3 C fresh strawberries, sliced and sweetened with 1 t sugar or artificial sweetener to taste
1 recipe "Nonfat Whipping Cream"✔ prepared
Pam no stick cooking spray

1. Sift together the first 4 ingredients in a large bowl; blend in evaporated milk. Knead dough lightly into 1 smooth log about 6" in diameter. Cut dough into 6 equal slices and place on a baking sheet that has been coated with Pam. Bake at 350° for 12 - 15 minutes; cool.
2. Combine strawberries with ½ - 1 C water to form a syrup.
3. To serve, split each biscuit and top 6 halves with ½ C strawberries. Spoon about ½ C whipped cream on top. Garnish with a whole fresh strawberry if desired. Save remaining halves for other shortcakes. Freezes well.

Serves: 6 (1 half per person plus ½ C each strawberries and whipped cream.

Per Serving: 0.46 g Fat, 171 Calories, 2 % Fat, 5 g Protein, 36.9 g Carb, 36.1 mg Sodium, 0.06 mg Cholesterol

MAMIE'S PINEAPPLE ORANGE CAKE

(Very moist and rich)

1 box lite yellow cake mix
1 large can lite mandarin oranges, undrained
½ C EACH unsweetened applesauce and Kraft Free mayonnaise
1 C Egg Beaters
1 large can unsweetened crushed pineapple, undrained
1 (3-oz.) package instant vanilla pudding mix
1 box Betty Crocker Fluffy White Frosting Mix, prepared

1. Mix together the first 4 ingredients. Spray 3 (9-inch round) cake pans with Pam and flour each. Divide batter between pans and bake at 325° for 20 minutes. Cool.
2. Mix pineapple with pudding mix. Refrigerate. When pudding is semi-set, mix in 1 C prepared frosting. Chill until firm. Ice cake and serve.

Serves: 16

Per Serving: 1.5 g Fat, 215 Calories, 7 % Fat, 5 g Protein, 45 g Carb, 377 mg Sodium, 0 mg Cholesterol

FRESH APPLE CAKE

2 C sugar
1 C applesauce
3 C flour
¾ C 1% buttermilk
1 C Egg Beaters
½ t salt (optional)
1½ t baking soda
1 C fresh apples, peeled, cored and grated
½ C Grape-Nuts cereal
1 t cinnamon
1 t nutmeg

1. In large bowl of mixer, at medium speed, mix applesauce and sugar. Continue to beat and add eggs one at a time.
2. Measure and sift flour, baking soda, salt, cinnamon and nutmeg.
3. Add flour mixture to sugar mixture alternately with buttermilk, add flour first and last. Fold in apples and Grape Nuts.
4. Pour into a tube pan which has been sprayed with Pam and floured. Bake at 325° for about 1 hour. Do not overbake. Remove from pan onto cooling rack.

Serves: 12

Per Serving: 0.6 g Fat, 287 Calories, 2 % Fat, 5.7 g Protein, 65 g Carb, 68 mg Sodium, 0.3 mg Cholesterol

PUDDING CAKE

1 C flour
½ C hot water plus 1 package Butter Buds
1 C Grape Nuts
1 box Betty Crocker Fluffy White Frosting Mix, prepared
8 oz. Healthy Choice Fat Free cream cheese, softened
1 small package instant sugar-free vanilla pudding
1 small package instant sugar-free chocolate pudding
3 C skim milk

1. Mix together the first 3 ingredients; press into a 9 x 13-inch pan and bake in 350° oven about 10 minutes. Let cool.
2. Beat together 2 C of prepared frosting with cream cheese; layer over cooled crust.
3. Mix the puddings and milk; chill until almost set; spread over cream cheese layer. Top with remaining frosting and chill thoroughly.

Serves: 16

Per Serving: 0 g Fat, 155 Calories, 0 % Fat, 7 g Protein, 26 g Carb, 205 mg Sodium, 3.4 mg Cholesterol

RUM CAKE

1 C Grape Nuts cereal
1 lite yellow cake mix
1 small package instant vanilla pudding mix
1 C Egg Beaters
½ C EACH cold water and unsweetened applesauce
½ C dark rum
2 packages Butter Buds plus ½ C hot water
1 C sugar
½ C dark rum
Pam no stick cooking spray

1. Preheat oven to 325°. Coat a bundt with Pam and flour. Shake off excess.
2. Sprinkle bottom of pan with Grape Nuts. Mix the next 5 ingredients together and pour over cereal. Bake 1 hour. Cool on wire rack and turn out on to cake plate.
3. Place Butter Buds liquid and sugar in saucepan. Boil and stir about 5 minutes. Remove from heat and mix in rum. Prick top and sides of cake with toothpick; drizzle boiled mixture on top and over sides of cake. Serve with "Nonfat Whipped Cream" if desired.

Serves: 16

Per Serving: 1.5 g Fat, 258 Calories, 5 % Fat, 4.25 g Protein, 45.6 g Carb, 410 mg Sodium, 0 mg Cholesterol

LILLIAN'S ANGEL FOOD CAKE

(Taste this and you'll never buy one at the grocery again)

11 large egg whites at room temperature
1¼ C cake flour (Swans or Soft Silk)
½ C sugar
¼ t EACH cream of tartar and salt (optional)
1 t vanilla
¼ t almond extract
1⅓ sugar (sift by itself 3 or 4 times)

1. Sift together the cake flour and ½ C sugar 4 or 5 times. Set aside.
2. Beat egg whites until stiff and add cream of tartar, salt and flavorings. Sprinkle in 1⅓ C sugar in 4 additions and stir by hand after each addition.
3. Using a wooden spoon, fold in flour/sugar mixture in 4 additions.
4. Put in ungreased 10-inch tube pan and bake at 375° for 35-40 minutes. Cool on cake rack.

Serves: 12

Per Serving: 0.1 g Fat, 165 Calories, 1 % Fat, 3.4 g Protein, 37 g Carb, 44 mg Sodium, 0 mg Cholesterol

STRAWBERRY-LOVERS CAKE

(Easy Prep)

1 (10-oz.) package unsweetened frozen strawberries
1 box lite white cake mix
½ C EACH water and Kraft Free mayonnaise
1 small package wild strawberry Jello
1 C Egg Beaters
1 box Betty Crocker Fluffy White Frosting mix, prepared
8 oz. Healthy Choice Fat Free cream cheese, softened

1. Slightly thaw strawberries. Mix half the strawberries with cake mix, water, mayonnaise, and jello. Beat 3 minutes; add Egg Beaters and beat 1 minute longer. Pour into sprayed and floured oblong cake pan; bake at 350° for 25-35 minutes.
2. Mix together 1½ C frosting with cream cheese and remaining strawberries. Spread on cooled cake.

Serves: 16

Per Serving: 1.5 g Fat, 184 Calories, 7 % Fat, 5.3 g Protein, 37.2 g Carb, 250 mg Sodium, 2.5 mg Cholesterol

FROSTINGS & TOPPINGS

HEAVENLY CREAM FROSTING

2½ C plus 1 T "Nonfat Whipping Cream"✔ (made as directed and set aside in refrigerator)
1 box Betty Crocker "Fluffy White" frosting mix (made as directed using clean beaters)
4 oz. container nonfat ready-to-eat chocolate pudding
1 T instant nonfat ready-to-eat vanilla pudding
½ t cinnamon
¼ t "Auto-Drip" canned coffee grounds
3 T Healthy Choice Fat Free cream cheese
1 t almond extract
¼ t butterscotch flavoring or 1 T nonfat Butterscotch pudding
2 T water
1 t unflavored gelatin

1. Add puddings, cinnamon, coffee, cream cheese, almond and butterscotch flavorings to prepared frosting, mixing at low to medium speed until blended. Set aside.
2. Sprinkle gelatin over water in a small saucepan. Let gelatin stand 1 minute. Stir over low heat until it dissolves. Cool to lukewarm.
3. Fold gelatin into prepared whipped cream. Fold frosting mixture into whipped cream mixture and frost cake. Chill. Serve with "Chocolate Lovers' Dream Torte."✔

Serves: 24 - Enough frosting for 2 cakes.
Note: You may want to chill frosting before icing cake.

Per Serving: 0 g Fat, 52 Calories,
0 % Fat, 1.17 g Protein, 10.9 g Carb,
187 mg Sodium, 0 mg Cholesterol

KAHLUA BERRIES
(Easy Prep)

1 quart large fresh strawberries, stems removed
1 box Betty Crocker "Fluffy White" Frosting Mix, prepared
1 C "Nonfat Yogurt Cheese"✔
½ t EACH vanilla and ground cinnamon
3 T Kahlua or coffee-flavored liqueur

1. Mix together 2 C prepared frosting with remaining ingredients except berries. Whip until smooth. Chill.
2. Serve as dip or spoon over strawberries in dessert dishes.

Serves: 6

Per Serving: 0.6 g Fat, 185 Calories,
3 % Fat, 4 g Protein, 36 g Carb,
100 mg Sodium, 0 mg Cholesterol

NONFAT WHIPPING CREAM
(Easy Prep)

½ C evaporated skim milk
1½ t unflavored gelatin
½ C plus 2 t water
½ t lemon juice
2 t vanilla
3 T sugar or artificial sweetener to taste

1. Pour milk in small, deep bowl and place in freezer until ice crystals form around the entire edge of the milk (about 20 minutes). Chill beaters in freezer as well.
2. Meanwhile place water in small saucepan; sprinkle gelatin over water. Let stand about one minute. Cook gelatin mixture over low heat until gelatin dissolves, stirring constantly. Chill in refrigerator until gelatin resembles unbeaten egg white, about 15 minutes.
3. Beat milk in mixer on high until foamy. Slowly add vanilla and sugar a little at a time until soft peaks form.
4. Immediately add gelatin mixture and lemon juice. Continue to beat until stiff peaks form. Be patient but continue to beat, depending on your mixer 5-8 minutes approximately.

Serves: 10 (Makes about 3 Cups)
Note: To make chocolate cream, add 2 T cocoa to 1 C whipped cream.

Per Serving: 0.41 g Fat, 8.8 Calories, 4 % Fat, 0.41 g Protein, 1.7 g Carb, 6.7 mg Sodium, 0.45 mg Cholesterol

VANILLA CREAM CHEESE FILLING

(Easy Prep and great for crepes or blintzes)

8 oz. Healthy Choice Fat Free cream cheese, softened
½ t vanilla
¼ C Butter Buds liquid
1 C powdered sugar
Dash cinnamon

1. Mix all ingredients except cinnamon together until smooth. For crepes or blintzes spoon 2 T mixture into crepe. Lay seam side down in glass baking dish; cover and bake at 350° for about 12-15 minutes. Top with your favorite dessert sauce or dust with cinnamon and serve immediately.
2. If not using with crepes, use as topping or dip for desserts or fruit.

Makes: about 2 C or enough filling for 16 crepes (2 T per crepe)

Per Serving: 0 g Fat, 39 Calories,
0 % Fat, 2.5 g Protein, 7.3 g Carb,
100 mg Sodium, 2.5 mg Cholesterol

NEVER FAIL MERINGUE

(Quick Fix)

2 T sugar
1 T cornstarch
½ C water
3 egg whites at room temperature
⅛ t salt
½ t vanilla
6 T sugar

1. Combine first 3 ingredients in a small saucepan. Cook over low heat, stirring constantly until mixture is thick and clear. Cool.
2. Beat egg whites, salt and vanilla until soft mounds form. Gradually add remaining sugar by spoonfuls beating well after each addition. Add cooled cornstarch mixture and continue beating until stiff peaks form.
3. Spread on pie and bake in a preheated 350° oven for 12-15 minutes or until meringue is browned.

Serves: 8

Per Serving: 0 g Fat, 58 Calories,
0 % Fat, 1.1 g Protein, 13.6 g Carb,
18 mg Sodium, 0 mg Cholesterol

BLUEBERRY APRICOT TOPPING

½ C sugar free apricot jam or jelly
1 C fresh blueberries
1 lb. fresh apricots, seeded and chopped
⅓ C apricot nectar
1 t Apricot brandy (optional)

1. Blend all ingredients in food processor or blender; chill and serve over cheesecake, meringues, or over shortcake and other desserts.

Serves: 12

Per Serving: 0 g Fat, 16 Calories, 0 % Fat, 0.2 g Protein, 4.1 g Carb, 0.3 mg Sodium, 0 mg Cholesterol

BERRY PUREE

(Quick Fix)

1 C fresh strawberries, your favorite fruit
1 scant T cornstarch

1. Mix together both ingredients in food processor or blender and blend until smooth. Heat in a microwave safe bowl on medium high until slightly thickened for about 5 - 8 minutes stirring frequently. May cook in saucepan for about 12 - 15 minutes.

Makes: 1 C or 16 (1 T) servings (Nutritional per T)

Per Serving: 0.06 g Fat, 3.4 Calories, 16 % Fat, 0.06 g Protein, 0.81 g Carb, 0 mg Sodium, 0 mg Cholesterol

PIES & PASTRIES

BASIC PIE CRUST

(Easy Prep)

3/4 C all-purpose flour
Dash salt (optional)
4 T Ultra Promise Fat Free margarine
1/4 C "Nonfat Yogurt Cheese"✔
Pam no stick cooking spray

1. Mix together the flour and salt in a large bowl; cut in margarine with 2 knives or pastry blender until mixture resembles small peas.
2. Blend in yogurt and form into a ball. Wrap in plastic wrap or wax paper and chill for about one hour (can remain in refrigerator for about 3-5 days). Also freezes well: chill, press in pan, and freeze.
3. To bake, roll dough out to size of pan, 1/8-inch thick. Place in pie pan sprayed with Pam and bake at 375° for 12-15 minutes. For filled crust, place filling in crust and bake as directed.

Serves: 8-16 (Nutritional analysis is for the entire crust.)

Note: Prepare ahead of time, make extras, and freeze.

Per Serving: 0 g Fat, 344 Calories,
0 % Fat, 11 g Protein, 70 g Carb,
1.5 mg Sodium, 0 mg Cholesterol

NUTTY GRAHAM CRACKER PIE CRUST

(Quick Fix)

11 large (5 1/2 X 2 1/2-inch) Honey Maid graham crackers
1/4 C Grape Nuts cereal
1 1/2 t cinnamon
3 T light corn syrup
3 T Butter Buds liquid
Pam no stick cooking spray

1. Puree crackers, cereal, and cinnamon in food processor or blender to a fine consistency. Drizzle corn syrup and Butter Buds liquid into crumbs while processor is running; mix well.
2. Spray a 9-inch pie plate with Pam. Press crumb mixture into plate. Use as is or bake in 350° for 5 minutes.

Makes: 1 crust (Nutritional analysis is for the entire crust.)

Per Serving: 11 g Fat, 685 Calories,
17 % Fat, 7.8 g Protein, 118.6 g Carb,
977 mg Sodium, 0 mg Cholesterol

HEARTY GRAINS PIE CRUST

(Quick Fix and definitely my favorite crust!)

1 (9-oz.) can Pillsbury Hearty Grains biscuits
Pam no stick cooking spray
1 slightly beaten egg white or 1 - 2 T Egg Beaters

1. Spray a pie pan with Pam. Remove and separate 8 biscuits from can. Pull each biscuit apart in the center, creating two biscuits from one.
2. Press all 16 biscuit circles into pie pan. Cover bottom of pan and sides forming 1 entire crust; crimp edges.
3. **For a pre-baked crust or filled pie:** Make crust; line pie crust with foil. Place 1 or 2 cups dried beans or pie weights in foil to keep crust from rising. Bake at 350° about 8 - 10 minutes. Watch closely If it browns too quickly, make a foil tent and place over crust. Cool; fill pie and serve.
4. **For a cooked pie:** Make crust; again line pie with foil and weight it down. Bake at 350° about 2-3 minutes. Remove crust from oven; remove foil and weights. Brush crust with egg white or Egg Beaters; fill with desired filling and bake as directed in pie recipe. If needed cover with foil to prevent crust from getting too brown.

Makes: 1 whole pie crust (nutritional analysis is for whole crust; ⅛ crust = 2 Fat g and 82 Calories)

Per Piecrust: 16 g Fat, 657 Calories, 22 % Fat, 16g Protein, 120 g Carb, 160 mg Sodium, 0 mg Cholesterol

KAREN'S FAVORITE CHOCOLATE PEANUT BUTTER PIE

2½ T Truly Lite Fat Free ricotta cheese
3 T crunchy peanut butter
1 C powdered sugar
½ C flour
1 large package instant sugar-free chocolate pie filling prepared with 2⅓ C skim milk plus 1 t vanilla
1 recipe "Never Fail Meringue"✔

1. Mix first four ingredients until smooth. Press into bottom and up sides of pie plate.
2. Make pie filling according to package directions using skim milk and vanilla; pour over peanut butter crust. Chill. Prepare meringue; spoon over pie and bake as directed. Chill and serve.

Serves: 12

Per Serving: 2 g Fat, 104 Calories, 17 % Fat, 3.5 g Protein, 17.5 g Carb, 73 mg Sodium, 1.1 mg Cholesterol

RUBY'S PECAN PIE

(The original recipe is included with substitutions beside it)

3 eggs or ¾ C Egg Beaters
2 T flour
1 t vanilla
Nutmeg to taste
1 t vinegar
1 dollop margarine, the size of an egg, or 2 packages Butter Buds plus ⅓ C water
¾ C white Karo syrup
¼ C dark Karo syrup
½ C sugar
1 C pecans or 1 C Grape Nuts
1 (9-inch) "Basic Pie Crust"✔

1. Mix all ingredients well. Pour into prepared pie crust; bake at 375° for 10 minutes. Turn oven down to 350° and bake until top is brown and filling is set.

Serves: 8 (using second set of ingredients)

Per Serving: 0.9 g Fat, 248 Calories, 3 % Fat, 1.7 g Protein, 59 g Carb, 297 mg Sodium, 0 mg Cholesterol

PENNEY'S PEACH-BANANA PIE
(Quick Fix)

1 recipe "Nutty Graham Cracker Pie Crust"✔, prepared
1 large can lite sliced peaches
2 medium bananas, sliced
½ C sugar
2 T cornstarch
Pinch EACH nutmeg and salt (optional)

1. Drain peaches; reserve juice. Measure juice, adding water if needed, to make 1 C. Place in a medium saucepan; bring to a boil. Combine the sugar, cornstarch, and spices; add to boiling juice mixture. Cook until clear, about 3 minutes.
2. Slice bananas into pie shell; top with peaches. Pour mixture over pie. When cool, top with "Nonfat Whipped Cream".

Serves: 8

Per Serving: 0.8 g Fat, 107 Calories, 0 % Fat, 0.8 g Protein, 24 g Carb, 1 mg Sodium, 0 mg Cholesterol

EASY LEMONADE PIE

1 t unflavored gelatin plus ¼ C water
1 box Betty Crocker Fluffy White Frosting mix, prepared
¼ C plus 2 T lemon juice, or to taste
A few drops of red food coloring (optional)
1 "Nutty Graham Cracker Pie Crust"✔, prepared

1. Sprinkle gelatin over water; let stand 1 minute. Cook and stir over medium heat 2-3 minutes or until dissolved.
2. Whisk in prepared frosting and lemon juice. Spoon into prepared crust and chill.

Serves: 10

Per Serving: 1 g Fat, 112 Calories, 8 % Fat, 2.4 g Protein, 20.9 g Carb, 78 mg Sodium, 0 mg Cholesterol

QUICK FRIED PIES
(Easy Prep)

1 (9-oz.) can Pillsbury Hearty Grains Biscuits
1 can Lite apple pie filling
½ t cinnamon
Dash nutmeg
Butter flavor Pam no-stick cooking spray

1. Puree pie filling with cinnamon and nutmeg. Set aside.
2. Separate biscuits, using 1 biscuit per pie. Roll out each biscuit to about ⅛-inch thick. Fill center with about 1 T of filling. Fold dough over and crimp edges with tines of a fork.
3. Coat a non-stick skillet with Pam; slowly cook each pie on both sides until brown and cooked through. (If desired, mix powdered sugar with enough skim milk to form an icing and drizzle over warm pies.)

Serves: 8

Sweet Variation: Use your favorite pie filling or unsweetened jam or jelly in pies, or use fresh fruit mixed with sugar or sugar substitute. May also make mini pies - see below.

Appetizer or Main Dish Variation: For appetizers, cut each biscuit in half making two pies from one biscuit. For a main dish, use one biscuit as in dessert pies. Fill with shredded lift meat, nonfat cheeses, or puree an entrée or vegetable dish and fill biscuits. Make mini beef or chicken pies with beef stew or chicken pot pie recipes.

Per Serving: 2 g Fat, 115 Calories,
15 % Fat, 2 g Protein, 2 g Carb,
7.5 mg Sodium, 0 mg Cholesterol

BASIC CREAM PIE FILLING

1¼ C sugar
1 C flour
¼ t salt (optional)
2 C EACH skim milk and evaporated skim milk
¾ C Egg Beaters
1 package dry Butter Buds
1½ t vanilla

1. Sift first 3 ingredients into a saucepan. Slowly add milk; stir until smooth. Cook over medium heat, stirring constantly, until thick.
2. Slowly drizzle the Egg Beaters into the hot mixture. Simmer and stir 2 minutes. Add Butter Buds and vanilla. Remove from heat. Pour into cups or pie crust.

Serves: 8

Variations: Lemon: Add 2 T fresh lemon juice. Coconut: Add 1 t coconut extract. Banana: Add 1 t banana extract. Chocolate: Add 4 T cocoa powder plus ½ t instant coffee.

Per Serving: 0.48 g Fat, 225 Calories,
2 % Fat, 6 g Protein, 49 g Carb,
144 mg Sodium, 3.3 mg Cholesterol

PARTY PEACH PIE

1 (9-inch) "Hearty Grains Pie Crust"✔, baked and cooled
1 can peach pie filling
½ t EACH cinnamon and almond extract
1 recipe "Nonfat Whipping Cream,"✔ prepared
1 C "Nonfat Yogurt Cheese"✔
Cherries for garnish (optional)

1. Combine pie filling, cinnamon, and almond extract; set aside.
2. Fold 2½ C whipped cream into yogurt cheese.
3. Spoon ½ of peach mixture into cooled crust; top with about 1¾ C whipped cream mixture.
   Gently spoon remaining pie filling on top. Chill about 2 hours or until set.
4. Serve each slice with 1 T of whipped cream and a cherry if desired.

Serves: 8

Per Serving: 0 g Fat, 85 Calories,
0 % Fat, 1.2 g Protein, 53 g Carb,
53 mg Sodium, 0 mg Cholesterol

COCONUT BANANA CREAM PIE

3 C evaporated skim milk, divided
¾ C sugar, divided
1 C Egg Beaters
3 T cornstarch
¼ C flour
2 drops yellow food coloring
2 t coconut extract
2 t vanilla
2 medium bananas, sliced
1 recipe "Never Fail Meringue"✔, prepared
1 recipe " Hearty Grain Pie Crust"✔, prepared

1. Mix together ¼ C sugar, Egg Beaters, cornstarch and flour. Gradually whisk in 1 C of the evaporated skim milk. Mix thoroughly and set aside.
2. Pour 2 C evaporated skim milk and ½ C sugar in a large saucepan; bring mixture to a its boiling point, not to boiling. When at this point, slowly add Egg Beater mixture. Cook and stir constantly until slightly thick.
3. Remove from heat; stir in vanilla and food coloring. Cover surface of pan with plastic wrap and cool.
4. Prepare pie crust following recipe directions; cool. Line bottom of pie crust with bananas and top with cooled filling. Chill while preparing meringue.
5. Prepare meringue following recipe directions, spoon over cream filling, and bake according to meringue directions; chill before serving.

Serves: 8

Per Serving: 2.4 g Fat, 165 Calories, 12 % Fat, 6.18 g Protein, 34 g Carb, 78 mg Sodium, 2.75 mg Cholesterol

NOONER'S SWEET POTATO PIE

2 C grated sweet potatoes
¾ C sugar
¼ t EACH allspice, cinnamon, and nutmeg
⅓ C evaporated skim milk
1 package Butter Buds
¼ C Egg Beaters
1 "Basic Pie Crust,"✔ prepared

1. Place potatoes in mixing bowl. Add remaining ingredients. Mix at medium speed for 3 minutes; pour into pie shell.
2. Bake in preheated 325° oven for one hour or until done.

Serves: 8

Per Serving: 0 g Fat, 195 Calories, 0 % Fat, 4.5 g Protein, 43 g Carb, 100 mg Sodium, 0.33 mg Cholesterol

GRASSHOPPER PIE

1 small package lemon pudding and pie filling, not instant
1 (3-oz.) package sugar-free lime jello
⅓ C sugar
2½ C water
½ C Egg Beaters
½ C Bacardi light rum
1 recipe prepared "Nonfat Whipped Cream"✔
1 "Nutty Graham Cracker Pie Crust"✔ prepared

1. Combine the first 5 ingredients in saucepan; mix well. Heat and stir over medium high heat until mixture comes to a full boil. Remove from heat and add rum. Chill until partially set.
2. When ready, blend jello mixture with whipped cream. Spoon into crust and chill until firm, about 2 hours. Top with more whipped cream and fresh strawberries if desired.

Serves: 12

Per Serving: 0.9 g Fat, 79 Calories, 10 % Fat, 1.91 g Protein, 0.7 g Carb, 80.5 mg Sodium, 0 mg Cholesterol

TOM'S FAVORITE PIE
(Easy Prep)

2 boxes SnackWell's Fat Free Devil's Food Cookie Cakes, crumbled
½ gallon frozen vanilla nonfat dairy dessert, softened
2 C "Nonfat Whipped Cream"✔
2 "Nutty Graham Cracker Pie Crusts,"✔ made as directed

1. Mix frozen dessert, whipped cream and crushed cookies.
2. Put in pie shells and freeze.

Serves: 8 (per pie)

Per Serving: 1.3 g Fat, 175 Calories, 3 % Fat, 7.7 g Protein,70.2 g Carb, 487 mg Sodium, 0.37 mg Cholesterol

COOKIES & CANDY

MILLIONAIRE COOKIES
(Easy Prep)

1 box Betty Crocker Fluffy White Frosting mix, prepared
½ C Egg Beaters
2 C lite yellow or white cake mix
2½ C oatmeal; blend in blender to a fine powder
¼ C peanut butter chips
2 C Honey Bunches of Oats cereal, crushed

1. Add Egg Beaters to prepared frosting. Beat in cake mix and oatmeal; blend well. Mix in remaining ingredients. Roll dough into balls, place 2-inches apart on sprayed cookie sheet, and bake 5-10 minutes at 375°.

Serves: 60

Per Serving: 0.4 g Fat, 56 Calories, 8 % Fat, 1.3 g Protein, 11 g Carb, 86 mg Sodium, 0 mg Cholesterol

CARROT COOKIES

1 box lite yellow cake mix
1 box Betty Crocker Fluffy White Frosting mix, prepared
¼ C Egg Beaters
¼ t EACH ground nutmeg and allspice
1 t almond flavoring
2 C finely shredded and chopped carrots

1. Prepare frosting according to package directions. Add cake mix, Egg Beaters, and flavorings; fold in carrots.
2. Drop by spoonfuls onto cookie sheet that has been coated with Pam and bake at 350° for 10-15 minutes.

Serves: 60

Per Serving: 0.4 g Fat, 49 Calories, 7 % Fat, 0.9 g Protein, 10.4 g Carb, 0.72 mg Sodium, 0 mg Cholesterol

COOKIE BARS
(Easy Prep)

1 box Betty Crocker Fluffy White Frosting Mix, prepared
7 (2½ x 5-inch) Nabisco graham crackers, crushed into crumbs
1 C Health Valley Fat-Free Granola
1 t EACH vanilla and baking powder
Pinch of salt (optional)

1. Make frosting according to package directions. Fold in remaining ingredients. Spray a square baking pan with Pam. Spoon in batter; bake at 325° for 30 minutes. Cool and cut into squares.

Serves: 20

Per Serving: 0.37 g Fat, 69 Calories, 5 % Fat, 1.1 g Protein, 15.6 g Carb, 60 mg Sodium, 0 mg Cholesterol

BARBIE'S LEMON CHEESE BARS
(Easy Prep)

1 box lite yellow cake mix
1 package Butter Buds plus ⅓ C hot water
½ C Egg Beaters, divided
8 oz. Healthy Choice Fat Free cream cheese
1 t lemon juice
⅓ C sugar
½ t vanilla
Pam no stick cooking spray

1. Combine dry mix, Butter Buds liquid and ¼ C Egg Beaters. Reserve 1 C of mixture; pat remaining mixture into 9 x 13-inch casserole that has been coated with Pam. Bake at 350° for 15 minutes.
2. Beat remaining ingredients, except reserved crumb mixture, until light and smooth. Spread over baked layer, sprinkle with reserved crumbs and bake at 350° for 15 minutes longer.

Serves: 16

Per Serving: 1.5 g Fat, 163 Calories, 8 % Fat, 5.3 g Protein, 31.5 g Carb, 375 mg Sodium, 2.5 mg Cholesterol

APRICOT COOKIE BARS

8 oz. dried apricots
1 box lite white or yellow cake mix
⅔ C flour
1 t baking powder
½ t salt (optional)
1 C Egg Beaters
¼ C sugar
2 t vanilla
1 C Grape Nuts cereal
Pam no stick cooking spray

1. Prepare cake mix using ¾ C water and ¼ C Egg Beaters. Spray an oblong baking dish with Pam; spread cake batter in pan and bake at 350° for about 15 minutes.
2. Place apricots in saucepan, cover with water and cook about 8 minutes; drain and chop. Set aside. Mix together the flour, baking powder, and salt. Stir in the Egg Beaters, sugar, vanilla and Grape Nuts; mix well and add the apricots.
3. Pour apricot mixture over cooked cake mixture and bake about 30 minutes at 350° or until firm but not overdone.

Serves: 24

Per Serving: 1.03 g Fat, 141 Calories, 6 % Fat, 3.02 g Protein, 24.9 g Carb, 170 mg Sodium, 0 mg Cholesterol

MY FAVORITE OATMEAL COOKIES
(Quick Fix)

1 box lite white or yellow cake mix
½ C Egg Beaters
2 C Raisin Bran cereal
1 ½ C quick cooking oats
½ t allspice
1 ½ t vanilla
1 t cinnamon
Butter flavor Pam

1. Combine all ingredients forming a stiff batter. Drop by heaping teaspoonfuls on a cookie that has been sprayed with Pam. Press down gently with a fork and bake at 375° for 5 - 7 minutes or until brown.

Note: Feel free to try other cereals besides Raisin Bran.
Makes: about 70 medium size cookies

Per Serving: 0.48 g Fat, 38 Calories, 11 % Fat, 0.78 g Protein, 7.7 g Carb, 52.6 mg Sodium, 0 mg Cholesterol

CAPTAIN CRUNCH COOKIES
(Quick Fix)

1 C Captain Crunch cereal
2 C Rice Krispies cereal
2 C thin pretzels, broken into 1-inch pieces
1½ C Health Valley Fat Free Granola
4 C miniature marshmallows
Pam no stick cooking spray

1. Combine first 4 ingredients.
2. Melt marshmallows in microwave-safe dish coated with Pam. Add cereal mixture; mix well. Drop on sprayed wax paper by spoonful or spread into dish.

Serves: 48

Per Serving: 0.10 g Fat, 22 Calories, 4 % Fat, 0.45 g Protein, 4.5 g Carb, 63 mg Sodium, 0 mg Cholesterol

LEMON WHIPPERSNAPS

(Easy Prep)

1 package lite yellow cake mix
½ t lemon extract
1 package Betty Crocker "Fluffy White Frosting" mix, prepared
¼ C Egg Beaters
½ C sifted powdered sugar
Pam no stick cooking spray sugar

1. Combine cake mix, lemon extract, and Egg Beaters in mixing bowl. Mix on medium speed until smooth. Add 2¼ C frosting; mix until well blended.
2. Drop by teaspoonfuls into powdered sugar and roll each into a small ball. Place each ball on sprayed cookie sheet about 1½-inches apart and bake at 350° for 10-17 minutes. (The longer they bake the crispier they are.) Remove from cookie sheet and cool.

Makes: 60

Variation: Chocolate Version - Repeat recipe as in Lemon Whippersnaps using lite chocolate cake mix or lite white cake mix plus ¼ C cocoa instead of the yellow cake mix. Omit lemon extract; add ½ t each vanilla and cinnamon.

Per Serving: 0.4 g Fat, 51 Calories, 7 % Fat, 0.88 g Protein, 11 g Carb, 71 mg Sodium, 0 mg Cholesterol

CHOCO BROWNIE BITES

(Easy Prep)

1 box lite brownie mix
½ C Egg Beaters
2 C Health Valley Fat Free granola
1½ C quick cooking oatmeal
1½ t vanilla
½ t EACH nutmeg, cinnamon, and ground coffee
Pam no stick cooking spray

1. Combine all ingredients to form a stiff batter. Drop by heaping teaspoonfuls on a cookie sheet that has been coated with Pam. Bake at 375° for 8 - 12 minutes or until done.

Makes: about 70 medium size cookies

Per Serving: 0.8 g Fat, 51 Calories, 14 % Fat, 0.97 g Protein, 10.3 g Carb, 29.7 mg Sodium, 0 mg Cholesterol

COCOA FORGET-ME-NOTS
(Easy Prep)

4 egg whites at room temperature
1 C sugar
1 t EACH vanilla and maple flavoring
1 C Grape Nuts cereal
6 C Cocoa Krispies
Pinch salt (optional)

1. Beat egg whites until foamy; add sugar and beat until stiff. Fold in remaining ingredients. Drop by spoonful onto foil lined cookie sheet.
2. Place in preheated 350° oven. Turn off oven. Forget them until they are completely cool. Remove from oven and store in an airtight container.

Serves: 75

Per Serving: 0 g Fat, 28 Calories, 0 % Fat, 0.76 g Protein, 5.96 g Carb, 51 mg Sodium, 0 mg Cholesterol

CORNFLAKE KISSES
(Easy Prep)

1 box Betty Crocker Fluffy White Frosting Mix, prepared
1 t EACH almond and vanilla extract
½ t coconut flavoring
Pinch of salt (optional)
6 C cornflakes

1. Make frosting according to package directions. Gradually add flavorings. When frosting is stiff, fold in cereal.
2. Drop by teaspoonful on a cookie sheet lined with wax paper. Bake at 325° for 10-15 minutes until light brown. Cool on wire rack.

Serves: 50

Note: Try a variety of healthy cereal in place of cornflakes.

Per Serving: 0 g Fat, 28 Calories, 0 % Fat, 0.48 g Protein, 6.3 g Carb, 39 mg Sodium, 0 mg Cholesterol

POWDERED SUGAR LOGS

(Delicious and fat-free too!)
(Easy Prep)

1 C sugar
¾ C flour
1 t baking powder
¾ C Egg Beaters
1 t vanilla
1 C chopped dates
½ C Grape Nuts cereal dusted with flour
Powdered sugar
Pam no stick cooking spray

1. Combine first 5 ingredients; mix well. Stir in eggs.
2. Fold in dates and cereal.
3. Heat oven to 325°. Coat a square baking pan with Pam, pour in batter and bake 35-40 minutes.
4. Cut into bars while still warm. Cool. Roll in powdered sugar if desired and serve.

Serves: 24

Per Serving: 0.7 g Fat, 78 Calories,
8 % Fat, 1.12 g Protein, 18.2 g Carb,
40 mg Sodium, 0 mg Cholesterol

UNCLE D'S MARSHMALLOW FUDGE

(Always a requested favorite from the Amarillo McLean's kitchen)

2½ C sugar
2 T cocoa
1 T Smart Beat margarine
¾ C skim milk
1 t vanilla
10 large marshmallows
1 C Grape Nuts, optional (original recipe calls for pecans)

1. Place first 5 ingredients in a saucepan and boil until a definite soft ball of chocolate is formed by dropping a little of the chocolate in a cup of cold water (usually about 10 minutes). Remove from heat, add marshmallows, and beat until fudge thickens. Add cereal or nuts if desired. (To make handling easier, you may place pan in cold water while you beat candy.) Pour into a sprayed pan; cool and cut into squares.

Serves: 16

Per Serving: 0.18 g Fat, 155 Calories,
1 % Fat, 1 g Protein, 38 g Carb,
69 mg Sodium, 0.23 mg Cholesterol

AUNT JODIE'S DIVINITY
(The Best)

2½ C sugar
¼ C white Karo syrup
½ C water
2 egg whites at room temperature, stiffly beaten
1 t vanilla
1 C Grape Nuts (optional) less fat than nuts

1. Cook the first 3 ingredients over medium heat until syrup spins a thread off of spoon.
2. Pour hot mixture slowly over egg whites, beating constantly at high speed until mixture begins to thicken and loses its glossy look.
3. Add vanilla and nuts (if desired); mix well.
4. Spoon soft mounds onto wax paper.

Serves: 48

Per Serving: 0 g Fat, 49 Calories, 0 % Fat, 0.31 g Protein, 13.6 g Carb, 22 mg Sodium, 0 mg Cholesterol

MARTHA'S PEANUT BRITTLE

2 C sugar
1 C Karo syrup
½ C water
1 C raw Spanish peanuts
2 t soda
3 T hot water plus 1 package Butter Buds
Pam no stick cooking spray

1. Cook the first 3 ingredients over medium heat until it spins a thread. Add peanuts and cook until mixture turns brownish gold.
2. Add soda and Butter Buds mixture; stir and pour out on foil coated with Pam.

Serves: 24

Note: Reduce amount of peanuts to reduce fat.

Per Serving: 3 g Fat, 141 Calories, 19 % Fat, 1.5 g Protein, 28 g Carb, 73 mg Sodium, 0 mg Cholesterol

DESSERTS

CHOCOLATE LOVERS' DREAM TORTE

(When you want to make a real impression)

2 boxes lite fudge brownie mix
6 T water
Pam no stick cooking spray
Flour
4 (9-inch) round cake pans (see note at end of recipe)
"Heavenly Cream Frosting,"✔ prepared
Lite cherry pie filling (optional)

1. Make brownie mix according to package directions adding water so mixture is not quite so thick. Mix well.
2. Preheat oven to 350°. Spray Pam on inverted cake pans and dust with flour. (You are using the outside bottom of the pan.)
3. Pour ⅓ cup of batter on bottom of each pan, spreading to within about ¼-inch of edge. They will resemble thin pancakes. Bake in center of oven for about 8 minutes. Cool 2 minutes; remove to wax paper. Repeat making 10-12 layers.
4. To assemble cake, place 1 layer on cake plate. Spread about ⅓ cup frosting over layer. Add next layer and repeat construction finishing with frosting on top. Garnish by spooning pie filling in a circle around the base of the cake. Store in refrigerator.

Serves: 24

Note: To make this dessert faster, have extra cake pans on hand. This cake may also be prepared in a 9 x 13-inch glass or ceramic dish. Using the same recipe, pour the batter into oblong baking pans, using about ½ cup batter or a little more per layer. It makes about 6 thin layers. Repeat using a little more frosting. VERY RICH AND DELICIOUS!

Per Serving: 2 g Fat, 212 Calories,
8 % Fat, 2.1 g Protein, 44.9 g Carb,
497 mg Sodium, 0 mg Cholesterol

MOCHA MOUSSE ROLL

4 egg whites at room temperature
½ C sugar
1 C Egg Beaters
1 t EACH cinnamon and vanilla
¼ C plus 2 T all-purpose flour
¼ C plus 2 T cocoa
¾ t baking powder
Pam no stick cooking spray
3 T powdered sugar

1. Beat the egg whites until foamy. Gradually add sugar 1 tablespoon at a time until stiff peaks form. Mix Egg Beaters with cinnamon and vanilla; fold in egg whites.
2. Sift the next 3 ingredients into the egg mixture; stir well. Spray a 9 X 13 X ¾-inch jelly roll pan with Pam; line with wax paper. Spray wax paper with Pam and dust with flour. Spread mixture evenly over wax paper and bake in 400° oven for 8-10 minutes.
3. Remove from oven immediately and turn out onto a dry tea towel that has been sprinkled with powdered sugar. Remove wax paper. Roll up cake and towel together starting at narrow end. Place seam side down on rack and cool completely. Prepare "Vanilla Cream Cheese Filling"✔ ; adding 1 t coffee granules. When cool, unroll cake, spread with filling, leaving about an inch margin from edge of cake and reroll. Wrap in wax paper and chill. Frost if desired or dust with more powdered sugar mixed with a little cinnamon. Freezes well.

Serves: 10 (Nutritional without filling) (165 Calories, 0.6 Fat with filling)

Per Serving: 0.7 g Fat, 29 Calories, 21 % Fat, 3 g Protein, 6.39 g Carb, 110 mg Sodium, 0 mg Cholesterol

HOMEMADE BANANA PUDDING

5 large bananas, sliced
40 vanilla Teddy Graham cookies
1¼ C sugar
1 C sifted flour
¼ t salt (optional)
2 C EACH skim milk and evaporated skim milk
¾ C Egg Beaters
1 package Butter Buds
1 t vanilla

1. Combine sugar, flour, salt and milk in a saucepan over medium heat; stir constantly until thickened.
2. Slowly add egg substitute and cook 2 minutes. Add Butter Buds and vanilla.
3. Line bottom of a 2½-quart dish with 8 cookies, then a little of the bananas and pudding. Repeat layers 5 times, ending with cookies.

Serves: 13 (¾ C servings without meringue)

Note: Top with "Never Fail Meringue"✔ if desired.

Per Serving: 0.16 g Fat, 111 Calories,
1 % Fat, 3.4 g Protein, 24 g Carb,
12 mg Sodium, 1.4 mg Cholesterol

BAKED CUSTARD

¾ C Egg Beaters
¾ C EACH skim milk and evaporated skim milk
1 C nonfat cottage cheese, drained
½ C sugar
1 t vanilla
Nutmeg

1. In a medium bowl mix the first 5 ingredients. Blend in a blender or food processor until smooth.
2. Pour into 6 custard cups; sprinkle with nutmeg. Place cups in a shallow pan. Pour hot water into pan about 1-inch deep. Bake in 350° oven for 30-40 minutes until a knife inserted near center comes out clean.

Serves: 6

Per Serving: 0.5 g Fat, 122 Calories,
4 % Fat, 8.8 g Protein, 21 g Carb,
213 mg Sodium, 3.5 mg Cholesterol

BLUEBERRY DELIGHT

1 (6-oz.) package blueberry jello
2 C boiling water
1 small can crushed pineapple
1 can blueberries
1 C Grape Nuts
1 C "Nonfat Yogurt Cheese"✔
½ C sugar
8 oz. Healthy Choice Fat Free cream cheese

1. Dissolve jello in water. Add next 3 ingredients and chill in refrigerator until set.
2. Beat together the remaining ingredients until smooth. Spread on top of chilled jello mixture; chill and serve.

Serves: 16

Per Serving: 0 g Fat, 87 Calories, 0 % Fat, 4.05 g Protein, 15 g Carb, 150 mg Sodium, 2.5 mg Cholesterol

FROSTY HOLIDAY PRETZELS
(Easy Prep)

Forty 3-ring medium-size low-salt pretzels
2 large egg whites at room temperature
⅛ t cream of tartar
1 C sifted powdered sugar
½ t EACH vanilla and almond extract
Confetti sugar sprinkles

1. Beat egg whites and cream of tartar on high speed until foamy. Add sugar a little at a time, beating well after each addition; stir in flavorings.
2. Carefully dip each pretzel into frosting mixture and lay on wire rack. Sprinkle with sugar sprinkles. Let dry and store in airtight container.

Serves: 8

Note: Wrap in colorful cellophane; tie up with festive ribbon. They make nice gifts!

Per Serving: 0.37 g Fat, 81 Calories, 4 % Fat, 1.5 g Protein, 18.2 g Carb, 162 mg Sodium, 0 mg Cholesterol

LITE BANANAS FOSTER

¼ C hot water plus 1 package Butter Buds
1½ C brown sugar
¼ t cinnamon
⅓ C banana liqueur
6 small, firm, ripe bananas, peeled and halved lengthwise then lengthwise again.
⅓ C plain or spiced rum (80 proof)
6 (½-C) scoops of nonfat frozen vanilla dairy dessert

1. Place Butter Buds liquid and next 3 ingredients in a large sprayed skillet, stirring well. Heat 1-2 minutes; add bananas and sauté until soft and lightly browned.
2. Pour rum over bananas - DO NOT STIR! Allow to heat through.
3. CAREFULLY - ignite sauce with a long match. Rotate pan to keep flame burning. Allow sauce to flame until it dies out.
4. Place 1 scoop of vanilla dessert into serving bowls. Spoon bananas and sauce on top.

Serves: 6

Per Serving: 0 g Fat, 378 Calories, 0 % Fat, 1.5 g Protein, 65 g Carb, 101 mg Sodium, 0.5 mg Cholesterol

SUGAR-FREE APPLESAUCE DESSERT
(Easy Prep)

2 C heated unsweetened applesauce
1 small package sugar-free lime jello
1 (6-oz.) bottle diet ginger ale
½ C Grape Nuts, chopped in food processor

1. Dissolve jello in hot applesauce. Add remaining ingredients and chill until firm.

Serves: 6

Per Serving: 0 g Fat, 60 Calories, 0 % Fat, 0.7 g Protein, 14.3 g Carb, 81 mg Sodium, 0 mg Cholesterol

COUSIN EMILY'S FAVORITE BROWNIES
(Quick Fix)

3/4 C sifted flour
5 T cocoa
1 C sugar
½ C Kraft Free mayonnaise or use ¼ C fat free chocolate syrup plus ¼ C Kraft Free mayonnaise
½ C Egg Beaters
1¼ t vanilla
½ C Grape Nuts
Pam no stick cooking spray

1. Have all ingredients at room temperature. Place in large mixing bowl; beat until blended, about 1 minute.
2. Coat an 8-inch square pan with Pam; dust with flour. Bake at 350° for about 30 minutes. Do not overbake.

Note: Serve plain or top with your favorite fat free or lowfat frozen dairy dessert; try Healthy Choice Mint Chocolate Chip lowfat frozen dairy dessert on top.
Serves: 16

Per Serving: 0.1 g Fat, 50 Calories, 2 % Fat, 1.7 g Protein, 52 g Carb, 32 mg Sodium, 0 mg Cholesterol

HELEN'S BLUEBERRY CRUNCH
(Easy Prep and great with other fresh fruits!)

4 C fresh blueberries
¾ C packed brown sugar
¾ C EACH flour and raw oatmeal
½ C liquid Butter Buds
Pam no-stick cooking spray

1. Spray a 2 quart casserole with Pam. Place blueberries in dish.
2. Combine remaining ingredients and spread over berries. Bake at 350° for about 45 minutes. Top with nonfat frozen vanilla yogurt if desired.

Note: If using lite pie filling, omit sugar.
Serves: 8

Per Serving: 0.58 g Fat, 159 Calories, 3 % Fat, 1.62 g Protein, 38 g Carb, 43.3 mg Sodium, 0 mg Cholesterol

RASPBERRY BOMBE

3 pints frozen raspberry nonfat yogurt
2 pints frozen strawberry nonfat yogurt
1 recipe "Nonfat Whipped Cream,"✔ prepared
¼ C finely chopped dates
¼ C Grape Nuts
½ t EACH rum and almond flavorings

1. Chill a 2½ quart metal salad mold in freezer.
2. Stir raspberry yogurt just to soften. With chilled spoon, quickly spread yogurt over bottom and sides of mold. Be sure yogurt is spread up to top. Freeze until firm.
3. Stir strawberry yogurt to soften. Spread completely over raspberry yogurt. Freeze until firm.
4. Fold dates, nuts and flavorings into 1½ C whipped cream. Pile into mold; smooth evenly. Cover with foil; freeze 6 hours.
5. Remove foil; invert on chilled plate. Rub mold with hot, damp cloth to loosen. Lift off mold. Garnish with additional whipped cream if desired.

Serves: 16

Per Serving: 0 g Fat, 56 Calories,
0 % Fat, 4.7 g Protein, 9.3 g Carb,
50.9 mg Sodium, 5.6 mg Cholesterol

CRANBERRY FLUFF

(Very pretty, perfect for holidays)

1 (8-oz.) carton vanilla frozen nonfat yogurt, thawed
2 (16-oz.) cans whole cranberry sauce
1 (15-oz.) can crushed pineapple, drained
3-4 bananas, sliced
½ C Grape Nuts, dusted with flour

1. Combine all ingredients, blending well.
2. Spoon into a 13 x 9 x 2-inch pan or into 16 individual molds.
3. Freeze until firm. Let stand at room temperature 10-15 minutes before serving.

Serves: Approximately 16 (½ C servings)

Per Serving: 0.25 g Fat, 187 Calories,
1% Fat, 1.6 g Protein, 46.5 g Carb,
24.1 mg Sodium, 1.2 mg Cholesterol

LIME FLUFF
(Easy Prep)

1 (6-oz.) package sugar-free lime jello
1 C EACH boiling water and cold water
½ C Kraft Fat Free mayonnaise
1 C prepared Betty Crocker Fluffy White frosting (box mix)
1 (8-oz.) can unsweetened crushed pineapple, drained
1 C Grape Nuts dusted with flour

1. Dissolve jello in boiling water; stir in cold water.
2. Beat mayonnaise and jello together. Chill until the consistency of unbeaten egg white. Fold in the next 3 ingredients; pour into a glass dish, cover, and chill.

Serves: 12

Per Serving: 0 g Fat, 80 Calories, 0 % Fat, 1.1 g Protein, 19 g Carb, 215 mg Sodium, 0 mg Cholesterol

FROZEN LEMON CRUNCH

1 box lite yellow cake mix; prepare batter
1 package Butter Buds
½ C Grape Nuts
1 (13-oz.) can evaporated skim milk, well chilled
1 small can frozen pink lemonade
Pam no stick cooking spray

1. Mix 1½ C batter with next 2 ingredients. Press into a sprayed baking dish; bake at 400° about 12 minutes. Remove from oven and crumble with spoon; cool. Reserve ¼ C crumbs. Press remaining crumbs into sprayed pie plate.
2. Beat until stiff the chilled milk. Stir in lemonade concentrate. Pour into crust, top with reserved crumbs, and freeze until firm. (Remove 10 minutes before serving.)

Serves: 12

Per Serving: 2.1 g Fat, 220 Calories, 8.5 % Fat, 5.7 g Protein, 44 g Carb, 44.5 mg Sodium, 2.5 mg Cholesterol

HOLIDAY CREAM

8 oz. plain "Nonfat Yogurt Cheese"✔
1 T cornstarch
1 C prepared "Nonfat Whipping Cream"✔
¾ C sugar
1 envelope unflavored gelatin
¼ C boiling water
8 oz. Healthy Choice Fat Free cream cheese, softened
½ t vanilla
Pam no stick cooking spray

1. Combine yogurt, cornstarch and whipping cream in mixer; beat at medium speed. When blended, gradually add sugar; beat well. Transfer to a saucepan and cook over low heat.
2. Dissolve gelatin in boiling water and stir into mixture. Remove from heat.
3. In mixer, beat cream cheese and vanilla until light and fluffy. Fold in yogurt mixture.
4. Pour into 4-cup mold sprayed with Pam. Chill until firm.
5. Unmold on serving platter and garnish with fresh fruit.

Serves: 10

Per Serving: 0 g Fat, 93 Calories, 0 % Fat, 5.4 g Protein, 18.7 g Carb, 164.1 mg Sodium, 4 mg Cholesterol

BANANAS WITH RUM
(Quick Fix)

½ C brown sugar, packed
¼ C light rum
¼ C hot water mixed with 1 package Butter Buds
2 large firm bananas
Vanilla nonfat dairy dessert (or) nonfat frozen yogurt

1. In a microwave-safe dish, mix the first 3 ingredients. Microwave on high about 2 minutes; stir. Cook on high 2 to 3 more minutes or until sugar is dissolved.
2. Cut bananas in half cross-wise and length-wise making 8 pieces. Place bananas in sugar mixture; coat evenly.
3. Microwave 1 minute. Spoon each serving over ½ C frozen vanilla yogurt or fat free cake.

Serves: 4 (with yogurt)

Per Serving: 0 g Fat, 239 Calories, 0 % Fat, 0.5 g Protein, 41.5 g Carb, 178 mg Sodium, 0 mg Cholesterol

CREAMY APPLE DELIGHT

(Easy Prep)

2 cans lite apple pie filling
1 (11-oz.) can Pillsbury soft bread sticks
1½ C "Nonfat Yogurt Cheese"✔ plus 1½ T cornstarch
½ C firmly packed brown sugar
¼ t EACH nutmeg, cinnamon and allspice
Pam no stick cooking spray

1. Spray a long rectangular baking dish with Pam. Spoon pie filling evenly into bottom of pan. Separate breadsticks and lay each side by side over filling.
2. Mix together yogurt cheese, cornstarch, brown sugar, and spices; spoon over breadsticks. Bake at 350° for 30 - 40 minutes or until done. Serve with "Nonfat Whipping Cream"✔ or nonfat frozen vanilla yogurt if desired.

Serves: 12

Per Serving: 1 g Fat, 152 Calories, 6 % Fat, 3 g Protein, 32 g Carb, 166 mg Sodium, 0.6 mg Cholesterol

DEB'S CHOCOLATE CHERRY SURPRISE

1 lite chocolate cake mix or lite white cake mix plus ½ C cocoa
½ C "Nonfat Yogurt Cheese"✔
1 package Betty Crocker Fluffy White Frosting Mix, prepared
1 can lite cherry pie filling
1 recipe "Nonfat Whipped Cream"✔

1. Prepare cake according to directions. Bake in layers or as sheet cake.
2. Mix together the yogurt cheese and about 2 C of frosting. Spread between layers or on top of sheet cake.
3. To serve, top with pie filling and nonfat whipped cream.

Serves: 12

Note: Add 1 t of your favorite liqueur to pie filling for a change.

Per Serving: 1.25 g Fat, 277 Calories, 4 % Fat, 5.08 g Protein, 59 g Carb, 356 mg Sodium, 0 mg Cholesterol

CREAMY RICE PUDDING
(Easy Prep)

1⅔ C cooked rice mixed with 1 package Butter Buds
1 C Egg Beaters
7 T sugar
Dash of allspice
1 t vanilla
¼ t cinnamon
1⅓ C evaporated skim milk

1. Mix together all the above ingredients.
2. Pour into a 2-quart deep casserole coated with Pam.
3. Bake at 325° for 50-60 minutes until set.
4. Do not over cook. Serve warm with raisins if desired.

Serves: 6

Per Serving: 0.16 g Fat, 159 Calories, 1 % Fat, 5.8 g Protein, 32 g Carb, 388.5 mg Sodium, 1.75 mg Cholesterol

SURPRISE PEACH COBBLER
(Easy Prep)

1½ C flour
1 package dry Butter Buds
4 t baking power
1 C sugar
1½ C skim milk
½ C EACH light corn syrup & Butter Buds liquid
4 C fresh sliced, peeled peaches (or) 2 (16-oz.) canned peaches without sugar, drained, liquid reserved
Pam no stick cooking spray

1. Preheat oven to 350°. Pam a 9 x 13-inch glass casserole dish; set aside.
2. Sift together the first three ingredients and mix in sugar. Add milk slowly to make the batter.
3. Pour the corn syrup into the casserole dish. Carefully pour batter on corn syrup. DO NOT MIX or STIR!!!
4. Spoon peaches gently over the batter keeping a little of the juice, if any in each spoonful.
5. Bake 1 hour. Serve with nonfat frozen yogurt if desired.

Serves: 10

Note: Add ½ - ¾ cup of sugar to peaches if the peaches are not very sweet, depending on your taste.

Per Serving: 0.15 g Fat, 205 Calories, 0.7 % Fat, 2.3 g Protein, 49 g Carb, 234 mg Sodium, 0 mg Cholesterol

CHERRY MERINGUE DESSERT

1 box Betty Crocker Fluffy White frosting mix, prepared
1 C Grape Nuts cereal
2 C Premium Fat Free cracker crumbs
1 recipe "Nonfat Whipping Cream"✔
2 cans lite cherry pie filling
1 t almond flavoring

1. Prepare frosting mix as directed on box; fold in cereal and crackers. Spray an oblong baking dish with Pam; spread frosting mixture evenly in bottom of pan. Bake at 350° until crisp and light brown, 5 - 10 minutes. Cool.
2. Prepare whipped cream without the sugar. Spread on top of baked frosting mixture. Spoon pie filling over whipped cream and serve.

Serves: 12

Per Serving: 0 g Fat, 194 Calories,
9 % Fat, 2.5 g Protein, 45.06 g Carb,
100.9 mg Sodium, 9 mg Cholesterol

BASIC LITE CREPES OR BLINTZES

1 egg white at room temperature
¾ C skim milk
1 C sifted cake flour
1 t Butter Buds liquid
Butter Flavor Pam no stick cooking spray

1. Beat egg white until it forms soft peaks; beat in water. Slowly stir in remaining ingredients.
2. Spray a nonstick skillet with Pam. Heat pan over medium heat until hot. Pour about ¼ C of batter into skillet; swirl around to let batter cover bottom of pan. Cook about 1 minute, gently turn over and cook about 45 seconds more or until sides are light brown. Remove to plate; stack crepes between wax paper. Repeat with remaining batter.
3. To serve, spoon about 3-4 T favorite main dish or dessert filling down center of crepe. Roll up and serve.

Makes: about 8 crepes (nutritional information per crepe without filling)

Per Serving: 0.12 g Fat, 54 Calories,
2 % Fat, 2 g Protein, 10.6 g Carb,
20.5 mg Sodium, 0.46 mg Cholesterol

CREAMY ALMOND FLOAT
(Quick Fix)

8 C skim or ½% fat milk
⅔ C sugar (or add artificial sweetener last, to taste)
2 t almond extract
1½ t vanilla extract
¼ t ground nutmeg
4 C vanilla nonfat frozen yogurt or nonfat dairy dessert
Reddi Wip Lite (optional)
Almond slivers (optional)

1. Blend together the first 5 ingredients, making sure sugar is dissolved.
2. Spoon frozen yogurt into 6 glasses and pour milk mixture over it. Garnish with whipped topping and almonds if desired.

Serves: 8 (1 C each)

Per Serving: 1 g Fat, 110 Calories, 8 % Fat, 12 g Protein, 18 g Carb, 189 mg Sodium, 1.8 mg Cholesterol

EASY MERINGUES

3 egg whites at room temperature
¼ t EACH cream of tartar and salt (optional)
¾ C sugar

1. Beat egg whites in large mixing bowl with electric mixer until foamy. Add cream of tartar and salt; beat until just stiff. Add sugar gradually, about a spoonful at a time, until very stiff.
2. Drop by tablespoonfuls on sprayed baking sheet. Bake in preheated 250° oven for 1 hour and 15 minutes. Turn oven off; leave meringues in oven 15 minutes. Remove from oven and cool on wire rack. (May also spread meringues into larger shapes before cooking. For example, spoon meringues in a circular shape about the size of a medium size bagel. Bake and top with fresh fruit and nonfat whipping cream.)

Serves: 24

Per Serving: 0 g Fat, 26 Calories, 0 % Fat, 0.37 g Protein, 6.2 g Carb, 6.04 mg Sodium, 0 mg Cholesterol

STRAWBERRY SURPRISE DESSERT

7 oz. no fat low-sodium or no salt pretzels
½ C Butter Buds liquid
2 T corn syrup
1 (6 oz.) package sugar-free strawberry jello
2 C boiling water
3 (10 oz.) packages unsweetened frozen strawberries, undrained
8 oz. Healthy Choice Fat Free cream cheese
1 box Betty Crocker Fluffy White Frosting Mix, prepared
Pam no stick cooking spray
7 oz. no fat low sodium or no salt pretzels

1. Puree pretzels in food processor or blender; drizzle Butter Buds liquid and corn syrup. Press into an oblong pan that has been coated with Pam. Bake at 350° for 5 minutes. Cool.
2. Dissolve jello in boiling water; stir in strawberries. Chill until slightly thickened.
3. Prepare frosting; beat in cream cheese until smooth. Spread over cooled crust. Top with jello mixture; chill until firm.

Serves: 16

Per Serving: 0 g Fat, 141 Calories, 0 % Fat, 6 g Protein, 29.2 g Carb, 562 mg Sodium, 2.5 mg Cholesterol

FRESH FRUIT COMPOTE

1 ¾ C cold skim milk
1 T orange liqueur or orange juice
1 package (4 serving size) sugar-free vanilla instant pudding, dry
1 C "Nonfat Whipped Cream,"✔ prepared
6 C fresh fruits (blueberries, melon balls, raspberries,sliced strawberries, bananas, peaches, etc.)

1. Pour milk and liqueur into a bowl; add pudding mix. Beat slowly with hand beater or at lowest speed of electric mixer for 1 minute.
2. Add whipped cream; beat 1 minute longer, or until blended.
3. Arrange ½ the fruits in a deep glass serving bowl. Add the pudding mixture and top with remaining fruit.
4. Garnish with additional whipped cream and fruit if desired.

Serves: 10

Per Serving: 0.37 g Fat, 73 Calories, 4 % Fat, 2.2 g Protein, 20.4 g Carb, 28.9 mg Sodium, 1 mg Cholesterol

Notes and Extra Recipes:

Notes and Extra Recipes:

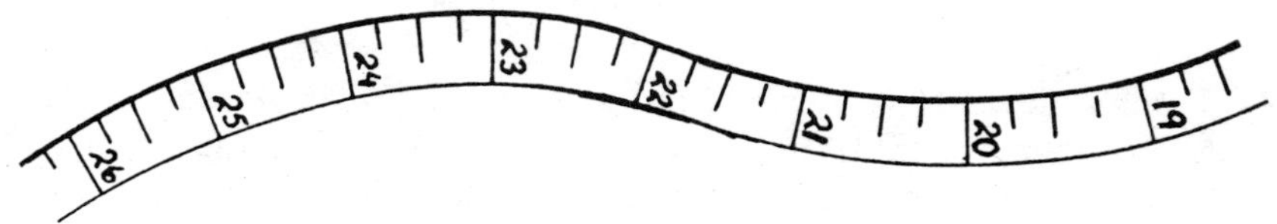

KID'S STUFF & SANDWICHES

STARTING THEM OUT RIGHT

Research shows that because children are fed a high amount of saturated fat, mainly found in fast foods and quick frozen foods, they become candidates for heart disease at a very early age. This also sets them up for weight problems which can affect self-esteem and physical performance. Many of our children today are actually obese or overfat; they do not eat healthy and get very little exercise. Don't we owe it to them, especially with all they are faced with this day and time, to help them live healthy, happy, somewhat stress-free lives? It is so important for all of us to try to eat healthy and keep fit. If we, as adults, can set a good example for our children, then perhaps they will not ever have to be concerned about losing weight, hypertension, heart disease, gaining weight, etc. Hopefully they will develop sensible, healthy eating and exercise habits for a lifetime.

Children over age 2 do not need any more than 30% of their daily caloric intake coming from fat. Many adults believe they need more. As with adults, complex carbohydrates are the main fuel needed followed by fat and protein. (See the nutrition section for recommended daily food requirements for children.) Make sure kids eat a good breakfast to get them going and keep them going. A breakfast high in sugar will rev them up quickly only to drop them into a slump when it is used up. Try a low protein, high carbohydrate breakfast instead, followed by a well-balanced lunch and dinner. Kids need snacks too. Don't let them nibble all day. When it is meal or snack time, provide healthy appealing food choices, let them eat as much as the want, then, nothing between meals until the next snack or meal time. So many children today are overweight or overfat; this can only lead to future health and social problems. Help them develop good habits that will stay with them for a lifetime. You could be saving their lives.

Teach children to read labels and to spot hidden fats and saturated fats. Give them the tools they need so they can do well on their own as well as at home. Be careful to guide, not nag, your kids about what they eat and about their exercise habits. You can show them by example. Present the facts and consequences of eating healthy and exercising as opposed to poor eating and not exercising; but, they must learn to make their own choices. Present the choices and praise them when they make the right decision. Also remember, children need to be children. Let them know it's okay occasionally if they choose to splurge. If we deprive them totally, they might go in completely the opposite direction going on binge after binge, especially when they're away from home where healthy choices may not be available.

Make healthy eating and exercise a family affair; make it your lifestyle. Here are some tips for making eating and exercise a more fun, pleasant family experience:

- Make food appealing when serving: For example, cut nonfat cheese, whole wheat bread, and Healthy Choice lunchmeat into shapes such as Christmas trees, squares, triangles, etc. Make a picture on your plate. Serve on colorful dishes with festive napkins, colored toothpicks, and light candles.
- Give names to some of your children's foods, especially the hard-to-eat ones. Example: broccoli/trees, cauliflower/ clouds, green beans/beaver logs, etc.
- Make a picnic for one meal, outside or inside.
- Let the kids plan and prepare dinner or a part of the dinner by themselves if age permits, or let them help you.
- When food shopping, let each child choose one item to buy. As you know all children are drawn to the high sugar cereals on the grocery store shelves. At our house, we call them Saturday cereals. My children may have one of those cereals and eat it only on Saturday mornings as long as they do not contain saturated fat. This is one way they learn to read labels.
- Have a taste test. Pretend to be anyone of your choice (a famous person or one you've made up); try new foods and beverages. This is a great way to have kids try new foods. Be prepared to test their concoctions as well.
- Because peanut butter is so high in fat, but a great source of protein, don't omit it from your child's foods, simply use less of it or mix it with unsweetened jelly or a little nonfat ricotta cheese.
- Make birthdays special. Let each child select anything he or she wants to eat for the whole day. If you are setting a good

example, you might just be surprised at his/her choice.

- If you want kids to associate exercise with good feelings, never use it as a punishment.
- If you want your kids to keep fit, make exercise something you do together as a family. Try walking, skipping, dancing, playing follow the leader as you do various exercises, swimming, skating, jogging, biking, aerobics, bench stepping, climbing stairs, skiing, or any fun activity you all enjoy that keeps you moving for about 30 minutes. Try a little warm-up before you start moving and be sure to cool down slowly using this simple activity: walk for 3-5 minutes, then stretch your muscles without bouncing. Never bend all the way forward or sideways from your waist; always make sure your back is supported. Exercise at a pace and intensity that is right for you. If you are able to continue talking as you exercise, not huff and puff, you are probably working at your proper level of intensity. See the "Exercise" section for more information on this topic.
- Set family exercise goals and award non-food prizes.
- For some kids, a variety of activities done at different intervals works better because it keeps their attention longer. For example, you might walk around the block, skate in the driveway, then go for a bike ride.
- Make sure kids know that the reason you exercise is because it's fun, it makes you feel good, it's good for you, and because you enjoy being together as a family.
- Keep kids moving; let T.V. be a special time that they choose to watch a favorite program, not part of their daily routine. For example, you may say that your child is allowed one hour of T.V. or one movie per day. Let him/her check the television schedule with you to select the programs he/she would like to choose for that day Try not to make eating in front of the T.V. a habit. It's best to avoid it entirely if possible.
- As for desserts, help your children satisfy their sweet tooth with fresh fruit and other natural sugar-free desserts. (See "Sweet Treats" - Time Savers and Helpful Hints Section).

Lastly, good mental health is extremely important to you and your family. If affects the way we feel about ourselves, thus affecting how we deal with life and other people. Keeping ourselves healthy helps our self-esteem and helps us have a more positive outlook on life. Bringing up confident, happy, well-adjusted children is so important, especially in today's world. Children are faced with so many pressures that they must feel good about themselves to be able to make right choices for their lives. Even one wrong choice this day and time can be fatal, for example, whether or not he/she chooses to take drugs. By making a healthy lifestyle a family affair, you can teach your children to respect their bodies. You can also use the family exercise time to air feelings and concerns, thus keeping the lines of communication open. Be a good listener. Always tell your kids that you love them, even when they do not always do the things they should. Show your love and concern with kind words and lots of hugs. As my friend Deb Biggs always says, "Twelve hugs a day - minimum!" and she means it - so should you!

KID'S STUFF

Time Savers:

- Caramel corn: Stir together 2 T melted Smart Beat margarine, 6 T liquid Molly McButter, ¾ C firmly packed brown sugar, ¼ C light corn syrup; cover and heat in microwave 3½-4 minutes. Remove and stir in ½ t vanilla and ¼ t baking soda. Combine well with 3 quarts air popped popcorn. Place all in microwave-safe dish coated with Pam and microwave on high for 2½-3½ minutes, stirring about every minute. Remove from oven, spread on sprayed wax paper; cool and break into pieces.
- Quiche for kids: Mix together ½ C each Kraft Free mayonnaise and evaporated skim milk, 1 T cornstarch, dash of mace, and 1½ C grated nonfat cheese; add to ½ lb. cooked, rinsed, and drained Healthy Choice ground beef and bake in low-fat pie crust for about 35 minutes.
- Beans N' Franks: Mix together ½ package cubed Healthy Choice hot dogs plus 1 (16-oz.) can pinto beans; add ketchup and brown sugar to taste.
- Puppy Dogs: Pour cornbread batter into sprayed muffin tins. Cut Healthy Choice hot dogs into thirds; place a popsicle stick in center of each third. Place hot dog end down in muffin tin and bake according to cornbread directions, reducing cooking time by about ½ or ⅓.
- Alternate fresh or canned unsweetened fruit with low-fat yogurt in clear parfait glasses.
- Top low-fat waffles with fresh strawberries or your favorite fruit, a little Reddi Wip whipped topping, and a sprinkle of powdered sugar for great Belgian waffles.
- Nachos: Top Guiltless Gourmet tortilla chips with vegetarian refried beans and nonfat cheese; bake. May add cooked Healthy Choice ground beef, sliced, cooked chicken breast strips, diced Healthy Choice ham, diced tomatoes, "Great Guacamole"✔ (my kids love it!), plain yogurt, and a few sliced

black olives.

- Granola Bars: Mix ¼ C each brown sugar and Butter Buds liquid with 1⅓ C Health Valley fat free granola and ¼ C Grape Nuts; stir in 4 large peeled and sliced apples, 1 t cinnamon, ½ t vanilla and bake covered at 375° for 30 minutes; uncover and bake 10-12 minutes more.
- Slice Healthy Choice hot dogs in half lengthwise; dip in Egg Beaters and roll in crushed crispy rice bites or rice cereal. Bake at 375° until crisp. Do with cooked chicken breast strips, also.
- Stir frozen blueberries or your favorite unsweetened frozen fruit into hot oatmeal.
- Place 1 slice Healthy Choice ham on top of 1 slice fat free cheese; wrap (ham-side out) around 1 cooked stalk broccoli and secure with toothpick. Microwave until cheese melts.
- For special occasions, buy cotton candy. Remove from bag or stick and place on individual plates forming a small circle like a bird's nest. Top with nonfat frozen yogurt, sugar sprinkles, and a dab of Reddi Wip whipped topping.
- Top unsweetened applesauce with marshmallows and cinnamon.
- Place grapes in freezer-safe container; freeze and eat.
- Fold Hearty Grain biscuits over Healthy Choice hot dogs and nonfat cheese and cooked veggies if desired; bake as directed on biscuit can.
- Make popsicles from your favorite unsweetened juice or a mixture of reserved canned juices. Pour into molds and freeze.
- Use different shaped pasta when making low-fat macaroni and cheese, spaghetti, etc.
- Big Birdwich - Flatten a piece of bread with rolling pin; spread with nonfat cream cheese and unsweetened jelly. Roll up, spray with butter-flavor Pam, and roll in sesame seeds. Bake at 350° for 12-15 minutes. Use different fillings if desired.
- Make low-fat banana splits using sliced bananas, nonfat frozen yogurt, lite chocolate syrup, butterscotch syrup, or any lite syrup, Grape Nuts or any fat free crunchy cereal or fat free granola, marshmallow topping, Reddi Wip lite whipped topping, cherries, and any unsweetened preserves or fresh fruit.
- Make low-fat ice cream sandwiches - Prepare lite brownie mix according to directions on box. Spread in 1 very thin layer in a long large baking dish that has been coated with Pam. Bake, cool, and cut into 2½ X 5-inch rectangles. Spoon about ¼ C of your favorite fat free frozen yogurt or ice cream on 1 rectangle; top with another brownie rectangle.
- Roll sliced bananas in egg white, then in nonfat bread crumbs; sauté in liquid Butter Buds and lemon juice.

- Best Popcorn!! - Air popped popcorn will not taste like cardboard any more if you'll follow these easy steps. Air pop popcorn and coat with Butter flavor Pam no stick cooking spray; sprinkle dry Butter Buds over popcorn and toss to coat. Season with lite salt, chili powder, garlic powder, cinnamon, Parmesan cheese, etc. or a combination of seasonings.

Helpful Hints:

- When preparing lunches for children to take to school, place nonfat mayonnaise or mustard between lite lunch meat slices or nonfat cheese to keep bread from getting soggy.
- Keep a container of ice cold water with a pouring spout on it in the refrigerator so children are always able to get a drink.
- Never use food as a reward. This creates bad habits that some of us still have today as adults.
- Never make a child clean his plate. Children eat when they are hungry. Provide 3 well-balanced meals with several healthy snacks in between.
- Make fresh fruit and cut up vegetables available to kids so when they do want to snack, they reach for something healthy.
- Have emergency foods on hand in case you accidently get up late and have to rush the kids to school. They need a good start in the morning. Toasted bagels with a little fat free or low-fat cream cheese and honey, low-fat waffles, ziploc bags full of cereal mix and raisins, a cup of low-fat yogurt, lite cheese between 2 bread slices, low-fat muffins (they freeze well and thaw quickly), fruit smoothies they can drink on the way, leftover pizza, egg sandwich (using Egg Beaters) cooked quickly in the microwave, peanut butter sandwich, and other nutritious foods make a good breakfast.
- For lunches, try to avoid those prepackaged lunches found in the dairy case. Although convenient, they are usually high in fat and expensive. Take a little extra time and prepare a healthy lunch. Also avoid most of the "Kid" T.V. frozen dinners. They, too, are usually high in fat.

Suggestions for lunches for children over age 2:

- Sandwiches on low-fat whole wheat or white bread filled with your choice of the following - low-fat lunchmeat or low-fat chicken or tuna salad, low-fat cheese, low-fat pimiento cheese, peanut butter and honey or unsweetened jelly (light on the peanut butter), fat free cream cheese with or without unsweetened jelly or honey. Any of the previous can be spread on low-fat crackers, bagels, pita bread, or muffins.

- Serve sandwiches with: low-fat yogurt, cholesterol free chips containing no partially hydrogenated oils such as Charles Chips or some Eagle Chips or other acceptable brands (read labels), flavored rice chips, rice cakes, or rice crackers, low sodium pretzels, low-fat crackers, homemade "Pita or Bagel Chips"✔, fresh fruit, canned unsweetened fruit or applesauce, cut up raw carrots or other vegetables served with nonfat salad dressing as a dip, low-fat pasta salad, etc. Any of these served in the right combination can provide a healthy lunch for your child. (Make sure the meats are properly chilled.) Water or skim milk make a great ending.

Healthy Snacks:

- Many of the foods listed above are perfect for snacks as well as air popped popcorn, low-fat milkshakes and smoothies, nonfat frozen yogurt, soft pretzels, low-fat hot dogs, peanut butter spread on fruits and vegetables such as celery, carrots, bananas, pears or apples, Healthy Choice Fat Free cheese sticks or cheese singles, low-fat breadsticks dipped in Healthy Choice spaghetti sauce or nonfat salad dressing or yogurt, cherry tomatoes, marshmallows, Hearty Grains biscuits wrapped around fat free cream cheese or low-fat hot dogs, unsweetened fresh or canned fruit, low-fat lunchmeat, low-fat no lard corn or flour tortillas wrapped around similar toppings as in Healthy Grains biscuit, low-fat cookies such as graham crackers, Fig Newtons, animal crackers, etc. (read the labels) low salt, dried peanuts, popsicles, baked potatoes, Cracker Jacks, Nutrigrain Bars, low-fat pudding, low-fat macaroni and cheese or pasta, low-fat soup, cold oven-fried chicken, nonfat cottage cheese, low-fat low sugar cereal and skim or 1% milk, no cholesterol devilled eggs and egg salad, oven fried french fries, leftover pizza, Healthy Choice fish sticks, or any of your healthy leftovers, etc. The list can go on and on. Obviously, some high sugar snacks should be limited to once a day or less. Find the ones right for your child/children and remember that too much of anything is not good. Variety and moderation is the key. Normal healthy children over age 2 need no more that 30% of their calories from fat just like adults. Check the cookbook index for many of the salad and sandwich spreads mentioned as well as for other healthy foods.
- Try serving breakfast foods for lunch or supper and lunch or supper foods for breakfast. This makes a nice change and may encourage lighter meals in the evening which is a very positive habit to get into.

SANDWICHES

Time Savers:

- Grilled cheese - Coat low-fat whole wheat bread with Butter flavor Pam or a smear of Smart Beat margarine. Top with nonfat cheese and grill in a hot skillet coated with Pam.
- Make a meatball or meatloaf sandwich from the meatloaf or meatball recipes in the cookbook. Lightly toast low-fat sourdough or French bread. Heat meatloaf or meatballs with a little Healthy Choice spaghetti sauce; spoon onto bread and top with fat free mozzarella cheese. Make a vegetarian sandwich using lettuce, thin slices of cucumber, green and red pepper, tomatoes, pickles, and a few sprouts. Place between 2 slices of whole wheat low-fat bread that have been spread lightly with Healthy Choice Fat Free cream cheese, garlic and herb cream cheese, or fat free salad dressing. May also top with fat free cheese slices.
- Fresh tomato slices and nonfat mayonnaise with a little salt (optional) and a lot of pepper between whole wheat low fat bread slices make a great sandwich. A variety of nonfat cheese slices on whole wheat bread with nonfat mayonnaise makes a great cold or hot sandwich .
- Make great sandwiches from Healthy Choice lunchmeats and cooked, rinsed, and drained ground beef, cooked boneless, skinless chicken breast, drained water-packed tuna, crab, salmon, etc.; add your favorite fat free condiments such as nonfat mayonnaise, fat free salad dressings, Pam (Butter or Olive Oil flavor) no stick cooking spray, picanté sauce, yellow, Dijon or Creole mustard, ketchup, nonfat bar-b-que sauce, flavored wine vinegars, nonfat yogurt, fat cheeses, etc. Add sliced vegetables or fruits such as apple or pineapple, fat free cheese slices and your favorite low fat breads such as bagels, whole wheat, sourdough, pita pocket, English muffins, French, Italian, rye, pumpernickel, cracked wheat, oatmeal, oatbran, etc. Experiment with different combinations of breads, meats, vegetables, fruits, and condiments.
- Stuff pita pocket bread with whole or vegetarian refried beans, top with cooked, rinsed, and drained Healthy Choice ground beef, fresh sliced tomatoes, diced nonfat cheese, "Great Guacamole"✔ and nonfat yogurt. Serve warm or cold. Top half of a plain bagel with thin sliced apple and nonfat cheese; sprinkle with cinnamon and bake about 5 minutes at 350°. Vegetarian refried beans mixed with nonfat yogurt and picanté sauce makes a great sandwich spread.

KID'S STUFF

PARTY POTATO CHIPS

2 large baking potatoes, scrubbed and peeled if desired
Pam no stick cooking spray
Molly McButter (any flavor) sprinkles
Any of your favorite nonfat seasonings (Good Seasons Fat Free salad dressing mix, chili or garlic powder, etc.)

1. Slice potatoes paper thin (A food processor with a slicing blade works well.) Line a cookie sheet with parchment paper or a brown paper sack that has been cut into a single layer. Place each potato slice in a single layer on paper. (Note - Potatoes may also be cooked in nonstick skillet instead of the oven.)
2. Coat potatoes with Pam, sprinkle with seasonings, and bake at 350° for 8-10 minutes. Turn each slice over and spray and season again. Continue to cook 8-10 more minutes or until potatoes are crisp.

Serves: Approximately 6 @ 25 chips each

Per Serving: 0.06 g Fat, 73 Calories,
0.7 % Fat, 1.5 g Protein, 17 g Carb,
5.3 mg Sodium, 0 mg Cholesterol

OSCAR'S TRASH CAN MIX

1 C unsalted peanuts
4 C unsalted pretzel twists
5 C Cheerios
3 C Quaker Oat Squares
4 C Raisin Squares cereal
3 C bite size shredded wheat squares
1 C raisins
2 t EACH garlic powder and salt or salt free alternative
2 T EACH Worcestershire sauce and Butter Buds liquid

1. Mix together the first 7 ingredients and place in a large roasting pan coated with Pam. Stir in remaining ingredients, mixing well. Coat mixture with Pam. Bake in a 250° oven for 1½ - 2 hours; stir slowly every 15 - 20 minutes so it will bake evenly. Cool and store in an air tight container.

Makes: 20 (1 C) servings
Note: It tastes great without cooking at all.

Per Serving: 3.2 g Fat, 160 Calories,
18 % Fat, 9.1 g Protein, 23.7 g Carb,
324 mg Sodium, 0 mg Cholesterol

SHAKEY SHARKS

(Easy Prep and great for parents too!)

1 lb. cod or flounder fillets
1 C "Better Baker's Mix"✔
1 C skim milk
2 - 4 T prepared mustard
¼ C Egg Beaters
½ - 1 C self-rising flour
Pam no stick cooking spray

1. Cut fish fillets into strips. Sprinkle with salt to help draw the moisture out of the fish. Let stand 10 minutes; pat dry.
2. Place remaining ingredients except self-rising flour in a medium size mixing bowl. Mix just until blended; batter will be thin. Add fish to batter and let marinate about 30 minutes in refrigerator.
3. Spread self-rising flour in a long pan or baking sheet. Carefully remove fish from batter and roll in flour, coating evenly and completely. Place on a baking sheet that has been coated with Pam and bake at 500° for about 5 - 6 minutes or until golden brown and fish flakes easily with a fork.

Serves: 6

Per Serving: 0.2 g Fat, 63 Calories, 3 % Fat, 4.5 g Protein, 8.6 g Carb, 213 mg Sodium, 3 mg Cholesterol

MEMA'S CRAZY P B & PICKLE SANDWICH

1½ t Peanut butter
1 medium dill pickle, sliced
2 slices Wonder Light Reduced Calorie Fat Free bread

1. Spread peanut butter on 1 slice of bread. Top with sliced pickle and remaining bread slice.

Serves: 1

Per Serving: 2.4 g Fat, 113 Calories, 19 % Fat, 5.2 g Protein, 13.9 g Carb, 1186 mg Sodium, 0 mg Cholesterol

DOGGIE BAG
(Quick Fix)

4 Healthy Choice hot dogs
2 slices Healthy Choice Fat Free cheese slices
8 EACH cooked broccoli and cauliflower florets
4 Wonder Lite hot dog buns

1. Starting about ¼-inch from the end of each hot dog, make a slit lengthwise forming a pocket. Slice each piece of cheese into fourths and stuff each pocket with two of these strips. Place on a microwave safe dish and heat about 30 seconds or until hot dog is heated and cheese is melted.
2. Remove from oven, stuff each pocket with 2 each of broccoli and cauliflower florets. Serve immediately with fresh fruit.

Serves: 4

Per Serving: 2.2 g Fat, 166 Calories, 12 % Fat, 16.2 g Protein, 21.2 g Carb, 268 mg Sodium, 0 mg Cholesterol

FLYING SAUCERS

1 (9-oz.) can Hearty Grains biscuits
1 C tomato soup
2 C (8 oz.) grated Healthy Choice Fat Free mozzarella cheese
¼ C Parmesan cheese
Optional toppings: ½ C EACH sliced black olives, Healthy choice ham cut into strips, Healthy Choice cooked ground beef, mushrooms, green pepper, etc.
Olive oil flavored Pam no stick cooking spray

1. Separate biscuits and roll out to about a 4-inch circle. Place each biscuit on a cookie sheet that has been coated with Pam. Spoon 1 T soup on each biscuit, top with 2 T mozzarella cheese and ½ T Parmesan cheese. Add other toppings if desired. Bake at 400° for about 10 minutes.

Serves: 8

Note: Make extra and freeze by placing wax paper between each pizza. Freeze before baking; remove pizzas when needed and bake as directed.

Per Serving: 2.3 g Fat, 156 Calories, 13 % Fat, 12.6 g Protein, 19.8 g Carb, 447 mg Sodium, 8.7 mg Cholesterol

BRAVO BURRITOS

(Soft or crispy, Quick Fix and always a hit!)

1 (16-oz.) can Old El Paso vegetarian refried beans
8 (7-inch) flour tortillas, softened
2 oz. EACH grated Healthy Choice Fat Free Cheddar cheese and cheese singles
½ C picanté sauce
Butter flavor Pam no stick cooking spray

Directions for Soft Burritos:

1. Spread an equal amount of beans, about 4 T each, down center of each tortilla. Fold tortilla, and place seam-side down in sprayed casserole. Sprinkle with cheeses; microwave until cheese melts. Top with salsa, "Great Guacamole,"✔ and "Nonfat Yogurt Cheese,"✔ etc.

Directions for Crisp Burritos:

1. Stir cheeses into bean-meat mixture. Fill and roll each tortilla as before.
2. Coat each tortilla with Pam; place on sprayed baking sheet. Bake at 375° for 20 minutes or until crisp, or brown in skillet.

Serves: 8

Note: Healthy Choice ground beef or ground turkey breast (½-lb. cooked, rinsed and drained) may be added if desired.

Per Serving: 3 g Fat, 139 Calories, 19 % Fat, 5.7 g Protein, 22 g Carb, 580 mg Sodium, 2.5 mg Cholesterol

MINTA CHEESE

(Quick Fix)

8 oz. Healthy Choice Fat Free cream cheese
¼ C nonfat cottage cheese
8 oz. Healthy Choice Fat Free cheese singles, shredded
1 (4-oz.) jar pimientos, undrained
Dash of garlic salt

1. Mix and serve on celery stalks or with crackers or bread.

Serves: 12 (2 oz. or ¼ C servings)

Per Serving: 0 g Fat, 114 Calories, 1 % Fat, 18 g Protein, 8.5 g Carb, 810 mg Sodium, 16.8 mg Cholesterol

MOO STEW

½ recipe "Lite Meatballs"✔, prepared
1 (26-oz.) jar Healthy Choice spaghetti sauce
1½ C evaporated skim milk
1 C water
½ C dinosaur or fun shaped pasta
¼ C rice
1 large potato and 1 large carrot, peeled and sliced like shoe strings
½ of a (15-oz.) can pinto beans, undrained
½ C cut green beans, drained
10 pieces miniature or baby corn
Parmesan cheese (optional)

1. Pour spaghetti sauce, evaporated milk, and water into a large pan. Bring to a boil. Add pasta, rice, potato, and carrot slices; return to a boil. Reduce heat and simmer until tender.
2. Add remaining ingredients, including about 25 cooked meatballs, and simmer until heated through. Add more liquid if needed. Top each serving with a sprinkle of Parmesan cheese.

Makes: about 12 (1 C servings with 2 meatballs each)

Per Serving: 1.9 g Fat, 121 Calories, 14 % Fat, 7.5 g Protein, 24.9 g Carb, 196 mg Sodium, 169 mg Cholesterol

FRUIT FREEZERS

(Easy Prep)

1 quart frozen nonfat vanilla yogurt, softened
1 pint nonfat vanilla yogurt
1½ C sugar
1 C Grape Nuts
4 T lemon juice
1 (20-oz.) can crushed pineapple, drained
5 large bananas (diced or mashed)
1 C maraschino cherries, chopped

1. Mix all ingredients and pour into muffin tins with paper liners. Place in freezer.

Makes 18 regular size muffin cups.

Per Serving: 0 g Fat, 152 Calories, 0 % Fat, 2.5 g Protein, 36.7 g Carb, 37.3 mg Sodium, 2 mg Cholesterol

YUM YUM DESSERT
(Quick Fix)

1 can lite mandarin oranges
1 can lite pineapple chunks
1 can lite peaches
1 can lite cherry pie filling
3 sliced bananas

1. Drain fruit; reserve juice to drink or use in making Jello at another time. Mix fruit and pie filling. Chill and serve.

Serves: 16

Per Serving: 0 g Fat, 59 Calories, 0 % Fat, 0.75 g Protein, 15.3 g Carb, 5 mg Sodium, 0 mg Cholesterol

SHEPHERD'S PIE

4 C cooked mashed potatoes plus 1 package Butter Buds plus 2 T grated fresh onion
¼ C Egg Beaters
1 lb. Healthy Choice ground beef, cooked, rinsed and drained
½ C finely chopped celery
1 T parsley
1 (6-oz.) can mushroom pieces, drained
1½ t salt (optional)
¼ t pepper
½ C Weight Watcher's cream of mushroom soup, heated
1 t Parmesan cheese
Pam no stick cooking spray

1. Mix potato mixture with Egg Beaters. Spoon ½ mixture into bottom of a sprayed pie plate.
2. In another bowl, mix beef and next 6 ingredients. Spoon beef on top of potato mixture; top with remaining potato mixture. Sprinkle with cheese and bake in preheated 400° oven 20 minutes or until golden brown.

Serves: 8

Per Serving: 2.1 g Fat, 156 Calories, 12 % Fat, 13.6 g Protein, 20.3 g Carb, 267 mg Sodium, 27.8 mg Cholesterol

PRETTY FRUIT PIZZA

½ recipe "Lemon Whippersnaps"✔
2 (8-oz.) containers Healthy Choice Fat-Free cream cheese
¼ C favorite fruit juice, unsweetened
1 t EACH coconut and almond flavorings
1½ C EACH sliced strawberries, kiwi fruit, pineapple, grapes, and mandarin oranges, drained
1 canister Reddi Wip Lite whipped cream, (optional)
Pam no-stick cooking spray

1. Prepare cookie dough and spread on a pizza pan that has been coated with Pam. Bake as directed allowing a little extra time to make sure entire cookie is done. Cool completely.
2. Beat together the cream cheese, fruit juice, and flavorings. Spread over cooled cookie. Decorate the pizza with the sliced fruit beginning at the outside of the pizza and circling in toward the middle by alternating fruits, or create your own designs. Better yet, let the kids do their own decorating. Dot each slice with 1 T of whipped topping if desired.

Serves: 16

Per Serving: 1.5 g Fat, 252 Calories, 5 % Fat, 6.01 g Protein, 53.9 g Carb, 356 mg Sodium, 2.45 mg Cholesterol

SLOPPY JO'S
(Quick Fix)

1 lb Healthy Choice ground beef
1½ C tomato sauce
½ C ketchup
1 t minced onion
1 t Worcestershire sauce
1-2 t chili powder
½ of (10-oz.) package frozen corn
8 Wonder Light hamburger buns

1. Cook meat, rinse, and drain. Place in saucepan or microwaveable dish and add remaining ingredients. Simmer until heated through, about 5 minutes.
2. Divide mixture evenly and serve over warmed buns. Serve with "Non-fat Potato Chips"✔

Serves: 8

Variations: Serve Sloppy Jo mix over pasta or baked potatoes or in pita bread. Also great for nachos using Guiltless Gourmet Tortilla Chips.

Per Serving: 3.3 g Fat, 199 Calories, 15 % Fat, 16.5 g Protein, 38.3 g Carb, 211 mg Sodium, 28.7 mg Cholesterol

MADISON'S APPLE TREAT
(Easy Prep)

6 Red Delicious medium size apples, cored and sliced
1 T cinnamon
¼ C unsweetened apple juice
2 squirts lemon juice
½ C Butter Buds liquid
½ C sugar or to taste
¾ C flour
Pinch allspice
¼ t salt (optional)
Pam no stick cooking spray

1. Spray an oblong, shallow casserole with Pam; place apples in dish. Pour apple juice over apples and sprinkle liberally with cinnamon.
2. Combine remaining ingredients; work together until crumbly and sprinkle over apples. Bake uncovered at 350° for 30 - 40 minutes. Serve with frozen nonfat vanilla yogurt if desired.

Serves: 6

Per Serving: 1.1 g Fat, 205 Calories, 5 % Fat, 1.5 g Protein, 49.5 g Carb, 58 mg Sodium, 0 mg Cholesterol

FRUIT SMOOTHIES
(Quick Fix)

8 oz. nonfat yogurt, any flavor
1 (6-oz.) can frozen unsweetened orange juice concentrate
¼ C honey
½ C EACH skim milk and water
1½ t vanilla
Ice cubes
Artificial sweetener (optional)

1. Combine all ingredients in blender, adding enough ice cubes to make 5 cups of liquid. Add artificial sweetener if desired. May add 2 C fresh or frozen fruit in place of the orange juice if desired.

Makes 5 (1-C) servings

Per Serving: 0.48 g Fat, 247 Calories, 2 % Fat, 5.2 g Protein, 56.4 g Carb, 38.4 mg Sodium, 4 mg Cholesterol

PLAY DOUGH

1 C EACH flour and water
½ C salt (optional)
2 t cream of tartar
Food coloring

1. Mix and cook all ingredients over medium heat until mixture pulls away from sides of pan. It will become the consistency of play dough. Knead until cool.

Makes: Happy children

TINY TEDDY BEAR CHEESECAKES
(Quick Fix)

1 (8-oz.) carton Healthy Choice Fat Free cream cheese
½ C sugar
½ C Egg Beaters
1½ t lemon juice
1 t vanilla
12 Teddy Graham cookies
Pam no stick cooking spray

1. Beat together the first 5 ingredients until smooth.
2. Spray mini muffin tins with Pam, place one Teddy Graham in the bottom of each muffin tin, and spoon equal amounts of cream cheese mixture on top of each cookie.
3. Bake for 15-20 minutes or until toothpick inserted in middle comes out clean. Do not overbake. Cool on rack. Drizzle with nonfat chocolate syrup or top with fruit, if desired

Serves: 12 (Makes 1⅓ C batter)

Per Serving: 0.5 g Fat, 144 Calories, 3 % Fat, 1.3 g Protein, 18.6 g Carb, 539 mg Sodium, 13.3 mg Cholesterol

BUTTERMILK PANCAKES
(Easy Prep)

2 C all purpose flour
1 t baking soda
1 T sugar
1 t salt (optional)
½ C Egg Beaters
1 C EACH 1% fat buttermilk and evaporated skim milk
1-2 T Butter Buds liquid
Pam no stick cooking spray

1. Sift together the dry ingredients. Mix together the liquid ingredients and stir into dry ingredients. Mix well.
2. Spray a large skillet or griddle with Pam and cook until done.

Makes: 20 medium size pancakes

Per Serving: 0.24 g Fat, 57 Calories, 4 % Fat, 2.5 g Protein, 10.8 g Carbs, 34 mg Sodium, 0.9 mg Cholesterol

BERRY GOOD SYRUP

2 C berries (strawberries, blueberries, blackberries, etc.)
2 T apple juice concentrate
½ t vanilla

1. Blend berries in blender or food processor until smooth.
2. Pour remaining ingredients into saucepan, add berries and bring to a boil. Simmer 20-30 minutes.

Serves: 4

Per Serving: 0.5 g Fat, 50 Calories,
9 % Fat, 0.5 g Protein, 12 g Carb,
0.5 mg Sodium, 0 mg Cholesterol

CHEERY CHERRIES

3 oz. Healthy Choice Fat Free cream cheese, softened
½ t vanilla or almond extract
1 T EACH evaporated skim milk and grated orange peel
1 lb. fresh cherries, pitted

1. Mix all ingredients except cherries and spoon into decorating bag with a small tip on end.
2. Keeping one finger on the bottom of each cherry to prevent mixture from coming through, pipe cream into and on top of each cherry.

Serves: 50

Note: Flavored liqueurs may be used in place of the extracts if desired.

Per Serving: 0 g Fat, 11 Calories,
1 % Fat, 0.3 g Protein, 2.6 g Carb,
10 mg Sodium, 0.31 mg Cholesterol

HAPPY CLOWN
(Quick Fix)

1 canister Reddi-Wip Lite whipped topping
½ C, scooped into a ball, vanilla nonfat frozen dessert
1 Keebler sugar ice cream cone
3 maraschino cherries, halved, for mouth
2 whole pecan halves, for ears
8 mini chocolate chips, for eyebrows
2 raisins, for eyes
1 peanut M & M candy, for nose
1 small doily, for clown collar (may use whipped topping)

1. Place doily on a dessert plate. Top with scoop of vanilla dessert. Place inverted ice cream cone on top of scoop for the clown's hat.
2. Use fruit and/or candy, or use your own ideas, to create the clown's face and decorate his hat. Suggestions at left. Use 3 small squirts (about 3 T)of whipped topping for little balls on the front of his hat if desired.

Serves: 1

Per Serving: 7.7 g Fat, 263 Calories, 26 % Fat, 4.04 g Protein, 49.6 g Carb, 85 mg Sodium, 6 mg Cholesterol

SKINNY BITES
(Quick Fix)

2 (10-count) rolls Pillsbury Breadsticks in dairy case
¼ C hot water mixed with ½ package Butter Buds
Cinnamon and sugar mixture or any seasonings

1. Coat a small cake or bundt pan with Pam.
2. Tear each breadstick into 10 pieces. Layer bread, then water mixture, then seasoning in pan, repeating layers. Bake at 350° for 20-30 minutes. Serve immediately.

Serves: 20

Per Serving: 2 g Fat, 101 Calories, 18 % Fat, 3 g Protein, 17.2 g Carb, 247 mg Sodium, 0 mg Cholesterol

EGG IN A GLASS
(Quick Fix)

- **¼ C Egg Beaters plus 1 large egg white**
- **2 slices nonfat reduced calorie whole wheat bread**
- **1 package Butter Buds**
- **Butter flavor Pam no stick cooking spray**
- **1 fat beer or tulip-shape mug with stem**

1. Toast bread to a dark golden brown, not burned. Spray with Pam and tear into bite-size pieces.
2. Coat a small skillet with Pam or use microwave and cook egg mixture with Butter Buds over medium heat until soft.
3. Immediately place egg in glass; top with toast pieces and stir well to coat toast with egg. If mixture in glass is too dry, cook a little more egg and add to glass.

Serves: 1

Per Serving: 0 g Fat, 88 Calories,
0 % Fat, 8 g Protein, 8 g Carb,
808 mg Sodium, 0 mg Cholesterol

KID-KABOBS
(Easy Prep)

- **4 Healthy Choice hot dogs**
- **2 ears of corn cut into 1-inch pieces**
- **12 pineapple chunks**
- **¼ C Butter Buds liquid**

1. Cut hot dogs into fourths and thread onto skewers alternating with corn pieces and pineapple chunks. Brush with Butter Buds mixture and grill until corn is tender.

Serves: 4

Per Serving: 1.5 g Fat, 146 Calories,
9 % Fat, 7.5 g Protein, 26 g Carb,
352 mg Sodium, 10 mg Cholesterol

CHEESEBURGER PIE

1 C plus 2 T "Best Baker's Mix"✔
¼ C cold water
1 lb. Healthy Choice ground beef, cooked, drained, and rinsed
½ C onion, finely chopped
Salt (optional) and pepper to taste
1 T Worcestershire sauce
½ C Egg Beaters
1 C nonfat cottage cheese
4 oz. Healthy Choice Fat Free cheese singles, diced
2 medium tomatoes, optional
Pam no stick cooking spray

1. Mix 1 C baker's mix with the water until soft dough forms. Beat vigorously about 20 strokes. Gently form into a ball; knead 5 times. Make into pie crust and ease into sprayed pie plate.
2. Place cooked beef into large skillet; sauté with onion, salt and pepper. Stir in 2 T baker's mix and Worcestershire sauce. Mix well and spoon into crust.
3. Mix Egg Beaters, cottage cheese and diced cheese; pour over meat mixture. Sprinkle with tomatoes if desired. Bake 30 minutes at 350° or until set.

Serves: 8

Per Serving: 2.2 g Fat, 121 Calories, 16 % Fat, 18.3 g Protein, 6.3 g Carb, 462 mg Sodium, 31.2 mg Cholesterol

BIRD NESTS
(Quick Fix)

1 medium can sweet green peas, warmed
1 package instant mashed potatoes
Skim milk
1 package Butter Buds

1. Prepare potatoes as directed using skim milk and Butter Buds; omit butter.
2. Place a "nest" of potatoes on each plate, spoon peas in center of potatoes and serve.

Serves: 6

Per Serving: 0.25 g Fat, 108 Calories, 4 % Fat, 4 g Protein, 18.5 g Carb, 726 mg Sodium, 0 mg Cholesterol

MOMMY'S MACARONI AND CHEESE

1-2 T cornstarch
¾ C (half skim milk - half evaporated skim milk)
½ C Egg Beaters
1 C (4 oz.) shredded Healthy Choice Fat Free cheese singles
½ C nonfat cottage cheese
½ C (2 oz.) Healthy Choice Fat Free mozzarella cheese
Salt (optional) and pepper to taste
12 oz. macaroni, cooked and drained

1. Mix cornstarch with milk; add Egg Beaters. Add milk mixture to remaining ingredients; stir well.
2. Coat a medium baking dish with Pam. Pour macaroni into dish and bake at 375° for about 20 minutes.

Serves: 8

Per Serving: 0.17 g Fat, 219 Calories, 3 % Fat, 14 g Protein, 36 g Carb, 358 mg Sodium, 5.3 mg Cholesterol

HONEY-SICLES
(Easy Prep)

1 medium ripe banana, peeled and cut in half crosswise
2 popsicle sticks
¼ C honey
½ C Grape Nuts or your favorite lowfat topping

1. Insert a popsicle stick into each banana slice. Freeze.
2. Spread frozen banana with honey; roll in topping.

Serves: 2

Per Serving: 0 g Fat, 260 Calories, 0 % Fat, 2.8 g Protein, 64 g Carb, 242 mg Sodium, 0 mg Cholesterol

PINK ELEPHANT SHAKES
(Quick Fix)

1 C pink lemonade
1 C skim milk
2 C nonfat vanilla frozen yogurt
Ice cubes

1. Blend together and serve.

Serves: 4

Per Serving: 0 g Fat, 130 Calories, 0 % Fat, 10.5 g Protein, 21.5 g Carb, 126 mg Sodium, 10.25 mg Cholesterol

JUNE'S MIDNIGHT SNACK
(Quick Fix)

2 Healthy Choice Fat Free cheese singles
8 fat free saltine crackers, salt-free if desired

1. Break each cheese slice into 4 squares. Place each square on 1 cracker and broil on a cookie sheet until edges are lightly browned and cheese is melted. Serve with skim milk and a lot of "TLC"!!

Serves: 2

Note: (My dad sometimes fixed this for me when I was a child if I was awake after a bad dream or if I was sick during the middle of the night. Making it and the special time we shared was more fun than eating it. The ingredients now are a little different.)

Per Serving: 0 g Fat, 60 Calories, 0 % Fat, 5.5 g Protein, 8 g Carb, 260 mg Sodium, 5 mg Cholesterol

CHICKEN LITTLE
(This requires a little more thought, but is sure to make a hit!)

1 small ceramic hen dish with lid (can be found at most dime stores - usually white with a little red)
⅔ C cooked rice, mixed with 1 t Butter Buds
¼ C green peas, drained
2 oz. cooked boneless, skinless, chicken breast, cubed
⅓ C Weight Watcher's cream of mushroom soup

1. Mix together all ingredients; heat and serve in "Chicken Little" dish.

Serves: 1

Per Serving: 1.5 g Fat, 297 Calories, 4 % Fat, 29 g Protein, 45 g Carb, 238 mg Sodium, 37.5 mg Cholesterol

EGG WITH A HOLE IN IT
(Quick Fix)

1 slice nonfat reduced calorie whole wheat bread
¼ C Egg Beaters
Butter flavor Pam no stick cooking spray

1. Coat bread on both sides with Pam. Cut a hole about the size of a half dollar out of the center of the bread; remove and set aside.
2. Coat a small skillet with Pam; heat over medium heat. When medium hot, place large piece of bread in skillet; pour Egg Beaters in center. Cook to desired doneness turning once. Remove from skillet. Place reserved hole in pan to toast; spread with sugar-free jelly if desired.

Serves: 1

Per Serving: 0 g Fat, 65 Calories, 0 % Fat, 8 g Protein, 8 g Carb, 207 mg Sodium, 0 mg Cholesterol

PEPPERMINT CHOCOLATE
(Quick Fix)

3 T cocoa
2 T sugar
10 round peppermint candies, crushed
4 C skim milk, divided
1 C hot water

1. Combine first 3 ingredients in microwave-safe bowl. Gradually add the milk and water; mix well. Cook on medium until heated through. Stir frequently during cooking.

Serves: 5

Per Serving: 0.14 g Fat, 128 Calories, 1 % Fat, 6.4 g Protein, 24.6 g Carb, 112 mg Sodium, 4 mg Cholesterol

PEACHY QUICK CAKE

1 box lite white cake mix
1 can peach pie filling plus 1 T almond extract
¾ C Egg Beaters
Pam no stick cooking spray

1. Combine all ingredients and pour into an oblong cake pan that has been sprayed with Pam; bake at 350° for 40-45 minutes. Serve with frozen nonfat vanilla yogurt. (May use other flavors of lite cake mix and pie fillings.)

Serves: 12

Per Serving: 2 g Fat, 194 Calories, 10 % Fat, 4.2 g Protein, 39 g Carb, 333 mg Sodium, 0 mg Cholesterol

GRANNY'S SCRAMBLED EGG SANDWICH
(Quick Fix)

½ C Egg Beaters
1 scant T skim milk
2 slices nonfat reduced calorie wheat bread
Butter flavor Pam no stick cooking spray
2 t Bac-Os artificial bacon bits

1. Coat a small skillet with Pam and warm over medium heat. Do not get it too hot!
2. Mix all ingredients except Bac-Os and pour into skillet; cook slowly over medium heat. Fold over once and cook until done.
3. Lightly toast bread and spray with Pam. Place egg mixture on top of 1 slice of bread; sprinkle with bacon bits. Top sandwich with remaining slice of bread, slice into triangles and serve.

Serves: 1

Per Serving: 1 g Fat, 155 Calories, 6 % Fat, 14 g Protein, 17 g Carb, 250 mg Sodium, 0 mg Cholesterol

HELEN'S FRUIT SLUSH

1 small can EACH frozen orange juice and lemonade
3 C water
2 (10-oz.) packages frozen unsweetened strawberries
1 (15-oz.) can unsweetened crushed pineapple
1 medium jar maraschino cherries
2 medium bananas, diced

1. Mix all ingredients and pour into freezer-safe cups, (may use plastic cups); freeze. Take out 2-3 hours before serving and place in refrigerator.

Serves: 12

Per Serving: 0 g Fat, 199 Calories, 0 % Fat, 1.1 g Protein, 50 g Carb, 3.25 mg Sodium, 0 mg Cholesterol

WAFFLES
(Quick Fix)

2 C cake flour
1 package Butter Buds
1 scant ½ C Egg Beaters
½ t salt (optional)
1 T sugar
½ t vanilla
2 T water
1½ C skim milk
Pam no stick cooking spray

1. Spray waffle iron with Pam and heat to cooking temperature.
2. Mix all ingredients well and spoon into waffle iron.

Serves: 12

Per Serving: 0.16 g Fat, 77 Calories, 2 % Fat, 3 g Protein, 14.8 g Carb, 86 mg Sodium, 0.62 mg Cholesterol

JANE'S GELATIN SQUARES
(Easy Prep)

2 C warm water
6 T unflavored gelatin
12 oz. unsweetened frozen juice concentrate

1. Pour water into a bowl; sprinkle gelatin over water to soften and dissolve. Microwave 1½-2 minutes to further dissolve gelatin.
2. Stir concentrate into water mixture and pour into a 9 X 13-inch glass pan; chill and cut into squares or shapes. Serve cold or at room temperature.

Serves: 16 (using orange juice)

Per Serving: 0 g Fat, 46 Calories, 0 % Fat, 1 g Protein, 10.8 g Carb, 0 mg Sodium, 0 mg Cholesterol

TRIPLE TREATS
(Quick Fix)

Butter flavor Pam no stick cooking spray
6 C crispy rice cereal
7 C miniature marshmallows

1. Coat a large microwave-safe bowl with Pam. Place marshmallows in bowl and microwave about 2 minutes until melted.
2. Coat a wooden spoon with Pam and stir cereal into marshmallows. Coat hands with Pam; press into a sprayed glass dish. Cool and break into squares.

Serves: 16

Per Serving: 0 g Fat, 183 Calories, 0 % Fat, 2.1 g Protein, 38 g Carb, 135 mg Sodium, 0 mg Cholesterol

CONEY BALONEY
(Quick Fix)

1 (5-oz.) can chunk chicken breast, rinsed and drained
1 (8-oz.) can crushed pineapple, well drained
⅓ C Grape Nuts cereal
3 T Kraft Free mayonnaise
1½ T chopped maraschino cherries
4 low-fat, flat-bottom ice cream cones

1. Mix all ingredients except cones and chill.
2. Press about ½ C mixture into each cone and serve.

Serves: 4

Per Serving: 2.2 g Fat, 210 Calories, 9 % Fat, 9.25 g Protein, 32 g Carb, 243 mg Sodium, 21.5 mg Cholesterol

GO FISH FOR FRUIT

1 medium red watermelon, halved
Fresh fruits cut into chunks or balls

1. Scoop out fruit from watermelon to ¼-inch of rind; remove seeds. Place melon in bowl and set aside.
2. Place remaining fruit in watermelon "bowl"; add watermelon. Place long wooden skewers in container next to fruit and let everyone "fish" for fruit.

Serves: a large group of children and/or adults

Note: You may do this with veggies, low-fat cheeses, chicken, etc.

DOG ON A LEASH
(Quick Fix)

4 Pillsbury soft uncooked breadsticks, cut in half
1 package Healthy Choice hot dogs
8 wooden popsicle sticks
Pam no stick cooking spray

1. Place 1 stick inside each hot dog vertically, like a corn dog. Wrap hot dog with ½ breadstick; start at the bottom and wind it up to the top.
2. Place on a sprayed cookie sheet and bake according to breadstick directions.

Serves: 8

Per Serving: 2 g Fat, 100 Calories, 18 % Fat, 7.5 g Protein, 12.5 g Carb, 575 mg Sodium, 15 mg Cholesterol

CHIPS 'N CHILI CRUNCH
(Quick Fix)

4 oz. Guiltless Gourmet Baked tortilla chips, divided
2 cans Health Valley Fat Free vegetarian chili
1 C (4 oz.) Healthy Choice Fat Free mozzarella cheese, grated
4 oz. Healthy Choice Fat Free cheese slices, diced
Pam no stick cooking spray

1. Coat a square baking dish with Pam. Crush half of the chips, about 48, and sprinkle in the bottom of the baking dish. Top with 1 can chili. Crush remaining chips; sprinkle over chili. Top chips with remaining chili, sprinkle cheese over entire casserole, and bake at 350° about 10 minutes or until heated through.

Serves: 6

Per Serving: 0.7 g Fat, 84 Calories, 5 % Fat, 12 g Protein, 21 g Carb, 338 mg Sodium, 3.3 mg Cholesterol

OVEN FRIED HONEY CHICKEN

½ C 1% buttermilk plus ½ C Egg Beaters
6 (4-oz.) boneless, skinless chicken breasts (may be cut into chunks)
¾ C flour (1 T to coat each side), plus 1 package dry Butter Buds
½ t salt (optional) plus ¼ t EACH garlic powder and pepper
¼ C Butter Buds liquid plus 2 T honey
Pam no stick cooking spray

1. Dip each chicken breast into buttermilk/egg mixture. Coat with mixture of flour, salt, garlic and pepper.
2. Coat an oblong baking dish with Pam. Pour Butter Buds/corn syrup mixture into pan. Place chicken pieces on top and bake uncovered at 425° for 20 minutes. Turn chicken and bake another 5-10 minutes or until tender.

Serves: 6

Per Serving: 2.5 g Fat, 265 Calories, 8 % Fat, 39 g Protein, 18.5 g Carb, 146 mg Sodium, 97 mg Cholesterol

P B SHAKE
(Quick Fix)

3 C skim milk
¼ C honey
3 T creamy peanut butter
½ t vanilla extract
1 medium banana
Ice cubes

1. Combine all ingredients in a blender. Process until smooth. Serve in tall glasses.

Serves: 6

Per Serving: 4 g Fat, 150 Calories, 24 % Fat, 6.1 g Protein, 23 g Carb, 28 mg Sodium, 0.6 mg Cholesterol

FANTASTIC FRENCH FRIES
(Easy Prep)

2 large baking potatoes
Butter flavor Pam no stick cooking spray
Seasoning of your choice (garlic powder or salt, chili powder, paprika, chives, etc.

1. Bake potatoes in microwave about 4 minutes or until halfway cooked (crisp-tender). Remove from oven and slice into thin strips. Coat baking sheet and potato slices with Pam and bake at 400° until golden brown on one side. Turn potatoes and continue to bake until crisp. Total cooking time about 30 minutes. Watch closely; do not overcook.

Serves: 4

Variation: Sauté potato slices in nonstick skillet coated with Pam until crisp.

Per Serving: 0 g Fat, 72 Calories, 0 % Fat, 2 g Protein, 16.5 g Carb, 3 mg Sodium, 0 mg Cholesterol

DR. MAC'S POPCORN BALLS #1

3 quarts air-popped corn, discard unpopped kernels
1 C EACH sugar and water
⅓ C white corn syrup
¼ t salt (optional)
1 t lemon or vanilla extract
Pam no stick cooking spray

1. Place popcorn in large bowl coated with Pam; set aside.
2. In a medium saucepan, cook sugar, water and syrup to medium-crack stage (280° F).
3. Add flavoring and salt; pour over corn, stirring to coat evenly. Shape into balls and wrap in wax paper.

Serves: 12

Per Serving: 0.25 g Fat, 86 Calories, 3 % Fat, 0.6 g Protein, 21.25 g Carb, 0.16 mg Sodium, 0 mg Cholesterol

DR. MAC'S POPCORN BALLS #2

3 quarts air-popped corn, discard unpopped kernels
1 C EACH honey and sugar
⅔ C water
½ package Butter Buds, mixed with hot corn
¼ t salt (optional)

1. Follow same directions as in recipe #1.

Serves: 12

Per Serving: 0.25 g Fat, 158 Calories, 3 % Fat, 0.6 g Protein, 38.9 g Carb, 0.16 mg Sodium, 0 mg Cholesterol

SANDWICHES

LITE MONTE CRISTO SANDWICH
(Quick Fix)

4 egg whites, well beaten
1 C skim milk
4 slices Wonder Lite Fat-Free Reduced Calorie day old bread slices
2 (1-oz.) slices Healthy Choice turkey or ham
¾ C (3 oz.) Healthy Choice Fat Free mozzarella cheese, divided
Butter flavor Pam no stick cooking spray

1. Mix egg and milk. Set aside.
2. Spray bread slices on both sides with Pam. Top two of the slices with half the meat and cheese. Top with another slice of bread and press together.
3. Spray a skillet with Pam and heat. Dip each sandwich gently into egg mixture and sauté in skillet until golden brown on each side and cheese is melted. Serve hot with lite syrup, powdered sugar or lite jam.

Serves: 2

Per Serving: 3.5 g Fat, 270 Calories, 15 % Fat, 37 g Protein, 18 g Carb, 770 mg Sodium, 36 mg Cholesterol

CHEESE PUFF SANDWICHES
(Quick Fix)

1 (8-oz.) loaf French bread (no more than 1 gram fat per serving)
2 t Creole mustard
¼ C Butter Buds liquid
3 oz. (8 thin slices) Healthy Choice ham
¼ t EACH chili and garlic powder (more if desired)
2 T flour mixed with 4 T white wine
½ t Worcestershire sauce
½ C Egg Beaters
5 oz. Healthy Choice Fat Free cheese singles, shredded

1. Slice bread horizontally to make 2 open-face slices. Combine mustard and Butter Buds mixture; spread on each slice. Top with meat.
2. Combine remaining ingredients; spoon on top of meat. Bake in 375° oven for 10 minutes. Cut each slice into 3 servings.

Serves: 6

Per Serving: 3.1 g Fat, 193 Calories, 14 % Fat, 16 g Protein, 26 g Carb, 678 mg Sodium, 0.23 mg Cholesterol

HAM SALAD FOR SANDWICHES

1 lb. Healthy Choice cooked lean ham, ground
3 hard cooked egg whites, chopped
½ C chopped celery
¼ C sweet pickle relish
½ C Kraft Free mayonnaise
1½ t creole mustard or to taste

1. Mix all ingredients and chill well.

Serves: 8

Per Serving: 2 g Fat, 170 Calories, 10 % Fat, 27 g Protein, 3.1 g Carb, 271 mg Sodium, 68 mg Cholesterol

PAT'S PICKLE SANDWICHES

(Easy Prep)

1 jar Vlasic regular dill spears, cut lengthwise in half
1 T Kraft Free mayonnaise
1 (8-oz.) carton Healthy Choice Fat Free cream cheese
1 t garlic salt
1 loaf Wonder Lite Reduced Calorie Fat Free bread

1. Drain pickles well and pat dry.
2. Mix mayonnaise, cream cheese, and garlic salt. Spread about 2 T on each slice of bread. Place pickle inside; roll up each slice and secure with a toothpick. Chill 2 hours.
3. Serve each slice whole or slice each roll into bite size pieces.

Serves: 20 (1 slice, prepared)

Per Serving: 0 g Fat, 62 Calories, 0 % Fat, 4.4 g Protein, 2 g Carb, 497 mg Sodium, 2 mg Cholesterol

TERRIFIC TUNA SALAD SANDWICHES
(Quick Fix)

1 (6½-oz.) can tuna in water, drained
2 hard boiled eggs, yolks removed
1 stalk celery, chopped
1 t onion juice
2 small sweet pickles, chopped
¼ C Kraft Free mayonnaise

1. Combine all ingredients. Serve on nonfat toasted bread as a sandwich or with "Pita or Bagel Chips"✔.

Makes: 6 (¼ C) servings of salad only

Per Serving: 0.18 g Fat, 61 Calories, 3 % Fat, 6.1 g Protein, 4 g Carb, 262 mg Sodium, 5.5 mg Cholesterol

LUNCHEON SANDWICH SPREAD
(Quick Fix)

8 oz. Healthy Choice Fat Free cream cheese
1 loaf fat free Wonder light bread, crust removed
1 t Worcestershire sauce
2 shakes celery salt
1 t parsley flakes
2-3 T Lawry's Salad Sprinkle
2 T Fat-Free Ranch Dressing
½ t salt (optional)

1. Mix all ingredients. Spread mixture on 10 bread slices. Top with another slice, cut each sandwich into 4 triangles, and serve.

Serves: 40

Per Serving: 0 g Fat, 31 Calories, 0 % Fat, 2.2 g Protein, 4.2 g Carb, 105 mg Sodium, 1 mg Cholesterol

Notes and Extra Recipes:

Notes and Extra Recipes:

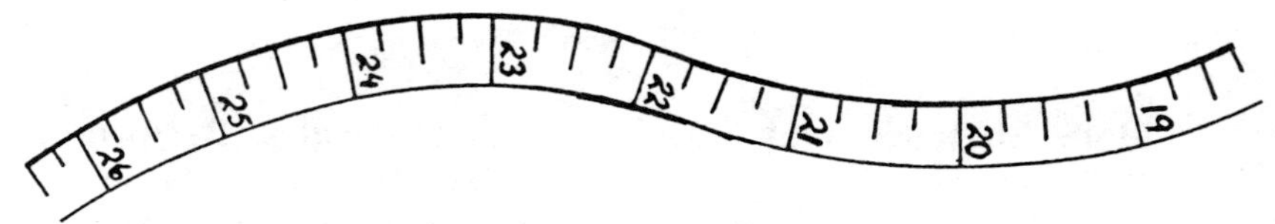

FINISHING TOUCHES

Time Savers:

- Marinate fish, chicken, or lean beef in Madeira wine for 2-8 hours; grill as directed. (See grilling tips in Main Dish Section).
- Add a dash of grapefruit, orange, or lemon juice to bottled nonfat Bar-B-Que sauce for a different flavor.
- Mix unsweetened jam or jelly with orange or pineapple juice; brush on cooked meats about 5 minutes before they are done.
- Make your own chili mix - Stir a mixture of 1 T sugar (optional), 3 T paprika, 3 T flour, 5 T chili powder, 3 T cumin, and 6 T cornmeal into 1 lb. hot cooked, rinsed, and drained Healthy Choice ground beef plus ½-1 C canned diced tomatoes, 2 cans drained pinto beans, and 1 small chopped onion. Adjust seasonings to taste.
- For a spaghetti sauce with a creamier taste, mix Healthy Choice spaghetti sauce with a little Weight Watcher's cream of mushroom soup to your taste.
- Make a spicy sauce with ½ Healthy Choice spaghetti sauce and ½ picanté sauce.
- Check under "Pizza, Pasta, and Potato Toppers"✔ for other pasta sauces or toppers.
- Saute ½ C chopped onion and 1 T minced garlic in 1-2 T "Defatted Chicken Broth"✔. When tender, add 2½ C peeled and cubed eggplant, 1/3 C each diced yellow and red bell peppers and ¼ C water. Cook until vegetables are tender. Add 2½ C chopped tomatoes and simmer about 30 minutes. Serve over pasta.
- Heat and stir 1 C nonfat plain yogurt, ½ C evaporated skim milk, 2 t Dijon mustard, and 1 t Parmesan cheese. Heat to bubbling; stir in a mixture of ¼ C cold water and 1 T cornstarch and cook until thick. Serve over pasta, etc.
- To "Lite White Sauce"✔ add 4 oz. Healthy Choice diced ham, 1½ T minced onion, ½ C fat free ricotta cheese, and ⅓ C chopped tomatoes. Great over pasta, vegetables, or potatoes.
- Sauté 1 lb. scallops and a pinch of parsley in 1 T Bacon flavor

Molly McButter until browned, about 5 minutes. Remove scallops; add ½ C each "Defatted Chicken Broth"✔, and clam juice. Bring to a boil, reduce heat and simmer 2-3 minutes. Mix with pasta, scallops, and Bac-Os if desired.

- Brown ½ lb. ground turkey breast, 1 C chopped onion, and a dash of garlic powder in 2 T "Defatted Beef Broth"✔. Add ½ C each white wine and Butter Buds liquid; simmer 5 minutes. Season to taste. Serve over rice, pasta, etc.
- Sauté ½ C chopped onion, 1 t minced garlic and ½ t cayenne pepper in ¼ C Butter Buds liquid until crisp-tender. Add 1 bunch chopped broccoli or cauliflower and ½ C more Butter Buds liquid. Season to taste.
- Sauté 1 C diced onion in 2 T liquid Butter Buds until crisp-tender. Add ½ lb. each diced fresh or frozen asparagus (thawed) and sliced mushrooms in ½ C Defatted Chicken Broth"✔, salt (optional) and pepper. Cook 3-4 minutes; add ⅔ C evaporated skim milk and simmer until slightly thick. Stir in 1-1½ C cooked diced chicken breast, or lean fish. Serve over spinach pasta or rice.
- Bring evaporated skim milk to a boil; remove from heat and add a dash of your favorite seasoning. Add a pinch of parsley, 1 t dry Butter Buds, and 1 T lemon juice. Serve, with or without diced chicken breast or lean fish, over pasta or rice.
- Sauté fresh sliced vegetables in "Defatted Chicken Broth"✔, season to taste and serve over pasta, rice, etc.
- Microwave just until softened - 1 (15-oz.) container Truly Lite fat free ricotta cheese, 1 T Bacon flavor Molly McButter, 2 T each Parmesan cheese and parsley, and a dash of pepper and garlic. Serve over hot pasta.
- To ½ C "Defatted Chicken Broth"✔ add 1 package dry Butter Buds, a dash of garlic powder, 1 can plain artichoke hearts, (drained), 2 oz. diced Healthy Choice ham and 2 T Parmesan cheese. Serve over pasta or vegetables.
- Quick Hollandaise - Heat in microwave and stir frequently ½ C nonfat mayonnaise, 2 T evaporated skim milk, 1 t lemon juice, and 1 package dry Butter Buds. Serve over vegetables.
- Marinate 8 boneless, skinless chicken breasts overnight in a mixture of ½ C fat free mayonnaise, ⅓ C lemon juice, 3 T Worcestershire sauce, 1 t salt (optional), 2 t each onion powder and light corn syrup, and ½ t each dried basil, garlic powder and pepper. Grill until done.

Helpful Hints:

- To thicken gravies or sauces, try adding a little instant mashed potato flakes.

- If gravy or sauce is lumpy, place it in your food processor or blender and process until smooth.
- Use Butter Buds liquid, wine, "Defatted Chicken Broth"✔, "Defatted Beef Broth"✔, or vegetable broth in your own recipes in place of oil; experiment with seasonings.

GRAVIES & SAUCES

CHICKEN FRIED CHICKEN GRAVY
(Easy Prep)

2 T "Defatted Chicken Broth"✔
2 T Grape Nuts cereal plus 1 T flour
1 C evaporated skim milk
2 T cornstarch plus 3 T cold water to form a paste
2 T Weight Watcher's cream of mushroom soup
Salt (optional) and pepper to taste

1. Sauté Grape Nuts and flour in broth until cereal is soft. Slowly add evaporated milk; stir well. Heat to a slow simmer; slowly stir in cornstarch mixture and cook until thick. Add soup and season to taste. Serve with chicken fried chicken or chicken fried steak.

Makes: about 24 T (2 Cups) (Nutrition per T)

Per Serving: 0.1 g Fat, 9 Calories, 10 % Fat, 0.49 g Protein, 1.55 g Carb, 17.4 mg Sodium, .39 mg Cholesterol

MOTHER MARGARET'S BASIC GRAVY

2 C "Defatted Chicken Broth"✔
4 T flour
Salt (optional) and pepper to taste

1. Heat broth in medium-size pan to almost boiling. Gradually add flour by the spoonful until thickened. Add seasonings.
2. For large quantities, add 2 T flour to each C of liquid.

Serves: 8

Per Serving: 0.23 g Fat, 18 Calories, 11 % Fat, 1.7 g Protein, 5.2 g Carb, 86 mg Sodium, 5 mg Cholesterol

EASY CHICKEN GRAVY

⅔ C evaporated skim milk
1 can Weight Watcher's cream of mushroom soup
1 t cornstarch

1. Mix together; heat and serve with "Oven Fried Chicken"* or serve over rice, pasta, or potatoes.

Makes: About 2 C or 16 (2 T) servings.

Per Serving: 0.15 g Fat, 9 Calories, 0.01 % Fat, 0.5 g Protein, 1.3 g Carb, 83.2 mg Sodium, 0.34 mg Cholesterol

NONFAT YOGURT CHEESE

(You may substitute No Fat sour cream in place of Nonfat Yogurt Cheese)

2 Cups nonfat yogurt (Use a yogurt that has a culture in it; Using one that contains a gelatin base or carrageenan will not let the yogurt separate the way it should).
Yogurt strainer or cheesecloth (coffee filters work also)

1. Spoon yogurt into strainer or into cheesecloth. Gather cheesecloth at the top and suspend over a bowl to catch the whey.
2. Place in refrigerator for 8 to 12 hours to drain. The longer it drains, the more firm it becomes.
3. To cook with the yogurt cheese, add 1 Tbsp. cornstarch per cup of yogurt cheese to prevent mixture from separating.
4. Any flavor of yogurt may be used or your choice of seasonings may be mixed in to create different flavors of cheese.

Makes: 1 C
Note: Use "Nonfat Yogurt Cheese"✔ instead of sour cream, cream cheese, ricotta cheese, or mayonnaise. (2 cups yogurt = 1 cup yogurt cheese)

Per Serving: 0 g Fat, 220 Calories, 0 % Fat, 24 g Protein, 32 g Carb, 230 mg Sodium, 36 mg Cholesterol

MOCK SOUR CREAM

(Quick Fix)

¾ C nonfat cottage cheese
¼ C nonfat plain yogurt
2 T 1% or less fat buttermilk
1 packet Equal (optional)

1. Blend in blender until smooth.

Makes: 1 C (4 servings)

Per Serving: 0.17 g Fat, 14 Calories, 11 % Fat, 2.1 g Protein, 1.2 g Carb, 63 mg Sodium, 1.3 mg Cholesterol

QUICK BROWN GRAVY

2 T Butter Buds liquid
¼ t garlic powder
2 T flour
1 C boiling water plus 1 beef bouillon cube
Salt (optional) and pepper to taste
½ t Worcestershire sauce
Pam no-stick cooking spray

1. Coat a skillet with Pam. Pour liquid Butter Buds into skillet; slowly blend in flour, stirring well. Add bouillon and remaining ingredients; bring to a boil stirring constantly.

Makes: (about 1 cup or 8 (2 T) servings)
Variation: Sauté ½ C mushrooms in a skillet coated with Pam in 2 T liquid Butter Buds. Add to brown gravy.

Per Serving: 0.1 g Fat, 10 Calories,
1 % Fat, .2 g Protein, 2 g Carb,
125 mg Sodium, 0 mg Cholesterol

SPICY HOMEMADE MUSTARD
(Quick Fix)

¼ C Egg Beaters
¾ t dry mustard
1 T EACH sugar and vinegar

1. Beat Egg Beaters until very light and fluffy. Add remaining ingredients. Cook in double boiler or in microwave, stirring frequently until thick.

Note: Vary the hotness by the amount of dry mustard used. Serve as a mustard spread on sandwiches or with baked Healthy Choice ham or lean roast.
Makes: about 7 (1 T) servings

Per Serving: 0 g Fat, 9 Calories,
0 % Fat, 0.71 g Protein, 1.4 g Carb,
11.4 mg Sodium, 0 mg Cholesterol

LITE AND EASY BARBECUE SAUCE

2 C ketchup
2 T EACH brown sugar and dry mustard
3 T Worcestershire sauce

1. Combine all ingredients, mixing well. To serve on roast or chicken, pour sauce on top of precooked meat; cover and bake until heated.

Makes: (about 2¼ C) (per ¼ C serving)

Per Serving: 0.18 g Fat, 63 Calories,
3 % Fat, 0.9 g Protein, 15 g Carb,
493 mg Sodium, 0 mg Cholesterol

RODOLFO'S MARINARA SAUCE
(Quick Fix)

3 C peeled and coarsely chopped tomatoes
¼ C white wine
1 t pureed garlic
Oregano, salt (optional) and pepper to taste

1. In blender, mix all ingredients until slightly chunky.
2. Pour in pan and cook over medium heat stirring occasionally until sauce just comes to a boil. Use with "Rodolfo's Spinach Ricotta Dumplings"✔

Makes: 3 cups (Per Cup)

Note: From Rodolfo's Restaurant in Dallas and Arlington, Texas.

Per Serving: 0 g Fat, 32.6 Calories, 0 % Fat, 1.06 g Protein, 6.7 g Carb, 4.6 mg Sodium, 0 mg Cholesterol

BASIL CREAM SAUCE

1 quart evaporated skim milk
1 medium shallot, peeled and sliced
1 large or 2 small bunches fresh basil, chopped
Salt (optional) and white pepper to taste

1. Combine first 2 ingredients and bring to a boil. Reduce heat and simmer 12-15 minutes or until milk is reduced by half. Remove from heat; remove shallots with a slotted spoon and discard. Season with basil; salt and pepper to taste. Serve over pasta.

Serves: 6

Per Serving: 0.3 g Fat, 135 Calories, 2 % Fat, 13 g Protein, 19.8 g Carb, 197 mg Sodium, 7 mg Cholesterol

HELEN'S CADDO PICKLES

½ gallon small green tomatoes
1½ C EACH chopped onion and bell pepper
2 C white vinegar
2 C sugar
1 t salt

1. Heat liquid ingredients to a boil; add remaining ingredients. Simmer on low until tomatoes turn gray. (Do not boil.) Seal in sterile jars.

Makes: 6 pints (48 ¼ C servings)

Per Serving: 0 g Fat, 34 Calories, 0 % Fat, 0.12 g Protein, 8.8 g Carb, 1 mg Sodium, 0 mg Cholesterol

SEAFOOD & CHICKEN SAUCE

1 recipe "Lite White Sauce"✔
2 T EACH chopped green pepper and pimento
½ C chopped onion
1 C sliced cooked mushroom
½ C Egg Beaters mixed with ¾ C evaporated skim milk
½ t Worcestershire sauce
Salt (optional) & pepper to taste
Dash of red pepper
2¼ lbs. boneless, skinless chicken breasts or shrimp, lobster or lean white fish (cooked)

1. Prepare white sauce as directed in recipe, using a large pan. Stir in remaining ingredients a little at a time, adding your choice of chicken or seafood last. Serve over spinach pasta or rice.

Serves: 12

Per Serving: .5 g Fat, 68 Calories, 5 % Fat, 11.8 g Protein, .46 g Carb, 45.3 mg Sodium,33.1 mg Cholesterol

QUICK CHEESE SAUCE

9 oz. Healthy Choice Fat Free Pasteurized Processed Cheese, diced
⅓ C EACH evaporated skim milk and skim milk
¼ t dry mustard
1 T dry Butter Buds

1. Mix all ingredients in a small bowl. Cover and microwave about 3 minutes, stirring frequently during cooking time.

Makes: about 1½ C or 24 T (Nutr. per T)

Per Serving: 0.2 g Fat, 21 Calories, 1 % Fat, 2.4 g Protein, 2.1 g Carb, 192 mg Sodium, 2.04 mg Cholesterol

YOGURT SAUCE

(A Quick Fix that's good on fish or vegetables!)

1 C "Nonfat Yogurt Cheese"✔
1 T cornstarch
½ C Egg Beaters
1½-2 t tarragon vinegar
½ t paprika

1. Combine all ingredients and cook over hot heat stirring frequently until thick; do not boil.

Per Serving: 0 g Fat, 130 Calories, 0 % Fat, 16 g Protein, 12 g Carb, 160 mg Sodium, 0 mg Cholesterol

AMY'S SPECIAL REQUEST PESTO
(Quick Fix)

3 (½-oz.) cartons fresh basil leaves, discard stems, measure leaves only (about 1 C packed)
Olive oil flavored Pam no stick cooking spray
¼ C hot water plus 1 package dry Butter Buds

3 T Healthy Choice Fat Free garlic and herb cream cheese, softened
1 T Grape Nuts cereal
3-4 T Parmesan cheese
Salt to taste (optional)

1. Spray basil leaves with Pam. Mix basil leaves with Butter Buds, cream cheese and Grape Nuts in a blender or food processor. Process until it forms a smooth paste. Add Parmesan and season to taste. Serve over hot pasta. It freezes well so make extra and freeze for later.

Makes: about 4 C (2½ T) servings

Per Serving: 1.2 g Fat, 73 Calories, 15 % Fat, 7.5 g Protein, 5 g Carb, 40 mg Sodium, 12.5 mg Cholesterol

LITE WHITE SAUCE
(Quick Fix)

½ C EACH skim milk and evaporated skim milk
1 C "Defatted Chicken Broth"✔
Salt (optional) and pepper to taste
1 package dry Butter Buds
2 T plus 1½ t cornstarch mixed with ½ C plus 2 T water

1. Stir all ingredients together except cornstarch and water. Bring to simmer stirring constantly.
2. Slowly add in cornstarch mixture. Stir until thick.

Variations:

1. Add 1 small can drained mushrooms.
2. Add a pinch of poultry seasoning to use in chicken dishes.
3. For a béarnaise sauce, add tarragon to taste.
4. Add a dash of horseradish, mustard or fresh herbs.

Makes: 11 (¼ cup) servings

Per Serving: 0.22 g Fat, 20 Calories, 10 % Fat, 0.77 g Protein, 3.81 g Carb, 74 mg Sodium, 0.8 mg Cholesterol

ENCHILADA SALSA

(Easy Prep)

- **2 T defatted chicken or beef broth**
- **½ C minced or chopped onion**
- **1 T cumin**
- **1 (10-oz.) can Rotel tomatoes and green chiles**
- **¼ C evaporated skim milk**
- **16 oz. tomato sauce (may use chunky, if desired)**
- **1 C Weight Watcher's cream of mushroom soup**
- **½ t garlic powder**
- **Salt to taste (optional)**

1. In a medium saucepan, sauté onion in broth until crisp tender. Stir in remaining ingredients and heat through. Use in enchilada recipes and other Mexican dishes.

Makes: about 3½ C (Nutrition given per ½ C)

Per Serving: 0.27 g Fat, 50 Calories, 5 % Fat, 1.9 g Protein, 8.8 g Carb, 546 mg Sodium, 0.28 mg Cholesterol

WHITE WINE SAUCE

(An Easy Prep that's great for pasta, potatoes, crèpes, etc.)

- **½ lb. fresh mushrooms, chopped**
- **½ C Butter Buds liquid**
- **½ C flour**
- **½ C EACH skim milk and evaporated skim milk**
- **1 C "Defatted Chicken Broth"✓**
- **½ C white wine**
- **1 t Worcestershire sauce**
- **1 t crushed parsley flakes**
- **2 T Parmesan cheese**
- **Salt (optional) and pepper to taste**

1. Sauté mushrooms in Butter Buds liquid until tender; blend in flour. Slowly add remaining ingredients and cook until thickened, stirring constantly.

Variation: Add 2 C cooked boneless skinless cubed chicken breast to every 2 C sauce.

Makes: about 3½ C or 14 (¼ C) servings

Per Serving: 0.4 g Fat, 41 Calories, 8 % Fat, 1.2 g Protein, 5 g Carb, 63 mg Sodium, 1.8 mg Cholesterol

MISCELLANEOUS

BEST BAKER'S MIX

3 C unsifted all purpose flour
1¼ t baking powder
1 t baking soda
1 t salt (optional)

1. Sift all ingredients together and store in airtight container. Use in place of commercially prepared baking or biscuit mix.

Makes: 3 C (serving size per cup).

Variation: Chocolate baker's mix - Sift 1 C unsweetened cocoa powder into plain baker's mix. Sweet Version: add 1½ C sugar

Per Serving: 1 g Fat, 422 Calories, 2 % Fat, 9 g Protein, 88 g Carb, 138 mg Sodium, 0 mg Cholesterol

BASIC BREAD CRUMBS

(Quick Fix)

6 slices Wonder Light Reduced Calorie Fat-Free bread
Butter Flavor Pam no stick cooking spray

1. Spray both sides of each bread slice with Pam and bake in a 250° oven until toasted. Turn slices over and toast until brown and dry.
2. Crumb bread in food processor.
3. Store in air-tight container in freezer and use as needed.

Makes 3 (1 cup) servings

Per Serving: 0 g Fat, 80 Calories, 0 % Fat, 2.6 g Protein, 0.5 g Carb, 0 mg Sodium, 0 mg Cholesterol

CRUNCHY CROUTONS
(Easy Prep)

12 slices Wonder Light Reduced Calorie Fat Free day old bread
1 t EACH paprika, finely ground parsley, and garlic powder
½ t salt (optional)
Olive oil or butter flavor Pam no stick cooking spray

1. Mix seasoning and set aside. Spritz both sides of bread lightly with Pam. Sprinkle with seasonings; cut into cubes.
2. Spritz both sides of bread lightly with Pam. Sprinkle with seasonings; cut into cubes.
3. Bake at 250° on sprayed cookie sheet until brown and dry, about 30 minutes.

Serves: 24 (about 10 croutons each)

Per Serving: 0 g Fat, 20 Calories,
0 % Fat, 2 g Protein, 3 g Carb,
57 mg Sodium, 0 mg Cholesterol

ROSS'S SPECIAL SEASONING
(Quick Fix)

¼ C plus 1 t chili powder
½ C plus 2 t salt or lite salt
¼ C plus 1 t brown sugar
½ C (less ½ t) cumin
1¼ t ginger
½ t plus ⅛ t mace
2½ t garlic powder

1. Mix all ingredients and use as a marinade for meats. See "Ross's Chicken or Fajitas on the Grill"✔.

Makes: about 2 C

Per Serving: 0 g Fat, 180 Calories,
0 % Fat, 0 g Protein, 48 g Carb,
3.9 mg Sodium, 0 mg Cholesterol

CHRISTMAS SCENT

1 EACH lemon and orange, quartered
4 cinnamon sticks
3 bay leaves
¼ C whole cloves
1 quart water

1. Place ingredients in a medium saucepan or kettle. Bring to a boil; reduce heat and simmer adding water when needed.

Serves: A HAPPY HOME

SAVE $10.00!

ORDER BOTH COOKBOOK AND AUDIO SERIES!

FOR FAST ORDERING BY CREDIT CARD CALL: (817) 460-2280

Orders taken 24 hours a day. Have your credit card number and expiration date on hand. Sorry, no collect calls.

SEND MAIL ORDERS TO:

The Lite Switch • P.O. Box 121242 • Arlington, TX 76012

☐ Please send _______ copies of *The Lite Switch* cookbook at $19.95 each, plus $3.00 shipping and handling.

☐ Please send _______ copies of *The Lite Switch* audio series only at $39.95 each, plus $4.00 shipping and handling.

☐ Please send _______ copies of *The Lite Switch* cookbook AND audio series at **THE SPECIAL PRICE of $49.95** for both, plus $5.00 shipping and handling.

Additional orders are $1.00 for shipping and handling, if shipped together. **(Texas residents add 7.75% sales tax per order).** *Sorry, no C.O.D.s accepted.*

☐ I have enclosed a check or money order for $ _______________.

☐ Please charge my credit card number below:

VISA/MC: __________ - __________ - __________ - __________
(CIRCLE ONE)

EXPIRATION DATE: _______ / _______ / _______

Signature: ____
(REQUIRED ON CHARGE ORDERS)

NAME: (as it appears on card) ________________________________

ADDRESS: ____

CITY: ________________________ STATE: ______ ZIP: ________

PHONE: (__________) _____________________________________

For your convenience we will be glad to ship gift orders anywhere in the continental United States. Please indicate on a separate piece of paper if you want an order sent to an address other than above. A gift card will be enclosed.